JavaScript
A Beginner's Guide

Fourth Edition

John Pollock

Mc
Graw
Hill
Education

New York   Chicago   San Francisco
Lisbon   London   Madrid   Mexico City
Milan   New Delhi   San Juan
Seoul   Singapore   Sydney   Toronto

Cataloging-in-Publication Data is on file with the Library of Congress

McGraw-Hill books are available at special quantity discounts to use as premiums and sales promotions, or for use in corporate training programs. To contact a representative, please e-mail us at bulksales@mcgraw-hill.com.

JavaScript: A Beginner's Guide, Fourth Edition

1234567890 DOC DOC 109876543

ISBN   978-0-07-180937-5
MHID   0-07-180937-6

Sponsoring Editor   Brandi Shailer
Editorial Supervisor   Janet Walden
Project Manager   Harleen Chopra, Cenveo® Publisher Services
Acquisitions Coordinator   Amanda Russell
Technical Editor   Christie Sorenson
Copy Editor   Margaret Berson
Proofreader   Madhu Prasher
Indexer   Jack Lewis
Production Supervisor   George Anderson
Composition   Cenveo Publisher Services
Illustration   Cenveo Publisher Services
Art Director, Cover   Jeff Weeks
Cover Designer   Jeff Weeks

*To my wife Heather, daughters Eva and Elizabeth,
Bruce and Joy Anderson, and Dr. J. D. and Linda Andrews*

*In memory of James D. and Livian Anderson, John William and Edith Hopkins,
Burley T. and Aline Price, "Doc" Flores, and Clifton Idom*

About the Author

John Pollock is employed as a Web Administrator during the day and works on Web sites and other projects during the evening. He runs a Web site devoted to Web development and design: Script the Web (www.scripttheweb.com). He also is a contributor to Web Xpertz (www.webxpertz.net), a help community for Web developers. John holds a Bachelor of Arts in English from Sam Houston State University and currently lives in Huntsville, Texas with his wife, Heather, and his daughters, Eva and Elizabeth.

About the Technical Editor

Christie Sorenson is a senior software engineer at ZingChart. She has worked on JavaScript-based systems in analytics, content management, and business applications since 1997 and has been fascinated with the evolution of the language and its users. She has collaborated on several books, including *Ajax: The Complete Reference* and *HTML & CSS: The Complete Reference* and was also the tech editor on *JavaScript: The Complete Reference* and *HTML: A Beginner's Guide*. She holds a Bachelor of Science in Computer Science from University of California, San Diego, and now lives in San Francisco with her husband, Luke, and daughters, Ali and Keira.

Contents at a Glance

Contents

Acknowledgments

I would like to begin by thanking my wonderful wife, Heather Pollock, for all of her love, support, and encouragement in all I do. I love you! I would also like to thank my two daughters, Eva and Elizabeth. I love both of you!

I would like to thank my parents, Bruce and Joy Anderson, for their love and guidance, and for always supporting my endeavors.

I would like to thank Dr. J. D. and Linda Andrews for their love, guidance, and support.

In addition I would like to thank John and Betty Hopkins (grandparents), James D. and Livian Anderson (grandparents), Clifton and Juanita Idom (grandparents), Richard Pollock (brother) and family, Misty Castleman (sister) and family, Warren Anderson (brother) and family, Jon Andrews (brother) and family, Lisa and Julian Owens (aunt/uncle) and family, and every aunt, uncle, cousin, or other relation in my family. All of you have been a great influence in my life.

I would like to thank all of my editors at McGraw-Hill/Professional for their outstanding help and support throughout the writing of this book. Thanks to Brandi Shailer, Ryan Willard, Amanda Russell, and to all of the editors who worked on each edition of the book.

Thanks to my technical editor, Christie Sorenson, for editing and checking over all of the technical aspects of the book, and helping me provide clear explanations of the topics that are covered.

I would like to thank God for the ability He has given me to help and teach people by my writing. "In all your ways acknowledge Him, and He shall direct your paths." (Proverbs 3:6).

Introduction

Welcome to *JavaScript: A Beginner's Guide, Fourth Edition*! Years ago, I was surfing the Web and noticed that people were publishing pages about themselves and calling them homepages. After viewing a number of these, I decided to create a homepage myself. I had no idea where to begin but, through trial and error, I figured out how to code HTML and publish my documents on a Web server. Over time, I saw some interesting effects used on other homepages (like alert messages that popped up out of nowhere or images that would magically change when I moved my mouse over them). I was curious and just *had* to know what was being done to create those effects. Were these page creators using HTML tags I did not know about?

Eventually, one site revealed what they were using to create those effects: *JavaScript.* I went in search of information on it, and came across a few tutorials and scripts on the Web. Since I had programmed in other languages (such as a relatively obscure language called Ada), I was able to catch on to JavaScript fairly quickly by looking at these tutorials and scripts.

I learned enough that I decided to create a Web site that would teach HTML and JavaScript to beginners. As soon as I began the project, I received questions from visitors that were way over my head—forcing me to dig deeper and learn more about JavaScript. As a result, I became completely familiar with this scripting language and what it can do. Not only can you add fun effects to a Web page, you can create scripts that will perform useful tasks, like validate form input, add navigational elements to documents, or react to user events.

The goal of this book is to help you to learn the basics of the JavaScript language with as little hair pulling and monitor smashing as possible. You do not need any prior programming experience to learn JavaScript from this book. All you need is knowledge of HTML and/or XHTML, Cascading Style Sheets (CSS), and how to use your favorite text editor and Web browser (see Chapter 1 for more information).

What This Book Covers

The 16 chapters of this book cover specific topics on the JavaScript language. The first two chapters cover the most basic aspects of the language: what it is, what you need to know to begin using JavaScript, and how to place JavaScript into an HTML file. The middle of the book (Chapters 3–14) covers beginning JavaScript topics from variables all the way to using JavaScript with forms. The final two chapters (Chapters 15–16) introduce some advanced techniques, and point you toward resources if you want to learn more about JavaScript once you have completed the book.

This book includes a number of special features in each chapter to assist you in learning JavaScript. These features include

- **Key Skills & Concepts** Each chapter begins with a set of key skills and concepts that you will understand by the end of the chapter.

- **Ask the Expert** The Ask the Expert sections present commonly asked questions about topics covered in the preceding text, with responses from the author.

- **Try This** These sections get you to practice what you have learned using a hands-on approach. Each Try This will have you code a script through step-by-step directions on what you need to do to in order to accomplish the goal. You can find solutions to each project on the McGraw-Hill/Professional Web site at www.mhprofessional.com/computingdownload.

- **Notes, Tips, and Cautions** Notes, Tips, and Cautions call your attention to noteworthy statements that you will find helpful as you move through the chapters.

- **Code** Code listings display example source code used in scripts or programs.

- **Callouts** Callouts display helpful hints and notes about the example code, pointing to the relevant lines in the code.

- **Self Test** Each chapter ends with a Self Test, a series of 15 questions to see if you have mastered the topics covered in the chapter. The answers to each Self Test can be found in the appendix.

That is it! You are now familiar with the organization and special features of this book to start your journey through JavaScript. If you find that you are stuck and need help, feel free to get online and visit the JavaScript discussion forums on the Web Xpertz Web site at www.webxpertz.net/forums. The forums will allow you to interact with other JavaScript coders who may be able to help you with your questions. If you would like to contact me, you can send me a message on my Web site (www.scripttheweb.com/about/contact.html) or you can find me on Twitter (@ScripttheWeb).

Now it is time to learn JavaScript. Get ready, get set, and have fun!

Chapter 1

Introduction to JavaScript

Key Skills & Concepts

- Using Text Editors, WYSIWYG Editors, and Web Browsers
- Defining JavaScript
- Differences Between JavaScript and Other Languages

Welcome to *JavaScript: A Beginner's Guide, Fourth Edition*! You're obviously interested in learning JavaScript, but perhaps you're not sure what you need to know to use it. This chapter answers some basic questions about what JavaScript is, discusses its advantages and limitations, explains how you can use it to create more dynamic and inviting Web pages, and provides a brief history of the language.

JavaScript is ubiquitous on the World Wide Web. You can use JavaScript both to make your Web pages more interactive, so that they react to a viewer's actions, and to give your Web pages some special effects (visual or otherwise).

JavaScript often gets thrown in with Hypertext Markup Language (HTML) and Cascading Style Sheets (CSS) as one of the recommended languages for beginning Web developers (whether you build Web sites for business or pleasure). Of course, you can build a Web page by using only HTML and CSS, but JavaScript allows you to add additional features that a static page of HTML can't provide without some sort of scripting or programming help.

What You Need to Know

Before you begin learning about JavaScript, you should have (or obtain) a basic knowledge of the following:

- HTML and Cascading Style Sheets (CSS)
- Text editors
- Web browsers
- The different versions of JavaScript

If you have this basic knowledge (the different versions of JavaScript will be discussed in this chapter), then you'll do just fine as you work through this book. Knowing another programming/scripting language or having previous experience with JavaScript isn't required. This book is a *beginner's* guide to JavaScript.

If you think you don't have enough experience in one of the aforementioned areas, a closer look at each one may help you decide what to do.

Basic HTML and CSS Knowledge

While you don't need to be an HTML guru, you do need to know where to place certain elements (like the head and body elements) and how to add your own attributes. This book will reference scripts in the head section (between the <head> and </head> tags) and the body section (between the <body> and </body> tags).

Sometimes, you will also need to add an attribute to a tag for a script to function properly. For example, you may need to name a form element using the id attribute, as shown in the following code:

```
<input type="text" id="thename">
```

If you know the basics of using tags and attributes, the HTML portion shouldn't pose any problems in learning JavaScript.

If you don't have a basic knowledge of HTML, you can learn it fairly quickly through a number of media. For example, you can buy a book or look for some helpful information on the Web. A good book is *HTML: A Beginner's Guide, Fourth Edition* by Wendy Willard (McGraw-Hill Professional, 2009). To find information about HTML on the Web, check out these sites: www.scripttheweb.com/html and www.w3.org/wiki/The_basics_of_HTML.

Occasionally, you will need to use CSS to add or change presentation features on a Web page. We will mainly use CSS for the purposes of dynamically changing CSS properties via JavaScript in this book. Two good places to learn CSS are www.scripttheweb.com/css/ and www.w3.org/wiki/CSS_basics.

Basic Text Editor and Web Browser Knowledge

Before jumping in and coding with JavaScript, you must be able to use a text editor or HTML editor, and a Web browser. You'll use these tools to code your scripts.

Text Editors

A number of text editors and HTML editors support JavaScript. If you know HTML, you've probably already used an HTML editor to create your HTML files, so you might not have to change.

However, some HTML editors have problems related to adding JavaScript code (such as changing where the code is placed or altering the code itself when you save the file). This is more often the case when using WYSIWYG (What You See Is What You Get) editors. It is best to use an HTML editor that allows the option to write your own code (such as Adobe Dreamweaver), a code editor such as NetBeans, or a plain text editor. Some examples of text editors are Notepad, TextPad, and Simple Text.

Web Browsers

Again, if you've been coding in HTML, you probably won't need to change your browser. However, some browsers have trouble with the newer versions of JavaScript. The choice of

Web browser is ultimately up to you, as long as it's compatible with JavaScript. I recommend one of the following browsers to test your JavaScript code:

- Microsoft Internet Explorer version 9.0 or later (or 8 if you are not able to upgrade on your operating system, for example, Windows XP)

- Mozilla Firefox version 14.0 or later

- Google Chrome version 20.0 or later

- Opera version 12.0 or later

New versions of these browsers continue to be produced. The newest versions will continue to support more features.

To give you an idea of what some browsers look like, Figure 1-1 shows a Web page when viewed in Microsoft Internet Explorer, and Figure 1-2 shows the same page when viewed in Mozilla Firefox.

If you have an older browser and you can't upgrade, a number of features (mostly discussed later in the book) may not work in that browser. Even so, the book can still help you learn the JavaScript language itself, so you don't need to give up if you have an older browser.

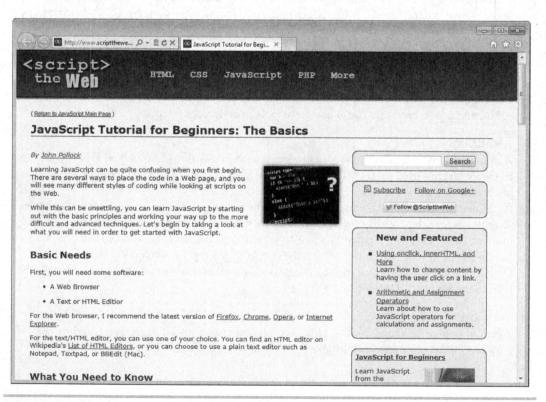

Figure 1-1 A Web page viewed in Microsoft Internet Explorer

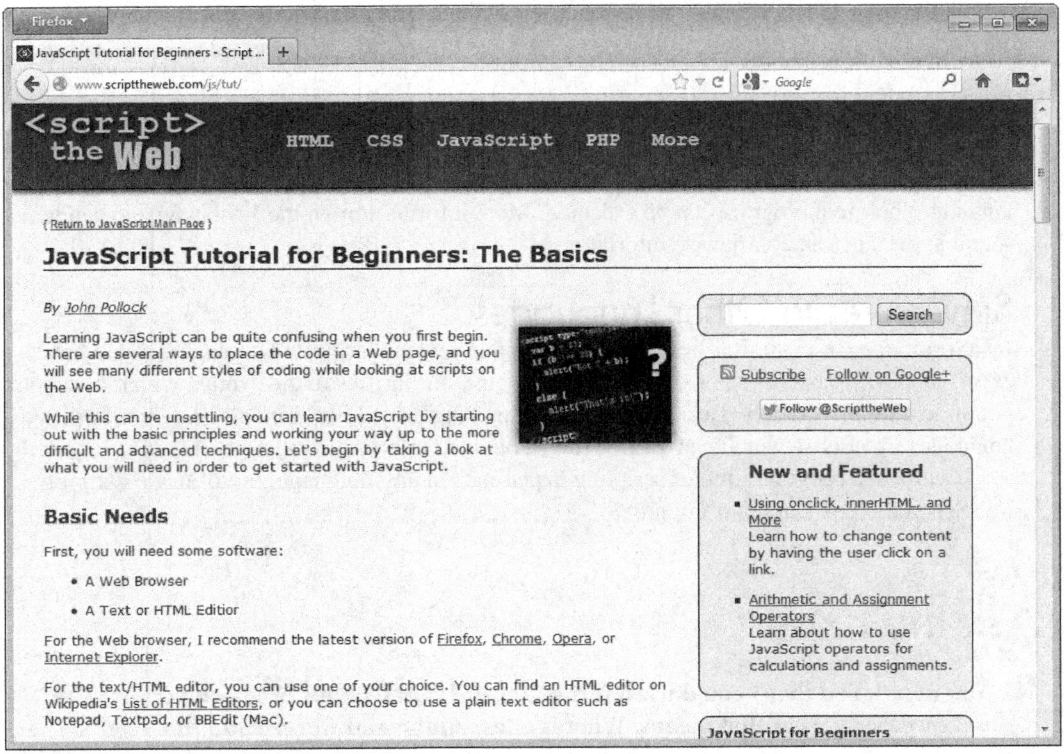

Figure 1-2 A Web page viewed in Mozilla Firefox

NOTE
Even if you have one of the latest browsers, your viewers may not, so it is always appropriate to understand what features may not be supported in older browsers. This book will cover how to handle a number of these issues.

Which Version?

The version of JavaScript being used by a browser (or other software) can be a difficult number to identify, since different browsers may have different names for the language (for example, JScript in Microsoft Internet Explorer) and each of these can follow its own set of version numbers. To find out what standard conventions are being followed, it is best to look at what version of ECMAScript is supported in each browser. You can see what versions are supported by each browser at en.wikipedia.org/wiki/ECMAScript#Dialects.

ECMAScript is the international standard name and specification used for the JavaScript language, so it's not a new language but a standard that is set for JavaScript, JScript, and other implementations of the language. For more on ECMAScript, see www.ecmascript.org/docs.php.

At the time of this writing, the browsers recommended earlier in this chapter should support at least ECMAScript 5.

Remember, It's Not Java

JavaScript and Java are two different languages. Java is a programming language that must be compiled (running a program through software that converts the higher-level code to machine language) before a program can be executed. More information on the Java language can be found at docs.oracle.com/javase/tutorial/.

Similarities to Other Languages

JavaScript does have similarities to other programming and scripting languages. If you have experience with Java, C++, or C, you'll notice some similarities in the syntax, which may help you to learn more quickly. Because it's a scripting language, JavaScript also has similarities to languages like Perl—which can also be run through an interpreter rather than being compiled.

If you have programming or scripting experience in any language, it will make learning JavaScript easier—but it isn't required.

Ask the Expert

Q: You mentioned that I could use a text editor or HTML editor of my choice, but I'm not quite sure what that means. What is a text editor and where can I find one?

A: A text editor is a program that you can use to save and edit written text. Text editors range from simple to complex, and a number of choices are available: Notepad, WordPad, and Simple Text, to name a few. You can also purchase and download some from the Web, like NoteTab or TextPad.

An HTML editor is either a more complex text editor or an editor that allows you to add code by clicking buttons or by other means—often called a What You See Is What You Get (WYSIWYG) editor. I recommend a plain text editor or an HTML editor that doesn't change any code you add to it manually. Some examples of HTML editors are Adobe Dreamweaver and Softpress Freeway.

For the purposes of JavaScript coding, you may decide to use a more code-oriented program that can offer features such as code highlighting, completion, debugging tools, and more, such as NetBeans IDE.

Q: What exactly do I need to know about using a text editor?

A: Basically, you only need to know how to type plain text into the editor, save the file with an .html, .css, or .js extension, and be able to open it again and edit it if necessary. Special features aren't needed because HTML, CSS, and JavaScript files are made up of plain text.

Q: **What do I need to know about using a browser?**

A: All you absolutely need to know is how to open a local HTML file on your computer (or on the Web) and how to reload a page. If you don't know how to open an HTML file from your own computer, open your browser and go to the File menu. Look for an option that says something like Open, or Open File, and select it. You should be able to browse for the file you want to open, as you would with other programs. The following illustration shows where the option is in Microsoft Internet Explorer:

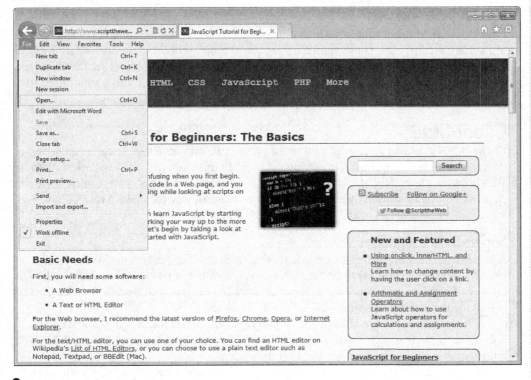

Q: **Where do I get those browsers you mentioned?**

A: Here are links for the browsers:

- **Microsoft Internet Explorer**   www.microsoft.com/ie
- **Mozilla Firefox**   www.mozilla.com/firefox
- **Google Chrome**   www.google.com/chrome/
- **Opera**   www.opera.com

Beginning with JavaScript

JavaScript came about as a joint effort between Netscape Communications Corporation and Sun Microsystems, Inc. The news release of the new language was issued on December 4, 1995, back when Netscape Navigator 2.0 was still in its beta version. JavaScript version 1.0 became available with the new browser. (Before its release as JavaScript, it was called LiveScript.)

JavaScript is a prototype-based, client-side scripting language that can be used in numerous environments. To make sense of such a definition, let's look at its important parts one by one.

Prototype-Based

Prototype-based means that JavaScript is an object-oriented programming language that can use items called *objects*. However, the objects are not *class-based*, so no distinction is made between a class and an instance; instead, objects inherit from other objects via the prototype property. You'll learn how to work with JavaScript objects in Chapter 8. You don't need to understand them in detail until you know a few other features of the language.

Client-Side

Client-side means that JavaScript runs in the *client* (software) that the viewer is using, rather than on the Web server of the site serving the page. In this case, the client will most often be a Web browser (though ECMAScript can be run in other environments as well, such as Adobe Acrobat, Adobe Flash, and others). To make more sense of this, let's take a look at how a server-side language works and how a client-side language works.

Server-Side Languages

A *server-side language* needs to get information from the Web page or the Web browser, send it to a program that is run on the host's server, and then send the information back to the browser. Therefore, an intermediate step must send and retrieve information from the server before the results of the program are seen in the browser.

A server-side language often gives the programmer options that a client-side language doesn't have, such as saving information on the Web server for later use, or using the new information to update a Web page and save the updates.

However, a server-side language is likely to be limited in its ability to deal with special features of the client that can be accessed with a client-side language (like the width of the browser window or the contents of a form before it's submitted to the server).

Client-Side Languages

A *client-side language* is run directly through the client being used by the viewer. In the case of JavaScript, the client is typically a Web browser. Therefore, JavaScript is run directly in the Web browser and doesn't need to go through the extra step of sending and retrieving information from the Web server.

With a client-side language, the browser reads and interprets the code, and the results can be given to the viewer without getting information from the server first. This process can make certain tasks run more quickly.

A client-side language can also access special features of a browser window that may not be accessible with a server-side language. However, a client-side language lacks the ability to save files or updates to files on a Web server as a server-side language can.

NOTE

Using the XMLHttpRequest object allows JavaScript to send and request data from the server. This will be covered briefly in Chapter 15.

A client-side language is useful for tasks that deal with the content of a document or that allow information to be validated before it is sent to a server-side program or script. For instance, JavaScript can change the content of one or more elements on a Web page when the user clicks a link or presses a button (many other user actions can also be activated).

JavaScript can also be used to check the information entered into a form before the form is sent to a server-side program to be processed. This information check can prevent strain on the Web server by preventing submissions with inaccurate or incomplete information. Rather than running the program on the server until the information is correct, that data can be sent to the server just once with correct information.

NOTE

While JavaScript is able to *help* validate information sent to the server, it cannot replace server-side validation since users may have JavaScript disabled or unavailable in the device being used (which allows them to bypass the JavaScript validation). For security reasons, you should always use server-side validation, regardless of whether or not you incorporate JavaScript validation.

Scripting Language

A scripting language doesn't require a program to be compiled before it is run. All the interpretation is done on-the-fly by the client.

With a regular programming language, before you can run a program you have written, you must compile it using a special compiler to be sure there are no syntax errors. With a scripting language, the code is interpreted as it is loaded in the client. Thus, you can test the results of your code more quickly. However, errors won't be caught before the script is run and could cause problems with the client if it can't handle the errors well. In the case of JavaScript, the error handling is up to the browser or other client being used by the viewer.

Putting It All Together

With all this in mind, you might wonder how JavaScript is run in a browser. You might wonder where to write your JavaScript code and what tells the browser it is different from anything else on a Web page. The answers are general for now, but the next chapter provides more details.

JavaScript runs in the browser by being added into an existing HTML document (either directly or by referring to an external script file). You can add special tags and commands to the HTML code that will tell the browser that it needs to run a script. When the browser sees these special tags, it interprets the JavaScript commands and will do what you have directed it to do with your code. Thus, by simply editing an HTML document, you can begin using JavaScript on your Web pages and see the results.

For example, the following code adds some JavaScript to an HTML file that writes some text onto the Web page. Notice the addition of <script> and </script> tags. The code within them is JavaScript.

```
<html>
<body>
<script>◄──────────────┘
document.write("This writes text to the page");◄──────
</script>◄──────────────┐
</body>
</html>
```

This tag tells the browser
that JavaScript follows

This line writes the
text inside the quote
marks on the page

This line tells the browser that
this is the end of the script

The next chapter looks at how to add JavaScript in an HTML file by using the <script> and </script> HTML tags. This will be your first step on the road to becoming a JavaScript coder!

Online Resources

To find additional information online to help you with JavaScript, here are some useful resources:

● A place to find tutorials with working examples of the results: www.scripttheweb.com/js/

● An excellent tutorial site that includes cut-and-paste scripts: www.javascriptkit.com

● A place where you can address questions about JavaScript to fellow coders: www.webxpertz.net/forums

Try This 1-1 Use JavaScript to Write Text

pr1_1.html

This project shows you JavaScript in action by loading an HTML document in your browser. The script writes a line of text in the browser using JavaScript.

Step by Step

1. Copy and paste the code shown here into your text editor:

```
<html>
<body>
<script>
document.write("This text was written with JavaScript!");
</script>
</body>
</html>
```

2. Save the file as pr1_1.html and open it in your Web browser. You should see a single line of text that was written with JavaScript. (To open a file in your Web browser, go to the File menu and look for an option that says something like Open, or Open File, and select it. You should be able to browse for the file you want to open as you would with other programs.)

Try This Summary

In this project, you copied and pasted a section of code into a text editor and saved the file. When you opened the saved file in your Web browser, a line of text was displayed in the browser. This text was written in the browser window using JavaScript. You will see more about how this type of script works in Chapter 2.

Chapter 1 Self Test

1. You must know which of the following to be able to use JavaScript?

   A. Perl

   B. C++

   C. HTML

   D. SGML

2. Which of the following is something you should have to use JavaScript?

   A. A Web browser

   B. A C++ compiler

   C. A 500GB hard drive

   D. A DVD-RW drive

3. The choice of a Web browser is up to you, as long it's compatible with _____.

   A. Flash

   B. VBScript

   C. JavaScript

   D. Windows XP

4. JavaScript and Java are the same language.

   A. True

   B. False

5. _____ is the international standard name and specification used for the JavaScript language.

   A. JScript

   B. LiveScript

   C. ECMAScript

   D. ActionScript

6. JavaScript has similarities to other programming and scripting languages.

   A. True

   B. False

7. Before its release as JavaScript, JavaScript was called _____.

   A. Java

   B. JavaCup

   C. LiveScript

   D. EasyScript

8. JavaScript is _____.

   A. prototype-based

   B. class-based

   C. object deficient

   D. not a language that uses objects

9. A client-side language is run directly through the _____ being used by the viewer.

   A. server

   B. client

   C. monitor

   D. lawyer

10. How can a client-side language help when using forms on a Web page?

   A. It can save the information on the server.

   B. It can validate the information before it is sent to the server.

   C. It can update a file and save the file with the new information.

   D. It can't help at all.

11. A _____ language doesn't require a program to be compiled before it is run.

    A. programming

    B. server-side

    C. scripting

    D. computer

12. With a scripting language, the code is interpreted as it is loaded in the client.

    A. True

    B. False

13. In JavaScript, what handles errors in a script?

    A. The Web server

    B. A compiler

    C. A program on the Web server

    D. The client/Web browser

14. How is JavaScript added to a Web page?

    A. It isn't. It must be compiled and loaded separately.

    B. It is taken from a compiled program on the server.

    C. You place the code in a file by itself and open that file.

    D. It is added to an HTML document.

15. What is added to a Web page to insert JavaScript code?

    A. <script> and </script> HTML tags

    B. The JavaScript code word

    C. <javascript> and </javascript> HTML tags

    D. <java> and </java> HTML tags

Chapter 2

Placing JavaScript in an HTML File

Key Skills & Concepts

- Using the HTML Script Tags
- Creating Your First Script
- Using External JavaScript Files
- Using JavaScript Comments

N ow that you have been introduced to JavaScript, you're ready to start coding. Since JavaScript code is run from HTML documents, you need to know how to tell browsers to run your scripts. The most common way to set off a script is to use the HTML <script> and </script> tags in your document. You can place your script tags in either the head or the body section of an HTML document.

This chapter first shows you how to use the script tags to begin and end a segment of JavaScript code. Then, you will get started creating and running your first scripts. At the end of the chapter, you will learn how to add JavaScript comments to document your scripts.

Using the HTML Script Tags

Script tags are used to tell the browser where code for a scripting language will begin and end in an HTML document. In their most basic form, script tags appear just like any other set of HTML tags:

```
<script>◄──────────────  Tells the browser where
JavaScript code here         script code begins
</script>◄──────────────  Tells the browser where
                             script code ends
```

As you can see, there is the opening <script> tag, the JavaScript code, and then the closing </script> tag. When you use just the basic opening and closing tags like this, almost all browsers will assume that the scripting language to follow will be JavaScript.

In HTML, the script tag is not case sensitive. However, in XHTML, the script tag must be in lowercase. JavaScript is case sensitive in all versions, so you will need to be more careful with it. In this book, I will use HTML5 for the HTML code (even though HTML5 is not case sensitive, I will write the tag and attribute names in lowercase). For the JavaScript code, I will use the case that is needed for it to function correctly.

The <script> tag has six possible attributes: *type*, *language* (deprecated), *charset*, *src*, *defer*, and *async*. These attributes give the browser additional information about when the script should load, the scripting language, and the location of an external JavaScript file (if any).

Identifying the Scripting Language

The scripting language between the opening and closing script tags could be JavaScript, VBScript, or some other language, though JavaScript is almost always set as the default scripting language in browsers. If desired, you can explicitly identify JavaScript as the scripting language by adding the type attribute with the value of "text/javascript" to the opening script tag:

```
<script type="text/javascript">◄─────────────── Tells the browser the scripting
JavaScript code here                              language will be JavaScript
</script>
```

NOTE

The type attribute in the opening script tag is required in XHTML in order for the Web page to validate, but is optional in HTML.

In the past, the language attribute was used to identify the scripting language, but is ignored in modern browsers and will cause the page to be invalid in XHTML and HTML5. It should no longer be used.

The charset attribute, which allows for the character set of the JavaScript code to be specified, is not recognized by most browsers and is not recommended.

Calling External Scripts

Script tags allow you to call an external JavaScript file in your document. An *external JavaScript file* is a text file that contains nothing but JavaScript code, and it is saved with the .js file extension. By calling an external file, you can save the time of coding or copying a long script into each page in which the script is needed. Instead, you can use a single line on each page that points to the JavaScript file with all of the code.

You can call external scripts by adding the src (source) attribute to the opening script tag:

```
<script type="text/javascript" src="yourfile.js"></script>
```

This example calls a JavaScript file named yourfile.js from any page on which you place this tag. Be sure there are no spaces or code between the opening and closing script tags, as this may cause the script call to fail.

If the script is extremely long, using the src attribute to add the script to multiple pages can be much quicker than inserting the entire code on each page. Also, the browser will cache the external JavaScript file the first time it is loaded, making subsequent Web pages that use the script render faster. Using an external script is also helpful when dealing with page validation and when trying to keep script code separated from markup (HTML) code.

By default, script files are loaded in the order in which they are placed in the HTML code (synchronously). There are some options for altering this behavior, which are described in the next section.

Specifying When the Script Should Load

The last two attributes, defer and async, allow you to specify when an external script should be loaded. These attributes are not fully supported by older browsers, or may behave differently, so be aware that an older browser may not execute the script when it is expected to do so.

The defer Attribute

The defer attribute allows you to specify that an external script file should be loaded, but should not execute until the page has completed parsing (the </html> tag has loaded). The following <script> tag would defer the execution of the external JavaScript code:

```
<script type="text/javascript" src="file.js" defer></script>
```

NOTE

If you are using XHTML, set this attribute using defer="defer".

Support for this attribute is available in Internet Explorer 4+, Firefox 3.5+, and Chrome 7+. Internet Explorer 4–7 will allow this attribute to work on inline scripts as well, but versions 8 and above only support this attribute on external scripts as other browsers do.

The async Attribute

When the async attribute is set, the page can continue to load without waiting for the script to load, and the script will execute before the document completes loading. Here is an example:

```
<script type="text/javascript" src="file.js" async></script>
```

NOTE

If you are using XHTML, set this attribute using async="async".

Support for this attribute is available in Firefox 3.5+ and Chrome 7+.

Using <noscript></noscript> Tags

One way of providing alternate content for those viewers without JavaScript (or with JavaScript turned off) is to use the noscript tag. The <noscript></noscript> tags may be placed anywhere in the HTML document and can contain any content needed for those viewers browsing without JavaScript. For example:

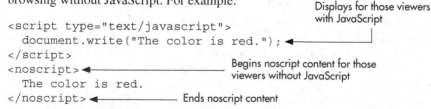

```
<script type="text/javascript">
  document.write("The color is red.");
</script>
<noscript>
  The color is red.
</noscript>
```

Displays for those viewers with JavaScript

Begins noscript content for those viewers without JavaScript

Ends noscript content

This example displays the phrase "The color is red." to the viewer either through JavaScript or through the text within the <noscript></noscript> tags.

CAUTION

Some older browsers may not handle the noscript tag correctly and won't display the content in either section. If your users have older browsers, another alternative is to display the content on the page and then use JavaScript to enhance the content for those who are able to display it with JavaScript on.

The <noscript> tag can be useful at times, but there are often better ways to provide the same content to those without JavaScript (avoiding the document.write() method, for instance). You will learn more about accessible JavaScript as you progress through this book.

Ask the Expert

Q: Do I always need to use script tags to add JavaScript to a page?

A: It's possible to use *event handlers* that allow you to write short bits of script within the event-handling attribute of an HTML tag. You'll learn about event handlers in Chapter 8.

Q: What about the language attribute?

A: The language attribute once was used to specify the scripting language to be used, and for a time some browsers allowed a JavaScript version to be specified (for example, language="JavaScript1.2"). This is no longer the case, and the attribute has been deprecated. Since it is completely ignored in modern browsers and causes pages not to validate in XHTML and HTML5, it should no longer be used.

Q: My page won't validate in XHTML strict (or transitional) when I add a script to it. How do I get the page to validate?

A: If the script contains characters used in XHTML such as < (which is used for "less than" in JavaScript but is seen as the beginning of a new tag in XHTML), then the page won't validate with the script directly in the document without adding a CDATA section:

```
<script type="text/javascript">
<![CDATA[ ◄─────────────────────── Begins the CDATA section
var x  = 5;
var y = 10;
if (x < y) {
window.alert("x is less than y");
}
]]> ◄─────────────────────── Ends the CDATA section
</script>
```

(continued)

This will allow the page to validate, but because the <![CDATA[and]]> characters are in the script, the script will no longer work. To fix this, you need JavaScript comments (/* and */) around those characters when they are within the script tags:

```
<script type="text/javascript">
/*<![CDATA[*/
var x = 5;
var y = 10;
if (x < y) {
window.alert("x is less than y");
}
/*]]>*/
</script>
```

Opening and closing JavaScript comments are placed around <![CDATA[

Opening and closing JavaScript comments are placed around]]>

As you can see, this can get quite tedious very quickly! Typically, the better option is to use an external script file, which eliminates this problem because only the script tags themselves are needed in the XHTML document.

Creating Your First Script

Now that you know how to use the HTML script tags to tell browsers about the JavaScript in a document, you're ready to learn how to add the actual JavaScript code between those script tags. The first coding example often given to teach any language is one that writes some sort of text to the default output area, commonly known as a basic "Hello World" script. Following that convention, your first script will write a string of text to a Web page.

Writing a "Hello World" Script

Rather than write "Hello World," you'll use another line of text for this script: "Yes! I am now a JavaScript coder!" This requires only a single line of code, using the document.write() method, which writes a string of text to the document:

```
<script type="text/javascript">
  document.write("Yes! I am now a JavaScript coder!");
</script>
```

Notice the parentheses and the quotation marks around the text. The parentheses are required because the document.write() method is a JavaScript *function*, which takes an *argument* contained in parentheses. You will learn more about JavaScript functions in Chapter 4.

The quotation marks denote a *string* of text. A string is a type of variable that is defined in JavaScript by placing it inside quotation marks. Chapter 3 provides details on strings and other types of JavaScript variables.

The last thing to notice about your script is the semicolon at the end of the line. The semicolon signals the end of a JavaScript statement. A *statement* is a portion of code that does not need anything added to it to be complete in its syntax (its form and order). A statement can be used to perform a single task, to perform multiple tasks, or to make calls to other parts of the script that perform several statements. Most JavaScript statements end with a semicolon, so it is a good idea to get in the habit of remembering to add one.

NOTE

In later chapters, you will see various lines that do not end in semicolons because they open or close a block of code. Also, many scripts you encounter may not end statements with semicolons. JavaScript is lenient about the use of a semicolon in most cases; however, it is best to use the semicolon to end a statement because it can prevent possible errors and aid in debugging (removing errors from) the script later.

So, to write a text string to the page, you use the document.write() method, followed by the text, surrounded by quotation marks and enclosed in parentheses. End the line (the statement) with a semicolon. JavaScript will handle the rest of the job.

Creating an HTML Document for the Script

In order to make this example complete and test the script, you need to insert it into an HTML document. First, create the following HTML document with the basic tags (using any text editor you prefer):

```
<!DOCTYPE html>
<html>
<head>
<title>Untitled Document</title>
</head>
<body>
</body>
</html>
```

Save the document as test1.html in your text editor. You will call it later with a Web browser to see the results of the script. Next, you'll add the script to this HTML document, so leave the file open.

Inserting the Script into the HTML Document

Now you need to insert the script in the document. Where should it go? You can place a script between the <head> and </head> tags, or between the <body> and </body> tags. Since this example writes a text string directly to the page, you want to insert the script between the <body> and </body> tags, wherever you want the text string to appear. It can come before, after, or between any HTML code on the page.

To make it clear how the script results appear, you'll add HTML code to write lines of text before and after the script. The script tags and the script itself are inserted between those lines. Add the lines shown next between the <body> and </body> tags:

```
<p>This is the first line, before the script results.</p>
<p>
<script type="text/javascript">
  document.write("Yes! I am now a JavaScript coder!");
</script>
</p>
<p>This line comes after the script.</p>
```

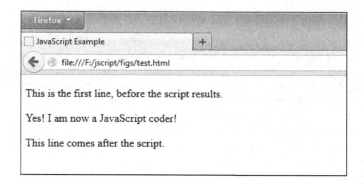

Figure 2-1 The test.html file in a Web browser

Save the test1.html document again. You should now be able to open the document in your Web browser to see the results of the script. Figure 2-1 shows how the text should look in your browser when you load the Web page.

Congratulations, you have now finished your first script!

NOTE
The example code in this section uses the entire HTML document and all of its tags. In order to keep things as relevant as possible, from this point on the example code will use only the HTML tags involved with the scripts rather than the entirety of its tags. Project code may use entire HTML documents as needed.

Ask the Expert

Q: Why is there a dot (.) in the document.write() command?

A: Document is one of JavaScript's predefined objects, and write() is a predefined method of the document object. The dot puts the object and the method together to make the function work. Chapter 9 explains JavaScript objects, and Chapter 10 is devoted to the document object.

Q: How do I know when to add the script inside the head section and when to add it inside the body section?

A: In the past, JavaScript code was almost always placed inside the head section, which kept it in a separate area from the rest of the HTML code. Modern coding practice is typically to place all JavaScript code in an external .js file and to place the <script> tag(s) right before the closing </body> tag. This ensures that the HTML page has loaded in the browser (since large scripts can delay the loading of the page if placed elsewhere), giving the user a better experience.

Try This 2-1 Insert a Script into an HTML Document

pr2_1.html

This project gives you practice adding a script to your page. You will create an HTML document and insert a script that displays a short sentence in the browser window when the page loads.

Step by Step

1. Set up an HTML document so that you have a simple file with nothing between the <body> and </body> tags yet.

2. Put the following line of text into the Web page within a paragraph:

    I am part of the HTML document!

3. Insert a <p> tag after this line.

4. After the <p> tag, insert a script that will write the following line on the page:

    This came from my script, and is now on the page!

5. After the script, add a </p> tag. Add another opening <p> tag.

6. Put the following line of text into the Web page after the last <p> tag, and make it emphasized (using <em></em> tags):

    I am also part of the HTML document, after the script results!

7. Add a </p> tag to complete the paragraph.

8. Here is what your HTML document should look like:

```
<!DOCTYPE html>
<html>
<head>
<title>JavaScript Project 2-1</title>
</head>
<body>
<p>I am part of the HTML document!</p>
<p>
<script type="text/javascript">
  document.write("This came from my script, and is now on the page!");
</script>
</p>
<p><em>I am also part of the HTML document, after the script results!</em></p>
</body>
</html>
```

9. Save the file as pr2_1.html and view the page in your browser to see the results.

(continued)

Try This Summary

In this project, you created an HTML file. Using the knowledge that you acquired thus far in this chapter, you inserted within the HTML file a script that writes a specific line of text on the page. When the HTML page is opened in a Web browser, the result of the script is displayed between two lines of text.

Using External JavaScript Files

Now suppose that you want to use your "Hello World" script (the one you created earlier in this chapter) on more than one page, but you do not want to write it out on each page. You can do this by putting the script in an external script file and calling it with the src attribute of the script tag. For this method, you need to create a JavaScript text file to hold your script. You also need one or more HTML files into which you will place the script tags to call your external script file.

Creating a JavaScript File

For this example, you will create a JavaScript file that contains only one line. For practical applications, you would use this approach for lengthier scripts—the longer the script is, the more useful this technique becomes (especially if you are trying to validate your Web pages or you are separating your script code from your markup).

Open a new file in your text editor and insert only the JavaScript code (the document.write() statement) itself. The script tags are not needed in the external JavaScript file. The file should appear like this:

```
document.write("Yes! I am now a JavaScript coder!");
```

Save the file as jsfile1.js in your text editor. To do this, you may need to use the Save As option on the File menu and place quotation marks around your filename, as shown in Figure 2-2 (using Notepad with Windows).

Once the file has been saved, you can move on to the next step, which is to create the HTML files in which to use the script.

Creating the HTML Files

You will create two files in which to place your script. The technique should work for any number of HTML files, though, as long as you add the required script tags to each file.

For the first file, create your base HTML document and insert the script tags into the body section of the document, using the src attribute to point to the jsfile1.js file, and add some HTML text to the body of the page to identify it as the first HTML document:

```
<body>
<script type="text/javascript" src="jsfile1.js"></script>
<p>
  This is page 1, and the script works here!
</p>
</body>
```

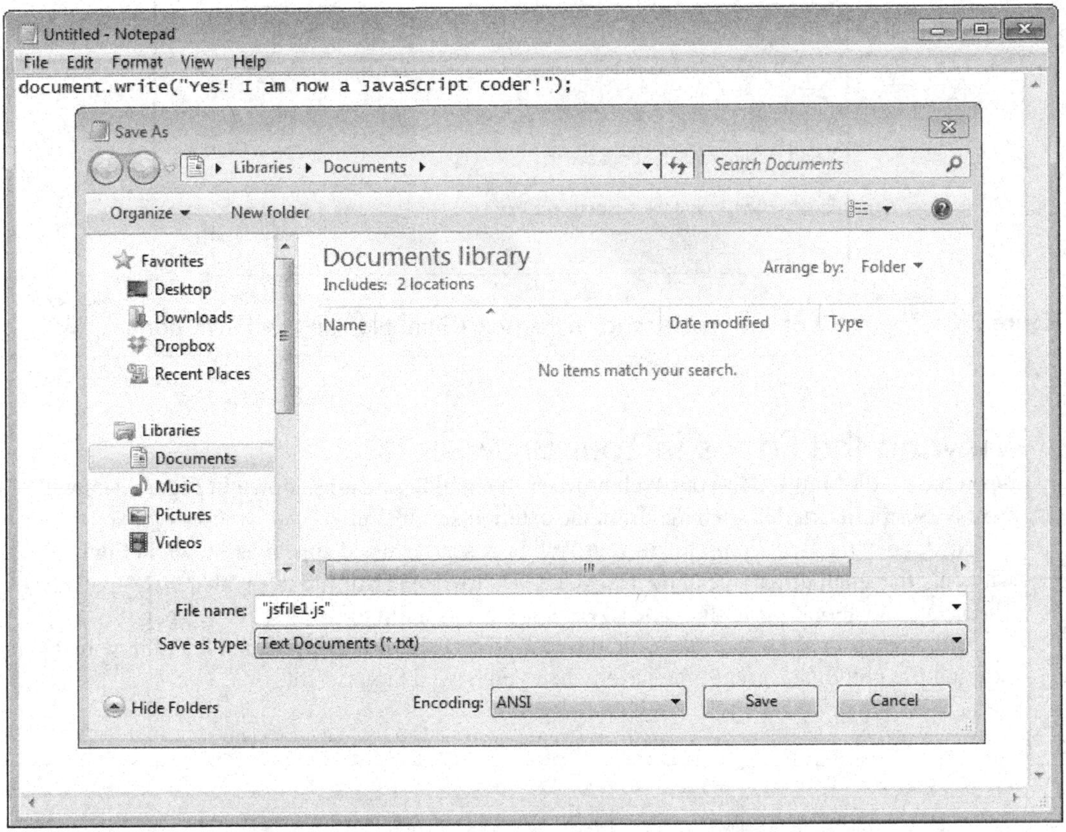

Figure 2-2   An example of saving a file with a .js extension using quote marks so it will save with the correct file extension

Save this file as jsext1.html in your text editor. Be sure to save it in the same directory as your jsfile1.js file.

The second HTML document looks the same as the first one, except that the HTML text says that it's page 2:

```
<body>
<script type="text/javascript" src="jsfile1.js"></script>
<p>
  This is page 2, and the script also works here!
</p>
</body>
```

Save this file as jsext2.html in your text editor. Again, be sure to place it in the same directory as the other files.

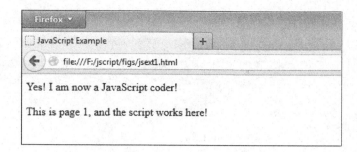

Figure 2-3 The result of calling the script in the jsext1.html file, the first HTML page

Viewing the Pages in Your Browser

Open the jsext1.html file in your Web browser. It should appear as shown in Figure 2-3, with the JavaScript inserted in the page from the external script file.

Next, open the jsext2.html file in your Web browser. It should appear as shown in Figure 2-4, with only the small difference of the text you added to the HTML file to say that this is page 2. The JavaScript should write the same text to this page as it did to the first HTML page.

Although we used a short script in this example, it should give you an idea of how using an external file could be a great time-saver when you have a large script.

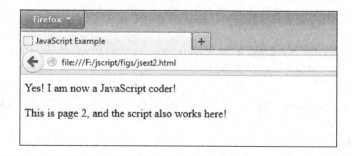

Figure 2-4 The result of calling the script in the jsext2.html file, the second HTML page

Try This 2-2   ## Call an External Script from an HTML Document

pr2_2.html
prjs2_2.js

This project will allow you to practice creating external JavaScript files and using them to insert a script into a Web page.

Step by Step

1. Set up a simple HTML document with nothing between the <body> and </body> tags.

2. Place the following line of text between the body tags of the page:

    This text is from the HTML document!

3. Place a <p> tag after this text.

4. Save it as pr2_2.html.

5. Create an external JavaScript file that will write the following line when it is executed:

    I love writing JavaScript and using external files!

6. Here is how your JavaScript file should look:

```
document.write("I love writing JavaScript, and using external files!");
```

7. Save the JavaScript file as prjs2_2.js.

8. Go back to the HTML document. Place the script tags after the <p> tag in the document so that the external JavaScript file will write its sentence on the page.

9. Insert a </p> tag after the script tags.

10. The body of your HTML document should look like this:

```
<body>
This text is from the HTML document!
<p>
<script type="text/javascript" src="prjs2_2.js"></script>
</p>
</body>
```

11. Save the HTML file and view the results in your browser.

Try This Summary

In this project, you created an HTML page. Using your knowledge of external JavaScript files from the previous section, you created an external JavaScript file and placed the necessary code into the HTML file to include the external JavaScript file. When the HTML file is displayed in a Web browser, a line of plain text is shown, followed by the results of the external JavaScript file.

Using JavaScript Comments

You may need to make notes in your JavaScript code, such as to describe what a line of code is supposed to do. It's also possible that you will want to disable a line of the script for some reason. For instance, if you are looking for an error in a script, you may want to disable a line in the script to see if it is the line causing the error. You can accomplish these tasks by using JavaScript comments. You can insert comments that appear on one line or run for numerous lines.

Inserting Comments on One Line

If you want to add commentary on a single line in your code, place a pair of forward slashes before the text of the comment:

```
// Your comment here
```

In this format, anything preceding the two slashes on that line is "live" code—code that will be executed—and anything after the slashes on that line is ignored. For example, suppose that you wrote this line in your code:

```
document.write("This is cool!"); // writes out my opinion
```

The document.write() method will be run by the browser, so the text "This is cool!" will be written to the page. However, the comment after the slashes will be ignored by the browser.

If you place the forward slashes at the beginning of a line, the browser will ignore the entire line. Suppose that you move the slashes in the previous example to be the first items on the line:

```
// document.write("This is cool!"); writes out my opinion
```

In this format, the entire line is ignored, since it begins with the two slashes that represent a JavaScript comment. The text will not be written to the page, since the code will not be executed by the browser. In effect, you are disabling the document.write() statement. You may wish to do this if the script containing this line has an error and you want to know whether or not this line is causing the problem.

Adding Multiple-Line Comments

Comments denoted by a pair of forward slashes apply only to the line on which they appear; their effects are cut off at the end of the line. You can span multiple lines with this type of comment by adding the slashes to each line of code, as in this example:

```
// Deleted my commentary.
// document.write("This is cool!"); writes out my opinion
// End of commentary deletion.
```

To add comments that span any number of lines without placing slashes on every line, you can use a different comment format: a forward slash followed by an asterisk at the beginning of the comment, then the text of the comment, and then an asterisk followed by a forward slash at the end of the comment. Here's an example:

```
/*
My script will write some text into my HTML document!
All of this text is ignored by the browser.
*/
document.write("You can see me!");
```

Using this format, you can begin the comment on one line and end it on another line.

Multiple-line comments can be handy when you want to insert lengthier descriptions or other text, but you need to be careful when you use them. Look at this example to see if you can find a problem with it:

```
<script type="text/javascript">
/*
This code won't work for some reason.
document.write("I want someone to see me!");
</script>
```

Did you notice that the closing JavaScript comment symbols are missing? When you use multiple-line comments, you need to be careful to close them. Otherwise, you might accidentally comment out code you need executed! In this example, the comment just keeps going on with no end in sight. To fix this, you need to close the JavaScript comments before the document.write() method is used:

```
<script type="text/javascript">
/*
The JavaScript code is now working! This text is hidden.
*/
document.write("Now everyone can see me!");
</script>
```

Note, however, that multiple-line comments cannot be placed inside other multiple-line comments, since the closing comment code for the inner comment will close the comment early. For example, consider this code:

```
/* ◄─────────── Outside comment started
Comment out some code
document.write("I cannot be seen!"); ◄──
/* ◄──
document.write("I also cannot be seen."); ◄─────── This code also won't be executed
*/ ◄────────────────────────────────── This ends the entire comment!
document.write("Oops! I can be seen!"); ◄───┐
*/                                           This code will execute!
```

This code won't be executed

Inside comment started (isn't recognized as a new comment, since it is already commented out)

As you can see, the first instance of the ending */ causes the entire comment to end, and the code afterward could be executed.

In the preceding examples, you saw how comments can be used to provide some documentation of what to expect from each script. In Chapter 16, you will learn how using comments can help you debug your JavaScript code. For now, you should get in the habit of adding comments to your scripts as short documentation or instructions.

✓

Chapter 2 Self Test

1. What is the purpose of the <script> and </script> tags?

    A. To tell the browser where a script begins and ends

    B. To let the browser know when the script should be loaded

    C. To point to an external JavaScript file

    D. All of the above

2. Why would you use the type attribute in the opening script tag?

    A. To let the browser know what type of coder you are

    B. To ensure the Web page validates when using XHTML

    C. To create a typing script

    D. To make sure the script does not make a grammatical error

3. Is JavaScript code case sensitive?

    A. Yes

    B. No

4. The noscript tag provides _____ for those without _____.

5. An external JavaScript file commonly uses a filename extension of _____.

    A. .js

    B. .html

    C. .jav

    D. .java

6. Which of the following correctly points to an external JavaScript file named yourfile.js?

    A. <extscript type="text/javascript" src="yourfile.js"></extscript>

    B. <script type= "text/javascript" src="yourfile.js"></script>

    C. <script language="yourfile.js"></script>

    D. <script type="text/javascript" link="yourfile.js"></script>

7. In HTML, the script tag is not case sensitive. However, with XHTML, the script tag must be in _____.

8. The _____ signals the end of a JavaScript statement.

   A. colon

   B. period

   C. question mark

   D. semicolon

9. To write a string of text on a Web page, the _____ method can be used.

   A. document.write()

   B. document.print()

   C. document.type()

   D. window.print()

10. When would it be a good idea to use an external JavaScript file?

   A. When the script is short and going to be used in only one HTML document

   B. When your Web site viewers have older browsers

   C. When the script is very long or needs to be placed in more than one HTML document

   D. External files are not a good idea

11. JavaScript comments can be very useful for the purpose of _____ or _____ your code.

12. Which of the following indicates that a single line of commentary will follow it within JavaScript code?

   A. /*

   B. /-

   C. //

   D. <!--

13. Which of the following indicates that more than one line of commentary will follow it within JavaScript code?

   A. /*

   B. /-

   C. //

   D. <!--

14. Which of the following indicates the end of a multiple-line JavaScript comment?

    A. \\

    B. -->

    C. /*

    D. */

15. When you use multiple-line JavaScript comments, you need to be careful to _____ them.

    A. close

    B. read

    C. program

    D. compile

Chapter 3

Using Variables

Key Skills & Concepts

- Understanding Variables

- Why Variables Are Useful

- Defining Variables for Your Scripts

- Understanding Variable Types

- Using Variables in Scripts

Now that you have learned the basics of adding JavaScript to a Web page, it is time to get into the inner workings of the language. Since variables are an important part of JavaScript coding, you will need to know as much as possible about what they are and why they are useful in your scripts. Once you have an understanding of how variables work and what they can do, you will be able to move on to other topics that build on the use of the various types of variables.

In this chapter, you will begin by learning what variables are and why they are useful. You will then move on to find out about the methods that are used to declare variables and how to assign a value to a variable. Finally, you will see how to use variables in your scripts.

Understanding Variables

A *variable* represents or holds a value. The actual value of a variable can be changed at any time. To understand what a variable is, consider a basic statement that you may recall from algebra class:

```
x=2
```

The letter x is used as the name of the variable. It is assigned a value of 2. To change the value, you simply give x a new assignment:

```
x=4
```

The name of the variable stays the same, but now it represents a different value.

Taking the math class example one step further, you probably had to solve a problem like this one:

```
If x=2, then 3+x=?
```

To get the answer, you put the value of 2 in place of the variable x in the problem, for 3+2=5. If the value of x changes, so does the answer to the problem. So, if $x=7$, then the calculation turns into 3+7, and now the result is 10.

Variables in JavaScript are much like those used in mathematics. You give a variable a name, and then assign it values based on your needs. If the value of the variable changes, it will change something that happens within the script.

Why Variables Are Useful

Using variables offers several benefits:

- They can be used in places where the value they represent is unknown when the code is written.

- They can save you time in writing and updating your scripts.

- They can make the purpose of your code clearer.

Variables as Placeholders for Unknown Values

Often, a variable will hold a place in memory for a value that is unknown at the time the script is written. A variable value might change based on something entered by the viewer, or it may be changed by you later in the script code.

For instance, you might have a function that takes in certain values based on user input (functions will be discussed in Chapter 4). Since the value of user input is unknown at the time the script is written, a variable can be used to hold the value that will be input by the user. This is true for any sort of user input, whether it be in the form of a JavaScript prompt/confirm box, input fields in a form, or other methods of input.

Variables as Time-Savers

Variables speed up script writing because their values can change. When you assign a value to a variable at the beginning of a script, the rest of the script can simply use the variable in its place. If you decide to change the value later, you need to change the code in only one place—where you assigned a value to the variable—rather than in numerous places.

For instance, suppose that back in math class, you were asked to solve this problem:

```
If x=2, then 3+x-1+2-x=?
```

You know that you need to substitute the value of 2 for each x that appears, for 3+2–1+2–2=4. Now if the teacher wants you to do this problem again with a different value for x, the whole problem does not need to be rewritten. The teacher can just give you the following instruction:

```
Solve the above problem for x=4.
```

The longer and more complex the problem gets, the more useful the variable becomes. Rather than rewriting the same thing over and over, you can change one variable to offer an entirely new result.

Variables as Code Clarifiers

Since variables represent something, and you can give them meaningful names, they are often easier to recognize when you read over (and debug) your scripts. If you just add numbers, you may forget what they stand for. For example, consider this line of code:

```
TotalPrice = 2.42 + 4.33;
```

Here, the numbers could mean almost anything. Instead, you might assign 2.42 as the value of a variable named CandyPrice and 4.33 as the value of a variable named OilPrice:

```
TotalPrice = CandyPrice + OilPrice;
```

Now, rather than trying to remember the meaning of the numbers, you can see that the script is adding the price of some candy to the price of some oil. This is also useful in debugging, because the meaningful variable names make it easier to spot errors.

Defining Variables for Your Scripts

Now that you understand what variables are and why you want to use them, you need to learn how to make them work in your scripts. You create variables by *declaring* them. Then you assign values to them using the JavaScript *assignment operator*. When you name your variables, you need to follow the rules for naming variables in JavaScript, as well as consider the meaningfulness of the name.

Declaring Variables

To declare text as a variable, you use the var keyword, which tells the browser that the text to follow will be the name of a new variable:

```
var variablename;
```

For example, to name your variable coolcar, the declaration looks like this:

```
var coolcar;
```

In this example, you have a new variable with the name coolcar. The semicolon ends the statement. The variable coolcar does not have a value assigned to it yet (JavaScript will give it a value of *undefined*).

To declare multiple variables, one option is to use the var statement each time:

```
var coolcar;
var cooltruck;
var coolvan;
```

Alternatively, you can use a single var statement and separate each variable name with commas, making sure the last one ends in a semicolon (to end the var statement):

```
var coolcar,
    cooltruck,
coolvan;  ◄─────────────
```

The last variable declared must end in a semicolon rather than a comma.

As described in the next section, you can give your variables a value at the same time that you declare them, or you can assign them a value later in your script.

Assigning Values to Variables

The code for giving a variable a name is simple, but there are some restrictions on words that you can use for variables and the cases of the letters. To assign a value to a variable, you use the JavaScript assignment operator, which is the equal to (=) symbol. If you want to declare a variable and assign a value to it on the same line, use this format:

```
var variablename = variablevalue;
```

For example, to name your variable paycheck and give it the numeric value 1200, use this statement:

```
var paycheck = 1200;
```

The statement begins with the keyword var, followed by the variable paycheck, just as in the plain variable declaration described in the previous section. Next comes the assignment operator (=), which tells the browser to assign the value on the right side of the operator to the variable on the left side of the operator. To the right of the assignment operator is 1200, which is the numeric value being assigned to the variable paycheck. The line ends with a semicolon to mark the end of the statement.

CAUTION

Be careful not to think of the assignment operator (=) as having the meaning "is equal to." This operator only assigns a value. The operator for "is equal to" is two equal signs together (==), as you'll learn in Chapter 5.

To declare and assign another variable, you use the same format. For example, to set up a variable named spending to track the amount of money you are spending from the paycheck variable, use these statements:

```
var paycheck = 1200;    ──── Assigns a value of 1200 to the variable paycheck
var spending = 1500;    ──── Assigns a value of 1500 to the variable spending
```

Of course, you will also notice that this financial situation is headed for trouble, since the money being spent in the spending variable is more than what is being brought in with the paycheck variable. Oddly, it is starting to look like the budget for my Web site!

The method you used earlier to declare multiple variables with a single var statement will also work to declare and assign values to multiple variables. Commas are used to separate each variable assignment, as shown in the following code:

```
var paycheck = 1200,
    bonus = 50,        ──── A comma is used to separate each variable assignment.
    spending = 1500;   ──── The last variable assignment ends with a semicolon.
```

Again, remember that the last variable that is declared and assigned a value will end with a semicolon to complete the var statement.

The examples you've seen illustrate the proper and safe way to code variable declarations and assignments. However, JavaScript allows a certain amount of flexibility when it comes to variables. In many cases, the code will work without using precise coding syntax. For example, you may see some scripts written without using the var keyword the first time a variable is used. JavaScript will often declare the variable the first time it is used even if it is previously undeclared. An example is shown here:

```
paycheck = 1200;
```

This works since the variable is being assigned a value (JavaScript will simply declare the variable and assign it the value of 1200). However, if you were trying to declare the variable without an assignment, the following would not be valid:

```
paycheck;
```

This declaration would still require the var keyword to be valid, as in the following code:

```
var paycheck;
```

You may also see a script that leaves off the ending semicolon:

```
var paycheck = 1200
```

And in some scripts, both features are left out of the variable assignment:

```
paycheck = 1200
```

All of these shortcuts may seem handy, but it is best to go ahead and define each variable before using it, use the var keyword, and include the semicolon. Not doing so can cause errors in some browsers and may give people the impression the code was not written well. Also, any of these omissions can be really troublesome if you need to debug the script. Giving variables the correct declarations and assignments will avoid problems, and your code will be easier to read and understand.

Naming Variables

Before you start naming your own variables, you need to be aware of JavaScript's naming rules. The factors you need to consider when choosing names are case sensitivity, invalid characters, and the names that are reserved by JavaScript. Additionally, you should try to give your variables names that are both easy to remember and meaningful.

Using Case in Variables

JavaScript variables are case sensitive—paycheck, PAYCHECK, Paycheck, and PaYcHeCk are four different variables. When you create a variable, you need to be sure to use the same case when you write that variable's name later in the script. If you change the capitalization at all, JavaScript sees it as a new variable or returns an error. Either way, it can cause problems with your script.

Here are a couple of suggestions for using case in your variable names:

- If you are using a variable name that consists of only one word, it is probably easiest to use lowercase for the entire name. It will be quicker to type, and you will know when you use it later to type it all in lowercase.

- For a variable name with two words, you might decide to capitalize the first letter of each word. For example, you may name a variable MyCar or My_Car (you will see more on the underscore character, _, in the next section). You also might use what is called "camelCase," where you leave the first word in lowercase and make each subsequent word uppercase. For example, you may name a variable myCar or myCoolCar.

The capitalization of variables is entirely up to you, so you should use whatever style you are most comfortable with. It is best that you adopt a convention and continue to use it. For instance, if you name a variable using lowercase characters only, you should do the same throughout the script to avoid accidentally switching the case when using the variable later. In this book, I use only lowercase characters for variable names, to keep the code clear.

Using Allowed Characters

An important rule to remember is that a variable name must begin with a letter, underscore (_), or dollar character ($). The variable name cannot begin with a number or any other character that is not a letter (other than the underscore and dollar). The other characters in the variable name can be letters, numbers, underscores, and dollar characters. Blank spaces are not allowed in variable names. So, the following variable names would be valid:

- paycheck
- _paycheck
- pay2check
- pay_check
- $pay_245

However, the following variable names are not valid:

- #paycheck
- 1paycheck
- pay check
- pay_check 2
- _pay check

The hardest rule to remember may be that you cannot begin the name with a number (it's the one I forget most often). While such a name may look valid, JavaScript doesn't allow it.

Avoiding Keywords and Reserved Words

Another rule to keep in mind when naming your variables is to avoid the use of JavaScript keywords and reserved words. Keywords are special words that are used for a specific purpose in JavaScript. For instance, you've learned that the reserved word var is used to declare a JavaScript variable. Using it as a variable name can cause numerous problems in your script, since this word is meant to be used in a different way. Reserved words are special words that are reserved to be used as keywords at a later date, so they should also not be used as variable names, in order to prevent your code from having potential problems in the future.

Table 3-1 lists the keywords and reserved words in JavaScript. Note that all of these words are in all lowercase letters. In later chapters, you will use a number of the keywords, so they will become more familiar over time.

Giving Variables Meaningful Names

Although x is an acceptable variable name, it is unlikely that you will be able to remember what it stands for if you need to debug the program later. Also, if someone else is trying to help you debug the code, their job will be even harder.

You should try to give your variables names that describe what they represent as clearly as possible. Suppose that you want to use a variable to hold a number of an example on a page. Rather than use x, ex, or another short variable, use something more descriptive:

```
var examplenumber = 2;
```

abstract	delete	goto	package	throws
boolean	do	if	private	transient
break	double	implements	protected	try
byte	else	import	public	typeof
case	enum	in	return	var
catch	export	instanceof	short	void
char	extends	int	static	volatile
class	final	interface	super	while
const	finally	let	switch	with
continue	float	long	synchronized	yield
debugger	for	native	this	
default	function	new	throw	

Table 3-1 JavaScript Keywords and Reserved Words

The variable examplenumber will be easy for you to recognize later, and other coders will be more likely to understand its use quickly.

The more variables you use in a script, the more important it becomes to use meaningful and memorable names.

Understanding Data Types

So far, you've seen examples of variable values that are numbers. In JavaScript, the variable values can be one of several data *types*, which include number, string, Boolean, null, and undefined.

Unlike stricter programming languages, JavaScript does not force you to declare the type of variable when you define it. Instead, JavaScript allows virtually any value to be assigned to any variable. It also allows you to change the data type if you change the value. Although this gives you flexibility in coding, you need to be careful because you can end up with some unexpected results—especially when adding numbers (see Chapter 5 for more on this topic).

Number

Number variables are just that—numbers. JavaScript does not require numbers to be declared as integers, floating-point (decimal) numbers, or any other number type. Instead, any number is seen as just another number, whether it is 7, –2, 3.453, or anything else. The number will remain the same type unless you perform a calculation to change the type. For instance, if you use an integer in a variable, it won't suddenly have decimal places unless you perform a calculation of some sort to change it (dividing unevenly, for instance).

As you've seen, you define a number variable by using the keyword var:

```
var variablename = number;
```

Here are some examples:

```
var paycheck = 1200;
var phonebill = 29.99;
var savings = 0;
var sparetime = -24.5;
```

If you need to use a particularly long number, JavaScript has exponential notation. To denote the exponent, use a letter *e* right after the base number and before the exponent. For example, to create a variable named bignumber and assign it a value of 4.52×10^5 (452,000), put the letter *e* in place of everything between the number and the exponent (to represent the phrase "times 10 to the power of"):

```
var bignumber = 4.52e5;
```

NOTE

JavaScript may return an answer to a calculation using exponential notation (like many calculators).

String

String variables are variables that represent a string of text. The string may contain letters, words, spaces, numbers, symbols, or most anything you like. Strings are defined in a slightly different way than numbers, using this format:

```
var variablename = "stringtext";
```

Here are some examples of string variables:

```
var mycar = "Corvette";
var oldcar = "Big Brown Station Wagon";
var mycomputer = "Pentium 3, 500 MHz, 128MB RAM";
var oldcomputer = "386 SX, 40 mHz, 8MB RAM";
var gibberish = "what? cool! I am @ home 4 now. (cool, right?)";
```

As you can see, strings can be short, long, or anything in between. You can place all sorts of text and other characters inside string variables. However, the quotation marks, some special characters, and the case sensitivity of strings need to be considered.

Matching the Quotation Marks

In JavaScript, you define strings by placing them inside quotation marks (quotes, for short), as you saw in the examples. JavaScript allows you to use either double quotes or single quotes to define a string value. The catch is that if the string is opened with double quotes, it must be closed with double quotes:

```
var mycar = "Red Corvette";
```

The same goes for single quotes:

```
var myhouse = 'small brick house';
```

Trying to close the string with a nonmatching type of quotation mark, or leaving out an opening or closing quotation mark, will cause problems.

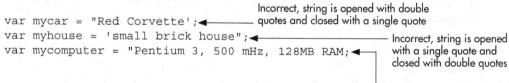

```
var mycar = "Red Corvette';
var myhouse = 'small brick house";
var mycomputer = "Pentium 3, 500 mHz, 128MB RAM;
```

Incorrect, string is opened with double quotes and closed with a single quote

Incorrect, string is opened with a single quote and closed with double quotes

Incorrect, string does not have a closing quote

These mistakes will result in an "Unterminated String" error in the Web browser.

NOTE

If you use double quotes to enclose the string, you can use single quotes inside the string and vice versa.

Watching the Case

JavaScript strings are case sensitive. This may not seem important now, but it matters when you need to compare strings for a match. It only takes one character in a different case to make the strings different:

```
"My car is fun to drive!"
"my car is fun to drive!"
```

You'll learn more about string comparisons in Chapter 5.

Using Special Characters

Special characters enable you to add things to your strings that could not be added otherwise. For example, suppose that you need a tab character between each word in a string. If you press the TAB key on the keyboard, JavaScript will probably see it as a bunch of spaces. Instead, use the special character \t, which places a tab in the string, as in this example:

```
var mypets="dog\tcat\tbird";
```

In each spot where the special character \t appears, JavaScript interprets a tab character.

The special characters all begin with a backslash character (\). Thus, if you want a single backslash character in your string, you need to use the special code for a backslash: \\. For instance, suppose you wish to write the following sentence on a Web page: "Go to the directory c:\javascript on your computer." If you use the string as it is written, your code would look like this:

```
<script type="text/javascript">
  document.write("Go to the directory c:\javascript on your computer.");
</script>
```

The single backslash won't be printed to the browser

The problem is that the single backslash would not be printed on the Web page. It would appear as

```
Go to the directory c:javascript on your computer
```

Unless the backslash is followed with the code for a special character, JavaScript prints the character after the slash as it appears (you will see this in the escape technique discussed in the next section). To fix this, use the \\ special code to print a single backslash on the page:

```
<script type="text/javascript">
  document.write("Go to the directory c:\\javascript on your computer.");
</script>
```

Using the special code for the backslash character allows it to be printed to the browser

Now you get the sentence you want printed to the browser, like this:

```
Go to the directory c\:javascript on your computer.
```

The special characters used in JavaScript are shown in Table 3-2.

Suppose that you want to print a sentence on a Web page with strong emphasis. JavaScript allows you to print HTML code to the page as part of a string in the document.write() method (which you used for your first scripts in Chapter 2). To do this, you can add in the <strong> and </strong> tags from HTML, as in this sample code:

```
<script type="text/javascript">
  document.write("<strong>JavaScript Rules!</strong> This is fun.");
</script>
```

Note the HTML <strong> and </strong> tags within the JavaScript string

Now suppose that you want the code itself to appear on two lines when it is viewed (via "View Source" in the browser), like this:

```
<strong>JavaScript Rules!</strong>
This is fun.
```

You can do this by adding the newline special character to the code:

```
<script type="text/javascript">
  document.write("<strong>JavaScript Rules!</strong>\n This is fun.");
</script>
```

The \n special code is only a newline in JavaScript; it will not result in an HTML line break. The JavaScript newline code does not add a new line to the result of the code shown in the browser display. So, the end result of the preceding code is a sentence like this one:

JavaScript Rules! This is fun.

If you want to add a line break in the browser display, you need to use the HTML <br /> tag to produce it.

Output Character	Special Code to Use
Backslash (\)	\\
Double quote (")	\"
Single quote (')	\'
Backspace	\b
Form feed	\f
Newline	\n
Carriage return	\r
Tab	\t
Vertical tab	\v

Table 3-2 Special JavaScript Characters

Keep in mind that the JavaScript newline affects only the appearance of the source code; it is not a factor in the end result. However, it does help later when you want to format the output of JavaScript alert boxes and various other JavaScript constructions.

Escaping Characters

JavaScript allows you to *escape* certain characters, so that they will show up correctly and avoid causing errors. Like special characters, escape sequences use the backslash character (\), which precedes the character that needs to be escaped.

As noted earlier, JavaScript checks each string for the presence of special characters before rendering it. This is useful if you want to have a quote within a string. For example, suppose that you want to print the following sentence on a Web page:

```
John said, "JavaScript is easy."
```

What would happen if you just threw it all into a document.write() command?

```
<script type="text/javascript">
  document.write("John said, "JavaScript is easy."");
</script>
```
The extra set of quote marks here will cause an error

If you look near the end of the document.write() line, you will see that the two double quotes together could cause trouble, but the browser will actually get upset before that point. When the double quote is used before the word *JavaScript*, the browser thinks you have closed the string used in the document.write() command and expects the ending parenthesis and semicolon. Instead, there is more text, and the browser gets confused.

To avoid problems with quotes, use the backslash character to escape the quotation marks inside the string. By placing a backslash in front of each of the interior double quote marks, you force them to be seen as part of the text string, rather than as part of the JavaScript statement:

The backslashes allow the inner quote marks to become part of the string

```
<script type="text/javascript">
  document.write("John said, \"JavaScript is easy.\"");
</script>
```

This fixes the problem with the string, and the sentence will print with the quotation marks.

CAUTION

Also watch for single quotes and apostrophes within strings. Escaping these is required for strings enclosed within single quotes.

The escape technique also works for HTML code in which you need quotation marks. For instance, if you want to put a link on a page, you use the anchor tag and place the URL in quotes. If you escape the quotes in the anchor tag, JavaScript allows you to write the HTML code to the page within the document.write() method, as in this example:

```
<script type="text/javascript">
  document.write("<a href=\"http://someplace.com\">Text</a>");
</script>
```

This does the job, but there is also an easier way to make this work if you do not want to escape quotation marks all of the time.

To avoid escaping the quotes in the preceding code, you could use single quotes around the URL address instead, as in this code:

Single quotes within double quotes are okay

```
<script type="text/javascript">
   document.write("<a href='http://someplace.com'>Text</a>");
</script>
```

You can also do this the other way around if you prefer to use single quotes on the outside, as in this example:

Double quotes inside single quotes are also okay

```
<script type="text/javascript">
   document.write('<a href="http://someplace.com">Text</a>');
</script>
```

The important point to remember here is to be sure that you do not use the same type of quotation marks inside the string as you use to enclose the string. If you need to go more than one level deep with the quotes, you need to start escaping the quotes; this is because if you switch again, it will terminate the string. For example, look at this code:

```
document.write("John said, 'Jeff says, \"Hi!\" to someone.'");
document.write("John said, 'Jeff says, "Hi!" to someone.'");
```

The first one would work, since the quotes are escaped to keep the string going. However, the second line only switches back to double quotes when inside the single quotes within the string. Placing the double quotes there without escaping them causes the string to terminate and gives an error.

As you can see, quotation marks can be a real pain when you need to use a large number of them within a string. However, remembering to use the backslash to escape the quotes when necessary will save you quite a few headaches when you are looking for a missing quote. I've had to look for missing quotes in my code a number of times, and my head was spinning after a few of those encounters! Later in this chapter, you will see that you can add strings together, which can simplify the use of quotes for you.

Boolean

A *Boolean* variable is one with a value of true or false. Here are examples:

```
var johncodes = true;
var johniscool = false;
```

Notice that the words *true* and *false* do not need to be enclosed in quotes. This is because they are literal values that JavaScript recognizes.

Boolean variables are useful when you need variables that can only have values of true and false, such as in event handlers (covered in Chapter 7).

NOTE

When we talk about the concept of a Boolean variable, the first letter of the word *Boolean* is capitalized (because it is derived from the name of the mathematician George Boole). However, the JavaScript reserved word boolean is written in all lowercase letters when you use the keyword in a script.

Null

Null is used to indicate an empty object (you will learn about objects in Chapter 9). If you need to define an object with a value of null, use a declaration like this:

```
var variablename = null;
```

As with the Boolean variables, you do not need to enclose this value in quotation marks as you do with string values, because JavaScript recognizes the special value of null. The null data type can only have one value: null.

Undefined

The undefined data type is similar to null, in that it only has one possible value: undefined. This value occurs when a variable has not been assigned an initial value, or when a previously undeclared variable is used. For example, both of the following examples make use of undefined variables (you will see more on how to use variables later in this chapter):

```
var myname;  ◄──── The variable myname is declared, but is not assigned a value
document.write(myname);  ◄──────┐
            Since the variable has no assigned value, it is undefined and the code will not work as expected.
```

```
document.write(myname);  ◄──── The myname variable was not previously declared, so myname
            is undefined and the code will not work as expected.
```

Ask the Expert

Q: Why do I need to learn about variables? Couldn't I just put in the number or text I want to use right where I'm going to use it?

A: You can do that; however, it will make longer scripts much harder to write, read, and debug. It also makes it much more difficult to update your scripts because, in order to change that number or text, you would need to change every line where it appears. When you use variables, you can modify just one line of code to change the value of a variable every place it is used. As you gain more experience with JavaScript, you will see just how useful variables are.

(continued)

Q: **Why don't I need to define the type of number I am using (such as float or integer) when I declare a numeric variable?**

A: JavaScript doesn't require this, which can be a good or bad feature depending on your perspective. To JavaScript, any number is just a number and can be used as a number variable.

Q: **Why do I need to put quotation marks around the text in a string?**

A: This is done so that JavaScript knows where a string begins and ends. Without it, JavaScript would be unsure what should be in a string and what should not.

Q: **But doesn't a semicolon end a statement? Why not use that and lose the quote marks?**

A: A variable declaration or any command involving strings can become more complex when the addition operator is used to add two strings and/or variables together. When this happens, JavaScript needs to know when one string stops and another begins on the same line.

Q: **What does the backslash (\) character do, in general?**

A: If the backslash is followed by a code to create a special character, the special character is rendered in its place. Otherwise, the first character after a single backslash is seen "as-is" by JavaScript and treated as part of the string in which it resides.

Try This 3-1   Declare Variables

pr3_1.html

This project gives you the opportunity to practice declaring variables with various values. It also prints a short line of text on the page.

Step by Step

1. Create an HTML page, leaving the space between the <body> and </body> tags open.

2. Between the <body> and </body> tags, add the <script> and </script> tags as you learned in Chapter 2.

3. Create a numeric variable named chipscost and give it the value 2.59.

4. Create a Boolean variable named istrue and give it the value false.

5. Create a variable named nada and give it the value null.

6. Create a JavaScript statement to write to the Web page the string value that follows. Remember to escape quotation marks when necessary:

   John said, "This project is fun!"

7. The body section of the HTML document should look like this when you are finished:

```
<body>
<script type="text/javascript">
  var chipscost=2.59;
  var istrue=false;
  var nada=null;
  document.write("John said, \"This project is fun!\"");
</script>
</body>
```

8. Save the file as pr3_1.html and view it in your Web browser.

You should see only the text that you output with the document.write() command. The variable definitions won't be printed on the browser screen. You can view the page source code to see how the variable definitions look in the code.

Try This Summary

In this project, you were able to use your skills to declare different types of variables in a script. This project included a numeric variable, a Boolean variable, and a variable with a value of null. You were also able to use skills learned in Chapter 2 to write a line of text to the page with JavaScript.

Using Variables in Scripts

To make a variable useful, you need to do more than just declare it in the script. You need to use it later in the script in some way, perhaps to print its value or even just to change its value. To use a variable, you make the call to a variable after it has been declared.

Making a Call to a Variable

The following code shows how to write the value of a variable to a Web page using the document.write() method:

```
<script type="text/javascript">
  var mycar="Corvette";
  document.write(mycar); ◄——— Prints the value of the mycar
                              variable to the browser
</script>
```

The script begins by declaring a variable mycar and giving it a value of "Corvette". Then, in the document.write() command, you see that just the variable name mycar is enclosed within the parentheses. The result of this script is simply to write "Corvette" to the browser.

There are no quotation marks around the mycar variable that is being written to the page. The reason for this is that the mycar variable has already been given a string value, so it does not need to be within quotes to print its value to the page in the document.write() command. Already, you can see how using a variable has the advantage of making a short document.write() command easier to code.

Adding Variables to Text Strings

The preceding code just prints the value of the variable in the browser. If you want that variable to print along with some other text in a string, the document.write() command becomes more complex. The text string needs quotes around it if it has not been defined as a variable, and the variable needs to be on its own. You use the addition operator (+) to add the value of the variable to the string, as shown in this example:

```
<script type="text/javascript">
  var mycar="Corvette";
  document.write("I like driving my "+mycar);
</script>
```

A variable is added to the string that is written to the browser

This code prints the following sentence in the browser window:

```
I like driving my Corvette.
```

Notice the space after the word "my" in the code. This ensures that a space appears before the variable is added to the string. If you used the line

```
document.write("I like driving my"+mycar);
```

the result would be

```
I like driving myCorvette.
```

When adding strings, you need to be careful to add the spaces that you want to appear in the output.

The addition operator enables you to place a variable before, after, or even into the middle of a string. To insert a variable into the middle of a string (so that it shows with text on both sides of it), just use another addition operator to add whatever you need to the right of the variable, as in this example:

```
<script type="text/javascript">
  var mycar="Corvette";
  document.write("I like driving my "+mycar+" every day!");
</script>
```

The variable is added between two strings

Now the variable sits inside two text strings, putting a single string together from three pieces. This code prints the following sentence to the browser:

```
I like driving my Corvette every day!
```

When using the variable, you need to make sure that the variable and addition operators are not inside the quotation marks of a string. If they are, you will not get the results you intended. For example, look at this code:

```
<script type="text/javascript">
  var mycar = "Corvette";
  document.write("I like driving my +mycar+ every day!");
</script>
```

The addition operator must also be outside the quote marks to work

JavaScript will not recognize the operators and variables here; they are seen only as part of the text string because they are inside the quotes. Instead of using the variable, JavaScript takes everything literally and prints this sentence in the browser:

```
I like driving my +mycar+ every day!
```

To make this code easier to write, you could place every string involved into a variable, so that you only need to add the variable values together rather than dealing with the quotes, like this:

```
<script type="text/javascript">
  var firststring = "I like driving my ";
  var mycar = "Corvette";
  var secondstring = " every day!";
  document.write(firststring+mycar+secondstring);
</script>
```

Three variables are added together and printed to the browser

This prints the same sentence but allows you to change its parts later without needing to edit the document.write() command.

The techniques you've learned in this section will become useful as your strings become more complex, especially when you use HTML code within the strings.

Writing a Page of JavaScript

Now that you know how to use variables and write basic HTML code to the page using JavaScript, you will create a page that is almost entirely written with JavaScript (everything inside the <body> and </body> tags), as a way to reinforce the techniques you have learned up to this point.

Creating the Framework

The first thing you need is a basic framework for the page so that you know where to insert your script. Since you are writing information onto the page, the script tags will be placed within the <body> and </body> tags. In this case, an external script file named ch3_code.js will be used. The body section of your HTML document will look like this:

```
<body>
<script type="text/javascript" src="ch3_code.js"></script>
</body>
```

The script tags are inserted here to call the external JavaScript file

The code you place in the ch3_code.js file will determine what shows up in the browser when you have finished.

Defining the Variables

To begin your script file, use some JavaScript code to write an HTML heading. You could write the code as a string directly into the document.write() command, as shown here:

```
document.write("<h1>A Page of JavaScript</h1>");
```

On the other hand, you could place the string inside a variable and use the variable inside the document.write() command later in the script:

```
var headingtext = "<h1>A Page of JavaScript</h1>";
Other code may be placed here...
document.write(headingtext);
```

For this example, you will go with the second method, since it uses a variable. You will see how this can be a handy feature as you get further into the script.

In fact, along with the headingtext variable, you'll create a bunch of variables to hold the strings of HTML code to add to the page. The next one will add a short sentence of introduction to the page. The variable declaration for the introduction will look like this:

```
var myintro = "Hello, welcome to my JavaScript page!";
```

Next, you'll add a link to the page. The variable declaration for the link looks like this:

```
var linktag = "<a href=\"http://www.scripttheweb.com\">Link to a Site</a>";
```

Next, you'll put in some red text to add a little color. Here's the redtext variable definition:

```
var redtext="<span style=\"color:red\">I am so colorful today!</span>";
```

Finally, you'll add in some variables that give you just the opening and closing strong tags and paragraph tags:

```
var begineffect = "<strong>";
var endeffect = "</strong>";
var beginpara = "<p>";
var endpara = "</p>";
```

The code for all of the variables in the ch3_code.js file is as follows:

```
var headingtext = "<h1>A Page of JavaScript</h1>";
var myintro = "Hello, welcome to my JavaScript page!";
var linktag = "<a href=\"http://www.scripttheweb.com\">Link to a Site</a>";
var redtext = "<span style=\"color:red\">I am so colorful today!</span>";
var begineffect = "<strong>";
var endeffect = "</strong>";
var beginpara = "<p>";
var endpara = "</p>";
```

Adding the Commands

Now, following the variable declarations, you can add some document.write() commands to the ch3_code.js file to write the contents of the variables back to the HTML document:

```
document.write(headingtext);
document.write(begineffect + myintro + endeffect);
document.write(beginpara + linktag + endpara);
document.write(beginpara + redtext + endpara);
```

This writes the heading at the top of the page. Adding the begineffect and endeffect variables to the left and right of the myintro variable writes the introductory text in bold under the heading. After that is a new paragraph with a link, and then another new paragraph with the red text message.

Here is the entire code for the ch3_code.js file up to this point:

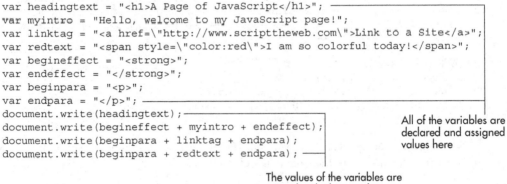

```
var headingtext = "<h1>A Page of JavaScript</h1>";
var myintro = "Hello, welcome to my JavaScript page!";
var linktag = "<a href=\"http://www.scripttheweb.com\">Link to a Site</a>";
var redtext = "<span style=\"color:red\">I am so colorful today!</span>";
var begineffect = "<strong>";
var endeffect = "</strong>";
var beginpara = "<p>";
var endpara = "</p>";
document.write(headingtext);
document.write(begineffect + myintro + endeffect);
document.write(beginpara + linktag + endpara);
document.write(beginpara + redtext + endpara);
```

All of the variables are declared and assigned values here

The values of the variables are printed to the browser here

Save the ch3_code.js file and then load your HTML document. The end result of this code in the browser is shown in Figure 3-1. Note the strong introduction text and the use of paragraphs between sections.

Figure 3-1   The result of the JavaScript code in a Web browser

Modifying the Page

Now suppose that you do not like the layout as it appeared on the Web page. Instead, you want the strongly emphasized introduction to be normally emphasized. If you had written the document.write() commands with plain strings rather than variables, you would need to search through the code to find the <strong></strong> tags and change them to <em></em> tags.

However, since you used the variables, all you need to do is change the values of the appropriate variables at the top of the script file rather than looking for the strong tags inside a bunch of code.

The code that follows shows the changes that you could make to the script file to get the new effect. Notice how you only need to change the values of the begineffect and endeffect variables to change the format of the text on the page:

```
var headingtext = "<h1>A Page of JavaScript</h1>";
var myintro = "Hello, welcome to my JavaScript page!";
var linktag = "<a href=\"http://www.scripttheweb.com\">Link to a Site</a>";
var redtext = "<span style=\"color:red\">I am so colorful today!</span>";
var begineffect = "<em>";          ◄──────────────── Changed to <em>
var endeffect = "</em>";          ◄──────────┐
var beginpara = "<p>";                       │
var endpara = "</p>";               Changed to </em>
document.write(headingtext);
document.write(begineffect + myintro + endeffect);
document.write(beginpara + linktag + endpara);
document.write(beginpara + redtext + endpara);
```

Save the ch3_code.js file and reload your HTML document. Figure 3-2 shows how these changes affect the display of the page in a Web browser.

Figure 3-2   The page after changing some JavaScript variables

Try This 3-2   Create an HTML Page with JavaScript

pr3_2.html
prjs3_2.js

In this project, you will create an HTML page with JavaScript, similar to the one you created in this chapter. The variables will be given new values, and the differences should be noticeable.

Step by Step

1. Create an HTML page, leaving the space between the <body> and </body> tags open.

2. Between the <body> and </body> tags, add the <script> and </script> tags to link to a file named prjs3_2.js. Save the HTML file as pr3_2.html.

3. Open a file to use as your JavaScript file. Save it with the filename prjs3_2.js. Use this file to add the JavaScript code in steps 4–10.

4. Create a variable named myheading and give it this value:

   This is My Web Page!

5. Create a variable named linktag and give it this value:

   <a href=\"http://www.webxpertz.net\">Web Site Link!</a>

6. Create a variable named sometext and give it this value:

   This text can be affected by other statements.

7. Create a variable named begineffect and give it the value .

8. Create a variable named endeffect and give it the value .

9. Create a variable named beginpara and give it the value <p>.

10. Create a variable named endpara and give it the value </p>.

11. Place all of the variable definitions into a single var statement so that you do not need to keep repeating the var keyword (remember to end the last one with a semicolon).

12. Write the value of each variable back to the HTML document in this order:

    myheading
    begineffect
    sometext
    endeffect
    beginpara
    linktag
    endpara
    beginpara
    sometext
    endpara

(continued)

When you have finished, save the prjs3_2.js file. It should look like this:

```
var myheading = "<h1>This is My Web Page!</h1>",
linktag = "<a href=\"http://www.webxpertz.net\">Web Site Link!</a>",
sometext = "This text can be affected by other statements.",
begineffect = "<em>",
endeffect = "</em>",
beginpara = "<p>",
endpara = "</p>";
document.write(myheading);
document.write(begineffect + sometext + endeffect);
document.write(beginpara + linktag + endpara);
document.write(beginpara + sometext + endpara);
```

13. Open the pr3_2.html page in your Web browser and view the results.

14. Reopen the prjs3_2.js file and make the changes in steps 15–16.

15. Change the value of begineffect to .

16. Change the value of endeffect to .

17. When you have finished, save the prjs3_2.js file. It should look like this:

```
var myheading = "<h1>This is My Web Page!</h1>",
linktag = "<a href=\"http://www.webxpertz.net\">Web Site Link!</a>",
sometext = "This text can be affected by other statements.",
begineffect = "<strong>",
endeffect = "</strong>",
beginpara = "<p>",
endpara = "</p>";
document.write(myheading);
document.write(begineffect + sometext + endeffect);
document.write(beginpara + linktag + endpara);
document.write(beginpara + sometext + endpara);
```

18. Reload the pr3_2.html page in your Web browser. Notice the differences resulting from the changes in the variable values in the JavaScript file.

Try This Summary

In this project, you combined your new skills in using variables with earlier skills in writing to a Web page with JavaScript. You created a Web page with a script that uses variables to write the HTML code on the page. You then changed the values of two variables and resaved the script file. The changes to the variables made visible changes to the page.

✓ Chapter 3 Self Test

1. A variable _____ or _____ a value.

2. What are two of the benefits of using variables?

    A. They can save you time in writing and updating your scripts, and they can make the purpose of your code clearer.

    B. They make the purpose of your code clearer, and they make it harder for noncoders to understand the script.

    C. They can save you time in writing and updating your scripts, and they make it harder for noncoders to understand the script.

    D. They offer no advantages whatsoever.

3. To declare a variable, you use the _____ keyword.

4. What symbol is used as the assignment operator in JavaScript?

    A. +

    B. –

    C. :

    D. =

5. Which of the following declares a variable named pagenumber and gives it a value of 240?

    A. var PageNumber=240;

    B. pagenumber=220;

    C. var pagenumber=240;

    D. int named Pagenumber=240;

6. Variable names are not case sensitive.

    A. True

    B. False

7. A variable name must begin with a(n) _____, a(n) _____, or a(n) _____ character.

8. You should avoid using JavaScript keywords and reserved words as variable names.

    A. True

    B. False

9. Which of the following variable declarations uses a variable with a valid variable name in JavaScript?

   A. var return;

   B. var my_house;

   C. var my dog;

   D. var 2cats;

10. In JavaScript, the data _____ include number, string, Boolean, null, and undefined.

11. To denote an exponent in JavaScript, you use a letter _____ right after the base number and before the exponent.

12. Which of the following string declarations is invalid?

   A. var mytext = "Here is some text!";

   B. var mytext = 'Here is some text!';

   C. var mytext = "Here is some text!';

   D. var mytext = "Here is \n some text!";

13. Which of the following statements would be valid in JavaScript?

   A. document.write("John said, "Hi!"");

   B. document.write('John said, "Hi!"");

   C. document.write("John said, "Hi!"");

   D. document.write("John said, \"Hi!\"");

14. _____ characters enable you to add things to your strings that could not be added otherwise.

15. Which of the following successfully displays the value of a variable named myhobby by adding it to a string?

   A. document.write("I like to +myhobby+ every weekend");

   B. document.write("I like to " +myhobby+ " every weekend");

   C. document.write("I like to myhobby every weekend");

   D. document.write("I like to 'myhobby' every weekend");

Chapter 4

Using Functions

Key Skills & Concepts

- What a Function Is

- Why Functions Are Useful

- Structuring Functions

- Calling Functions in Your Scripts

As a JavaScript coder, you need to know how to use functions in your scripts. Functions can make your scripts more portable and easier to debug.

This chapter covers the basics of using functions. First, you will find out what a function is and why functions are useful. Then, you will learn how to define and structure functions. Finally, you will learn how to call functions in your scripts.

What a Function Is

A *function* is basically a little script within a larger script. Its purpose is to perform a single task or a series of tasks. What a function does depends on what code you place inside it. For instance, a function might write a line of text to the browser or calculate a numeric value and return that value to the main script.

As you may recall from math class, a function can be used to calculate values on a coordinate plane. You may have seen calculations like these:

```
f(x)=x+2
y=x+2
```

Both are commonly used to calculate the *y* coordinate from the value of the *x* coordinate. If you need the *y* coordinate when *x* is equal to 3, you substitute 3 for *x* to get the *y* value: 3+2=5. Using the function, you find that when *x*=3, *y*=5.

The function itself is just sitting on the paper (or, in our case, the script) until you need to use it to perform its task. And you can use the function as many times as you need to, by calling it from the main script.

Why Functions Are Useful

Functions help organize the various parts of a script into the different tasks that must be accomplished. By using one function for writing text and another for making a calculation, you make it easier for yourself and others to see the purpose of each section of the script, and thus debug it more easily.

Another reason functions are useful is their reusability. They can be used more than once within a script to perform their task. Rather than rewriting the entire block of code, you can simply call the function again (they are even used to create objects in JavaScript).

Consider the simple function $y=x+2$. If you use it only once, the function doesn't serve much purpose. If you need to get several values, however, the function becomes increasingly useful. Rather than writing out the formula for each calculation, you can just substitute the x values each time you need to get the y value. So, if you need the y value when x is 3, 4, and 5, you can use the function three times to get the y values. The function will calculate 5, 6, and 7, respectively. Instead of writing the content of the function three times, you only need to write it once to get three answers.

Functions can perform complex tasks and can be quite lengthy. In the examples in this and later chapters, you'll see just how useful and time-saving they are in JavaScript.

Structuring Functions

Now that you understand what functions are and why you want to use them, you need to learn how to structure them in your scripts. A function needs to be declared with its name and its code. There are also some optional additions you can use to make functions even more useful. You can import one or more values into the function, which are called *arguments*. You can also return a value to the main script from the function using the *return* statement. You will start by looking at how the function begins.

Declaring Functions

On the first line of a function, you declare it as a function, name it, and indicate whether it accepts any arguments. To declare a function, you use the keyword function, followed by its name, and then a set of parentheses:

```
function functionname()
```

The keyword function tells the browser that you are declaring a function and that more information will follow. The next piece of information is the function's name. As with variable names, you cannot use JavaScript keywords or reserved words as function names (refer to Table 3-1 in Chapter 3 for a list of these). After that, the set of parentheses indicates whether the function accepts any arguments.

For example, to name your function reallycool and indicate that it does not use any arguments, the first line looks like this:

```
function reallycool()
```

Because the function does not use any arguments, the parentheses are left empty.

You may have noticed that there is no semicolon at the end. The semicolon is absent because you use a different technique to show where the function's code begins and ends, as described next. However, each of the separate lines of code within the function does end with a semicolon, as you will see in the examples in this chapter.

Defining the Code for Functions

Curly brackets ({ }) surround the code inside the function. The opening curly bracket marks the beginning of the function's code; then comes the code; and, finally, the closing curly bracket marks the end of the function, in this format:

Function is defined with the name reallycool, and an opening curly bracket shows the beginning of code within the function

```
function reallycool() {
   JavaScript code here
}
```

JavaScript code to be executed is placed here, between the brackets

Closing curly bracket ends the function

The browser will execute all of the code inside the curly brackets when the function is called (as you will learn later in this chapter). When the browser gets to the closing curly bracket, it knows the function has ended. The browser will move to the next line of code or continue whatever it was doing before the function was called.

The most common and recommended format for placing the curly brackets is to put the opening bracket on the same line as the function declaration, as shown in the previous code example. In this format, the opening brackets of code blocks are seen to the right, and closing brackets appear on the left. This is a useful technique to count how many brackets have been opened and/or closed within a segment of code.

Of course, if you have a particularly short function, you can also place the entirety of the function on a single line, like this:

```
function reallycool() { JavaScript code here }
```

The curly brackets are flexible in this way because white space, tabs, and line breaks that appear between tokens in JavaScript are ignored (tokens are such things as variable or function names, keywords, or other parts of the code that must remain intact). Thus, the following code would be valid:

```
function reallycool() {
var
          a
       =
          5; var b = 3; var c = 6; }
```

Though it may be more difficult to read and isn't the recommended formatting, JavaScript will still see it as valid code since the proper syntax is otherwise in place.

In the examples in this book, I will place the opening bracket on the same line as the function declaration and may occasionally place the entirety of a function on one line if it is particularly short.

Naming Functions

As with variables, functions need to be named carefully to avoid problems with your scripts. The same basic rules that applied to variables apply to the naming of functions: case sensitivity, using allowed characters, and avoiding keywords and reserved words. Refer to Chapter 3 for a list of these naming rules.

Your functions will be easier to remember and to debug if you choose names that reflect their purpose. As you learned in Chapter 3, for a variable, you should use a name that represents its value, such as examplenumber to stand for the number of an example on a page. A function name should tell you something about what the function will do. For example, suppose that you create a function that writes some text to the page. It could contain the following line of code:

```
document.write("<strong>This is a strong statement!</strong>");
```

You could just name the function *text*, but that might not be descriptive enough, because you could have other functions that also write text to the page. Instead, you might name it something like show_important_message, so that you know that the function is used to print a piece of strongly emphasized text to the browser. The full function is shown here:

This name helps describe the purpose of the function

```
function show_important_message() {
  document.write("<strong>This is a strong statement!</strong>");
}
```

This line is the code that will be
executed when the function is called

As with variables, the more functions you use in a script, the more important it becomes to use meaningful and memorable names for them.

Adding Arguments to Functions

Arguments are used to allow a function to import one or more values from somewhere outside the function. Arguments are set on the first line of the function inside the set of parentheses, in this format:

```
function functionname(variable1, variable2)
```

Any value brought in as an argument becomes a variable within the function, using the name you give it inside the parentheses.

For example, here is how you would define a function reallycool with the arguments (variables) coolcar and coolplace:

```
function reallycool(coolcar, coolplace) {
  JavaScript code here
}
```

Arguments are added to the first
line within the parentheses

Notice that in JavaScript, you do not use the var keyword when you set the arguments for a function. JavaScript declares the variables automatically when they are set as arguments to a function, so the var keyword is not used here. For example, a line like this one is invalid:

```
function reallycool(varcoolcar, varcoolplace)
```

Where do the arguments come from in the first place? They are obtained from outside the function when you make the function call. You will see how this works later in this chapter. For now, you just need to know how they are used as arguments to JavaScript functions.

NOTE
In other languages, it is often required that a variable have a declaration when set as an argument, but JavaScript will do this for you. However, when you declare variables outside of a function declaration, you need to use the var keyword.

Using Function Argument Values
When you assign arguments to a function, you can use them like any other variables. For example, you could give the value of the coolcar variable to another variable by using the assignment operator, as in this example:

```
function reallycool(coolcar, coolplace) {
  var mycar = coolcar;◄─────────────────────   The value of the coolcar variable is
}                                               assigned to the mycar variable
```

This assigns the value of the coolcar argument to a variable named mycar.

Instead of assigning its value to another variable, you could just use the coolcar argument in the function, as in this example:

```
function reallycool(coolcar, coolplace) {
  document.write("My car is a " + coolcar);◄───   The value of the coolcar variable is
}                                                  used in a document.write() command
```

If the value of coolcar is Corvette, then the function would print this line to the browser when it is called:

```
My car is a Corvette
```

The coolcar argument is given a value out of the blue here. As you will see later in this chapter, the value of coolcar is set when you call the function from elsewhere in the script.

Using Multiple Arguments
You may have noticed that the previous example had two arguments but used only one argument. A function can have as few or as many arguments as you wish. When you assign multiple function arguments, the function doesn't need to use all of them. It can use one argument, a few, or none. How many are used depends on what the function does and how it is called.

In the previous example, the second argument was not used. Here is how you could change the function to use both arguments:

```
function reallycool(coolcar, coolplace) {
  document.write("My car is a " + coolcar + " and I drive it to " + coolplace);◄┐
}                                                                               │
                                                   Both arguments are used as variables
                                                   in this document.write() command
```

Now, if the value of coolcar is Corvette and the value of coolplace is LasVegas, the function would print the following line to the browser when it is called:

```
My car is a Corvette and I drive it to Las Vegas
```

You can place as many arguments as your function needs within the parentheses on the first line of the function. Here is an example with four arguments:

```
function reallycool(coolcar, coolplace, coolfood, coolbreeze)
```

Remember to separate each argument with a comma when you have more than one.

Adding Return Statements to Functions

A return statement is used to return to the *scope* from which the function was called (for the time being, this is the main script), and can return a value. When executed, a return statement will return immediately, so it is often the last statement in a function or the result of a conditional statement (which you will learn about in Chapter 6). The value returned can be the value of a variable or another expression, using the following format:

```
return variablename or expression;
```

For example, to return the value of a variable cooltext, the return statement looks like this:

```
return cooltext;
```

This returns the value of cooltext to the scope where the function was called.

Suppose that you want to write a function that returns the result of adding two strings together. You could use a return statement, as in this example:

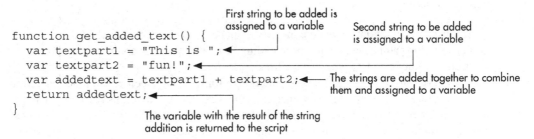

In this function, the first two variables are assigned string values, and the addedtext variable is given the value of the addition of those two strings. The new value is sent back to the script where it was called. It returns this string:

```
This is fun!
```

This returned value can be used in the scope that called the function. In its current form, this function is not very useful, because the strings were just defined in the function rather than being brought in as arguments.

In addition to returning a variable value, you can return a simple value, or even nothing. All of the following would be valid return statements:

```
return "This is cool";   ◄─── Returns a string value
return 42;   ◄───────────────── Returns a numeric value
return true;   ◄─────────────── Returns a Boolean value
return null;   ◄─────────────── Returns a null value
return;   ◄──────────────────── Returns nothing
```

All of these return the control back to the first JavaScript statement after the function call. Returning nothing does this without sending back a value.

You can also return an expression, such as the addition of numbers or strings (or any other expression you decide to build). The following would also be valid return statements:

```
return "This is " + "cool";   ◄──── Returns the result of the addition of two strings
return 21+20+1;   ◄───────────────── Returns the result of the addition of three numbers
```

These would return the values "This is cool" and 42, respectively.

You will see examples of more useful functions that use arguments and return statements in the next section.

Calling Functions in Your Scripts

Now that you know how the function itself works, you need to learn how to call a function in your script. A call to a function in JavaScript is simply the function name along with the set of parentheses (with or without arguments between the opening and closing parentheses), ending with a semicolon, like a normal JavaScript statement:

```
functionname();
```

You can call functions anywhere in your script code. You can even call a function inside another function. You have actually been calling functions since Chapter 1, since every time you used document.write(), you were calling a function.

A good rule to follow is to have the function definition come before the function call in the script. The easiest way to be sure that your function definition comes before your function call is to place all of your function definitions as close to the beginning of the script as possible (usually right after your variable declarations). For example:

```
var paycheck = 1200;   ◄──── A variable is defined
function send_alert() { ─────────────────────────────┐
   window.alert("This came from the function!");      ├──── The function is defined
} ───────────────────────────────────────────────────┘
send_alert();   ◄──── The function is called after it has been defined
```

You will notice the window.alert() method is used, which is yet another function. This method sends a pop-up alert to the viewer with the string sent to it as an argument. The user must click the OK button to close the alert box. This can be used for quick examples or to test code.

Defining a function before calling it is a suggestion for good coding practice, not a strict rule. A function can be called anywhere in JavaScript, due to *function declaration hoisting*. The JavaScript interpreter will first run through all of the JavaScript code looking for any function declarations. Any function declarations it finds are moved (hoisted) to the top of the code order. The code is then executed in the new order, which allows all of the hoisted functions to be called anywhere within the source code. For example, the following code will work due to function declaration hoisting:

```
send_alert();
function send_alert() {
  window.alert("This came from the function!");
}
```

CAUTION
Function declaration hoisting only works when functions are defined using a function declaration. For more information on this, see the "Other Ways to Define Functions" section later in this chapter.

Script Tags: Head Section or Body Section

When adding scripts directly to a Web page rather than using an external file, making sure that variable and function declarations are in the head section often helps to ensure they are available when the script calls them in the body section. However, since JavaScript often uses information from the document that may not have loaded yet, this could become problematic. On the other hand, having a lot of JavaScript code in the body section can also be troublesome when you need to edit your HTML code (and if the JavaScript code is in the body section, it needs to be after the element[s] that have the information JavaScript needs to use to ensure the necessary information is loaded).

A practice often used in modern JavaScript is to place the JavaScript code in an external file (keeping the script code separate from the HTML code), and then placing the script tags right before the closing </body> tag. The reason for this placement is that it allows the page to load and display before trying to load a JavaScript file. This makes the page appear to load faster, and permits the JavaScript code to make use of the HTML tags and CSS information provided by the document as soon as it executes, rather than causing an error or needing to wait for the page to load first.

As an example, you will create a script that sends an alert message to the viewer as soon as the page is loaded in the browser. To have a message pop up in a small message box, you use a JavaScript method called window.alert().

First, you'll learn how to create a JavaScript alert, and then you'll see how to build a function that uses that method and call the function in a script.

Creating a JavaScript Alert

Rather than writing something to the screen with the document.write() method, you can create a JavaScript alert that pops up in a message box by using the window.alert() method. Like the document.write() method, the window.alert() method takes the text string for the alert as an argument, using this format:

```
window.alert("alert_text");
```

The string of text will be displayed in the alert pop-up box.

For example, suppose that you want to display "This is an alert!" in the pop-up box. You write the command in your external JavaScript file (we will use the filename js_alert.js for this example) like this:

```
window.alert("This is an alert!");
```

Now you know how to make the alert pop up, but how can you get it to appear once the page has loaded? You can do this by making sure the script is called right before the </body> tag in the HTML code:

```
<body>
<h1>Hello</h1>                                              This line calls the
<p>This is some text...</p>                                 external JavaScript file
<script type="text/javascript" src="js_alert.js"></script>
</body>                  The closing </body> tag
```

Save the HTML file as js_alert.html and view it in your Web browser. As you can see, this would certainly be an easy way to show an alert when the page opens. However, because you are learning about functions, you will take another approach.

Using a Function for a JavaScript Alert

The following code uses a function in your external JavaScript file to pop up an alert box. In your js_alert.js file, change the code to the following:

```
                                        Names and begins
function show_message() {               the function
  window.alert("This is an alert!");                       The window.alert() command
}                                                          is used in the function
show_message();                         The function is called and executes,
                                        causing the alert to pop up
```

This example creates a function named show_message() to do the job of showing the alert. The alert will be shown only if you call the show_message() function somewhere in the code. In this case, the function is called right after its definition. The result is a small alert box with the message "This is an alert!"

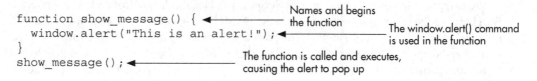

NOTE

When an alert box appears, you may see the page pause until you click the OK button, or it may continue to load while waiting for you to click OK. This depends on your browser.

Even though the function is defined first, it doesn't mean it will be executed first. A function is not executed until it is called; in other words, JavaScript will not use the function until it gets to the function call in the script.

Any commands that come before the function call (and that are not part of the function definition) will be executed before the function. For instance, we could change the code in the JavaScript file as follows:

```
                     The function is defined

function show_message() {
  window.alert("This is an alert!");          This alert doesn't happen
}                                             until the function is called
window.alert("I am first, ha!");          This alert shows up first
window.alert("I am second, ha ha!");
show_message();                               This alert is second

         This finally calls the function so
         that the alert inside it can display
```

This example defines the same function, show_message(), on the first line. The function is followed by two lone window.alert commands, and then the line that calls the function. Save the js_alert.js file with this new code and then reload the js_alert.html file in your Web browser. You should see an interesting result!

The two lone alert commands are the first executable statements JavaScript sees, and they come first. The call to our function is seen last, so the function is executed last. The result is three alerts, in this order:

- The user gets an alert, saying "I am first, ha!" and needs to click the OK button to get rid of it.

- Then the alert that displays "I am second, ha ha!" appears, and the viewer needs to click OK again.

- Finally, the function is executed, and the viewer sees the alert "This is an alert!" and needs to click OK a third time to end the alert frenzy.

Although this example goes overboard with its alerts, it helps you understand how a function call works.

As you gain more experience coding, choosing whether to place script tags in the head or body section will become easier. When scripts use information from the body of the HTML document, the script tags typically either are placed in the head section with a function set up to initialize variables and other functions when the page has loaded (this uses event handling, which will be discussed in Chapter 8) or are placed in the body section just before the ending </body> tag. I will use the latter method in this book.

Calling a Function from Another Function

Calling a function within another function can be a useful way to organize the sequence in which your events will occur. Usually, the function is placed inside another function that has a larger task to finish.

When you place a function call within a function, you should define the function that will be called before you define the function that calls it, per the earlier suggestion that a function should be defined before it is called.

Here is an example of two functions, where the second function calls the first one:

```
function update_alert(){                                            This function
   window.alert("Welcome! This site is updated daily!");            does the work of
}                                                                   displaying the alert
function call_alert() {
   update_alert();                      This function calls the
                                        update_alert() function
}
call_alert();                                                       This calls the call_alert()
                                                                    function to get things started
```

Notice that the update_alert() function is where all the real action happens. Everything else is a function call. The call_alert() function does nothing more than call the update_alert() function so that it is executed. Finally, you see the command that starts the entire sequence, which is the call to the call_alert() function. Since this is the first JavaScript statement outside a function, it is executed first. When it is executed, it just calls the update_alert() function, which does the work of displaying the alert.

NOTE

Most browsers would execute the preceding example without a problem even if you defined the update_alert() function after you called it, due to function declaration hoisting.

Now suppose that you want to create three functions to perform three tasks. To make sure that they occur in the correct sequence, you can call them in order from within another function. Here is an example of this technique with three functions that call alerts for various purposes:

```
function update_alert() {                                           This function
   window.alert("Welcome! This site is updated daily!");            pops up an alert
}                                                                   when called
function section_alert() {
   window.alert("Please visit the picture section!");               This function also pops
                                                                    up an alert when called
}
function links_alert() {
   window.alert("Also, check out my links page!");                  This function also pops
                                                                    up an alert when called
}
function get_messages() {
   update_alert();
   section_alert();                                                 This function calls the
   links_alert();                                                   other three functions into
                                                                    action when called
}
get_messages();                      Calling the get_messages()
                                     function starts the process
```

The code begins by defining the three functions to show each alert. Then it defines the get_messages() function, which just calls the previous three functions. Of course, the get_messages() function must be called to actually put this into action. This call happens as the first statement outside of a function.

Of course, creating a script that pops up message after message is not something you typically want to do. Although the example demonstrates the correct use of function calls, a script that does this would likely annoy your viewers! You'll see examples of practical uses of functions as you progress through this book.

Calling Functions with Arguments

The previous example used three different functions to show three alerts. Although it works, it would be nice if you did not need to write a new function for each alert. You can avoid doing this by using arguments. You can create a function to be used multiple times to do the same thing, but with the new information from the arguments each time.

As mentioned earlier in the chapter, variables are commonly used as arguments. However, you can also use a value as an argument. You'll learn about the different types of variable arguments first, and then take a look at value arguments.

The main rule is that if you have more than one argument, you need to separate each argument with a comma, so that the browser knows what to do. Also, arguments are read *in order*, so if you send one argument to a function that can take two arguments, it will always be used as the *first* argument.

If you want to send the values of certain variables to the function, you must first declare the variables and then be sure that they have the values you need before you send them. Here, the *scope* of a variable becomes important. The scope of a variable determines where it is and is not defined. JavaScript has both global and local variables.

Using Global Variables

Global variables are the variables that you learned about in Chapter 3. Because they are defined outside any functions, they can be changed anywhere in the script—inside or outside of functions. A global variable is declared anywhere outside of a function, as in the following code:

```
var mycar = "Honda";          These are global
var paycheck = "1200";        variables being declared
```

The variables in this example can be changed anywhere in the script. This means that they can even be accidentally overwritten or changed by a function.

To understand how global variables can be affected by a function, consider an example that shows two alerts. You want one alert to tell you how much money you need to get a certain car, and you want the other one to tell you how much money you currently have and what type of car you now own. What would happen if you used the following code?

```
var mycar = "Honda";          These are being declared as global variables
var paycheck = 1200;
function new_car() {
```

```
mycar = "Ferrari";
paycheck = 3500;
window.alert("You need $" + paycheck + " to get a " + mycar);
}
new_car();
window.alert("You make $" + paycheck + " and have a " + mycar);
```

Oops! The function assigns new values to the variables

The alert here is what you expect

The alert here is not what you expect, since the variables were accidentally changed

It may look as if you created new variables inside the function, even though they had the same name. However, the script would output the following text in the two alerts:

```
You need $3500 to get a Ferrari
You make $3500 and have a Ferrari
```

Obviously, this isn't right.

This example demonstrates why you need to use the var keyword when declaring variables. Without the var keyword, you are not creating new variables inside the function (which would make them local). Instead, you are changing the value of your global variables— you are issuing a reassignment command rather than a new variable command. If the variable is not already defined, then declaring it without the var keyword creates a global variable with that name—which can also cause problems. To clear this up, you need to either change one set of variable names or, better yet, use local variables instead.

Using Local Variables

A *local variable* can be used only within the function in which it is declared. It does not exist outside that function, unless you pass it along to another function by using an argument.

The key to creating a local variable in a function is to be sure that you declare it using the var keyword. Otherwise, any global variables by that name could be changed, as you saw in the previous example. To declare a local variable, you must place it inside a function and use the var keyword, as shown in this code:

```
function new_car() {
    var mycar = "Ferrari";
    var paycheck = "3500";
}
```

These variables are declared as local variables, using the var keyword inside a function

The mycar and paycheck variables are now local variables, which can only be seen and changed by the new_car() function.

Therefore, to correct the script in the previous section, you just need to add the var keyword to declare the local variables inside the function, like this:

```
var mycar = "Honda";
var paycheck = 1200;
function new_car() {
    var mycar = "Ferrari";
    var paycheck = 3500;
```

Adding the var keyword ensures that variables are declared locally and do not change the global variables by the same name

```
    window.alert("You need $" + paycheck + " to get a " + mycar);
}
new_car();
window.alert("You make $" + paycheck + " and have a " + mycar);
```

Now the alerts should appear as you intended:

```
You need $3500 to get a Ferrari
You make $1200 and have a Honda
```

As you can see, the scope of a variable may be important when you send certain variables as arguments to a function.

Using Variables As Function Arguments

The following example uses variable arguments. It sends a global variable along to the function.

```
function check_alert(pcheck) {  ◄─────────── The function accepts an argument
    window.alert("You make $" + pcheck);  ◄──────── The argument is used inside
}                                                    the function for the alert
var paycheck = 1200;  ◄────── The variable is assigned a value
check_alert(paycheck);  ◄────── The value is passed to the function as an argument
```

The script begins with the check_alert() function, which takes the argument pcheck. The function is then used to display an alert that uses the value of the argument sent to it (pcheck). After the function, in the outside script, the global variable paycheck is assigned a value of 1200. Then the code calls the check_alert() function and sends it the value of the paycheck variable.

When this code calls the check_alert() function, it sends that function the value of the paycheck variable. This is pulled into the function using the argument name within the parentheses: pcheck.

It is important to note that the pcheck variable becomes a local variable inside the check_alert() function. Since it is an argument, the var keyword is not needed within the parentheses to make it a local variable. Since the code sends a value of 1200, pcheck will be 1200 when beginning the function.

Using Value Arguments

You can also send a value as an argument directly. Instead of needing to declare a global variable in order to send an argument, you can just send a value that will be turned into a local variable inside the function. This allows you to send a value on the fly and eliminates the need to have a global variable handy.

The important thing to remember is that if you send a string value, you need to enclose it in quotes. The following function call sends a string value of "something" to a function named text_alert():

```
text_alert("something");
```

For example, the last example in the previous section can be modified to add more information while using one less line by using value arguments:

```
function check_alert(pcheck, car) {
   window.alert("You make $" + pcheck + " and have a " + car);
}
check_alert(1200, "Corvette");  ◄─────  The function is sent a numeric value and
                                         a string value instead of variable values
```

In this example, the function call sends two arguments to the function. The first one is a numeric value and does not need quotes. The second value is a string and needs to be enclosed in quotes. These values are then sent to the function, where they are read in as the local variables pcheck and car, respectively. They can now be used in the function to display this sentence in an alert:

```
You make $1200 and have a Corvette
```

Arguments can also be sent using expressions, such as the following:

```
check_alert(500+700, "Cor" + "vette");
```

JavaScript will evaluate each expression and send the results as arguments to the function. Thus, the preceding code would have the same end result (adding 500 and 700 gives 1200, and concatenating "Cor" and "vette" gives "Corvette"):

```
You make $1200 and have a Corvette
```

Arguments Are Optional

Another thing that should be mentioned is that sending arguments to a function is optional. The function will do its best to do its work without the argument values that are not sent. You could call the function check_alert() without any arguments:

```
function check_alert(pcheck, car) {
   window.alert("You make $" + pcheck + " and have a " + car);
}
check_alert();
```

Your result would be something like the following text:

```
You make $undefined and have a undefined
```

Thus, it is a good idea to set up some code to handle a situation where an argument is not sent. This can be done using conditionals. Here is one way to check if the arguments were sent to check_alert():

```
function check_alert(pcheck, car) {
   if (pcheck && car) {
      window.alert("You make $" + pcheck + " and have a " + car);
```

```
    }
    else {
      window.alert("My arguments are missing!");
    }
}
check_alert();
```

This essentially tells JavaScript to see if the arguments exist before writing the statement to the page. If they do exist, the statement is written on the page with the argument values. If they do not exist, then the viewer gets an alert that says "My arguments are missing!" The logical operator && will be discussed in more detail in Chapter 5, and the if/else statement will be discussed in more detail in Chapter 6.

Calling Functions with Return Statements

You can assign the result of a function as the value of a variable. In this way, the variable gets the value returned from the function and can be used later in the script. This is the format for declaring a variable that has the value returned by a function:

```
var variablename= functionname();
```

Consider this example, which has a function that returns the value of two text strings added together:

```
function get_added_text() {
  var textpart1 = "This is ";
  var textpart2 = "fun!";
  var addedtext = textpart1 + textpart2;
  return addedtext;◄———————— The result of the added text is returned to the script
}
var alerttext = get_added_text(); ◄——— The result of the function is assigned to a variable
window.alert(alerttext); ◄——— The value of the variable is used as the text for the alert
```

As you can see, the function returns the value of the added text variable to the script. By assigning the result of the get_added_text() function to the alerttext variable, you can use the added text later in the script. The variable is used to send an alert to the user with the result of the added text. The alert message reads

```
This is fun!
```

Now, isn't this fun? You'll see some more practical applications of return statements as you progress through this book.

Other Ways to Define Functions

There are several ways to define functions that you may come across while looking at scripts or may find useful in coding new scripts: the function declaration (already discussed), the function expression, and the function constructor.

The Function Declaration

This is the method you have been using up to this point and one that will be used often in this book. As you will recall, you simply declare the function as follows:

```
function functionname() {
  Code for function here
}
```

You can also add arguments and/or return statements as mentioned earlier in this chapter.

The Function Expression

The function expression is very similar to a function declaration, and uses this format:

```
var variablename = function(arguments) {
  Code for function here
};
```

Notice that there is a semicolon (;) after the closing curly bracket. Since the function is being assigned to a variable, the semicolon is required in order to complete the variable assignment statement. Note that the function itself is assigned to the variable in this case, and not the result of the function (as you have done previously). Also, the function is not being executed here, just assigned.

The main differences between a function declaration and a function expression are as follows:

- A function expression assigns the function to a variable and requires a semicolon to complete the statement.

- Since it has no name assigned after the function keyword, it is considered an *anonymous* function. The variable name can be used to call the function.

- A function expression does not make use of function declaration hoisting, so it cannot be called before it is defined in the code.

  As an example of the final point, take a look at the following code. It will cause an error:

```
send_alert("This is ", "broken!");
var send_alert = function(textpart1, textpart2) {
  window.alert(textpart1 + textpart2);
};
```

Notice that the function is called before it is defined. Since the function is defined as a variable assignment, it cannot be used until after the assignment is complete (it cannot make use of function declaration hoisting). Figure 4-1 shows the error that results from trying to run this in Mozilla Firefox.

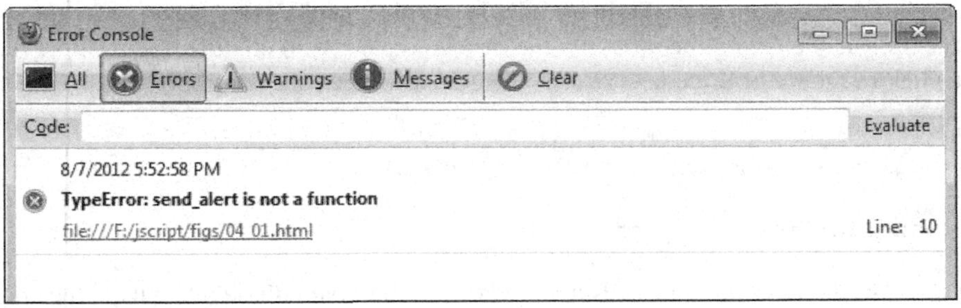

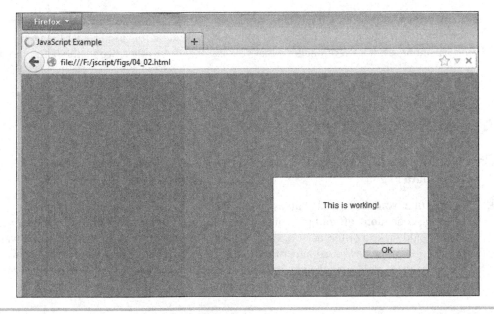

Figure 4-1 The function expression cannot make use of declaration hoisting, so calling it before it is defined caused an error.

In order to make this work, the function call must be moved to a point after the function is defined:

```
var send_alert = function(textpart1, textpart2) {
  window.alert(textpart1 + textpart2);
};
send_alert("This is ", "working!");
```

Now that the function call is after the function definition, the code will work as expected. This is an important difference to remember when using function expressions, as they cannot execute until they are defined. Figure 4-2 shows the alert that is displayed now that the function is called after being defined.

Figure 4-2 The alert now displays as expected.

Anonymous functions are quite useful when dealing with JavaScript events. For example, to react to a user clicking the mouse while on a Web page, you could write a simple function for a click event on the document and then call it, as in the following code:

```
function do_not_click() {
  window.alert("Do not click on my page!");
}
document.onclick = do_not_click;
```

This declares the function, then calls it afterward (without parentheses) to handle the click event.

However, you could combine these two steps into one using an anonymous function, as follows:

```
document.onclick = function() {
  window.alert("Do not click on my page!");
};
```

Since the reaction to this event will only be in one place in the JavaScript code, the anonymous function is a handy way to handle the event without the need to declare the function elsewhere and then call it. This technique and the type of code used for event handling (such as in the previous code listings) will be discussed in more detail in Chapter 8.

The Function Constructor

The function constructor creates a function object in the same way you would create a new instance of an object (this will be discussed in Chapter 9):

```
var functionname = new Function (arguments, code for function) ;
```

This will work like other functions, but the main drawback to this method is that it has poorer performance than the other methods (it is evaluated every time it is used rather than only being parsed once). It is recommended that you use one of the other two methods for defining functions.

Ask the Expert

Q: What if I put a function into my script but decide not to call it in the script? Will it matter?

A: The function won't be executed unless it is called. However, having unused functions makes the code more difficult to maintain and will increase the download time for viewers (which could make a difference on a slow connection such as dial-up or in situations where optimization of the download time of the code is desired). Also, if the function contains syntax errors, it could send the viewer JavaScript errors and keep other things on the Web page from working correctly.

Q: What happens if I decide to remove a function from my script later?

A: This can cause trouble if you do not also remove any calls you made to the function. The script may cause a JavaScript error; or it may run but give you unexpected results. Also, before you remove a function, make sure that it does not perform a necessary task somewhere in the script.

Q: So, what happens if I call a function that doesn't exist?

A: Either you will get a JavaScript error, or the browser will do nothing when the function is called, since it cannot find the function.

Q: What is the best way to determine when to use a function and when to just code what I want right into the script?

A: For the most part, you want to use a function if the code within the function will be reusable in some way. For instance, a function that performs a specific calculation might be useful in more than one spot in the script. Also, if you want to avoid using global variables, functions provide you a way to keep things out of the global context. You will see more about this as you progress through this book.

Try This 4-1   Create an HTML Page with Functions

```
pr4_1.html
prjs4_1.js
```

In this project, you create an HTML page with two JavaScript functions. One function uses arguments sent to it to pop up an alert box with a message. The other function uses a return statement to send a value back to the script. That returned value then is used in an alert message to the viewer.

Step by Step

1. Create an HTML page, leaving the space between the <body> and </body> tags.

2. Create an external JavaScript file and save it as prjs4_1.js.

3. Add the script tags necessary between the <body> and </body> tags of the HTML document to include the external JavaScript file. Save the HTML file as pr4_1.html.

4. Open the prjs4_1.js external JavaScript file and do steps 5–10.

5. Create a function named car_cost() that takes two arguments, mycar and paycheck. Create a window.alert() command that will display an alert with the following message:

   ```
   You have a <mycar variable here> and make $<paycheck variable here>
   ```

(continued)

6. Create a function named get_added_text() that returns the value of two strings added together inside the function. The two strings to add are these two separate strings:

```
This project<space here>
is almost fun!
```

7. In the main script (after the function definitions), call the car_cost() function, and send it the values of "Mustang" and 1500 as arguments.

8. In the main script (after the function definitions), assign the result of the get_added_text() function to a variable named alerttext. Create an alert that pops up with the value of that variable.

9. When you have finished, your external JavaScript file should look like this:

```
function car_cost(mycar, paycheck) {
   window.alert("You have a " + mycar + " and make $" + paycheck);
}
function get_added_text() {
   var textpart1 = "This project ";
   var textpart2 = "is almost fun!";
   var addedtext = textpart1 + textpart2;
   return addedtext;
}
car_cost("Mustang", 1500);
var alerttext=get_added_text();
window.alert(alerttext);
```

10. Save the external JavaScript file.

11. Open the pr4_1.html file and view it in your browser to see the result.

When you open the Web page, you should see two alert messages:

```
You have a Mustang and make $1500
This project is almost fun!
```

Try This Summary

In this project, you created a script that uses two JavaScript functions. The first function uses arguments and creates an alert box with a message based on the arguments that are sent to the function. The second function returns a value to the script after adding two strings together. The result of the script in the browser is two alert messages based on the information sent to the first function and the information returned to the script from the second function.

Scope/Context Basics

In JavaScript, there are some key things to remember when it comes to scope (the context in which a variable or function is usable and valid). For instance, you were able to create local variables earlier in this chapter by declaring them with the var keyword within a function. These local variables were only valid within the function in which they were defined, which kept them from being changed by something in the main script (the *global* context). The two main execution contexts in JavaScript are the global context and the function context.

Global Context

The global context in JavaScript includes any code that is not within a function. Consider this code:

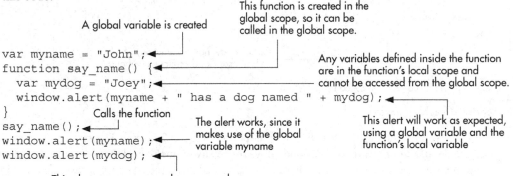

As you can see in the example, the global variable myname is usable anywhere in the code after it is defined. The say_name() function is defined in the global scope, so it can be called from anywhere in the code. The mydog variable, however, is only available within the say_name() function and cannot be used anywhere outside of this context. The attempt to use it within an alert at the end of the script will cause a JavaScript error.

In general, the more complex your script becomes, the better it is to move things out of the global context, since global variables can be accidentally overwritten from any other context. This concept will be discussed further in Chapter 9.

Function Context

In JavaScript, a function creates a new context. As you have seen, any variables declared with the var keyword inside a function are not available outside the function. One thing to remember, though, is that functions can have other functions nested inside them. Consider the following code:

```
var myname = "John";

function say_name() {
  var mydog = "Joey";

  function say_food() {
    var myfood = "Pizza";
    window.alert(myname + " and " + mydog + " like " + myfood);
  }

  window.alert(myname + " has a dog named " + mydog);
  say_food();
}

say_name();
```

The say_food() function can only be called within the say_name() function and is not available in the global context. It can use any variables from the say_name() context or the global context.

Calls the say_name() function, which calls the say_food() function within it.

The say_name() function can be called from the global context, but has a local variable mydog and a local function say_food()

This creates the say_food() function within the say_name() function. The say_food() function can make use of any variables defined either in the say_name() or global contexts. As you can see, this creates a scope chain based on the nested functions. The innermost function in the chain will have variables that are most well-protected from being altered, while the global context will have the least protected variables (they are public and can be used even in the innermost function).

Each context from the example and the variables/functions the context can use are shown here:

Global Context:
myname
say_name()

say_name() Context:
my_name (from global)
mydog
say_food()

say_food() Context:
myname (from global)
mydog (from say_name())
myfood

Notice that myname can be used in all three contexts, mydog can be used in two (say_name() and say_food() contexts), and myfood can be used only in one (the say_food() context).

It is important to remember how this works, as JavaScript only uses functions to create a context. Other block-level structures, such as conditional statements and loops, are not used for this purpose. You will see more on this topic in Chapter 6.

NOTE
A third type of execution context can be created by calling the eval() method; however, the eval() method can cause numerous problems (for example, speed and security issues) and should almost never be used.

Try This 4-2   Write Your Own Functions

pr4_2.html
prjs4_2.js

In this project, you again create an HTML page, but for this project, you will use a function to keep as much information out of the global context as possible (you will have a single global function that is called in the global context).

Step by Step

1. Create an HTML file, leaving the content of the body section empty, and save it as pr4_2.html.

2. Create an external JavaScript file and save it as prjs4_2.js. Use this file for steps 3–6.

3. Create a function named display_HTML().

4. Within the function, create a variable named myheading, and use it to hold this code:
   <h1>Hello, World!</h1>

5. Create a variable named mytext, and use it to hold the following code:
   <p>While it is nice to know you world, there are only some things that I am comfortable sharing in a global context. You can't alter the variable that holds this text outside of the function that contains it! Ha!</p>

6. Create a document.write() statement that will write both of the variable values on the page and end the function.

7. Insert code that will call the function.

8. When you are done, the JavaScript file should look like this:

```
function display_HTML() {
    var myheading = "<h1>Hello, World!</h1>";
    var mytext = "<p>While it is nice to know you world, there are only some
                  things that I am comfortable sharing in a global context.
                  You can't alter the variable that holds this text outside of
                  the function that contains it! Ha!</p>";
    document.write(myheading + mytext);
}
display_HTML();
```

9. In the body section of the HTML page, place the script tags in the document (pointing to the prjs4_2.js file) so that the script displays the HTML code on the page.

10. When you have finished, save the HTML and JavaScript files and view the HTML page in your browser to see how it works.

The results should be a heading saying "Hello, World!", followed by the long paragraph where the script explains its desire to keep some of its information from being altered by outside influences.

Try This Summary

In this project, you used your knowledge of functions and context to create a script. The result of the script is that the HTML page displays the information while protecting the variable values from being altered by anything that could potentially change in the global context.

Chapter 4 Self Test

1. In general, a function is a little _____ within a larger _____ that is used to perform a single _____ or a series of _____.

2. What are two reasons why a function can be useful?

   A. They make simple scripts more complex, and they make it harder for noncoders to read the script.

   B. They provide a way to organize the various parts of the script into the different tasks that must be accomplished, and they can be reused.

   C. They make simple scripts more complex, and they can be reused.

   D. They provide a way to organize the various parts of the script into the different tasks that must be accomplished, and they make it harder for noncoders to read the script.

3. On the first line of a function, you _____ it as a function, _____ it, and indicate whether it accepts any _____.

4. To declare a function, you use the keyword _____.

   A. var

   B. switch

   C. function

   D. for

5. What surrounds the code inside a function?

   A. Curly brackets – { }

   B. Colons – ::

   C. Square brackets – []

   D. Nothing

6. Function names are case sensitive.

   A. True

   B. False

7. JavaScript keywords can be used as function names.

   A. True

   B. False

8. Which of the following would be a valid function name in JavaScript?

   A. function my function()

   B. function var()

   C. function get_text()

   D. function 24hours()

9. _____ are used to allow a function to import one or more values from somewhere outside the function.

10. Arguments are set on the first line of a function, inside a set of _____.

   A. curly brackets – { }

   B. parentheses – ()

   C. square brackets – []

   D. nothing

11. Multiple arguments are separated by what symbol?

   A. Period

   B. Colon

   C. Semicolon

   D. Comma

12. Which of the following is a valid use of the window.alert() method?

    A. win.alt("This is text");

    B. window.alert("This is text);

    C. window.alert('This is text");

    D. window.alert("This is text");

13. Which of the following correctly calls a function named some_alert() and sends it two string values as arguments?

    A. some_alert();

    B. some_alert("some", "words");

    C. some_alert("some", "words);

    D. SOME_alert("some", "words");

14. Which of the following correctly assigns the result of a function named get_something() to a variable named shopping?

    A. var shopping = get_something();

    B. var shopping = "get_something";

    C. var Shopping = get_Something;

    D. shopping = getsomething;

15. A _____ variable can be used anywhere in JavaScript.

Chapter 5

JavaScript Operators

Key Skills & Concepts

- Understanding the Operator Types

- Understanding Arithmetic (Mathematical) Operators

- Understanding Assignment Operators

- Understanding Comparison Operators

- Understanding Logical Operators

- Understanding Order of Operations

Operators do much of the work in scripts. In the previous chapters, you have seen examples of the use of the assignment (=) and addition (+) operators. JavaScript offers many other types of operators to perform various operations.

This chapter begins by giving you an introduction to the different types of JavaScript operators. Then, you will learn about each operator and its use in scripts. Finally, you will learn about the order of precedence for operators, which determines which operations are performed before others.

Understanding the Operator Types

An *operator* is a symbol or keyword in JavaScript that performs some sort of calculation, comparison, or assignment on one or more values. In some cases, an operator provides a shortcut to shorten the code so that you have less to type.

Common calculations include finding the sum of two numbers, combining two strings, or dividing two numbers. Some common comparisons might be to find out if two values are equal or to see if one value is greater than the other. A shortcut assignment operator might be used to assign a new value to a variable so that the variable name does not need to be typed twice.

JavaScript uses several different types of operators:

- **Arithmetic**   These operators are most often used to perform mathematical calculations on two values. The arithmetic operators will probably be the most familiar to you. They use symbols such as +, −, and *.

- **Assignment**   These operators are used to assign new values to variables. As you learned in Chapter 3, one of the assignment operators is the symbol =.

- **Comparison**   These operators are used to compare two values, two variables, or perhaps two longer statements. They use symbols such as > (for "is greater than") and < (for "is less than").

- **Logical** These operators are used to compare two conditional statements (or to operate on one statement) to determine if the result is true and to proceed accordingly. They use symbols such as && (returns true if the statements on both sides of the operator are true) and || (returns true if a statement on either side of the operator is true).

- **Bitwise** These are logical operators that work at the bit level (ones and zeros). They use symbols like << (for left-shifting bits) and >> (for right-shifting bits).

- **Special** These are operators that perform other special functions of their own.

In this chapter, you will learn about each of these types of operators. This will be a general overview of the function of each type of operator, so that you will better know the purpose of all the operator types when you put them to use later. To begin, you'll look at the arithmetic operators in JavaScript.

Understanding Arithmetic Operators

For a mathematical calculation, you use an arithmetic operator. The values that you use can be any sort of values you like. For instance, you could use two variables, two numbers, or a variable and a number. A few of these operators are able to perform a task on a single value.

As a quick example, you will remember that you used the addition operator (+) to add two strings together in previous chapters. Here is an example of two string values being combined with the addition operator:

```
window.alert("I begin and " + "this is the end.");
```

You can also use the addition operator when one of the values is a variable, as in this example:

```
var part2 = "this is the end.";
window.alert("I begin and " + part2);
```

The addition operator also works when both values are variables, as in the next example:

```
var part1 = "I begin and ";
var part2 = "this is the end.";
window.alert(part1 + part2);
```

These examples illustrate how you can use many of the arithmetic operators with a number of values and/or variables. This allows you some flexibility in the way you code your scripts.

The operators that work on single values are the increment, decrement, unary plus, and unary negation operators. The increment and decrement operators are actually shortcuts to adding or subtracting 1, so learning how to use them could save you some coding time.

The arithmetic operators and their functions are summarized in Table 5-1. The following sections discuss each operator in more detail.

Operator	Symbol	Function
Addition	+	Adds two values
Subtraction	−	Subtracts one value from another
Multiplication	*	Multiplies two values
Division	/	Divides one value by another
Modulus	%	Divides one value by another and returns the remainder
Increment	++	Shortcut to add 1 to a single number
Decrement	−−	Shortcut to subtract 1 from a single number
Unary Plus	+	Leaves numeric values as-is, but will attempt to change non-numeric values into numbers
Unary Negation	−	Makes a positive negative or a negative positive

Table 5-1 The Arithmetic Operators

The Addition Operator (+)

As you have seen, the addition operator can be used to combine two strings. It is also used to add numbers in mathematical calculations.

Variables for Addition Results

One use of the addition operator is to add two numbers to get the mathematical result. When adding numerical values, you often assign the result to a variable and use the value of the variable later. For example, to calculate the value of 4 plus 7 and show the result, you could code it like this:

```
var thesum = 4 + 7;          Two numbers are added with the addition operator
window.alert(thesum);        The result of the addition is shown as an alert to the viewer
```

The result is an alert that says 11.

To make the example a little more complex, you could change one of the numbers to a variable:

```
var num1 = 4;                A number is assigned to a variable
var thesum = num1 + 7;       A number is added to the variable and
window.alert(thesum);        the total is assigned to a new variable
```

The result is the same as the previous example's code: an alert that says 11.

Taking the example one step further, you could make both of the numbers variables:

```
var num1 = 4,
    num2 = 7;
var thesum = num1 + num2;    Two variables are added using the addition operator
window.alert(thesum);
```

This example allows for the most flexibility, since you can change the values of the two number variables and get a new result without needing to dig deeper into the script to make the change.

Operands

Each value that is used with an operator is called an *operand*. Most operators in JavaScript work with two operands at a time. For instance, the following code contains two operands: 7 and 4.

```
var thesum = 7 + 4;
```

The values on either side of the operator are operands. This is also true when using other data types or when using variables:

```
var num1 = 7,          The variable num1 and the
    mytext = "Hello",  number 4 are operands
    thesum = num1 + 4,
    ans = mytext + " there!";   The variable mytext and the
                                string " there!" are operands
```

When using operators that take two operands in a statement multiple times, JavaScript will use the order of operations (this will be explained in the "Understanding Order of Operations" section in this chapter) and perform the tasks with one operator and two operands at a time. In the case of the addition operator, if no other operators or parentheses are present, then the order of operations will proceed from left to right. Consider the following code:

```
var thesum = 2 + 3 + 1;
```

First, the 2 + 3 portion of the expression will be calculated to get a result of 5. This result is then used as the first operand to complete the calculation, 5 + 1, which will give the final result of 6.

Some operators (called unary operators) use only one operand. The operator is placed directly before or after the lone operand. For example, take a look at this code:

```
var mymoney = 5;
mymoney++;    The lone operand is the mymoney variable.
```

In this case, the increment operator is used, and the only operand is the mymoney variable. You will see more about the increment operator and the remaining unary operators as you move through this chapter.

Type Coercions in Calculations

It is important to note that JavaScript performs *type coercion* (attempting to change the data type of a value if it is deemed necessary) when working with the arithmetic operators. When you use the addition and other arithmetic operators, you need to be aware that JavaScript automatically coerces different values, like an integer (a nondecimal numeric value) and a float (a decimal numeric value) to the appropriate type. For instance, you might have the following code:

```
var num1 = 4.73,      This variable has decimal places
    num2 = 7,         This variable is an integer
    thesum = num1 + num2;   The two variables are added, and JavaScript
window.alert(thesum);       will show the answer with the decimal places
```

When the script is run, you will see an alert with the result.

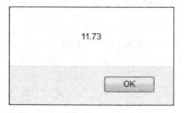

JavaScript added the integer and the float together and gave back a float: 11.73. JavaScript does this automatically, so you need to make sure that the values you use are going to give you the results you expect.

For example, if you add a number and a string, the result will come out as though you had combined two strings. Look at this example:

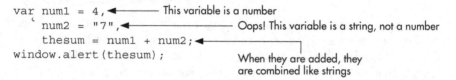

```
var num1 = 4,          This variable is a number
    num2 = "7",        Oops! This variable is a string, not a number
    thesum = num1 + num2;
window.alert(thesum);
                       When they are added, they
                       are combined like strings
```

This looks as if it would be adding the numbers 4 and 7, since they both appear to be numbers. The trouble is that the 7 is a string in this case, not a number, because it has quotes around it. This causes the 4 to be converted to a string, and then the two strings are added together (concatenated). The result that appears in the alert box may surprise you.

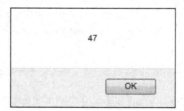

Rather than the expected answer of 11, you get 47. When the two values are added as strings, they are run together rather than added mathematically. With strings, "4"+"7"=47.

The other arithmetic operators also do conversions, much like the addition operator, so be aware of this possibility if you get unexpected results in a script.

Special Rules

The addition operator has some special rules it uses when trying to perform a calculation or concatenation. Here are some of the situations most commonly encountered:

- If one operand has the special value of NaN (Not a Number), and the other operand is a number, then the result will be NaN.

- If one operand is a string, the other operand is coerced into a string and the strings are concatenated.

- If both operands are strings, the strings are simply concatenated.

NOTE

If you have two numbers and then a string, the numbers will be added first and then converted. For example, 35 + 5 + "th Avenue" will first add 35+5 as numbers (since operators are evaluated from left to right), and then the result (40) will be concatenated as a string with "nth Avenue", resulting in "40th Avenue".

As an example of these rules in action, if NaN is added to a number, the result is NaN. If it is added to a string, the string value "NaN" will be concatenated to the other string value:

- 4 + NaN will be NaN

- "Hi" + NaN will be "HiNaN"

As you proceed through this chapter, you will see that the other operators also have special rules that may be helpful to understand if you should come across unexpected results in your scripts.

The Subtraction Operator (−)

The subtraction operator is used to subtract the value on its right side from the value on its left side, as in mathematics. Here is an example:

```
var theresult = 10 - 3;
```
⟵——————— Two numbers are subtracted using the subtraction operator

This code simply subtracts 3 (the number on the right of the operator) from 10 (the number on the left of the operator). The result is 7.

Special Rules

As with the addition operator, there are some special rules:

- If one of the operands is NaN, the result will be NaN.

- If one of the operands is of a data type other than number (for example, string, Boolean, and so on), then JavaScript attempts to coerce that value into a number and perform the subtraction. If it cannot coerce the value, the result will be NaN. For example, "7" − "3" will evaluate to 4, since these string values will be coerced into the numbers 7 and 3, respectively.

The Multiplication Operator (*)

The multiplication operator is used to multiply two operands. The next example shows this operator in action:

```
var num1 = 4 * 5;
```
⟵——————— Two numbers are multiplied using the multiplication operator

Special Rules

● If one of the operands is NaN, the result will be NaN.

● If one of the operands is of a data type other than number, it attempts to coerce that value and perform the multiplication. If it cannot coerce the value, the result will be NaN.

The Division Operator (/)

The division operator is used to divide the value on its left side by the value on its right side. For example, the code 4 / 2 means 4 divided by 2 and gives the result of 2. For a JavaScript example of this in action, take a look at this code:

```
var num1 = 10 / 2;        Two numbers are divided using the division operator
```

The result is 5, dividing 10 by 2.

Special Rules

● If one of the operands is NaN, the result will be NaN.

● If the number zero is divided by the number zero, the result will be NaN.

● If any other finite number is divided by the number zero, the result will be the special value of Infinity.

● If one of the operands is of a data type other than number, it attempts to coerce that value and perform the division. If it cannot coerce the value, the result will be NaN.

Division by Zero

When you use the division operator, you need to be careful that you do not end up dividing by zero in some way. If you do, the result is going to be Infinity. The code that follows shows an example of this happening (although it is unlikely to occur exactly in this way):

```
var num1 = 10,
    num2 = 0,
    theresult = num1 / num2;        Oh no! On this line you are dividing by zero
window.alert(theresult);        This alert won't be a number
```

If you placed this code in a document, you might see an alert box like this:

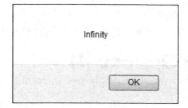

To avoid dividing by zero, be careful about what numbers or variables you place on the right side of the division operator.

The Modulus Operator (%)

The modulus operator is used to divide the number on its left side by the number on its right side, and then give a result that is the integer remainder of the division. Think back to when you learned long division and used remainders as part of the answer rather than converting to decimals or fractions. Dividing 11 by 2 gives 5 with a remainder of 1. The remainder of 1 is what the modulus operator gives you when you write 11 % 2.

The following is an example in JavaScript:

```
var num1 = 11 % 2;
window.alert(num1);◄──────── The modulus operator is used to get the remainder
```

The result is an alert box that shows the value of the remainder, which is 1. If the calculation had no remainder, the result would be 0.

This is the last of the arithmetic operators that work on two values at the same time. The unary operators, which work on only one value at a time, are next.

The Increment Operator (++)

The increment operator is unary and increases the value of its lone operand by 1. The effect of using it depends on whether the operator is placed before or after the operand.

The Increment Operator Before the Operand

When the increment operator is placed before the operand, it increases the value of the operand by 1, and then the rest of the statement is executed. Here is an example:

```
var num1 = 2,
    theresult = ++num1;
```

In this case, the variable num1 begins with a value of 2. However, when the code assigns the value to the variable theresult, it increments the value of num1 before the assignment takes place. The increment occurs first because the increment operator is in front of the operand. So, the value of num1 is set to 3 (2+1) and is then assigned to the variable theresult, which gets a value of 3.

The Increment Operator After the Operand

If you place the increment operator after the operand, it changes the value of the operand after the assignment. Consider this example:

```
var num1 = 2,
    theresult = num1++;
```

As in the previous example, num1 begins with the value of 2. On the next line, the increment operator is used after the operand. This means that the code assigns the current value of num1 to the variable theresult, and *after* that is done, it increments the value of num1. So, only after this assignment is complete do you have a new value for num1. The variable theresult is given a value of 2, and then num1 is changed to 3. If you use num1 after this, it will have a value of 3.

Another way to see how the increment operator works before and after the operand is to run the following script in your browser. Notice what the values are in the first alert and what they are in the second alert.

```
var num1 = 2;
   result = ++num1;
alert("num1= " + num1 + " result= " + result);
num1 = 2;
result = num1++;
alert("num1= " + num1 + " result= " + result);
```

In the first alert box, you will see num1= 3 result= 3. Since the ++ operator is used before the operand here, the value of num1 is increased by 1 and then assigned to the result variable. In the second alert box, you will see num1= 3 result= 2. This is because the ++ operator is used after the operand, so the value of num1 is increased after it has been assigned to the result variable. The result variable gets a value of 2, but num1 will be increased to 3.

Note also that you do not have to perform an assignment to use this operator. You can simply type num1++; or ++num1; and the value of num1 will be changed accordingly for later use.

The Decrement Operator (– –)

The decrement operator works in the same way as the increment operator, but it subtracts 1 from the operand rather than adding 1 to it. As with the increment operator, its placement before or after the operand is important.

If you place the decrement operator before the operand, the operand is decremented, and then the remainder of the statement is executed. Here is an example:

```
var num1 = 2,
   theresult = --num1;
```

Here, the variable num1 is given a value of 2. In the next line, the code subtracts 1 from num1 and then assigns the result to the variable theresult. Thus, the variable theresult ends up with a value of 1 (2–1).

When you place the operator after the operand, as in the next example, the rest of the statement is executed and the operand is decremented afterward:

```
var num1 = 2,
   theresult = num1--;
```

This time, the variable theresult is assigned a value of 2, and then num1 is decremented to 1. If you use num1 after this line, it will have a value of 1.

The Unary Plus Operator (+)

The unary plus operator is used to try to coerce a value into a number. If it cannot coerce the value, then the result will be NaN. This is a handy operator to use when you run into the situation mentioned earlier in the chapter:

```
var num1 = 4,
    num2 = "7",
    thesum = num1 + num2;
window.alert(thesum);
```

As you recall, this returned the string "47". The unary + operator could be used on the num2 variable to coerce the string "7" into its numeric value, which would then allow mathematical addition to take place rather than string concatenation.

```
var num1 = 4,
    num2 = "7",
    thesum = num1 + (+num2);
window.alert(thesum);
```

Notice the parentheses around the +num portion of the statement. As in math, you can use parentheses to set the order of operations (as you'll learn later in this chapter) or just to clarify the order visually. Here, the parentheses aren't necessary, but they help organize that code so that you can see that it is adding num1 to the result of using the unary plus operator on num2. You could have written this code as well:

```
var thesum = num1 + +num2;
```

This doesn't look as nice, but it still works. The updated code will return a result of 11 rather than "47", since the string "7" was able to be coerced into a numeric 7.

The Unary Negation Operator (−)

Unary negation is the use of the subtraction sign on only a single operand. This operator creates a negative number or negates the current sign of the number (positive or negative).

Here is an example of assigning a negative value to a number:

```
var negnum = -3;
```

This defines a variable with a value of negative 3. Basically, the operator tells the browser that the 3 is "not positive," because it negates the default sign of positive by placing the negation operator ahead of the number.

You can also use the unary negation operator to help show the addition or subtraction of a negative number, as in this example:

```
var theresult = 4 + (-3);
```

Notice the parentheses around the −3 portion of the statement. As mentioned with the unary plus operator, this is optional and merely provides additional clarity.

You may be thinking that an even easier way to write the same thing looks like this:

```
var theresult = 4 - 3;
```

You're right, this is the simplest way to write it; but it uses subtraction rather than unary negation.

You can also use this operator on a variable value, which simply negates the sign on the number represented by the variable:

```
var x = 4;
var y = 3;
var z = -y;
```

This assigns the variable z the unary negated value of y, which is –3.

Now that you've learned about the arithmetic operators, it's time to turn to the assignment operators.

Understanding Assignment Operators

Assignment operators assign a value to a variable. They do not compare two items, nor do they perform logical tests.

When you learned about variables in Chapter 3, you saw how the basic assignment operator, the single equal sign (=), is used to give an initial value or a new value to a variable.

The other assignment operators also give new values to variables, but they do so in slightly different ways because they perform a simple calculation as well. Table 5-2 summarizes the assignment operators, which are discussed in more detail in the following sections.

Operator	Symbol	Function
Assignment	=	Assigns the value on the right side of the operator to a variable
Add and assign	+=	Adds the value on the right side of the operator to the variable on the left side, and then assigns the new value to the variable
Subtract and assign	–=	Subtracts the value on the right side of the operator from the variable on the left side, and then assigns the new value to the variable
Multiply and assign	*=	Multiplies the value on the right side of the operator by the variable on the left side, and then assigns the new value to the variable
Divide and assign	/=	Divides the variable on the left side of the operator by the value on the right side, and then assigns the new value to the variable
Modulus and assign	%=	Takes the integer remainder of dividing the variable on the left side by the value on the right side, and assigns the new value to the variable

Table 5-2 The Assignment Operators

The Assignment Operator (=)

You have been using the direct assignment operator since Chapter 3. It assigns the value on the right side of the operator to the variable on the left side, as in this example:

```
var population = 4500;
```

This assigns the value of 4500 to the variable population.

The Add-and-Assign Operator (+=)

The += operator adds the value on the right side of the operator to the variable on the left side and then assigns that new value to the variable. In essence, it is a shortcut to writing the type of code shown here:

```
var mymoney = 1000;
mymoney = mymoney + 1;
```

Here, the variable mymoney is created and assigned a value of 1000. The code then changes the value by assigning it a value of itself plus 1. The value assigned to the mymoney variable is 1001.

Instead of writing the variable name an extra time, you can use the add-and-assign operator to shorten the code. The following code gives the same result as the previous example, but saves a little typing:

```
var mymoney = 1000;
mymoney += 1;
```

Using the add-and-assign operator, this code adds 1 (the value on the right) to mymoney (the variable on the left), assigning the new value of 1001 to the variable mymoney.

This operator can be used to add any value, not just 1. For example, you could add 5 in the assignment, as in this example:

```
var mymoney = 1000;
mymoney += 5;
```

This time, mymoney ends up with a value of 1005.

You can even use a variable rather than a plain number value on the right side, as in this example:

```
var mymoney = 1000;
var bonus = 300;
mymoney += bonus;
```

Here, bonus has a value of 300, which is added to the variable mymoney, and then mymoney is assigned the result of 1300. In this way, the value of the bonus variable can be changed to affect the result of the assignment.

This assignment operator, like the addition arithmetic operator, also allows you to concatenate strings. Thus, you could add on to the end of a string value using this operator:

```
var myname = "Bob";
myname += "by";
```

This adds the string "by" to the end of the string "Bob", which yields the string "Bobby".

The Subtract-and-Assign Operator (−=)

The −= operator works like the += operator, except that it subtracts the value on the right side of the operator from the variable on the left side. This value is then assigned to the variable. Here is an example of this operator in action:

```
var mymoney = 1000;
var bills = 800;
mymoney -= bills;
```

This example subtracts the value of the bills variable (800) from the mymoney variable and assigns the result to mymoney. In the end, mymoney has a value of 200.

The Multiply-and-Assign Operator (*=)

The *= operator multiples the value on the right side of the operator by the variable on the left side. The result is then assigned to the variable. The next example shows this operator at work:

```
var mymoney = 1000;
var multby = 2;
mymoney *= multby;
```

Here, the variable mymoney is multiplied by the value of the multby variable, which is 2. The result of 2000 is then assigned to the variable mymoney.

The Divide-and-Assign Operator (/=)

The /= operator divides the variable on the left side of the operator by the value on the right side. The result is then assigned to the variable. Here is an example:

```
var mymoney = 1000;
var cutpayby = 2;
mymoney /= cutpayby;
```

In this example, the variable mymoney is divided by the value of the variable cutpayby, which is 2. The result of 500 is then assigned to the mymoney variable.

The Modulus-and-Assign Operator (%=)

Like the other assignment variables that also perform math, the %= operator does a calculation for the variable assignment. It divides the variable on the left side of the operator by the value on the right side, takes the integer remainder of the division, and assigns the result to the variable. Here is how you might assign a value to the mymoney variable using the modulus-and-assign operator:

```
var mymoney = 1000;
var cutpayby = 2;
mymoney %= cutpayby;
```

Here, the variable mymoney is divided by the value of the variable cutpayby, which is 2. The result of that is 500 with no remainder, meaning that the end result of the calculation is 0. Thus, 0 is the value that gets assigned to the variable mymoney. (If they start cutting pay like this anyplace, it is probably time to leave!)

Try This 5-1 Adjust a Variable Value

pr5_1.html
prjs5_1.js

In this project, you create a page that uses some of the arithmetic and assignment operators and writes the results on an HTML page.

There is more than one solution that can be used for many of these steps, so feel free to use the method you prefer. You can also try to see which method requires the least typing. Be sure to write the results of each change to the page by using the document.write() command.

Step by Step

1. Create an HTML page and save it as pr5_1.html. Place script tags inside the body section to point to a script named prjs5_1.js.

2. Create an external JavaScript file and save it as prjs5_1.js. Use this file for steps 3–10.

3. Create a variable named paycheck and give it an initial value of 2000.

4. Use an operator to increase the value of paycheck to 4000.

5. Use an operator to decrease the value of paycheck to 3500.

6. Use an operator to decrease the value of paycheck to 0.

7. Use an operator to increase the value of paycheck to 500.

8. Finally, use an operator to decrease the value of paycheck to 420.

9. After you perform each action, write the value of the paycheck variable on the page.

10. Save the HTML and JavaScript files and view the HTML file in your browser to see the results.

11. A possible solution for the JavaScript file is shown in the following code, but keep in mind there are several ways to achieve the same results:

```
var paycheck = 2000;
document.write(paycheck + "<br>");
paycheck += 2000;
```

(continued)

```
document.write(paycheck + "<br>");
paycheck -= 500;
document.write(paycheck + "<br>");
paycheck *= 0;
document.write(paycheck + "<br>");
paycheck += 500;
document.write(paycheck + "<br>");
paycheck -= 80;
document.write(paycheck + "<br>");
```

Try This Summary

In this project, you were able to use your knowledge of arithmetic and assignment operators to display the results of several calculations on a Web page. This project could have been completed in numerous ways, depending on your preferences on the use of the various operators.

Understanding Comparison Operators

Comparison operators are often used with conditional statements and loops in order to perform actions only when a certain condition is met. Since these operators compare two values, they return a value of either true or false, depending on the values on either side of the operator. In later chapters, you will learn how to create a block of code to be performed only when the comparison returns true.

Table 5-3 summarizes the comparison operators, which are discussed in more detail in the following sections.

The Is-Equal-To Operator (==)

For the == operator to return true, the values or statements on each side must be equal. If the values do not return as equal, the == operator returns false. Note, however, that when using this operator, type coercion is still in place, so a statement such as "4"==4 will return true because JavaScript will convert the string "4" to a number for you. If you want this statement to return false, you should use the strict is-equal-to operator (===), discussed later in this section.

Special Rules

Since this operator performs type coercion, there are some special rules:

- If one operand is a number and the other is a string, it will try to convert the string into a number before testing for equality.

- If an operand is a Boolean, then it will convert it into a numeric value before testing for equality. In such cases, true is converted to 1 and false is converted to 0.

- If one operand is null and the other is undefined, the comparison will return true.

- If one or both of the operands is NaN, the comparison will return false.

Operator	Symbol	Function
Is equal to	==	Returns true if the values on both sides of the operator are equal to each other
Is not equal to	!=	Returns true if the values on both sides of the operator are not equal to each other
Strict is equal to	===	Returns true if the values on both sides are equal and of the same type
Strict is not equal to	!==	Returns true if the values on both sides are not equal or not of the same type
Is greater than	>	Returns true if the value on the left side of the operator is greater than the value on the right side
Is less than	<	Returns true if the value on the left side of the operator is less than the value on the right side
Is greater than or equal to	>=	Returns true if the value on the left side of the operator is greater than or equal to the value on the right side
Is less than or equal to	<=	Returns true if the value on the left side of the operator is less than or equal to the value on the right side

Table 5-3 The Comparison Operators

The following table shows examples of statements that use the is-equal-to operator, their return values, and the reason why they return true or false.

Comparison	Return Value	Reason
4 == 4	true	Two equal numbers
(4+2) == (3+3)	true	Result on both sides is 6, and 6 is equal to 6
"my socks" == "my socks"	true	Both strings are exactly the same
1 == true	true	The Boolean value of true is converted to 1
4 == 5	false	4 and 5 are not equal numbers
(4+3) == (2+2)	false	Result on left is 7, result on right is 4, and these are not equal
"My socks" == "my socks"	false	Strings are not exactly alike (capitalization)
1 == false	false	The Boolean value of false is converted to 0

NOTE

You will notice the addition of parentheses around some of the statements in the previous table, as well as in some of the tables that come later. Here, they are used mainly for readability. You will learn more about parentheses and the order of operations near the end of this chapter.

As with the other operators, you can use variables with comparison operators. If the values of the variables are equal, the comparison will return true. Otherwise, it will return false. Suppose that you have declared the following variables:

```
var num1 = 2,
    num2 = 5,
    num3 = 5;
```

The following comparison would return true:

```
num2 == num3
```

The next comparison would return false:

```
num1 == num3
```

CAUTION
Remember that the is-equal-to operator (==) is for comparison. Be careful not to accidentally use the assignment operator (=) in its place, because that will perform an assignment instead of a comparison and it will return the result of the assignment, so you may get some unexpected results.

The Is-Not-Equal-To Operator (!=)

The != operator is the opposite of the == operator. Instead of returning true when the values on each side of the operator are equal, the != operator returns true when the values on each side of it are *not* equal. This operator returns a false value if it finds that the values on both sides of the operator are equal.

As with the == operator, type coercion is in place for the != operator, and there are some special rules:

● If one operand is a number and the other is a string, it will try to convert the string into a number before testing.

● If an operand is a Boolean, then it will convert it into a numeric value before testing (true is converted to 1 and false is converted to 0).

● If one operand is null and the other is undefined, the comparison will return false.

● If one or both of the operands is NaN, the comparison will return true.

The following table shows some examples of statements that use the != operator, their return values, and the reason they return true or false.

Comparison	Return Value	Reason
4 != 3	true	4 and 3 are not equal numbers
"CooL" != "cool"	true	Strings do not have the same capitalization, so they are not equal

Comparison	Return Value	Reason
4 != 4	false	4 is equal to 4
"cool" != "cool"	false	Strings are exactly alike, so they are equal

The Strict Is-Equal-To Operator (===)

For the === operator to return true, the operands on each side must be equal and must be of the same type (no type coercion is performed). This means that if you use a statement such as 3 === "3", the operator will return false because the value on the left is a number and the value on the right is a string.

The following table shows examples of statements that use the === operator.

Comparison	Return Value	Reason
4 === 4	true	Two equal numbers
(4+2) === (3+3)	true	Result on both sides is 6, and both values are numbers
"my socks" === "my socks"	true	Both values are strings, and are exactly the same
7 === "7"	false	The number and string are different types
"My socks" === "my socks"	false	Strings are not exactly alike (capitalization)
"2" === (1+1)	false	The values are of different types

The Strict Is-Not-Equal-To Operator (!==)

For the !== operator to return true, the values or statements on each side must not be equal or must not be of the same type (no type coercion is used). This means that if you use a statement such as 3 !== "3", the operator will return true because the value on the left is a number and the value on the right is a string.

The following table shows some examples of statements that use the !== operator.

Comparison	Return Value	Reason
4 !== 3	true	4 and 3 are not equal numbers
"4" !== 4	true	Values on each side are of different types
4 !== 4	false	4 is equal to 4
"cool" !== "cool"	false	Strings are exactly alike, so they are equal

The Is-Greater-Than Operator (>)

When the is-greater-than operator is used, the comparison returns true if the value on the left side of the operator is greater than the value on the right side. Type coercion is used, so there are some special rules:

● If both operands are strings, then the strings are compared by checking the character code of each character in both of the strings.

● If one operand is a number, then it will attempt to coerce the other operand into a number and perform the comparison.

● If an operand is a Boolean, then it is converted to a number (1 for true and 0 for false).

NOTE

The remaining comparison operators (<, >=, <=) also use these same rules.

In the case of strings, the character code of each character is used. The result is a situation where a lowercase letter is greater than an uppercase letter, and an uppercase letter is greater than a number. To look up the character code, you can use the tool at www.scripttheweb.com/js/ref/javascript-character-codes.html.

When comparing strings, JavaScript first checks the first letter of the string for a difference. If there is no difference, it moves on to the next character, then the next one, and so on, until it finds a difference or reaches the end of the string.

The following table shows some examples of statements that use the > operator.

Comparison	Return Value	Reason
5 > 2	true	5 is greater than 2
true > 0	true	Boolean value true is converted to 1
"a" > "A"	true	Character code for "a" is 97, and character code for "A" is 65
"A" > "1"	true	Character code for "A" is 65, and character code for "1" is 49
"10" < "2"	true	Character code for "1" is 49, and character code for "2" is 50
5 > 7	false	5 is less than 7, not greater
false > 0	false	Boolean value of false is converted to 0
2 > 2	false	These are equal, so the value on the left is not greater

The Is-Less-Than Operator (<)

The is-less-than operator works in reverse from the is-greater-than operator. Rather than returning true when the value on the left is greater, the < operator returns true when the value on the left side of the operator is less than the value on the right side of the operator.

You can see some examples of the < operator by looking at the following table.

Comparison	Return Value	Reason
2 < 10	true	2 is less than 10
"A" < "a"	true	Character code for "A" is 65, and character code for "a" is 97
10 < 2	false	10 is greater than 2, not less
"a" < "A"	false	Character code for "a" is 97, and character code for "A" is 65
10 < 10	false	These are equal, so the value on the left is not less

The Is-Greater-Than-or-Equal-To Operator (>=)

The >= operator is slightly different from the comparison operators you've read about so far. This operator adds an option for the values on both sides to be equal and still have the comparison return true. So, to return true, the value on the left side of the operator must be greater than or equal to the value on the right side. The following table shows some examples of statements that use the >= operator.

Comparison	Return Value	Reason
5 >= 2	true	5 is greater than 2
2 >= 2	true	2 is equal to 2
"a" >= "A"	true	Character code for "a" is 97, and character code for "A" is 65
"A" >= "A"	true	The character codes are both 65
1 >= 2	false	1 is less than 2
"A" >= "a"	false	Character code for "A" is 65, and character code for "a" is 97

The Is-Less-Than-or-Equal-To Operator (<=)

Much like the >= operator, the <= operator adds the possibility for the values on each side to be equal. With the is-less-than-or-equal-to operator, a value of true is returned if the value on the left side of the operator is less than or equal to the value on the right side of the operator. The following table shows examples of statements that use the <= operator.

Comparison	Return Value	Reason
2 <= 5	true	2 is less than 5
2 <= 2	true	2 is equal to 2
"A" <= "a"	true	Uppercase letters are less than lowercase letters
"A" <= "A"	true	The strings are equal

(continues)

Comparison	Return Value	Reason
5 <= 2	false	5 is greater than 2, not less than or equal to
"a" <= "A"	false	Lowercase letters are greater than uppercase letters, not less than or equal to

You'll get some practice using the comparison operators when you learn about conditional statements and loops in Chapter 6. Next up are the logical operators, which can be helpful to you when checking conditions.

Understanding Logical Operators

The three logical operators allow you to compare two conditional statements to see if one or both of the statements is true and to proceed accordingly. The logical operators can be useful if you want to check on more than one condition at a time and use the results. Like the comparison operators, the logical operators return either true or false, depending on the values on either side of the operator.

Table 5-4 summarizes the logical operators, which are discussed in the following sections.

The AND Operator (&&)

The logical operator AND returns true if the comparisons on both sides of the && operator are true. If one or both comparisons on either side of the operator are false, a value of false is returned. Some statements that use the AND operator are shown in the following table.

Statement	Return Value	Reason
(1==1) && (2==2)	true	Comparisons on both sides are true: 1 is equal to 1, and 2 is equal to 2
(2>1) && (3<=4)	true	Comparisons on both sides are true: 2 is greater than 1, and 3 is less than 4
("A"<="A") && ("c"!="d")	true	Comparisons on both sides are true: "A" is equal to "A", and "c" is not equal to "d"
(1==1) && (2==3)	false	Comparison on the right is false
("a"!="a") && ("b"!="q")	false	Comparison on the left is false
(2>7) && (5>=20)	false	Comparisons on both sides are false

The OR Operator (||)

The logical operator OR returns true if the comparison on either side of the operator returns true. So, for this to return true, only one of the statements on one side needs to evaluate to true.

Operator	Symbol	Function
AND	&&	Returns true if the statements on both sides of the operator are true
OR	||	Returns true if a statement on either side of the operator is true
NOT	!	Returns true if the statement to the right side of the operator is not true

Table 5-4   The Logical Operators

To return false, the comparisons on both sides of the operator must return false. The following table shows some examples of comparisons using the OR operator.

Statement	Return Value	Reason
(2==2) || (3>5)	true	Comparison on the left is true
(5>17) || (4!=9)	true	Comparison on the right is true
(3==3) || (7<9)	true	Both comparisons are true
(4<3) || (2==1)	false	Both comparisons are false
(3!=3) || (4>=8)	false	Both comparisons are false

The NOT Operator (!)

The logical operator NOT can be used on a single comparison to say, "If this is not the case, then return true." Basically, it can make an expression that would normally return false return true, or make an expression that would normally return true return false. The following table shows some examples of this operator at work.

Comparison	Return Value	Reason
!(3 == 3)	false	3 is equal to 3 is true, but the NOT operator makes this statement false
!(2 > 5)	true	2 is greater than 5 is false; the NOT operator makes the statement true

Now that you have the regular logical operators down, take a quick look at the bitwise logical operators.

The Bitwise Operators

Bitwise operators are logical operators that work at the bit level, where there is a bunch of ones and zeros. You will not be using them in the examples presented in this book, but you may see them in some scripts on the Web. The following table lists some of the bitwise operators and their symbols, which should help you spot a bitwise operator if you see one.

Operator	Symbol
AND	&
XOR	^
OR	|
NOT	~
Left Shift	<<
Signed Right Shift	>>
Unsigned Right Shift	>>>

Special Operators

There are a number of special operators in JavaScript that are used to perform specific tasks, or to aid in shortening code. Table 5-5 lists the special operators and their purposes.

Don't be discouraged if many of the terms used in this table look unfamiliar. Objects, arrays, and other unfamiliar terms are discussed in later chapters. Many of these operators will be reintroduced at the appropriate point in the later chapters, where their purpose can be expressed more clearly.

Operator	Symbol	Purpose
Conditional	?:	Often used as a short if/else type of statement. A condition is placed before the question mark (?) and a value is placed on each side of the colon (:).
Comma	,	Evaluates the statements on both sides of the operator, and returns the value of the second statement.
Delete	Delete	Used to delete an object, a property, or an element in an array.
In	In	Returns true if a property is in a specified object.
Instanceof	instanceof	Returns true if an object is of a specified object type.
New	New	Creates an instance of an object.
This	This	Refers to the current object.
Typeof	Typeof	Returns a string that tells you the type of the value being evaluated.
Void	Void	Allows an expression to be evaluated without returning a value.

Table 5-5 Special Operators

Ask the Expert

Q: **Why are there so many assignment operators? If I can write x=x+1 instead of x+=1, why do I need to know about the extra assignment operators?**

A: They are provided as shortcuts, so that you don't need to type the variable name a second time in the same line. They also cut down the overall size of the script a bit, which helps with the loading time of the Web page. You can use either method; it just depends on how much you want to trim the script size or avoid extra typing. Also, it is good to know what these assignment operators do, so that you can recognize their purpose in scripts.

Q: **Can I use more than one operator at a time in a statement? What will happen if I do that?**

A: Yes, you can use multiple operators in a single statement. The operators will be executed according to their precedence in the order of operations, which is covered in the next section.

Q: **What is with all of the parentheses? Why are they used in some cases but not in others? Is there a reason for them?**

A: The parentheses used so far have been added for the readability of the statements. In some cases, it is necessary to use parentheses to get a desired result. This is something else that is covered in the next section.

Q: **Are there any common typos that are made with all of these operators?**

A: Often, the assignment operator (=) gets used in place of the is-equal-to operator (==) because the second equal sign is left off by accident. Also, forgetting to use && and typing just & is another common typo that can cause trouble in a script. The same sort of mistake can occur with the logical OR (||) and bitwise OR (|) operators.

Understanding Order of Operations

In JavaScript, the operators have a certain order of precedence. In a statement with more than one operator involved, one may be executed before another, even though it is not in that order in the statement. For instance, look at this example:

```
var answer = 8 + 7 * 2;
```

If you remember how this works in mathematics, you will know that the multiplication is performed first on the 7*2 part of the statement, even though it does not look like that is the right order when you read from left to right. The reason the multiplication is performed first is that the multiplication operator has a higher precedence in the order of operations than the addition operator. So, any multiplication done within a statement will be performed before any addition, unless you override it somehow.

As with math problems, in JavaScript, the way to override the order of operations is through the use of parentheses to set off the portion of the statement that should be executed first. Thus, if you wanted to be sure the addition was performed first in the preceding example, you would write it as shown here instead:

```
var answer = (8 + 7) * 2;
```

If you use more than one set of parentheses or operators of the same precedence on the same level, then they are read from left to right, as in this example:

```
var answer = (8 + 7) - (4 * 3) + (8 - 2);
```

Since the parentheses are all on the same level (not nested), they are read from left to right. The addition and subtraction operators outside the parentheses have the same precedence, and thus are also read from left to right.

The precedence of the JavaScript operators is shown in Table 5-6, ranked from highest precedence (done first) to lowest precedence (done last).

As you can see in Table 5-6, parentheses override the other operators. Parentheses are handy when you are unsure of the precedence of various operators or if you want to make something more readable.

Type of Operator	Example of Operators
Parentheses (overrides others)	( )
Unary (mathematical, logical, or bitwise)	- ++ -- ! ~ typeof void delete
Multiplication, division, modulus	* / %
Addition, subtraction	+ -
Shifts (bitwise)	>>> >> <<
Relational comparison	> >= < <= in instanceof
Equality comparison	== != === !==
AND (bitwise)	&
XOR (bitwise)	^
OR (bitwise)	|
AND (logical)	&&
OR (logical)	||
Conditional	?:
Assignment	= += -= *= /= %= <<= >>= >>>= &= ^= |=
Comma	,

Table 5-6 Operator Precedence, from Highest to Lowest

Try This 5-2   True or False?

pr5_2.html
prjs5_2.js

This project will allow you to experiment with some of the comparison operators to see how they work. You will create a script that shows an alert stating whether or not a statement or comparison will return true. The script will use a conditional if/else statement, which is explained in detail in the next chapter.

Step by Step

1. Create an HTML file and save it as pr5_2.html.

2. Create an external JavaScript file and save it as prjs5_2.js. Use this file for editing in steps 3–13.

3. Insert the code that follows into your JavaScript file:

```
var num1 = 0;
var num2 = 0;
if (num1 == num2) {
  window.alert("True");
}
else {
  window.alert("False");
}
```

4. Open the HTML page in your browser. You should instantly see an alert saying "True."

5. Change the value of the variable num1 to 5. Resave the JavaScript file and refresh your browser. You should now get an alert saying "False."

6. In the following line of code, change the == operator to the > operator:

```
if (num1 == num2) {
```

7. Resave the JavaScript file and refresh your browser. You should get "True" again.

8. Change the value of the variable num2 to 7.

9. Resave the JavaScript file and refresh your browser. You should now get "False" again.

10. In the following line (which you changed in step 4), change the operator to the < operator:

```
if (num1 > num2) {
```

11. Resave the JavaScript file and refresh your browser. You should get "True" again.

12. Try to change the value of the num1 variable so that you get an alert that says "False" instead.

13. Try your own tests with the other comparison operators to see what the results will be.

(continued)

Try This Summary

In this project, you were able to use your knowledge of the comparison operators to create an alert that displayed "True" or "False" depending on whether the comparison statement would return true or false. You were also able to try testing your own variations of values and operators if you desired.

✓ Chapter 5 Self Test

1. A(n) _____ is a symbol or word in JavaScript that performs some sort of calculation, comparison, or assignment on one or more values.

2. _____ operators are most often used to perform mathematical calculations on two values.

3. The _____ operator adds two values.

4. When the increment operator is placed _____ the operand, it increases the value of the operand by 1, and then the rest of the statement is executed.

5. Which of the following is not a JavaScript operator?

    A. =

    B. ==

    C. &&

    D. $#

6. What does an assignment operator do?

    A. Assigns a new value to a variable

    B. Gives a variable a new name

    C. Performs a comparison

    D. Nothing, because assignment operators are useless

7. The add-and-assign (+=) operator adds the value on the _____ side of the operator to the variable on the _____ side and then assigns that new value to the variable.

8. What does a comparison operator do?

    A. Performs a mathematical calculation

    B. Deals with bits and is not important right now

    C. Compares two values or statements, and returns a value of true or false

    D. Compares only numbers, not strings

9. Which of the following comparisons will return true?

    A. 4 != 3

    B. 4 == 3

    C. 4 < 3

    D. 4 <= 3

10. Which of the following comparisons will return false?

    A. 4 != 3

    B. 3 == 3

    C. 4 > 3

    D. 4 <= 3

11. The _____ operators allow you to compare two conditional statements to see if one or both of the statements are true and to proceed accordingly.

12. Which of the following statements will return true?

    A. (3 == 3) && (5 < 1)

    B. !(17 >= 20)

    C. (3 != 3) || (7 < 2)

    D. (1 == 1) && (2 < 0)

13. Which of the following statements will return false?

    A. !(3 <= 1)

    B. (4 >= 4) && (5 <= 2)

    C. ("a" == "a") && ("c" != "d")

    D. (2<3) || (3<2)

14. _____ operators are logical operators that work at the bit level.

15. In JavaScript, the operators have a certain order of _____.

Chapter 6

Conditional Statements and Loops

Key Skills & Concepts

- Defining Conditional Statements
- Using Conditional Statements
- Defining Loops
- Using Loops

Now that you have seen how the various operators work in JavaScript, this chapter will instruct you in how to put them to good use. This chapter begins by introducing you to conditional statements and why they are useful to you in scripts. Then, you will learn about all the conditional statement blocks and how to use them. After that, you will learn what loops are and learn how to use the various types of loops within your scripts.

Defining Conditional Statements

In order to use conditional statements, you need to know what they are and why they are useful to you in your scripts.

What Is a Conditional Statement?

A conditional statement is a statement that you can use to execute a bit of code based on a condition or to do something else if that condition is not met. You can think of a conditional statement as being a little like cause and effect. Perhaps a good way to parallel it would be to use something a parent might say, as in the following text:

```
"If your room is clean, you will get dessert. Otherwise, you will go
to bed early."
```

The first cause would be a clean room, which would have the effect of getting dessert. The second cause would be an unclean room, which would have the effect of an early bedtime.

In your scripts, you may want to create a similar statement. Perhaps something more like the following line:

```
"If a variable named mymoney is greater than 1000, send an alert that
says my finances are OK. Otherwise, send an alert saying I need more
money!"
```

In this case, the first cause would be a variable having a value greater than 1000, which would have the effect of an alert that says things are OK. The second cause is the variable being 1000 or less. If this happens, you get an alert saying you need more money.

As you can see, if you can create statements like these in your scripts, you will be able to do quite a bit more than you have with your scripts in the past.

Why Conditional Statements Are Useful

As you saw in the previous section, a conditional statement can be quite useful to you. Rather than executing every single line of code in the script as is, you could have certain sections of the script only be executed when a particular condition is met. You could even expand that single condition into a combination of conditions that need to be met for parts of the code to run.

With conditionals, you can tell JavaScript to do things like the following:

- If a variable named yourname is equal to John, then write a line to the page that says hello to John. Otherwise, write a line to the page that says hello to Unknown Surfer and have it be in bold type.

- If a variable named mycar is equal to Corvette or Mustang, then send an alert saying "Cool Car" to the browser. If a variable named mycar is equal to Corvette, then if a variable named yourname is equal to Marty, send an alert that says "Marty is cool and drives a cool car" to the browser. Otherwise, send an alert that says "Unknown Surfer drives a car of some sort" to the viewer.

I don't really drive a Corvette or a Mustang, so that leaves me out of the cool crowd here; however, these examples do show how you can make your scripts more useful by adding a way to check for certain conditions before an action takes place in the script. These types of statements provide what is known as "flow control" to your scripts.

Using Conditional Statements

Now that you know what conditional statements are, it's time to look at them in more detail and learn how to code them. You will be looking at the two types of conditional statement blocks used in JavaScript: the if/else statement and the switch statement. You will also learn about the use of the conditional operator.

Using if/else Statements

While using conditional statements, you will see that they have a familiar syntax. Most notable are the curly brackets ({ }) that surround the sections of code that will be executed based on a given condition.

The if/else Statement Block Structure

The first thing you must deal with in an if/else statement is the first line, which tells the browser to continue or move along. You begin an if/else statement with the JavaScript keyword if, followed by a comparison in parentheses. The following line shows a sample of the format of the if statement:

```
if (comparison here) {
  JavaScript Code
}
```

You replace the *comparison here* text with an actual comparison. To do this, you need to remember the comparison operators from the previous chapter. Suppose you want to see if a variable named boats is equal to 3 and to send an alert "Yes, there are 3 boats" if the condition is true. You could use the following code:

```
if (boats === 3) {
   window.alert("Yes, there are 3 boats");
}
```

Remember that a comparison will return a value of true or false. This is where the return value becomes useful. If the comparison of boats === 3 returns true, the code within the curly brackets will be executed. If it returns false, the code inside the brackets is ignored and the line of code after the closing curly bracket is executed.

If you wish to use an else block to execute a different set of statements when the comparison returns false, you place the else keyword on the next line and then follow it with its own set of curly brackets, as in the following code:

This alert is executed if the comparison on the first line returns true

```
if (boats === 3) {
   window.alert("You have the right number of boats");  ←
}
else {
   window.alert("You do not have the right number of boats");  ←
}
```

This alert is executed if the comparison on the first line returns false

This code will send an alert that says "You have the right number of boats" if the variable boats is equal to 3. If it is not, it will send an alert that says "You do not have the right number of boats" instead.

Now that you have the statements set up, you need to know whether or not the comparison returns true so that you can determine which block of code is executed. To do so, you need to declare the boats variable and assign it a value before the comparison takes place. This will give you the value to determine what happens in the script. See if you can guess which block of code is executed (first or second) if you use the following code:

```
var boats = 3;
if (boats === 3) {
   window.alert("You have the right number of boats");
}
else {
   window.alert("You do not have the right number of boats");
}
```

If you guessed the first code block would be executed, you got it! Since the variable boats is equal to 3, the comparison boats === 3 returns true. Since it returns true, the first code block is executed and the code block after the else keyword is ignored. You get the alert that says "You have the right number of boats" and nothing else.

CAUTION

Be careful when typing variable assignments (=), is-equal-to comparisons (==), and is strictly equal to comparisons (===), as they can be easily mistyped by accident and cause problems or unexpected results in your scripts.

Now take a look at how to set up the statement so that you have the opposite result. The following code will cause the comparison to return false:

```
var boats = 0;                          Assigning the variable a value of 0 will
if (boats === 3) {                      cause the comparison to return false
  window.alert("You have the right number of boats");
}
else {
  window.alert("You do not have the right number of boats");
}
```

With the value of the variable boats at 0, the comparison boats === 3 will return false; thus, the first code block is ignored and the code block after the else statement is executed instead. This time you get the alert that says "You do not have the right number of boats," while the alert in the first block is ignored.

Now that you know the basic structure of the if/else statement block, you are ready to look at the technique of nesting one block within another.

Block Nesting

If you *nest* something, you are basically putting one structure inside another structure of the same or a similar nature. With the if/else statement blocks, you are able to nest other if/else statements within the first block after the comparison (the "if block") or within the second block after the else keyword (the "else block").

For example, maybe you would like the browser to execute a statement such as the following: "If a variable named havecookbook is equal to yes, and if a variable named meatloafrecipe is equal to yes, send an alert that says 'Recipe found' to the browser. If havecookbook is equal to yes, but meatloafrecipe is not equal to yes, then send an alert 'Have the book but no recipe' to the viewer; otherwise, send an alert that says 'You need a cookbook' to the browser."

This is a somewhat long and complex statement, but you can accomplish what you are after by nesting an if/else statement within the if block of another if/else statement.

To see how this works, consider the following example, which puts the previous statement into JavaScript form:

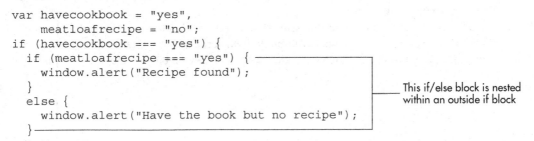

```
var havecookbook = "yes",
    meatloafrecipe = "no";
if (havecookbook === "yes") {
  if (meatloafrecipe === "yes") {
    window.alert("Recipe found");
  }                                        This if/else block is nested
  else {                                   within an outside if block
    window.alert("Have the book but no recipe");
  }
```

```
}
else {
  window.alert("You need a cookbook");
}
```

Oh no, nesting an if block requires curly brackets all over the place! To help you figure out what is going on with this piece of code, I will break it down into its individual parts.

The first thing you get is the main (first, or outermost) if block. You use it to find out whether the variable havecookbook is equal to yes or not. If this comparison returns true, you move along into the if block; however, the next thing you find is another if block! This is the nested if block, which means it is inside the outside if block. In the nested block, you check whether the variable meatloafrecipe is equal to yes or not. If this returns true, you finally are able to do something, which is to send the "Recipe found" alert.

When the nested if block is finished, you see that it has an else block to go with it in case the comparison meatloafrecipe === "yes" returned false. If it had returned false, the browser would have gone to this else block and executed the code within it. In the preceding code example, the comparison on the outside block (havecookbook === "yes") returned true, but the comparison on the nested block (meatloafrecipe === "yes") returned false. So, the nested else block is executed, sending the "Have the book but no recipe" alert.

After this nested else block, you see what looks like an extra closing curly bracket; however, this closing bracket is actually used to close the outside if block that contains all of this nested code. Looking at how the code is indented will help you see which brackets are closing which blocks. This is where using indentions or tabs can be helpful in your code, because—as opposed to the code being all in a straight line up and down—indentions can make the code easier to read.

TIP

When it comes indenting your code, some will recommend using four spaces, some two spaces, and others recommend using the tab key. The most important thing to do is to choose an indention method and to use it consistently in your code. This will help you if you need to read through the script or debug it later. See the following page: en.wikipedia.org/wiki/Indent_style for more information on spaces versus tabs in programming.

Finally, you get to the outside else block. This is the block that is executed only if the first comparison (havecookbook === "yes") returns false. If that comparison returns false, all the code within that outside if block is ignored (you never get to the nested if/else block) and the browser moves on to this outside else block. In this case, you get the "You need a cookbook" alert sent to the viewer.

The following example uses the same if/else code used in the preceding code example, but this time the variables are defined differently: both variables are given a value of yes. See if you can follow the code and name the alert that will show up on the screen when it is executed.

```
var havecookbook = "yes",
    meatloafrecipe = "yes";
if (have_cookbook === "yes") {
  if (meatloaf_recipe === "yes") {
    window.alert("Recipe found");
  }
  else {
    window.alert("Have the book but no recipe");
  }
}
else {
  window.alert("You need a cookbook");
}
```

The alert you should have chosen is the "Recipe found" alert. When the first comparison returns true, you are sent to the nested if block. Since the comparison for the nested if block also returns true, you execute the code within that block, which sends the "Recipe found" alert to the browser.

The last thing you should know about nesting is that you can nest as many blocks as you want inside other blocks. Rather than just nesting one if/else statement inside another, you could have a second nesting inside that statement, a third, or as many as you can track without going insane. For example, consider the following code:

This if/else block is nested within a nested if block

```
if (havecookbook === "yes") {
  if (meatloafrecipe === "yes") {
    if (ismomsmeatloaf === "yes") {
      window.alert("Recipe found");
    }
    else {
      window.alert("Recipe found, but not like what mom makes");
    }
  }
  else {
    window.alert("Have the book but no recipe");
  }
}
else {
  if (havewebaccess === "yes") {
    window.alert("Find the recipe on the Web");
  }
  else {
    window.alert("You need a cookbook");
  }
}
```

Now there is an if/else block within an if block within an if block. As you can see, yet another variable, ismomsmeatloaf, was added to check for an even more specific recipe. You could keep going on and on like this, until you cannot take it any more; however, this should be enough to allow you to build on it later if you need to do so.

Complex Comparisons

In addition to making a simple comparison such as $x === 2$ or $y < 3$, you can also build more complex comparisons using the logical operators discussed in Chapter 5. As you may recall, that chapter presented some of these comparisons in a form similar to the following example:

```
(2===2)||(3<5)
```

In Chapter 5, the only concern was whether the comparison would return true or false, and not with how to add it to an if/else statement. Notice the parentheses around each comparison. They are there mainly for organization; but given the order of operations, you could write the comparison as

```
2===2||3<5
```

The problem here is that this is harder to read, so it would be difficult to determine whether there is a problem with the code if you need to debug it later.

Recall that the first line of the if/else statement uses parentheses to enclose the comparison. If you write your complex comparisons without the organizational parentheses, as in the previous example, you could have the first line look like the line of code shown here:

```
if (2===2||3<5)
```

Although this is easy to type, it's pretty difficult to read because you are not sure if it should be read as "if 2 is equal to 2 or 3 and is less than 5" or as "if (2 is equal to 2) or (3 is less than 5)." The first thing you can do is add spacing, which can help the readability of the comparison:

```
if (2 === 2 || 3 < 5)
```

If you add the parentheses for organization, it becomes even easier to read; but you must be careful that you nest them correctly. The following example code shows the addition of parentheses for organization:

```
if ( (2 === 2) || (3 < 5) )
```

Which form you use will come down to personal preference. For now, this chapter uses the method with the extra parentheses for organization. It should make reading the code from the book easier for you.

Now you can create scripts that allow for more values to be included or allow a specific range of values that will return true. Suppose you want to show an alert when a variable named num1 is greater than 2 but less than 11, and another alert when num1 is not in that range. You could use the following code:

```
if ( (num1 > 2) && (num1 < 11) ) {        ← This complex comparison allows a
  window.alert("Cool number");              specific range of values to return true
}
else {
  window.alert("Not a cool number");
}
```

Your comparison is saying, "If num1 is greater than 2 and num1 is less than 11." If that comparison returns true, then you see the "Cool number" alert. If it returns false, you get the "Not a cool number" alert instead.

Of course, you can make the comparison line as complex as you want it to be. You can add *and* and *or* logical operators in one long line until you get what you need... or have a nervous breakdown. The following example adds an extra stipulation to the comparison to see if num1 is equal to 20:

```
if ( (num1 > 2) && (num1 < 11) || (num1 === 20 ) ) {
window.alert("Cool number");
}
else {
window.alert("Not a cool number");
}
```

This complex comparison adds an additional number that would cause the comparison to return true

Now, the comparison allows the numbers greater than 2, the numbers less than 11, and the number 20 to give the "Cool number" alert. The comparison now reads, "If num1 is greater than 2 *and* num1 is less than 11 *or* num1 is equal to 20." You could keep adding information to create more numbers that will return true, or even additional number ranges that will return true.

Of course, to see the preceding code in action, you would need to declare the num1 variable and assign it a value. See if you can figure out which alert will show up if the following code is used:

```
var num1 = 1;
if ( (num1 > 2) && (num1 < 11) || (num1 == 20) ) {
  window.alert("Cool number");
}
else {
  window.alert("Not a cool number");
}
```

Yes, you are stuck with the "Not a cool number" alert because the number 1 just doesn't cut it here (1 is not within the accepted range of numbers for the condition to return true). Of course, you can change it to something that fits to get the "Cool number" alert instead.

CAUTION
Complex expressions using && and || can cause unintended results in your script if not grouped correctly. For instance, the comparison ((u===v && w===x) || y===z) is going to be different than if it were grouped as (u===v && (w===x || y===z)). The first one will return true if u is equal to v and w is equal to x, or if y is equal to z. The second one will return true if u is equal to v and if either w is equal to x or y is equal to z.

Curly Brackets Shortcut

The if statement allows for a shortcut where curly brackets are not required if only one statement will be executed within an if or an else block. For example, consider the following code:

```
if (num1 === 1) {
   window.alert("The number is 1!");
}
else {
   window.alert("Not 1!");
}
```

Since the if and else blocks each contain only one statement, JavaScript allows them to be written without the curly brackets, as in the following code:

```
if (num1 === 1)
   window.alert("The number is 1!");
else
   window.alert("Not 1!");
```

While this does shorten the code in a situation like this, this technique is *not recommended* since it can cause confusion about what code is being executed for a condition. It is also best for forward compatibility to keep the curly brackets, since it makes it simpler to add a statement to one of the blocks at a later time. Consider this code:

```
if (num1 === 1)
   window.alert("The number is 1!");
else
   window.alert("Not 1!");
   window.alert("Ha Ha");   ◄──────── This line will execute even if the condition is true!
```

Given the formatting of the code, it appears that the "Ha Ha" alert is meant to display only when num1 is not equal to 1. However, the alert displays regardless of whether the condition is true or false. Since the brackets have been left off, the "Ha Ha" alert is not part of the else block, but is simply the first statement that follows the if/else statement and is always executed.

To fix this, you simply add the curly brackets to clarify what the code should do. The following code will work as intended:

```
if (num1 === 1) {
   window.alert("The number is 1!");
}
else {
   window.alert("Not 1!");
   window.alert("Ha Ha");
}
```

With the brackets in place, the "Ha Ha" alert will only display if num1 is not equal to 1.

Chaining if/else Statements

In some cases, you will want to set up an "elseif" type of statement. While JavaScript doesn't have an "elseif" keyword, it does allow you to create this type of statement by chaining if/else statements together, as in the following code:

```
if (num1 === 1) {
  window.alert("Number 1! Yes!");
}
else if (num1 === 2) {          An else keyword followed directly by the
 window.alert("Number 2.");     if keyword creates an "elseif" statement
}
else {
 window.alert("The number is not 1 or 2.");
}
```

This allows you to perform any number of tests before having to execute the final else statement as a final option. This can often be shortened further by using the switch statement, which is discussed in the next section.

Using the switch Statement

The switch statement allows you to take an expression and execute a different block of code based on whether a case is equal to the value of the expression. If you wish to check for a number of different values, this can be an easier method than using of a set of chained if/else statements.

The first line of a switch statement would have the following syntax:

```
switch (expression)
```

You can replace *expression* with a value, a variable, or some other sort of expression (for example, the addition of numeric values or the concatenation of string values). For the first example, you will just use a variable that has been assigned a value before the switch statement begins.

Now, you need to see the general syntax for a full switch statement. The following code is an example of how a switch statement looks:

```
var thename = "Fred";          The switch statement begins based
switch (thename) {             on the value of the thename variable
  case "George" :
    window.alert("George is an OK name");    A case is given with code
    break;                                   to execute it if it is true
  case "Fred" :
    window.alert("Fred is the coolest name!");   This is the case that is
    window.alert("Hi there, Fred!");             true and will be executed
    break;
  default :                                 The default is used
    window.alert("Interesting name you have there");   when none of the
}         The closing curly bracket closes the switch statement    cases is true
```

First, this example declares and assigns a variable named thename; it is given a value of Fred. Next, the switch statement begins, using the variable thename as the basis for comparison. Then, the block is opened with a curly bracket, followed by the first case statement. Written like this, it is saying, "If thename is equal to George, then execute the commands after the colon." If thename were equal to George, you would get an alert.

Next you see the break statement, which tells the browser to exit the code block and move on to the next line of code after the block. You use the break statement in the switch block to be sure only one of the case sections is executed; otherwise, you run the risk of having all the cases executed following the one that returned true, because, by default, the browser would continue to the next statement (called *fall through*) rather than exit the block entirely, even though it finds one of the cases to be true. To be sure that the browser exits the block, you add the break statement.

If you get back to the script, you see that thename is not equal to George, so this case is skipped; however, the next comparison returns true because thename is equal to Fred in the script. Thus, the set of statements in this case block will be executed. Note that two lines of JavaScript code appear before the break statement here. This shows that you could have any number of lines within a case.

Finally, you see the keyword default. This is used in the event that none of the case statements returns true. If this happens, the default section of code will be executed. Notice that you don't need the break statement after the default section of code, because it is at the end of the switch block anyway, so the browser will exit the block afterward, eliminating the need for the break statement.

Falling Through

Sometimes you want to execute the following case. This is called falling through, which will allow you to proceed to the next case statement. One use of this technique is when multiple cases would be suitable for a particular section of code. You could allow these cases to fall through until you get to the code to be executed:

```
switch (name) {
  case "Fred" : // fall through
  case "Frederick" : // fall through
  case "Freddie" :
    window.alert("Any version of Fred is a cool name");
    break;
  default:
    window.alert("I have not heard that name before");
}
```

This allows all cases where the name is some variation of "Fred" to be handled by the statements placed in the last case, rather than repeating them in each case with a break. When using a fall through, it is a good idea to note it using a comment, as shown in the example code.

You can still execute code on any case before falling through. The following code shows an example of this:

```
switch (name) {
  case "Fred" :
    window.alert("Your name is Fred"); // fall through
  case "Frederick" : // fall through
  case "Freddie" :
    window.alert("Any version of Fred is a cool name");
    break;
  default:
    window.alert("I have not heard that name before");
}
```

This time, if name is equal to "Fred", then the "Your name is Fred" alert will display. The case will then fall through and also display the "Any version of Fred is a cool name" alert. If name is equal to "Frederick" or "Freddie", then only the "Any version of Fred is a cool name" alert will display.

Using Expressions

Up to this point, you have used a variable value as the expression in the opening line of the switch statement. JavaScript allows you to use any type of expression, and this can be very useful when you use a Boolean value for the expression. Doing so allows you to write conditions that return a Boolean value, allowing you to test for more than a single value at a time. For example, consider the following code:

The condition used for this case returns true, which is equal to the expression used in the opening of the switch statement

```
var num1 = 17;
switch (true) {
  case (num1 < 20) :◄────────────────
    window.alert("The number is less than 20");
    break;
  case ( (num1 >= 20) && (num1 <= 100) ) :
    window.alert("The number is somewhere between 20 and 100");
    break;
  default :
    window.alert("The number is negative or more than 100");
}
```

By using the Boolean value of true as the expression, each case can in turn be a condition. If a case condition returns true, then it is a match and that case will be executed. In the previous code, the first case will be executed because the condition num1 < 20 will return true, creating a match with the initial expression.

Using the Conditional Operator

The conditional operator (also called the ternary operator) is one that can be used as a short way to assign a value based on a condition. For instance, you might decide you want to assign a value to a variable based on the result of a conditional statement. You could do it using the following code:

```
var mynum = 1,
    mymessage = "";
if (mynum === 1) {
```

```
  mymessage = "You win!";
}
else {
  mymessage = "Sorry! Try again!";
}
```

This works, and gives mymessage a value of "You win!" since mynum is equal to 1. However, the conditional operator allows you to shorten the amount of code required for this type of test. It allows you to place a condition before the question mark (?) and place a possible value on each side of the colon (:), like this:

```
var name = (condition) ? value1 : value2;
```

JavaScript evaluates the conditional statement and if the statement returns true, the value on the left side of the colon (*value1* here) is assigned to the variable. If the statement returns false, the value on the right side of the colon (*value2* here) is assigned to the variable. As you can see, this operator takes three operands (the condition and the two values), which is why it is also sometimes called the ternary operator.

To apply this to our previous example, we could rewrite the entire piece of code as follows:

```
var mynum = 1,
    mymessage = "";
mymessage = (mynum === 1) ? "You win!" : "Sorry! Try Again!";
```

This works the same way as the previous if/else block, but allows you to write the code with a lot less typing (lessening the size of the script).

The conditional statements you have learned in this chapter will allow you to do much more with your code now that you know how to use them. You will be using these extensively in later chapters to create more complex scripts.

User Input from a Prompt

One way to obtain input from a viewer is to use the window.prompt() method. This method takes two arguments: the prompt text to be displayed and the default value for the text box that grabs the viewer's reply. For example, you could use the following code.

```
var username = window.prompt("Give me your name!", "");
```

In this case, the prompt text will be "Give me your name!" and the default value of the text box will be empty. The following illustration shows how the prompt dialog would look when this is run in Mozilla Firefox.

The window.prompt() method returns the contents of the text box if the user clicks OK or presses the ENTER key. If the Cancel button is clicked or the prompt is otherwise closed, then the value returned will be null. The returned value is stored in the variable the window.prompt() method is assigned to, if a variable is used. In this case, the returned value will be stored in the username variable.

To make use of this, suppose you want to display the viewer's name on the page to personalize it a bit. You want to display the viewer's name if it is entered, or display a default message if nothing is entered or the user cancels/closes the prompt in some way. The following code shows how this can be done:

```
var username = window.prompt("Give me your name!", "");
if ( (username === null) || (username === "") ) {
  document.write("Hello, Random Nameless Person!");
}
else {
  document.write("Hello, " + username + "!");
}
```

The value returned by the prompt is stored in the username variable. The value of this variable is checked using the if statement. If the value of username is null or an empty string, then the page displays the "Hello, Random Nameless Person!" message. Otherwise, the viewer is greeted with his/her typed name. Figure 6-1 shows the result of entering "Brent" in the prompt text box.

As you can see, the if/else conditional statement allowed you to perform some basic testing on the user input. This kept you from displaying a message with null or an empty string as the viewer's name. Technically, the user could still enter blank spaces, but you can prevent this by using regular expressions with your conditional statements. Regular expressions will be covered in more detail in Chapter 13.

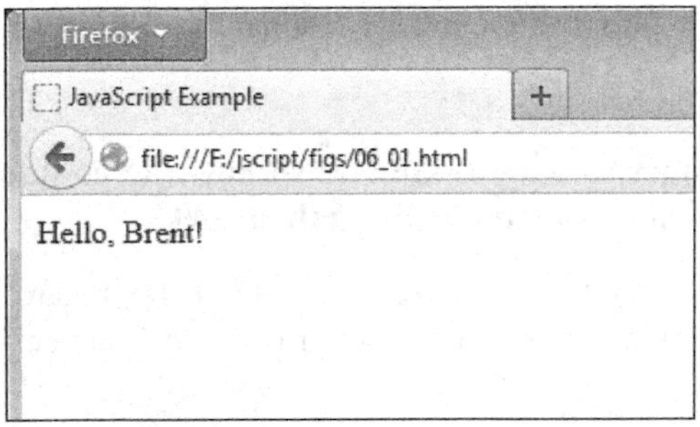

Figure 6-1 A greeting is displayed to the viewer.

Ask the Expert

Q: **Do I need to use curly brackets on every if/else block? I have seen them used in code on the Web without the brackets. Why?**

A: There is a shortcut that allows you to omit the curly brackets if you are only going to execute a single JavaScript statement in the if block and the else block (see the "Curly Brackets Shortcut" section of this chapter), and this may be used in free scripts on the Web. As explained earlier, this technique is not recommended as it can cause confusion when you are looking over or debugging the code.

Q: **Why I am bothering with conditional statements if all I can do is assign the variable a value and then test it? If I already know what the value of the variable is, why use a conditional?**

A: In the next section, you will get to the point where you are getting information from the viewer. This information can vary depending on the viewer (for example, if the viewer needs to enter his/her name into a text box or a prompt), thus making the conditional blocks more useful since you will be able to perform one action for one viewer, and another task for a different user. With user input, you won't know the value of the variable beforehand, and you will need to handle the possibilities using conditional blocks. Also, you will recall that functions can be passed different values as arguments, which you may need to test with conditionals before executing certain sections of code.

Q: **Do I *need* to use the switch statement or the conditional operator?**

A: While it is not absolutely necessary to use them (you could use if/else statements instead), it is a good idea to learn them since they can help you save time and optimize your code. It is also helpful to know them when you are reading through other scripts to see what the code is doing.

Q: **I tried entering a number into a prompt and adding it to another number, but it ran the two numbers together instead of adding them. Why?**

A: Data entered into the prompt text box is returned as a string, regardless of what type of data was entered. You can use the unary plus operator (refer to Chapter 5) to coerce the string into a numeric value:

```
var num1 = window.prompt("Enter a number","");
num1 = +num1 + 5;
```

If the value can be coerced, it will become numeric and the addition will take place as expected. You will learn more about validating input in Chapter 13.

Try This 6-1   Work with User Input

pr6_1.html
prjs6_1.js

This project will help you work with the window.prompt() method, if/else statements with nesting, and the switch statement. Suppose you just started an online store that offers a product for sale. Unfortunately, you are on a tight budget and only able to deliver products to certain cities. You want to prompt the customer for a city name and display a message stating whether or not delivery is available to the customer.

Step by Step

1. Create an HTML page and save it as pr6_1.html. Add script tags to point to an external JavaScript file named prjs6_1.js.

2. Create an external JavaScript file and save it as prjs6_1.js. Use this file for steps 3–6.

3. Create a variable named msg with an initial value of an empty string (""). This will be used to hold the message that will be displayed to the customer.

4. Create a variable named city and assign it the return value of a prompt that asks "What is the name of your city?"

5. If the value of city is null or an empty string (""), then assign the value "No city entered. Cannot determine delivery availability." to the msg variable. Otherwise (else), create a switch statement (this will be nested within the else block).

6. In the switch statement, assign the following values to the msg variable, depending on the name of the city:
   "We can have items delivered to you in 3 days." if the city is Johnstown.
   "We can have items delivered to you in 1 week." if the city is Donville.
   "We can have items delivered to you in 2 weeks." if the city is Danieltown or Martyville.
   "Sorry! We do not deliver to your city yet." for any other city name that is entered.

7. Write the value of the msg variable on the page.

8. When you are done, your JavaScript file should have the following code (other solutions are possible as well):

```javascript
var msg = "",
    city = window.prompt("What is the name of your city?", "");
if ( (city === null) || (city === "") ) {
  msg = "No city entered. Cannot determine delivery availability.";
}
else {
  switch (city) {
    case "Johnstown" :
      msg = "We can have items delivered to you in 3 days.";
      break;
    case "Donville" :
```

(continued)

```
        msg = "We can have items delivered to you in 1 week.";
        break;
      case "Danieltown" : // fall through
      case "Martyville" :
        msg = "We can have items delivered to you in 2 weeks.";
        break;
      default :
        msg = "Sorry! We do not deliver to your city yet.";
    }
  }
  document.write(msg);
```

9. Save the JavaScript file and the HTML file and view the HTML page in your browser.

10. Try entering one of the named cities. You should get the appropriate message written on the page. You can reload the page to try out different city names.

Try This Summary

In this project, you used your new skills with the window.prompt() method, if/else statements, and switch statements to create a script that allows the user to enter a city name and then see whether delivery is available to that city.

Defining Loops

To begin using loops, you will want to know what loops are, what they can do, and why they can be useful to you in your scripts.

What Is a Loop?

A loop is a block of code that allows you to repeat a section of code a certain number of times, perhaps changing certain variable values each time the code is executed. By doing this, you can often shorten certain tasks into a few lines of code, rather than writing the same line over and over again within the script and tiring your fingers.

Why Loops Are Useful

Loops are useful because they allow you to repeat lines of code without retyping them or using cut and paste in your text editor. This not only saves you the time and trouble of repeatedly typing the same lines of code, but also avoids typing errors in the repeated lines. You can also change one or more variable values each time the browser passes through the loop, which again saves you the time and trouble of typing a line that is only slightly different than the previous line.

As a simple example, suppose you wanted to write a sentence onto a Web page ten times in a row using JavaScript. To do this normally, you might have to write something like the following:

```
document.write("All this typing gets tiring after a while!<br>");
document.write("All this typing gets tiring after a while!<br>");
document.write("All this typing gets tiring after a while!<br>");
document.write("All this typing gets tiring after a while!<br>");
document.write("All this typing gets tiring after a while!<br>");
document.write("All this typing gets tiring after a while!<br>");
document.write("All this typing gets tiring after a while!<br>");
document.write("All this typing gets tiring after a while!<br>");
document.write("All this typing gets tiring after a while!<br>");
document.write("All this typing gets tiring after a while!<br>");
```

Ouch! Cut and paste can make the task easier, but it would still be a bit tedious, especially if you decide to write the sentence 50 times instead. With a loop, you could write that document.write() statement just one time and then adjust the number of times you want it to be written. It would be something like the following example. This is not actual code, but you will see the actual code needed to repeat a statement multiple times when you look at the loop structures in more detail in the next section, "Using Loops."

```
Do this block 10 times {
   document.write("I only had to type this once!<br>");
}
```

Of course, you will replace the "Do this block 10 times" text with an actual statement that JavaScript will understand. You will see what statements you can use to form loops in the following section.

Using Loops

In order to see how loops can really be helpful to you, you need to take a look at the different loop structures that you can use in JavaScript. The loop structures covered in this section are the *for*, *while*, and *do while* loops.

for

To use a for loop in JavaScript, you need to know how to code the basic structure of the loop and how to nest a for loop within another for loop. To begin, take a look at the basic structure of a for loop.

Structure of a for Loop

The structure of a for loop is very similar to that of the conditional blocks. The only major differences are that a loop serves a different purpose and, as a result, the first line is different. After that, you use the familiar curly brackets to enclose the contents of the loop.

The first line of a for loop would look similar to the following line:

```
for (var count= 1; count< 11; count++)
```

The first thing you see is the for keyword. This is followed by a set of parentheses with three statements inside. These three statements tell the loop how many times it should repeat by giving it special information.

The first statement (*var count*= 1) creates a variable named *count* and assigns it an initial value of 1. This initial value can be any number. This number is used as a starting point for the number of times the loop will repeat. Using the number 1 will help you see more easily the number of times the loop will repeat. The preceding code begins the loop with *count* having a value of 1. Note that if the count variable had been initialized earlier in the script, the var keyword would not be needed here.

The next statement (*count*< 11) tells the loop when to stop running. The loop will stop running based on this conditional statement. The condition here is to stop only when the variable *count* is no longer less than 11. This means that if you add 1 to the value of *count* each time through the loop, the loop's last run-through will be when *count* is equal to 10. When 1 is added to 10, it becomes 11; and that doesn't pass the conditional test, so the loop stops running.

The last statement in the set (*count* ++) determines the rate at which the variable is changed and whether it gets larger or smaller each time. In the preceding code, you add 1 to the variable each time you go back through the loop. Remember, the first time through, the variable has been set to 1. Since you add 1 each time, the variable will have a value of 2 the second time through, 3 the third time through, and so on, until the variable is no longer less than 11.

To finish the structure, you insert the curly brackets to enclose the code that you wish to use within the loop. An example of the full structure of a for loop is shown in the following code:

```
for (varcount=1; count< 11; count++) {          This line determines how many
   JavaScript Code Here                          times the loop will run
}
```

The JavaScript code for the loop will be inside the brackets here

Now, you just need to add a real variable and some JavaScript code to be executed, and you will have a full for loop put together. To do this, you'll begin with a script to write a sentence to the page ten times. Now that you can use a loop, you need to write the sentence itself only once, rather than ten times in a row. The following example code shows how this can be done using a for loop:

```
for (var count = 1; count < 11; count ++) {
   document.write("I am part of a loop!<br>");          This line of code is looped
}                                                        through ten times
```

The *count* variable is going to begin counting at 1, since it is assigned an initial value of 1. You are adding 1 to it each time through the loop. When the *count* variable has a value that is no longer less than 11, the loop will stop. In this case, the *count* will run from 1 to 10, thus running the loop ten times.

When 1 is added the next time the for statement is hit, the value of the *count* variable is 11, which is no longer less than 11; thus, the browser will skip over the loop and continue to the next line of code after the closing curly bracket for the loop. The <br> tag is used in the document.write command to be sure that each sentence will have a line break after it and will not write the next sentence on the same line.

To see this work on a page, you can add the script tags and insert an external JavaScript file into the body section of an HTML page. Create a JavaScript file named loops01.js, add the following code, and save the file. Add the necessary script tags to an HTML document and save it as loops01.html.

```
document.write("Get ready for some repeated text.<br>");
for (var count = 1; count < 11; count++) {
  document.write("I am part of a loop!<br>");
}
document.write("Now we are back to the plain text.");
```

This loop will display the text repeatedly in the HTML document

Here, a slight change was made to increment the *count* variable. Rather than typing count += 1, the increment operator (++) was used. When you are simply adding one to the variable, the increment operator can be a handy way to shorten the code. However, if you wanted to increment the variable by 2 or more, the add-and-assign operator would still need to be used (that is, count += 2).

The page represented by the preceding code has a short line of text that is followed by your repeating line of text. The page ends with a note, "Now we are back to the plain text." Figure 6-2 shows how this will appear in the browser window when viewed. Notice that the sentence "I am part of a loop!" is repeated ten times.

Figure 6-2 The loop displays the line of text ten times.

Now that you can do a basic loop, you are ready to add something to it that will make the loop even more useful. Within the loop, you can use the value of the count variable (or whatever variable is used) to do various things.

One thing you can do (this will become more apparent when you get to arrays later) is to make use of the fact that the variable is changing each time. With the variable going up by 1 each time through, you could use a loop to number the sentences from 1 to 10 and make the lines more readable. The following code does this:

```
document.write("Get ready for some repeated text.<br>");
for (var count = 1; count < 11; count++) {
   document.write(count + ". I am part of a loop!<br>");
}
document.write("Now we are back to the plain text.");
```

Now the variable is used to add line numbers each time the code is repeated

In the preceding code, you just added the value of the count variable to your string at the beginning. The period before the sentence will make the line of text appear with a period after the number, a space, and your sentence on each line. Figure 6-3 shows how the script would look in the browser with this addition.

The Comparison

When making the comparison, you are not limited to only the < operator. For example, you have been looping through ten times thus far. There are a number of ways to make a loop

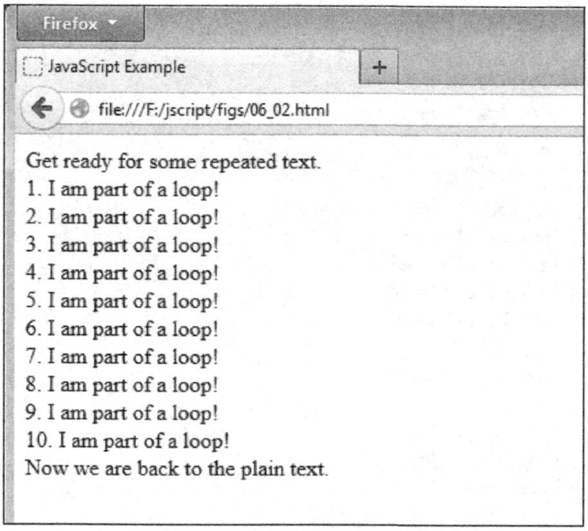

Figure 6-3 Now the repeated lines are numbered from 1 to 10.

execute ten times, though some will change what values the count variable uses (which can be handy when you do not want 1–10 as the count numbers). Some examples are shown here:

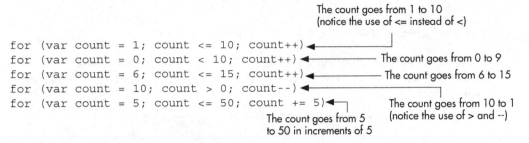

The count goes from 1 to 10
(notice the use of <= instead of <)

```
for (var count = 1; count <= 10; count++)
for (var count = 0; count < 10; count++)
for (var count = 6; count <= 15; count++)
for (var count = 10; count > 0; count--)
for (var count = 5; count <= 50; count += 5)
```

The count goes from 0 to 9
The count goes from 6 to 15
The count goes from 5 to 50 in increments of 5
The count goes from 10 to 1 (notice the use of > and --)

Keep this in mind, as this type of flexibility can help to save you time or additional calculations based on the count variable. The second method shown in the example, for instance, is used often with arrays. You will learn more about this in Chapter 7.

Block Nesting

Yes, you now have to deal with nested loops. As with if/else blocks, you can nest as many levels deep as you can handle. For now, you will just nest one loop within another. The following example shows a for loop within a for loop:

```
for (var count = 1; count < 11; count++) {
  document.write(count + ". I am part of a loop!<br>");
  for (var nestcount = 1; nestcount< 3; nestcount++) {
    document.write("I keep interrupting in pairs!<br>");
  }
}
```

This nested loop interrupts the outside loop

CAUTION
Be careful when you nest loops to be sure that each nested loop has its own counter on its first line, such as for (count = 1; count < 11; count ++). A counter will need to be unique to its own loop in most cases. Also, errors may occur if the curly brackets are not included or paired correctly.

Now you get a loop that interrupts your outer loop text with text of its own. Each time you go through the outer loop, you write out the "I am part of a loop!" line. Then, you encounter another loop that writes out "I keep interrupting in pairs!" to the screen.

The inner loop is set up to repeat twice; so each time you have one sentence from the outside loop, it is immediately followed by two sentences from the inside loop. In order to see this more clearly, consider the following example, which updates the code you used earlier in the loops01.js file:

```
document.write("Get ready for some repeated text.<br>");
for (var count = 1; count < 11; count++) {
  document.write(count + ". I am part of a loop!<br>");
```

```
   for (varnestcount = 1; nestcount< 3; nestcount++) {
      document.write("I keep interrupting in pairs!<br>");
   }
}
document.write("Now we are back to the plain text.");
```

Figure 6-4 illustrates how this nested loop affects the appearance of the page in the browser. You can now see how nested loops are useful to add even more information along the way if you need to do so.

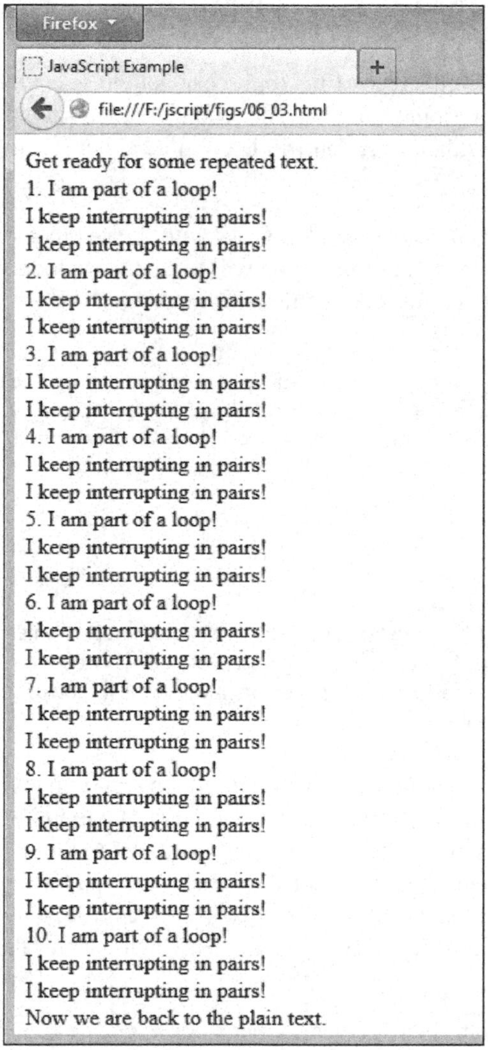

Figure 6-4 The nested loop inserts text within the outside loop's text.

To further complicate matters, you can also nest different types of blocks inside one another. For example, you can put an if/else statement block inside a loop, or a loop inside the if block or the else block of an if/else statement. The following example creates an if/else block within a for loop:

```
for (var count = 1; count < 11; count++) {
  if (count === 5) {
    document.write("The loop is halfway done!<br>");
  }
  else {
    document.write("I am part of a loop!<br>");
  }
}
```

In this case, the browser will check whether or not the count variable has a value of 5. If it does, the browser will print a different message to the screen than the browser would otherwise. You can best see the effects of this by adjusting your JavaScript file to have the following code:

```
document.write("Get ready for some repeated text.<br>");
for (var count = 1; count < 11; count++) {
  if (count === 5) {
    document.write("The loop is halfway done!<br>");
  }
  else {
    document.write("I am part of a loop!<br>");
  }
}
document.write("Now we are back to the plain text.");
```

Figure 6-5 shows the result of this code when run in the browser. Notice how the fifth line is different based on the conditional statement within the loop.

As you can see, you can do quite a bit with nesting. Using the same techniques you just learned, you can nest all the other statement blocks covered in this book; therefore, I won't be as detailed about the nesting techniques with the rest of the statements that are covered.

Infinite Loops

When writing any type of loop, it is possible to create what is known as an *infinite loop*, which is a loop that never completes. Such a loop can potentially continue to run until it crashes the user's computer. Though most modern browsers can detect this after a time and prompt the user to stop the execution of the script, it is not guaranteed and could cause issues for those running the script.

To avoid programming an infinite loop, you will need to be sure that the condition you set will at some point return false. For example, the following for loop creates a condition that never returns false when the loop runs, creating an infinite loop:

```
// DO NOT USE - Creates an infinite loop
for (var i = 25; i > 10; i++) {          Oops! The variable i will never be less than 10!
  document.write("This sentence can repeat forever...<br>");
}
```

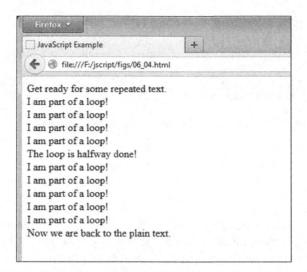

Figure 6-5 The nested if/else block causes the fifth line to be different from the other lines.

As you can see here, the variable i is assigned an initial value of 25 and is incremented by one each time through the loop. This means that i will always be greater than 10 and the condition i > 10 will never return false, creating an infinite loop.

To fix this, be sure to make an adjustment in the loop so that the condition will eventually return false. Here are two examples of how this loop can be fixed:

```
for (var i = 25; i > 10; i--) {
  document.write("This sentence can be stopped!<br>");
}
```

Here, i is decremented rather than incremented, which will eventually bring the value of i down to 10 to make the condition false.

```
for (var i = 25; i < 50; i++) {
  document.write("This sentence can be stopped<br>");
}
```

In this case, the condition is altered to i < 50 while keeping the increment in place. When i reaches 50, the condition will return false and end the loop.

Multiple Statements

A for loop can also contain multiple statements when it is initialized. This gives you the ability to have more than one variable for counting that can be altered through the loop. For example, if you want to count by tens, you could use the following code to go from 10 to 100.

```
for (var i = 1, j = 10; i < 11; i++, j += 10){
  document.write(j + "<br>");
}
```

Here, both i and j variables are initialized (i is 0 and j is 10) and incremented. The value of i is incremented by one, while j is incremented by 10. The condition i < 11 will stop the loop after it runs ten times. The end result is that the numbers 10, 20, 30, 40, 50, 60, 70, 80, 90, and 100 will be displayed on the page.

while

A while loop tests a comparison and repeats until the comparison is no longer true. The following code shows the general structure of a while loop:

```
var count = 1; ◄───────────── A variable is assigned a value to count the loop
while (count < 6) { ◄────────── The while statement begins with a comparison
JavaScript Code Here
   count++; ◄───────────────── The count variable is adjusted so that
}                               you do not have an endless loop
```

First, notice that the value of 1 is assigned to the variable count before the loop begins. This is important to do, since you cannot declare the variable when initializing a while loop as you can with a for loop. This loop is set up to repeat five times, given the initial value of the variable and the increase in the value of the variable by 1 each time through (count++).

In a while loop, you must also remember to change the value of the variable you use so that you do not get stuck in a permanent loop. If the previous sample loop had not included the count++ code, the loop would have repeated indefinitely, and you do not want that to happen. So, the main things you must remember with a while loop are to give a counting variable an initial value before the loop and to adjust the value of the variable within the loop itself.

For an example of the while loop in action, you can recode your sentence-repeat script to work with a while loop:

```
document.write("Get ready for some repeated text.<br>");
var count = 1;                                This line is written on the page ten
while (count < 11) {                          times, just as with the for loop
   document.write(count + ". I am part of a loop!<br>"); ◄──────┐
   count++;                                                      │
}
document.write("Now we are back to the plain text.");
```

The preceding code will produce the same result as your for loop did, just with a different look, as shown in Figure 6-6. In many cases, you can choose to use a for loop or a while loop based on personal preference, since they can perform many of the same tasks.

As far as nesting with while loops, it works the same as with the for loops. You can insert another while loop, a for loop, or an if/else block within a while loop. You can also insert a while loop within the other statement blocks if you wish.

do while

The do while loop is a special case because the code within the loop is performed at least once, even if the comparison used would return false the first time. A comparison that returns false in other loops on the first attempt would cause them never to be executed. In the case of a do

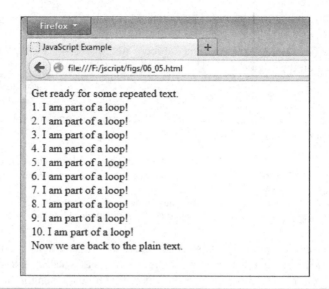

Figure 6-6 A line of text is repeated ten times using a while loop.

while loop, the loop is executed once, and then the comparison is checked each time afterward to determine whether or not it should repeat.

The following is an example of a do while loop that will run five times:

```
var count = 1;
do {                                    ──── The do keyword begins the do while loop
  document.write("Hi!");
  count++;
} while (count < 6);  ────  The while statement runs the comparison
                            each time after the first run-through
```

Notice that the keyword do and the opening curly bracket are the only things on the first line of the block in the preceding code. Then, when the block is complete, you see the while statement and comparison. The do keyword is how you ensure the code block is executed at least once.

After that, the browser checks to see that the comparison returns true before repeating. In this case, the loop repeats five times since the variable count starts at 1 and is increased by 1 each time through. When the value of count reaches 6, the loop is skipped and no longer executed. Also notice that there is a semicolon at the end of the loop to end the statement, unlike with other types of loops.

To see an example of a do while loop that gets executed at least once even though the initial comparison would return false, look at the following example code:

```
var count = 11;
do {
  document.write("Hi!");  ────  This is only written to the page once,
  count++;                      since the comparison will return false
} while (count < 10);
```

The loop in the preceding code will only run the first time. When the comparison is checked (count will be 12 by this time, since 1 is added to it in the execution of the loop), it returns false and the loop is no longer run.

A do while loop is most useful when you have some code that you need to have executed at least once but need repeated only if certain conditions are met; otherwise, one of the other two loops would be sufficient for the task.

for in and for each in

The for in loop allows you to loop over all the names of the properties of an object, while the for each in loop allows you to loop over the value of each of the properties. These loops will be covered in more detail in Chapter 8.

Using break and continue

The break and continue statements allow you to stop what a loop is currently doing, but they work in different ways. As you will recall from the use of a break statement within a switch block earlier in the chapter, the break statement stops the loop at that point and completely exits the loop, moving on to the next JavaScript statement after the loop. For instance, break could be used in this manner:

This will end the loop when count is equal to 5, rather than allowing the loop to complete

```
var stopnumber = 5;
for (var count = 1; count < 11; count++) {
  if (count === stopnumber) {
    document.write("Sorry, the loop stops here!<br>");
    break;
  }
  else {
    document.write(count + "I am part of a loop!<br>");
  }
}
```

This loop will go through normally until count is equal to the value of stopnumber (in this case, 5). When this happens, a special message is written to the page and the break statement is used to end the loop entirely. Thus, rather than going through the loop ten times, the loop will only be executed five times.

If you decided that you did not want to completely leave the loop when that condition occurs, you could modify the loop to use the continue statement. The continue statement will stop the loop from executing any statements after it during the current trip through the loop. However, it will go back to the beginning of the loop and pick up where it left off, rather than exiting the loop entirely. For example, you could use the following code:

```
var skipnumber = 5;
for (count = 1; count < 11; count++) {
  if (count === skipnumber) {
    continue; // do nothing
  }
  document.write(count + ". I am part of a loop!<br>");
}
```

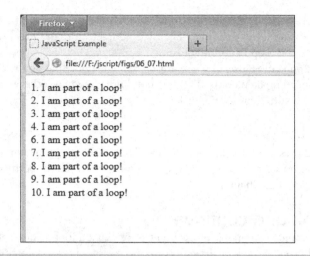

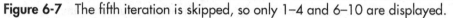

Figure 6-7 The fifth iteration is skipped, so only 1–4 and 6–10 are displayed.

This time, nothing is written to the page when count is equal to the value of skipnumber (in this case, 5). Instead, the loop is told to go back to the beginning and continue from there. The result is that the "I am part of a loop!" message will be written to the page only nine times (effectively skipping the fifth time the text would be written and going on to the sixth). Figure 6-7 shows how this would look when run in a browser.

Ask the Expert

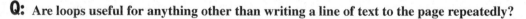

Q: Are loops useful for anything other than writing a line of text to the page repeatedly?

A: Yes, you will see their usefulness more as you progress through the chapters. You will see in Chapter 7 that they can be especially useful when dealing with arrays.

Q: Is it really okay to use the variable I have counting the loop inside the loop? Couldn't that lead to problems?

A: It is okay to use that variable within the loop, as long as you do not somehow assign it a new value when using it. If you are worried that you might do this, assign its value to another variable and use that one in the code instead. For example, take a look at the following code:

```
var thenum = 0;
for (var count = 1; count < 11; count++) {
  thenum = count;
  document.write(thenum + ". I am part of a loop!<br>");
}
```

Here, you assign the value of the count variable to a variable named thenum. You then use the thenum variable in the code instead of the count variable.

Note, however, that it is okay to assign a new value to a count variable if that is what you intend to do. The preceding idea is only a method you can use if you do not intend to change the count variable and want to be sure you don't accidentally do so.

Q: **Should I use a for loop or a while loop when I want to use a loop? Which one is better?**

A: Use the type of loop you personally prefer. Often, the type of loop used depends upon the situation at hand. One type of loop might seem to make more sense than the other type under different circumstances.

Q: **Will the do while loop ever be useful to me?**

A: Although the do while loop does have its usefulness, it is unlikely that you will use it often unless you use scripts that need to have a loop run at least once before it is checked. However, the knowledge you gained about the do while loop in this chapter will help you if you should encounter a script that uses it on the Web or elsewhere.

The break and continue statements will prove helpful to you when special situations come up that require you to stop the loop entirely or to stop the loop and restart it at the beginning.

Try This 6-2 — Work with for Loops and while Loops

`pr6_2.html`
`prjs6_2.js`

In this project, you will make use of a for loop to add another feature to the script from Try This 6-1. Suppose your online store also could only deliver a certain number of items to each of the available cities. Unfortunately, you are still on a tight budget and do not have online ordering in place yet. The customer must print out a form, fill in each item number, and snail mail it to you. You want to display a printable form for the customer with enough lines that the customer can order up to the maximum amount of items for the city entered.

Step by Step

1. Create an HTML page and save it as pr6_2.html. Add the script tags to point to a script named prjs6_2.js.

2. Create an external JavaScript file and save it as prjs6_2.js. Use it to complete steps 3–5.

3. Copy and paste your JavaScript code from prjs6_1.js into your prjs6_2.js file.

(continued)

4. Add a new variable named items to the script and assign it a value of 0.

5. In the switch statement, add code to assign the following values to the items variable, depending on the name of the city:
10 if the city is Johnstown.
5 if the city is Donville.
2 if the city is Danieltown or Martyville.
0 for any other city name that is entered.

6. After the document.write(msg) statement, add additional code so that if the value of the items variable is greater than 0 (an if statement), then the following document.write() statements are executed.

```
document.write("<p>We can deliver up to " + items + " items to your
city.</p>");
document.write("<p>Print this out, write your item numbers below,
and mail it to us to order.</p>");
```

7. Right after these statements (still inside the if statement), create a for loop that will display a number followed by a series of underscores (_) to create a place to fill in an item number. The loop will run enough times to allow the maximum number of items to be ordered for the city that was entered.

8. When you are done, your JavaScript file should have the following code (other solutions are possible as well):

```
var items = 0,
    msg = "",
    city = window.prompt("What is the name of your city?", "");
if ( (city === null) || (city === "") ) {
  msg = "No city entered. Cannot determine delivery availability.";
}
else {
  switch (city) {
    case "Johnstown" :
      msg = "We can have items delivered to you in 3 days.";
      items = 10;
      break;
    case "Donville" :
      msg = "We can have items delivered to you in 1 week.";
      items = 5;
      break;
    case "Danieltown" :
      // fall through
    case "Martyville" :
      msg = "We can have items delivered to you in 2 weeks.";
      items = 2;
      break;
```

(continued)

```
    default :
       msg = "Sorry! We do not deliver to your city yet.";
       items = 0;
    }
  }
document.write(msg);
if (items > 0) {
   document.write("<p>We can deliver up to " + items + " items to
your city.</p>");
   document.write("<p>Print this out, write your item numbers below,
and mail it to us to order.</p>");
   for (var count = 1; count <= items; count++) {
      document.write(count + ". _____<br>");
   }
  }
}
```

9. Save the JavaScript file again and view the HTML page in the browser. Enter a city and view the results. You can reload the page to try different city names.

Try This Summary
In this project, you used your knowledge of loops and if statements to enhance your previous project by adding a customized "snail mail" order form for customers in different cities.

✓

Chapter 6 Self Test

1. A conditional statement is a statement that you can use to execute a bit of code based on a _____, or do something else if that _____ is not met.

2. You can think of a conditional statement as being a little like _____ and _____.

3. Rather than executing every single line of code within the script, a conditional statement allows certain sections of the script to be executed only when a particular condition is met.

    A. True

    B. False

4. Which of the following would be valid as the first line of an if/else statement?

    A. if (*x*=2)

    B. if (*y*<7)

    C. else

    D. if ((*x*==2 &&)

5. What do you use to enclose the blocks of code in conditionals and loops?

   A. Parentheses

   B. Square brackets

   C. Curly brackets

   D. Less-than and greater-than characters

6. The _____ statement allows you to take a single variable value and execute a different line of code based on the value of the variable.

7. A _____ is a block of code that allows you to repeat a section of code a certain number of times.

8. A loop is useful because it forces you to type lines of code repeatedly.

   A. True

   B. False

9. Which of these would be valid as the first line of a for loop?

   A. for (var $x = 1$; $x < 6$; $x \mathrel{+}= 1$)

   B. for (x==1;x<6;x+=1)

   C. for (int x=1;x=6;x+=1)

   D. for (var x+=1;x<6;x=1)

10. A _____ loop looks at a comparison and repeats until the comparison is no longer true.

11. Which of these would not be valid as the first line of a while loop?

    A. while (x<=7)

    B. while (x=7)

    C. while (x<7)

    D. while (x!=7)

12. A do while loop is special because the code within the loop is performed at least once, even if the comparison used would return false the first time.

    A. True

    B. False

13. The first line of a do while block contains the keyword do and a comparison.

    A. True

    B. False

14. The last line of a do while block contains only a curly bracket.

    A. True

    B. False

15. How many times can you nest a code block within another?

    A. None

    B. Once

    C. Three times, but no more

    D. As many times as you like (though enough nesting could make the browser run out of memory)

Chapter 7

JavaScript Arrays

Key Skills & Concepts

- Defining and Accessing Arrays

- Array Properties and Methods

- Using Arrays with Loops

- Nesting Arrays

In this chapter, you are going to learn about JavaScript arrays and what they can do to help you improve your scripts. You will begin with a basic overview of what arrays are and why they are useful, and you will learn how to define and access arrays in JavaScript. After that, you will learn about helpful properties and methods that can be used with arrays. Finally, you will learn how to nest arrays to provide additional levels of organization.

What Is an Array?

An *array* is a way of storing a list of data (for example, a list of favorite colors or favorite foods). These values are accessed through the use of an index number.

To get an idea of how an array works, suppose you have a class full of students and you want to be able to quickly display the name of every student. You could use regular variables to hold the name of each student, but typing each variable name into a document.write() statement would take a long time. Instead, you could store each student's name in an array, which will allow you to access it more easily with a few lines of code using a loop.

The array would allow you to put together a number and a name, such as in the following example:

- Student 0: Thomas

- Student 1: Roger

- Student 2: Amber

- Student 3: Jennifer

By storing it in a manner like this, you could use the numbers to get the name of each student. This is where arrays become useful as a way to store information and access it later.

NOTE

Notice that the first student in the array is Student 0 rather than Student 1. This is because arrays begin storing values with the number 0 rather than 1. This will be discussed in more detail as you move through this chapter.

Why Arrays Are Useful

Why would the use of numbers make it easier for you to access the stored information? Because, with the use of numbers, you can easily use a loop to cycle through the information instead of manually typing each entry. If the list of students in the example becomes long, the loop would save you quite a bit of typing when you want to have all the names displayed in the browser.

For instance, if you assigned the name of each student in your example list to a variable and then wrote the names to the screen, you would need to rewrite each variable name in the document.write() statements. The following code shows an example of this:

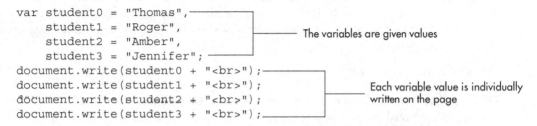

```
var student0 = "Thomas",
    student1 = "Roger",
    student2 = "Amber",
    student3 = "Jennifer";
document.write(student0 + "<br>");
document.write(student1 + "<br>");
document.write(student2 + "<br>");
document.write(student3 + "<br>");
```

The variables are given values

Each variable value is individually written on the page

If you were able to use a loop to repeat a single document.write() statement for each student, you could avoid writing four separate variable names. An array is a handy way to store the values (student names), because you can cycle through the values with a loop instead of writing out each value—even if you don't know the number of students beforehand (by using the length property of the array). You will see more on this as you move through this chapter.

Defining and Accessing Arrays

Now that you know what arrays are, you are ready to see how to name, define, access, and use arrays in JavaScript.

Naming an Array

You can name an array using the same rules you have already learned about naming variables. Refer to Chapter 3 for a list of these naming rules.

Defining an Array

JavaScript arrays are very versatile. You can choose whether or not to specify the number of items within an array, and you can use values of any data type in any position within an array (for example, you could have the first element be a number, the second a string, and so on). To see how this all works, you will first learn the two ways you can define arrays in JavaScript: the array constructor and array literal notation.

The Array Constructor

The array constructor defines an array using the following format:

```
var arrayname = new Array();
```

You replace *arrayname* with the name you wish to give to the array. You will notice that the keyword new is used with Array(). This code creates an empty array, but you can also place arguments within the parentheses to provide either the length of the array or the values of each of the individual array items.

To specify the length of the array, you place a single numeric value within the parentheses, as shown in this code:

```
var students = new Array(4);  ◄——————— Creates an array named students with four items
```

This array is named students and contains four items. All four values are set to undefined initially, but each item can be defined later in your code. Though you can do this, it is not necessary to set the array length, as it can vary as needed during your script execution.

To specify the values of each item in the array, you provide them as arguments, just as you would with a function:

```
var students = new Array("Thomas", "Roger", "Amber", "Jennifer");
```

This array has four defined items: "Thomas", "Roger", "Amber", and "Jennifer".

As you have read, JavaScript allows you to have various data types within the same array. The following code also produces a valid array:

```
var answers = new Array(42, "paper", -3, "plastic");
```

In this way, you have a great deal of flexibility, since you are not limited to one data type in an array.

CAUTION

When using the array constructor, providing a single numeric value as the argument will always create an array with that length, rather than an array with one item of that value. Thus, var students = new Array(4); will create an array with four items rather than an array with one item having a value of 4. If more than one argument is provided (whether numeric or not), then all arguments will be used as item values as expected.

Array Literal Notation

Array literal notation provides a shorter method for defining arrays, using square brackets ([]) rather than the constructor syntax. For example, you can create an empty array using the following code:

```
var students = [];
```

You can add items by simply providing them in a comma-separated list, as you do with arguments. The following examples all create valid arrays using array literal notation:

```
var answers = [42, "paper", -3, "plastic"];
var is_true = [true, false];
var nums = [4, 20, 19, 2, 2, 10056, -42, 3];
```

As with the array constructor, any data type is allowed as a value for an item. In this book, I will most often use array literal notation when defining arrays.

CAUTION

When using array literal notation, a single numeric value creates an array with that value as the only item, whereas the array constructor would create an array of that length. Thus, var students = [4]; will create an array with one item with a value of 4, rather than an array that contains four items.

Accessing an Array's Elements

To access the elements of an array, you use what is called an "index" that allows you access to each item in the array by its position. For instance, consider the following example code:

```
var students = ["Thomas", "Roger", "Amber", "Jennifer"];
```

You can access "Thomas" using the syntax students[0], "Roger" using students[1], and so on. Notice that square brackets are used immediately after the array name and that they contain the index of the item you wish to access in the array. You will also see that the first item is accessed using 0 as the index. This is because arrays begin counting at 0 instead of 1; thus, you need to be careful that you do not get confused about the index of an item in an array. The first item has an index of 0, the second has an index of 1, the third has an index of 2, and so on.

You can use an array item in your code just as you would a variable. For example, take a look at this code:

```
var students = ["Thomas", "Roger", "Amber", "Jennifer"];
alert(students[0]);
```

This code would send an alert saying "Thomas" to the viewer. You could display each student name in the array if needed, as in this code:

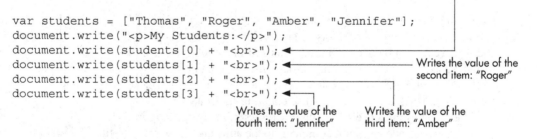

This will display the list of students on the Web page, in order. Unfortunately, as this list grows, you will have to continue adding lines of code for each new item. This is where the length property and the use of a loop can help you work with an ever-growing array.

Using the length Property and Loops

A very handy value to have is the number of items in an array. In JavaScript, this can be obtained by using the length property. To access the value of the length property, you use the name of the array, followed by a dot (.), followed by length, as in the following code:

```
var students = ["Thomas", "Roger", "Amber", "Jennifer"];
alert(students.length);
```

This will send an alert with the number 4 to the viewer, since there are four items in the array.

Since your array could have more items added to it at any time, the length property provides a way to find out how many items are currently in the array. One advantage of this is that you can create a loop to cycle through each item in the array.

Recall from the previous section that you had the following code:

```
var students = ["Thomas", "Roger", "Amber", "Jennifer"];
document.write("<p>My Students:</p>");
document.write(students[0] + "<br>");
document.write(students[1] + "<br>");
document.write(students[2] + "<br>");
document.write(students[3] + "<br>");
```

The value of each array item is written on the page with each index being typed separately

This code works, but it would be much better if you did not need to include a new line of code each time an item is added to the array. Since you now have the length attribute, you can use it to create a loop that will write each array item on the page, regardless of the length. The following code shows an example of this:

```
var students = ["Thomas", "Roger", "Amber", "Jennifer"];
document.write("<p>My Students:</p>");
for (var i = 0; i < students.length; i++) {
   document.write(students[i] + "<br>");
}
```

Notice that the for statement initializes a variable named i and gives it a value of 0. It is then compared to the value of students.length (which in this case is 4) each time through the loop, and is incremented by one each time. This allows the loop to cycle through each array item by its index, starting at 0 and running through the last item in the array (in this case, students[3], the fourth item in the array). Note that < is used and not <=, which would try to access students[4], which does not exist since counting starts at 0.

The result of this code when run in a browser is shown in Figure 7-1.

Now, we can add any number of items to the array and the script will still write all of the items on the page. For example, suppose you added some items to the array, as in the following code:

```
var students = ["Thomas", "Roger", "Amber", "Jennifer", "Joe", "Dawn"];
document.write("<p>My Students:</p>");
for (var i = 0; i < students.length; i++) {
   document.write(students[i] + "<br>");
}
```

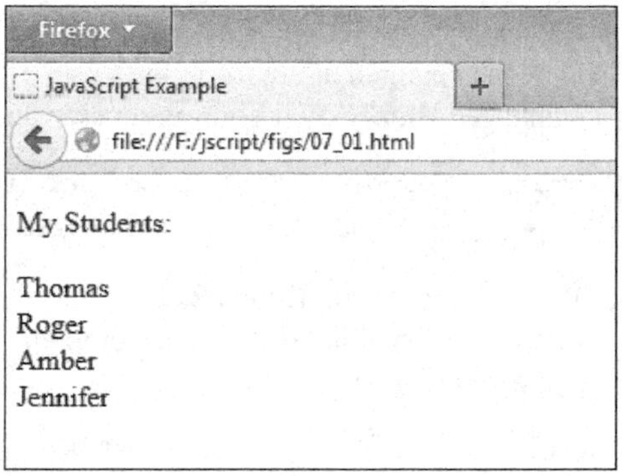

Figure 7-1   The name of each student is displayed using a loop.

This time, students.length will be 6, and the names of all six students will be written on the page. Figure 7-2 shows the result of this change when viewed in a browser.

As you can see, arrays and loops work extremely well together, giving you a way to access all of the items in an array and to perform any needed tasks without the need to repeat similar lines of code numerous times. Since the number of items and the values of items can be altered at any time, this technique can be an especially useful tool.

Changing Array Values and Changing the Length

You can alter arrays in a number of ways. Here, you will look at two things you can do to make changes to an array: changing values and changing the length.

Figure 7-2   The added array items are written on the page.

Changing Values

Each array item can have its value changed at any time in the script. Much like variables, the value of array items can be changed simply by assigning a new value, as in the following code:

```
var students = ["Thomas", "Roger", "Amber", "Jennifer"];
students[2] = "Dawn"; ◄———————— The value of the third array item is changed
```

This changes the value of the third array item (index 2) from "Amber" to "Dawn". You can also loop through the array and change every item as desired. For example, the following code will make the same alteration to the value of each array item:

```
var students = ["Thomas", "Roger", "Amber", "Jennifer"];
for (var i = 0; i < students.length; i++) {
   students[i] += " Doe");
}
```

This assigns all of the students a last name of "Doe": students[0] now has a value of "Thomas Doe", students[1] now has a value of "Roger Doe", and so on.

Changing the Length

Not only can you access the value of the length property, you can also change it. Doing so will either remove items from the end of the array or add items to the end of the array. For example, the following code would remove the last two items from the students array:

```
var students = ["Thomas", "Roger", "Amber", "Jennifer"];
students.length = 2;
```

The array originally had four items, but now has only the first two: "Thomas" and "Roger".

If you change the length value to a number that is greater than the array's current length, then items will be added to the end of the array. The following code shows an example of this:

```
var students = ["Thomas", "Roger", "Amber", "Jennifer"];
students.length = 7;
```

The array will now have seven elements, adding three elements to the end. The last three elements (students[4], students[5], and students[6]) will have a value of undefined until they are explicitly given a value.

One additional way to increase the length of an array is to assign a value to an index that is greater than any index currently in the array. For example, consider the following code:

```
                                                  The array has four elements
var students = ["Thomas", "Roger", "Amber", "Jennifer"]; ◄———┘
students[6] = "Marty"; ◄————————————————————  The array now has seven elements, with
                                              the item at index 6 defined as "Marty"
```

Defining an item at index 6 forces the array to expand in order to include the new item. The elements in between the end of the original array and the newly defined index will have a value of undefined until they are given a value. In this case, students[4] and students[5] will be undefined, while students[6] will be "Marty" as defined in the code.

If you are not sure where the last element is and want to add to the end of the array, you can use the length of the array in the brackets to do so, as in the following code:

```
var students = ["Thomas", "Roger", "Amber", "Jennifer"];
students[students.length] = "Marty";
```

Here, students[4] is added to the array and assigned a value of "Marty".

Other ways of adding or removing items are available using array methods, which you will learn about later in this chapter.

Try This 7-1   Use Loops with Arrays

pr7_1.html
prjs7_1.js

This project allows you to practice using loops with arrays. Suppose your company is selling specific computer parts and you want to display each part that you have for sale. All of your part names are stored in an array.

Step by Step

1. Create an HTML page with a heading with the text "Computer Parts Available". Add script tags that include an external JavaScript file named prjs7_1.js. Save the HTML file as pr7_1.html.

2. Create an external JavaScript file and save it as prjs7_1.js. Use it for steps 3–6.

3. Create a new array named computer_parts and assign the following list of parts as values for the items in the array:

   Monitors
   Motherboards
   Chips
   Hard Drives
   DVD-ROMs
   Cases
   Power Supplies

4. Display each computer part on its own line in the browser window (use a loop).

5. When complete, your JavaScript file should have the following code (more than one correct answer is possible):

```
var computer_parts = ["Monitors", "Motherboards", "Chips", "Hard Drives",
                      "DVD-ROMs", "Cases", "Power Supplies"];
for (var i = 0; i < computer_parts.length; i++) {
  document.write(computer_parts[i] + "<br>");
}
```

6. Save the JavaScript file and load the HTML file in a browser to view the results. You should see the current list of parts.

(continued)

Try This Summary

In this project, you used your knowledge of loops, arrays, and Array object properties to create two different results. One result lists the elements of an array, while the other adds some elements to the array and lists the elements in alphabetical order.

Array Properties and Methods

Arrays have a number of properties and methods available for use in your scripts. These allow you to do things such as add items, remove items, sort items, combine arrays, and more. Arrays have these properties and methods because arrays are objects in JavaScript (you will learn about objects in Chapter 8). To begin, you will take a look at the array properties, followed by the array methods.

Properties

Table 7-1 lists the properties of the Array object and provides a short description of each. Each property is discussed in more detail in the sections that follow.

The constructor and prototype Properties

The constructor property contains the value of the function code that created the array's prototype. It simply returns this value:

```
function Array() { [native code] }
```

The prototype property allows you to add properties and methods to all instances of an object that already exists, such as the Array object. Adding to the array prototype would affect all arrays used in the script, and is best to avoid for now. You will learn more about how constructor functions and prototypes work in Chapter 8.

The index and input Properties

To understand the index and input properties, you first need to understand regular expressions (which are used to match text strings), which requires a lengthy explanation, as provided in Chapter 13. Discussion of the index and input properties will be saved for that chapter.

Property	Description
constructor	Refers to the constructor function used to create an instance of the Array object
index	Used when an array is created by a regular expression match
input	Used when an array is created by a regular expression match
length	Contains a numeric value equal to the number of elements in an array
prototype	Allows the addition of properties and methods to the Array object

Table 7-1 Properties of the Array Object

The length Property

The length property, as you have seen, returns a number that tells you how many elements are in an array. Since you have already been using this, you can refer to previous sections in this chapter for more information.

Methods

Now that you know the properties of the Array object, this section presents the methods that you can use to do different things with your arrays. Table 7-2 lists the methods and provides a description of what each method does. Following the table, each method is described in more detail.

Method	Description
join()	Combines the elements of an array into a single string with a separator character
pop()	Removes the last element from an array and then returns the removed element if needed
push()	Adds elements to the end of an array and then returns the numeric value of the new length of the array if needed
shift()	Removes the first element from an array and then returns that element if needed
unshift()	Adds elements to the beginning of an array and returns the numeric value of the length of the new array if needed
reverse()	Reverses the direction of the elements in an array: the first element is moved to the last slot and the last element is moved to the first slot, and so on
sort()	Sorts the elements of an array into alphabetical order based on the string values of the elements
concat()	Combines the elements of two or more arrays into one new array
slice()	Pulls out a specified section of an array and returns the section as a new array
splice()	Removes elements from an array or replaces elements in an array
indexOf()	Finds the index of an item within an array
lastIndexOf()	Finds the last index of an item within an array
every()	Executes the function provided for every array item and returns true if the function returns true for all of the items
filter()	Executes the function provided for every array item and returns an array of items for which the function returns true
forEach()	Executes the function provided for every array item

(continues)

Table 7-2 Methods of the Array Object

Method	Description
map()	Executes the function provided for every array item and returns an array of the results of calling the function on each item
some()	Executes the function provided for every array item and returns true if the execution of the function returns true for any of the items
reduce() reduceRight()	Executes the function provided for every array item and returns a final result
toString() toLocaleString() valueOf()	Combines the elements of an array into a single string with a comma as a separator character

Table 7-2 Methods of the Array Object (*continued*)

The join() Method

The join([separator]) method is used to combine the items of an array into a single string, with each item separated by a comma (default) or a string sent to it as an argument.

CAUTION

Internet Explorer up through version 7 will use the string "undefined" by default if the argument is not provided. It is best to go ahead and provide the argument in order to prevent this from occurring.

To see how this method works, take a look at a bit of code. The following example defines an array and then calls the join() method on the array name:

```
var fruits = ["oranges", "apples", "pears"];
var fruit_string = fruits.join(",");
```

This code assigns the result of the join() method to the variable fruit_string. Notice that the method is called by using the name of the array (fruits), followed by a dot (.), followed by the method name. The fruit_string variable will have the following string value:

```
oranges,apples,pears
```

You can see this result by writing the string variable into a Web page. The following code will do this for you:

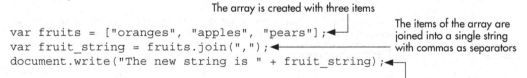

The array is created with three items

```
var fruits = ["oranges", "apples", "pears"];
var fruit_string = fruits.join(",");
document.write("The new string is " + fruit_string);
```

The items of the array are joined into a single string with commas as separators

The string is displayed on the screen

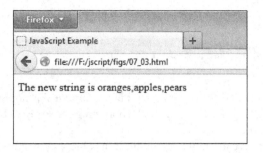

Figure 7-3   The new string is written on the page.

Now you can see the string that is returned from the join() method. Figure 7-3 shows what this code produces when run in a browser.

If you want to separate the items in the new string with something other than a comma, you can send the string you want to use as an argument. The following code uses a colon as a separator:

The array is created with three items

The items of the array are joined into a single string with colons as separators

```
var fruits = ["oranges", "apples", "pears"];
var fruit_string = fruits.join(":");
document.write("The new string is " + fruit_string);
```

The string is displayed on the screen

This time the string will be a little different from the previous one, because it has colons in place of the commas in the previous example. Figure 7-4 shows how this string would display in the browser window.

The pop() Method
The pop() method is used to remove the last item from an array. If you assign the result of the method to a variable, the popped element will be returned and assigned to the variable.

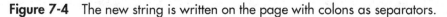

Figure 7-4   The new string is written on the page with colons as separators.

The following code creates an array and then removes the last item from the array using the pop() method:

```
var fruits = ["oranges", "apples", "pears"];
fruits.pop();
```

This creates an array named fruits with three items ("oranges", "apples", "pears"). Then, the last item is removed using the pop() method, shortening the array to have only the first two items ("oranges", "apples").

If you want to remove an item but still use it in some way later, you can assign the result of the method to a variable. The variable will be assigned the value of the item that was popped. The following example removes the last item of an array and then sends the popped item as an alert to the viewer:

```
var fruits = ["oranges", "apples", "pears"];
var picked_fruit = fruits.pop();
window.alert("You picked my " + picked_fruit);
```

This will pop up an alert that says "You picked my pears" to the viewer.

The push() Method

The push([item]) method is used to add items to the end of an array. The arguments sent to the method are the new items you wish to add to the array. If assigned to a variable, this method will return the new length of the array.

As an example, look at some code that adds one item to the end of an array:

```
var fruits = ["oranges", "apples"];
fruits.push("pears");
```

This code creates an array named fruits with two items ("oranges", "apples") and then uses the push() method to add a third item, "pears". The array now contains three items ("oranges", "apples", "pears"), with "pears" being the last item in the array.

You can add more than one element by sending more than one argument. The items will be added in the order in which they are sent in the argument list. The following code adds two elements to the fruits array:

```
var fruits = ["oranges","apples"];
fruits.push("pears", "grapes");
```

This code adds two items to the fruits array. In the end, the array contains four elements ("oranges", "apples", "pears", "grapes").

If you want the new length that is returned by the method, you can assign the result to a variable. The following code does this and then sends the viewer an alert with the returned value:

```
var fruits = ["oranges", "apples"];
var new_length = fruits.push("pears", "grapes");
window.alert("The array now has " + new_length + " items");
```

Since two items were added to the end of the array, the new length of the array will be four, and an alert saying "The array now has 4 items" will be sent to the viewer.

NOTE

For those who have programmed in other languages, push() and pop() treat an array like a stack (last in, first out). Combining these with the shift() and unshift() methods allows an array to work like a queue.

The shift() Method

The shift() method is used to remove the first item of an array. It returns the value of the item that was removed from the array.

The following code uses the shift() method to remove the first array item:

```
var fruits = ["oranges", "apples", "pears"];
fruits.shift();
```

This code creates an array with three items and removes the first item with the shift() method. This causes the array to have only two items remaining ("apples", "pears").

To use the value of the element that was removed, you can assign the result of the method to a variable. The following code assigns the removed element to a variable and then alerts the viewer about what was removed:

```
var fruits = ["oranges", "apples", "pears"];
var picked_fruit = fruits.shift();
window.alert("You picked my " + picked_fruit);
```

This code displays the alert "You picked my oranges" in the browser window.

The unshift() Method

The unshift([item]) method is used to add items to the beginning of an array. The items you wish to add to the array are sent as arguments. The value returned by the method is the new length of the array.

The following example adds one new item to the beginning of an array:

```
var fruits = ["apples", "pears"];
fruits.unshift("oranges");
```

This creates an array with two items and then adds an item to the beginning using the unshift() method. The array then contains three items ("oranges", "apples", "pears").

If you want to add more than one item at a time, you send them as arguments in the order in which you wish to add them. The following example adds two items to the beginning of the array:

```
var fruits = ["apples", "pears"];
fruits.unshift("oranges", "grapes");
```

This takes the initial array and adds two elements to the beginning. The array ends up containing four elements ("oranges", "grapes", "apples", "pears") after the unshift() method is called.

The reverse() Method

The reverse() method is used to reverse the order of the items in an array. To demonstrate how to use this method, the following code creates an array and then reverses the order of the items:

```
var fruits = ["oranges", "apples", "pears"];
fruits.reverse();
```

The initial order of the array is "oranges", "apples", "pears". When the reverse() method is called, the order of the items changes to "pears", "apples", "oranges". Note that this changes the original array, rather than returning a new array.

The sort() Method

The sort([sort_function]) method converts each array item into a string value, and then arranges the items in ascending order based on the string values. The following code shows an example of this method in action:

```
var fruits = ["oranges", "apples", "pears", "grapes"];
fruits.sort();
```

This will reorder the array so that the elements will be in alphabetical order: "apples", "grapes", "oranges", "pears".

Recall, however, that strings are compared based on their character codes (refer to the "The Is-Greater-Than Operator (>)" section in Chapter 5). If there is a difference in capitalization, this can cause an unexpected order to be returned:

```
var fruits = ["oranges", "apples", "pears", "Grapes"];
fruits.sort();
```

With the last item capitalized, the order of the array after the sort is "Grapes", "apples", "oranges", "pears". To fix this, you can use a method for strings named toLowerCase() to ensure all values are compared in lowercase and return in the order expected after the sort:

```
var fruits = ["oranges", "apples", "pears", "Grapes"];    ← The last item is capitalized
for (var i = 0; i < fruits.length; i++) {    ← A loop is created to cycle through the array
  fruits[i] = fruits[i].toLowerCase();    ← Each array item is put in lowercase by calling toLowerCase()
}    ← The array is sorted in the expected order
fruits.sort();
```

With this in place, the order will now be "apples", "grapes", "oranges", "pears".

Since the sort() method changes all values to strings, even an array containing only numeric values will be sorted based on their conversion to strings:

```
var fruits = [2, 3, 1, 20];
fruits.sort();
```

Instead of the expected order (numeric), the order is 1, 2, 20, 3 after the sort since the values are compared as strings. To work around this type of issue, JavaScript allows you to specify a *comparison function* as an argument of the sort() method.

A comparison function is a function with two arguments, which returns a positive number, negative number, or zero based on the result of comparing the two argument values. For example, a simple comparison function is shown here:

```
function mysort(first_value, second_value) {
  if (first_value > second_value) {
     return 1;
  } else if (first_value < second_value) {
     return -1;
  } else {
     return 0;
  }
}
```

Basically, a comparison function should return a positive number if the first argument is greater than the second, a negative number if the first argument is less than the second, or zero if the two arguments are equal. This will sort the items in ascending order. Using the function shown in the preceding code as the argument to the sort() method will place the numbers in the expected numerical order, since the greater-than operator will compare the numbers as numerical values instead of converting them to strings. Here is an example of this in action:

```
var fruits = [2, 3, 1, 20];
function mysort(first_value, second_value) {
  if (first_value > second_value) {
     return 1;
  } else if (first_value < second_value) {
     return -1;
  } else {
     return 0;
  }
}
fruits.sort(mysort);
```

The comparison function

The name of the comparison function is used as the argument in the sort() method

With this in place, the sort will place the items in the expected order: 1, 2, 3, 20.

The concat() Method

The concat([array]) method will concatenate the array with the arguments sent to it and return a new array containing all of the items. It does not affect the original array. You use array names or individual values as arguments and provide them in order.

The first example combines the elements of two arrays. To do this, only one argument needs to be used—the name of the array to be concatenated with the array that calls the method:

```
var fruits = ["oranges", "apples"];
var veggies = ["corn", "peas"];
var fruits_n_veggies = fruits.concat(veggies);
```

This code creates an array named fruits with two elements, and an array named veggies with two elements. Next, it defines fruits_n_veggies, which will receive the array returned by the concat() method. In this case, the fruits_n_veggies array will consist of "oranges", "apples", "corn", "peas".

If you instead want to have the items in the veggies array listed first, you can call the method using the veggies array name and send the fruits array name as the argument:

```
var fruits = ["oranges", "apples"];
var veggies = ["corn", "peas"];
var fruits_n_veggies = veggies.concat(fruits);
```

Now the items of the veggies array are listed first, and the new fruits_n_veggies array has the following items: "corn", "peas", "oranges", "apples".

If you combine three arrays, the items of the array with which you call the concat() method will come first, and then the items of each array sent as arguments will be added in the order in which they are sent:

```
var fruits = ["oranges", "apples"];
var veggies = ["corn", "peas"];
var meats = ["fish", "chicken"];
var three_groups = fruits.concat(veggies, meats);
```

Now you are combining three arrays, and the following are the items in the new three_groups array: "oranges", "apples", "corn", "peas", "fish", "chicken".

If you code it in the following way instead, you will get an array with the same elements, but in a new order:

```
var fruits = ["oranges", "apples"];
var veggies = ["corn", "peas"];
var meats = ["fish", "chicken"];
var three_groups = meats.concat(veggies, fruits);
```

The following is the order of the elements in the new three_groups array when using this code: "fish", "chicken", "corn", "peas", "oranges", "apples".

In addition to concatenating arrays, you can also concatenate strings, numbers, or other data types. These can all be done together if desired:

```
var fruits = ["oranges", "apples"];
var veggies = ["corn", "peas"];
var big_array = fruits.concat(veggies, "cat", 4, ["house","car"]);
```

This concatenation creates an array named big_array. It adds the veggies array, a string, a number, and another array to the fruits array. The final items in big_array are: "oranges", "apples", "corn", "peas", "cat", 4, "house", "car".

If you use concat() without any arguments, it will make a copy of the original array. So, the following code would simply give you a copy of the fruits array:

```
var fruits = ["oranges", "apples"];
var same_fruits = fruits.concat();
```

The slice() Method

The slice(start, [stop]) method is used to slice a specified section of an array and then to create a new array using the elements from the sliced section of the old array.

The following is the general syntax for using this method:

```
arrayname.slice(start, stop);
```

You replace *start* with the index where you will start the slice and replace *stop* with the index that comes after the last item you wish to slice.

For an example, the following code slices two items from an array and creates a new array with those items:

```
var fruits = ["oranges", "apples", "pears", "grapes"];
var somefruits = fruits.slice(1,3);
```

This slices the second item (index 1) and third item (index 2) of the array. It does not pull out the fourth item (index 3). The new array named somefruits contains the sliced items ("apples", "pears").

NOTE

If the second argument is not included, then the slice method will continue to the end of the array. This makes it a common solution to copy an array using slice(0), for example, var same_fruits = fruits.slice(0);

The splice() Method

The splice(begin, num_items, [add_item]) method allows you to remove or replace items in an array. The arguments that can be sent include the index at which to begin the splice, the number of items to remove, and the option to add new items to the array.

If you want to remove a single item from an array, you could use code such as the following:

```
var fruits = ["oranges", "apples", "pears", "grapes"];
var somefruits = fruits.splice(2, 1);
```

This begins removing items at index 2. The next argument is 1, so only one item will be removed; thus, only the element at index 2 ("pears") is removed here. After the splice, the array contains only three items: "oranges", "apples", "grapes".

To remove more than one item, you increase the value of the second argument. The following code removes two items, starting at index 2:

```
var fruits = ["oranges", "apples", "pears", "grapes"];
var somefruits = fruits.splice(2, 2);
```

This time the array is cut down to two items ("oranges", "apples"), since the last two items are removed by the splice() method.

You can also use the splice() method to replace spliced items in an array or to add items to an array. The following code replaces the spliced item at index 2 with a new item by sending an additional argument:

```
var fruits = ["oranges", "apples", "pears", "grapes"];
var somefruits = fruits.splice(2, 1, "watermelons");
```

This time, the item at index 2 is removed. Since the second argument is 1, only one item is removed. The next argument is added to the array at the index specified in the first argument (2). This value ("watermelons") replaces the value that was removed ("pears"). The array will now contain the following items: "oranges", "apples", "watermelons", "grapes".

If you want to use the splice() method to add one or more items to an array but not remove anything, you can set the second argument to 0 (thus removing zero elements). You set the first argument to the index at which you wish to begin adding elements. For example, take a look at the following code:

```
var fruits = ["oranges", "apples", "pears", "grapes"];
var somefruits = fruits.splice(2, 0, "watermelons", "plums");
```

The addition of items begins at index 2, as specified in the first argument, and nothing is removed, as specified in the second argument. Two items are added, after which the array will have six items: "oranges", "apples", "watermelons", "plums", "pears", "grapes".

The indexOf() and lastIndexOf() Methods

The indexOf([string]) and lastIndexOf([string]) methods were added in ECMAScript 5 and provide a way to search for an item in an array. The indexOf() method searches the array from front to back, while lastIndexOf() searches from back to front. If the item is found, the index of the item is returned. If the item is not found, −1 is returned.

The following code shows how both methods can be used:

```
var fruits = ["oranges", "apples", "pears", "apples"];
var found_apples = fruits.indexOf("apples");
window.alert(found_apples);  ◄──────────────── Alerts 1
found_apples = fruits.lastIndexOf("apples");
window.alert(found_apples);  ◄──────────────── Alerts 3
found_apples = fruits.indexOf("grapes");
window.alert(found_apples);  ◄──────────────── Alerts −1
```

Here, searching for the item "apples" from the front using indexOf() returns 1, since it will find the first instance of "apples" at index 1. If you use lastIndexOf() to search for "apples" from the back, then 3 will be returned, since the first instance of "apples" lastIndexOf() will detect is the last one in the array at index 3. Searching for "grapes" using either method will return −1, since "grapes" is not an item in the array.

Note that when the item is not in the array, −1 is returned instead of 0 since 0 is a valid index. Thus, you will want to avoid a construct such as: if (!fruits.indexOf("grapes")). Rather, you should use if (fruits.indexOf("grapes") === −1) to see if an item is not in the array.

A second argument can be provided to either method to specify an index from which to begin searching. This allows indexOf() or lastIndexOf() to skip previous instances of an item and only return the index of the first item it finds starting from the specified index. For example, consider this code:

```
var fruits = ["oranges", "apples", "pears", "apples"];
var found_apples = fruits.indexOf("apples", 2);
window.alert(found_apples);          ◄————————————— Alerts 3
found_apples = fruits.lastIndexOf("apples", 1);
window.alert(found_apples);          ◄————————————— Alerts 1
```

In this case, calling fruits.indexOf("apples", 2) begins the search from front to back at index 2 rather than index 0. This means that it will bypass the first instance of "apples" at index 1, start the search at index 2, and return 3, since the next instance of "apples" is at index 3. Calling lastIndexOf("apples", 1) begins the search from index 1 and proceeds toward the front. In this case, the "apples" at index 3 is skipped and the search begins at index 1, where it finds "apples" and returns 1.

Finally, it is important to note that both methods use the === operator rather than the == operator to determine whether an item was found. As a result, no type coercion is performed and there must be an exact match for a successful search. For example, consider the following code:

```
var nums = ["2", 5, 22, 3];————————————┐  The first item ("2") is a string and will
var found_two = nums.lastIndexOf(2);———┘  not match the numeric value of 2

alert(found_two);  ◄————————————————————— Alerts –1
```

Since "2" and 2 are not strictly equal, the item is not found and –1 is returned. Keep this in mind when making use of these methods in order to avoid unexpected results.

The every(), filter(), forEach(), map(), and some() Methods

The every(), filter(), forEach(), map(), and some() methods were added in ECMAScript 5 to provide a way to call a function as an argument to be run on each item in an array. These functions return a value based on the results of running the function called in the argument on each item in the array. These are called *iterative* functions, meaning that they cycle through (or iterate over) each item in an array. Here is what each of the iterative methods will do when called:

- **every()**   Executes the function provided for every array item and returns true if the function returns true for *all* of the items

- **some()**   Executes the function provided for every array item and returns true if the execution of the function returns true for *any* of the items

- **filter()**   Executes the function provided for every array item and returns an array of items for which the function returns true

- **map()** Executes the function provided for every array item and returns an array of the results of calling the function on each item

- **forEach()** Executes the function provided for every array item. No value is returned.

To use one of these methods, you would call it and provide a function name as an argument, as in the following example:

```
var grades = [94, 65, 71, 84, 99];
var the_result = grades.every(pass_grades);
```

The result returned after the every() method iterates over all of the array items running the named function (pass_grades) will be stored in the variable named the_result.

For example, suppose the function named pass_grades() is used to determine whether a student has made 70 or above on all recorded grades, as in the following code:

The function receives three arguments
from the every() method

```
function pass_grades(item_value, item_index, arr_name) {◀─┘
    return (item_value >= 70);◀─────────────────────── A return statement is used
}                                                       to return a Boolean value
var grades = [94, 65, 71, 84, 99];                     The result of calling the
var the_result = grades.every(pass_grades);◀────────── every() method on the grades
window.alert(the_result);◀──────── Alerts false        array using the pass_grades
                                                        function is assigned to a
                                                        variable named the_result
```

This will return a Boolean value based on whether or not the grade is greater than or equal to 70. You will notice that the function takes three arguments. The first is the value of the current array item, the second is the current array index, and the third is the array itself. These values are sent as arguments to the function specified (pass_grades here) when any of the iterative methods is called.

The pass_grade() function returns the following five results during the course of the iterations: true, false, true, true, true. Since the every() method requires *all* of the return values to be true in order to itself return true, it will return false in this case due to the single low grade at index 1 (65).

Calling each of the other methods in place of every() in the previous code will produce the following results:

- Calling some() will return true, since it only requires one of the return values to be true (four out of five are true in this case).

- Calling filter() will return an array with all of the items that returned true. In this case, the array would be [94, 71, 84, 99]. The item at index 1 in the original array (65) is left out since it returns false. The new array is assigned to the variable the_result.

- Calling map() will return an array with the result of each of the function calls. In this case, the array would be [true, false, true, true, true]. This new array is assigned to the variable the_result.

- Calling foreach() will not return anything. It will simply run the function for each item in the array.

The reduce()and reduceRight() Methods

The reduce() and reduceRight() methods were also added in ECMAScript 5. These methods also iterate over the items in an array, but they build toward a final value that is returned. These methods, much like the iterative methods, use a function as an argument. The argument function itself is passed two arguments: the previous value and the next item. The first iteration passes the first item and second item as previous and next, respectively.

As an example, consider the following code:

The function receives the arguments for the previous and next values

```
function sub_values(prev_value, next_value) {
    return (prev_value - next_value);
}
var nums = [2, 4, 8, 16, 32];
var the_result = nums.reduce(sub_values);
window.alert(the_result);                          Alerts -58
the_result = nums.reduceRight(sub_values);
window.alert(the_result);                          Alerts 2
```

The result of subtracting next_value from prev_value is returned

When reduce() is called, the values are iterated from front to back, which in this case will create a negative number (–58). The first time through, 2 and 4 are sent as arguments, and 2–4 = –2. The next time through the result (–2) is sent as prev_value and 8 is sent as next_value, and –2–8 = –10. This pattern continues until a final result of –58 is reached.

When reduceRight() is called, the same process occurs, but moving back to front. In this case, 32 and 16 are sent as arguments first, and 32–16 = 16. Next, 16 (the result) and 8 are sent as arguments, and 16–8 = 8. This pattern continues until a final result of 2 is reached.

The toString(), toLocaleString(), and valueOf() Methods

The toString(), toLocaleString(), and valueOf() methods effectively combine the elements of an array into a single string with a comma as a separator character (much like using the join method with a comma separator). The toLocaleString() method can be adjusted to return a localized version of an item value if desired. You will learn more about the toLocaleString() method when strings are discussed in Chapter 13.

Ask the Expert

Q: Among all the properties, are there any that are specifically useful for arrays?

A: The length property, as you have seen, is probably the most often used property. The index and input properties are handy when working with regular expressions, which will be discussed in Chapter 13.

(continued)

Q: Is there an easy way to remember all of these methods?

A: As with other lists, how well you remember them depends on how often you use the methods. One helpful thing is to look for the pairs that complement each other, like pop() and push(), or shift() and unshift().

Q: So, the reverse() method just turns everything around backward? Why would I want to do that?

A: You may want to reverse the order for numbers to create a list with the highest numbers displayed first (for example, grades or temperatures). You may also decide to have strings listed in reverse alphabetical order in some situations.

Q: Which is better to use, the array constructor or array literal notation?

A: Typically, array literal notation is preferred in modern JavaScript, as the syntax tends to be simpler and it avoids some potential confusion:

```
var nums = new Array(5); // nums[0] = undefined, array has a length of 5
var nums = [5]; // nums[0] = 5
var nums = new Array(4.225); // causes error trying to set length
var nums = [4.225]; // nums[0] = 4.225
```

The first example creates an array with five items, which can be confused with having 5 as the lone item. The second example creates an array with one item (5). The third example looks as if it might create an array with the lone value of 4.225, but this causes an error because a floating-point number cannot be used as an array length. The final example works as expected.

Nesting Arrays

Arrays can be nested, allowing you to use an array as an item within another array. Doing this provides the ability to create arrays of more than one dimension. To get an idea of how this might be used, go back to the students array used previously:

```
var students = ["Thomas", "Roger", "Amber", "Jennifer"];
```

Suppose that you also want to keep track of the last test grade and current average grade for each of the students. You could add them directly to the array, but this makes it more difficult to get the proper information from the array when needed:

```
var students = ["Thomas", 92, 90, "Roger", 87, 78,
                "Amber", 81, 85, "Jennifer, 99, 100"];
```

As you can see, looping through the array will put Thomas at index 0, his last test grade at index 1, and his current average at index 2. Roger uses indexes 3, 4, and 5; Amber 6, 7, and 8; and Jennifer 9, 10 and 11. Trying to associate the values with the proper students can be difficult, especially if you want to loop through the array. Trying to deal with which value is a student versus a grade can become tedious, as you would need to try to calculate based on every third position being a new student while the two indexes that follow are grades.

It would be nice if each student could be grouped with his/her own grades in separate arrays, each accessible through the main students array. This is where the ability to nest arrays can make life easier for you as a coder.

Defining Nested Arrays

Using array literal notation, you can nest arrays easily by using additional square brackets for each new array. The following code shows an example of this:

```
                                            Begins the outer array named students,
                                            and defines the students[0] inner array

var students = [ ["Thomas", 92, 90],◄──────────────────────┘
                 ["Roger", 87, 78], ◄────────────── Defines the students[1] inner array
                 ["Amber", 81, 85], ◄────────────── Defines the students[2] inner array
                 ["Jennifer", 99, 100] ◄─────────── Defines the students[3] inner array
               ];
```

Here, the outer array (students) includes four inner arrays. The first array is at index 0 in the students array (students[0]). You can access items in the inner arrays by adding a second set of square brackets immediately following the first. For example, students[0][0] will have the value "Thomas" and students[2][1] will have the value 81.

Note that this can also be done using the array constructor, though the syntax is a bit longer:

```
var students = new Array( new Array("Thomas", 92, 90),
                          new Array("Roger", 87, 78)
                          new Array("Amber", 81, 85)
                          new Array("Jennifer", 99, 100) );
```

This does the same thing, but you do have to be careful not to add arrays with a single numeric item with the constructor syntax. Remember that trying to do so will create an array with that number of items rather than an array with that number as the lone item (for example, new Array(3) will create an array with three items, not an array with one item that has a value of 3).

Loops and Nested Arrays

To loop through all of the arrays within an outer array, you need to create a nested loop: an outer loop to cycle through the outer array items and one to cycle through the inner array items. For example, the code shown next creates a nested for loop that will iterate over the nested array structure and display the value of each item within the inner arrays:

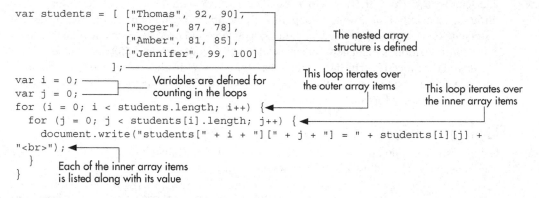

```
var students = [ ["Thomas", 92, 90],
                 ["Roger", 87, 78],
                 ["Amber", 81, 85],
                 ["Jennifer", 99, 100]
               ];
var i = 0;
var j = 0;
for (i = 0; i < students.length; i++) {
  for (j = 0; j < students[i].length; j++) {
    document.write("students[" + i + "][" + j + "] = " + students[i][j] +
"<br>");
  }
}
```

The nested array structure is defined

This loop iterates over the outer array items

This loop iterates over the inner array items

Variables are defined for counting in the loops

Each of the inner array items is listed along with its value

As you can see, the length property is used to determine how many times each loop will be executed. The outer loop gets executed four times (for students[0], students[1], students[2], and students[3]), and the inner loop gets executed three times in every iteration of the outer loop (a total of twelve iterations). Figure 7-5 shows the result of running this script in a browser.

With the information organized and loops at your disposal, you can now generate any number of reports based on the data in the arrays. For example, you could display each student's

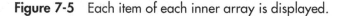

Figure 7-5 Each item of each inner array is displayed.

name along with the most recent grade earned (the last item in each of the inner arrays). The following code shows an example of this:

```javascript
var students = [ ["Thomas", 92, 90],
                 ["Roger", 87, 78],
                 ["Amber", 81, 85],
                 ["Jennifer", 99, 100]
               ];
var i = 0;
var j = 0;
for (i = 0; i < students.length; i++) {
  for (j = 0; j < students[i].length; j++) {
    if (j === 0) {
      document.write(students[i][j] + ": ");
    } else if (j === students[i].length -1) {
      document.write(students[i][j] + "<br>");
    } else {
      continue;
    }
  }
}
```

Checks to see if the item is at index 0, where the name of the student will be

Displays the student's name followed by a colon and a space

Displays the grade, followed by a line break

Checks to see if the item is at the last index in the array, where the most recent grade will be

Here, you are using the inner loop to gather the data you wish to display. The if statement is used to determine if the current index is one that contains needed data. The first thing needed is the student's name, which is at index 0 in each inner array. The other item needed, which is the most recent grade, will be the last item in the array. This is determined by checking whether the j variable is equal to the length of the array minus one (which will always be the last index in an array). At this point, you could simply use students[i][2] instead, but that would not account for the addition of new grades to the array. Using students[i].length–1 ensures that the most recent grade added to the array is used. You will also see that the final else statement simply tells the loop to continue to the next iteration, since you do not require any other data for this report. Figure 7-6 shows the result of running this in a browser.

As you can see, arrays are very helpful for storing and retrieving data, and you will find many uses for them as you continue coding.

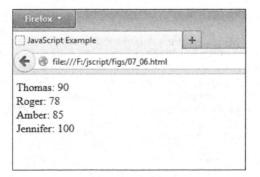

Figure 7-6   Each student and his/her most recent grade is displayed.

Nested Arrays Practice

```
pr7_2.html
prjs7_2.js
```

This project allows you to practice using nested arrays. Suppose, in your online store, you decide to display the features of each of your computer parts along with the part names. A nested array would help keep your information organized.

Step by Step

1. Create an HTML page with a heading with the text "Computer Parts Available". Add script tags to include an external JavaScript file named prjs7_2.js. Save the HTML file as pr7_2.html.

2. Create an external JavaScript file and save it as prjs7_2.js. Use it for steps 3–6.

3. Create a nested array named computer_parts with the inner arrays having these values:

   Inner array 0: Monitors, LCD Screens, Vibrant Colors
   Inner array 1: Motherboards, Fast
   Inner array 2: Chips, Pentium, Very Fast
   Inner array 3: Hard Drives, 100-500 GB, Fast Reading
   Inner array 4: DVD-ROMs, Burn CDs, Burn DVDs, Listen to both!
   Inner array 5: Cases, All Sizes, Choice of Colors
   Inner array 6: Power Supplies, We can get one for any computer!

4. Use nested loops to display each part and its features on one line. After the part name, display a colon and a space. Between part features, display a comma and a space. At the end of the last part feature, insert a line break.

5. When your JavaScript code is complete, you should have the following:

```javascript
var computer_parts = [ ["Monitors", "LCD Screens", "Vibrant Colors"],
                       ["Motherboards", "Fast"],
                       ["Chips", "Pentium", "Very Fast"],
                       ["Hard Drives", "100-500 GB", "Fast Reading"],
                     ["DVD-ROMs", "Burn CDs", "Burn DVDs", "Listen to both!"],
                       ["Cases", "All Sizes", "Choice of Colors"],
                       ["Power Supplies", "We can get one for any computer!"]
                     ];
var i = 0;
var j = 0;
for (i = 0; i < computer_parts.length; i++) {
  for (j = 0; j < computer_parts[i].length; j++) {
    if (j === 0) {
      document.write(computer_parts[i][j] + ": ");
    } else if (j === computer_parts[i].length -1) {
        document.write(computer_parts[i][j] + "<br>");
    } else {
        document.write(computer_parts[i][j] + ", ");
    }
  }
}
```

6. Save the JavaScript file and view the HTML file in your browser. You should see the list of parts and features.

Try This Summary

In this project, you used your knowledge of nested arrays and loops to create a page that displays the items within nested arrays.

Chapter 7 Self Test

1. An array is a way of storing a _____ of data.

2. In JavaScript, there are _____ ways to define an array.

3. In an array, access to an element is achieved through the use of a(n) _____.

4. You can use a _____ to cycle through all of the items in an array.

5. You can use JavaScript keywords as array names.

    A. True

    B. False

6. Which of the following does not correctly create an array?

    A. var myarray = new Array();

    B. var myarray = [3, 4, "Cool", 7];

    C. var myarray = new Array("hello","hi","greetings");

    D. var if = new Array[10];

7. To correctly access the fifth item of an array named "cool", you can write cool[5].

    A. True

    B. False

8. What does the following code do?

```
var s_list = new Array(5)
```

    A. Creates an empty array named s_list

    B. Creates an array named s_list with a single item that has a value of 5

    C. Creates an array with five items

    D. The code is invalid

9. What property of the Array object will return the numeric value of the length of an array?

   A. The length property

   B. The getlength property

   C. The constructor property

   D. The lengthOf property

10. Array _____ notation allows you to create an array using square brackets, without the need to write out "new Array".

11. The _____ method is used to combine the items of two or more arrays and return a new array containing all of the items.

12. The join() method is used to combine the items of an array into a single _____, with each item separated by a specified character.

13. The _____ method is used to remove the last element from an array.

14. By default, how does the sort() method sort the contents of an array?

   A. It reverses the contents of the array.

   B. It sorts the contents numerically.

   C. It sorts the contents using string character codes.

   D. It sorts it based on a random algorithm.

15. _____ arrays provide the ability to create arrays of more than one dimension.

Chapter 8

Objects

Key Skills & Concepts

- Defining Objects
- Creating Objects
- Using Prototypes
- Object Statements
- Understanding Predefined JavaScript Objects

Objects provide you with even more flexibility in your scripts. They can be used as another way to store data, or can be used to create reusable structures. In this chapter, you will learn what JavaScript objects are, how to create objects, and how to make use of some of the predefined objects.

Defining Objects

Since JavaScript is a prototype-based language, objects work differently than they do in class-based languages.

JavaScript objects are basically a collection of properties and values, what is called a *hash table* in programming. It is the values that give JavaScript a great deal of flexibility—a value can be any data type, including functions, arrays, and other objects.

You can use objects to pass multiple values around from one place to another (you will see that this can be quite handy when passing data between JavaScript and another language using JSON, discussed later in this book). You can also use them to describe a general type of object, which can have many specific *instances*. For example, you could have a general car object, which could be used to build specific car types (for example, sports car, work car, family car). Each car type could inherit property names from the general car object and then have its own specific property values.

Creating Objects

Now that you understand what objects are and their usefulness, you can begin creating your own JavaScript objects. To do this, you will learn about naming conventions, the structure of an object, and how to include methods in your objects.

Naming

As with variables and functions, there are certain rules you have to follow when naming your objects in JavaScript. They are the same rules you follow for naming variables and functions, which you can review in Chapter 3.

Single Objects

There are two ways to create single objects in JavaScript: by using the object constructor function or by using object literal notation. Single objects are good for specific purposes, such as creating name-value pairs or for creating unique objects that won't need to share code with other objects, where you might prefer to create a reusable structure instead.

The Object Constructor

The object constructor looks much like the array constructor. You simply give the object a name and define it as a new object. The following code shows an example of this:

```
var car = new Object();
```

This creates an empty object to which properties and values can be assigned, as in the following code:

```
var car = new Object();       The car object is defined
car.seats = "cloth";          The car object has a property named
                              seats assigned a value of "cloth"
```

Here, a property named "seats" is defined and assigned a value of "cloth". Notice the object name, followed by a dot, followed by the property name. In this way, you can define any number of properties. You can also assign a function to a property. This creates what is called a *method* (recall that you have already been using methods such as document.write() and window.alert() in your code). A method is a function that is part of an object and must be called using the name of the object. For example, the following code will create two properties ("seats" and "engine") and one method ("show_features"):

```
var car = new Object();
car.seats = "cloth";
car.engine = "V-6";
car.show_features = function() {                          A function is assigned, creating
   window.alert("car: " + car.seats + " seats, " + car.engine + " engine");   the car.show_features() method
};
car.show_features();          The method is called using the object
                              name, a dot, and the method name
```

As you can see, a function expression is used to define the car.show_features() method. The last line shows how the method is called using the object name, the dot, and the method name. Notice that the method accesses the value of each property by using the object name, a dot, and the property name. When the method is called, it sends an alert saying "car: cloth seats, V-6 engine".

You can also assign a named function as a method if desired, as in the following code:

```
var car = new Object();
car.seats = "cloth";
car.engine = "V-6";
function my_alert(){
    window.alert("car: " + car.seats + " seats, " + car.engine + " engine");
}
car.show_features = my_alert;
car.show_features();
```

If you use this method, be sure not to use parentheses in the assignment, as you want the function itself assigned as the method rather than its execution.

Object Literal Notation

Object literal notation uses curly brackets to enclose an object's properties and values. The syntax for this looks like this code:

```
var object_name = {
  property_name: value,
  property_name: value
};
```

You can have as many property-value pairs as needed; just be sure to separate each one with a comma. The last property-value pair does not have a comma afterward. Notice also that each property name is followed by a colon to separate it from its value.

Given the car object used in the previous section, you could rewrite it in object literal notation using the following code:

```
var car = {
  seats: "cloth",
  engine: "V-6",
  show_features: function() {
    window.alert("car: " + car.seats + " seats, " + car.engine + " engine");
  }
};
```

As you can see, this time all of the properties and values are separated by a colon (:), including the method function.

Object literal notation provides a straightforward way to create single objects and allows the properties and values to be contained within curly brackets ({}), which creates a good visual separation from other code in the script.

Accessing Property Values

JavaScript provides two ways to access the values of properties in objects: dot notation and bracket notation.

Dot Notation   As you have seen previously, you can use dot notation to access object property values. You use the object name, followed by a dot, followed by the property name, as in the following code:

```
var car = {
  seats: "cloth",
  engine: "V-6"
};
window.alert(car.seats);    ◄——————  The value of the seats property is alerted to the viewer
```

The value of the seats property is accessed by using the object name (car), followed by a dot (.), followed by the property name (seats). The viewer is shown an alert saying "cloth".

Bracket Notation   Bracket notation allows you to access property values by using square brackets ([]). This notation is similar to the notation used for arrays, but uses string values rather than numbers in the brackets. You use the object name, followed by the opening bracket ([), followed by the property name as a string, and end with the closing bracket (]).

The following code shows an example of bracket notation:

```
var car = {
  seats: "cloth",
  engine: "V-6"
};
window.alert(car["seats"]);
```

Here, the value of the seats property is accessed and alerted to the viewer.

Notice that this notation requires that the property name be inserted as a string value (using the quote marks in this case). Since the property name is inserted within the brackets as a string value, it can be put together via concatenation and/or using variables. For example, consider the following code:

```
var car = {
  seats: "cloth",
  engine: "V-6"
};
var s = "seats";
var start = "sea";
window.alert(car["seats"]);
window.alert(car["sea" + "ts"]);
window.alert(car[s]);
window.alert(car[start + "ts"]);
```

Variables are defined to hold all or part of the string "seats"

Uses the string "seats"

Concatenates "sea" and "ts" to insert the string "seats"

Uses the value of the variable s to insert the string "seats"

Uses the value of the variable start ("sea") concatenated with "ts" to insert the string "seats"

As you can see, each of these will produce the same result and get the value of the seats property from the car object. Four alerts saying "cloth" will be issued, since each combination evaluates to car["seats"].

This feature of bracket notation becomes quite useful when you need to use a property name, but it is stored in a variable (for example, when a value is sent as an argument to a function). Since dot notation only allows the use of the bare property name, it cannot use a variable value:

```
var car = {
  seats: "cloth",
  engine: "V-6"
};
var s = "seats";
function show_seat_type(sts) {
  window.alert(car.sts); // undefined
}
show_seat_type(s);
```

Here, rather than using the value of sts, a search for a property named sts within the car object ensues, which results in a value of undefined being returned when the property is not found. Using bracket notation, you can get this working:

```
var car = {
  seats: "cloth",
  engine: "V-6"
};
var s = "seats";
function show_seat_type(sts) {
  window.alert(car[sts]); // works
}
show_seat_type(s);
```

This time, the value of the variable sts is used, which is the string "seats", and "cloth" is alerted to the viewer.

Which Notation to Use?   The method to use depends on the situation. Dot notation is used most often, but when you need to put the property name together, use the value of a variable, or use a value that is not JavaScript-friendly such as seat-type, then bracket notation should be used in order to successfully access the property value.

Try This 8-1   Create a Computer Object

pr8_1.html
prjs8_1.js

In this project, you create objects on your own and develop the skills involved in object creation. The script will create a computer object and then use properties, methods, and instances of the object to create feature lists and price lists for the different types of computers.

Step by Step

1. Create an HTML page and save it as pr8_1.html. Add the necessary script tags to point to an external JavaScript file named prjs8_1.js.

2. Create an external JavaScript file and save it as prjs8_1.js. Use it for steps 3–5.

3. Create an object named computer that has three properties: speed with a value of "4GHZ", hd with a value of "500GB", and ram with a value of "8GB". Use object literal notation.

4. Display the value of each of the properties on the page in this format:

   Computer Speed: *speed value*
   Computer Hard Disk: *hd value*
   Computer RAM: *ram value*

When complete, your JavaScript file should look like this:

```
var computer = {
  speed: "4GHZ",
  hd: "500GB",
  ram: "8GB"
};
document.write("Computer Speed: " + computer.speed + "<br>");
document.write("Computer Hard Disk: " + computer.hd + "<br>");
document.write("Computer RAM: " + computer.ram);
```

5. Save the JavaScript file and view the HTML file in your browser. You should have a list of the properties of the computer object you created.

Try This Summary

In this project, you were able to use your new knowledge of objects to create an object with properties using object literal notation. You were able to create a Web page that displays the properties of the computer in the browser.

Object Structures

When you program objects in particular ways, you can build an object that acts as a structure, or model, for other objects. To get an understanding of how this works, you will look at constructor functions and learn how prototypes are used.

Constructor Functions

A constructor function can be used to create reusable code for objects. For instance, you could have a Car object created by a constructor function that would allow its code to be reused for any number of car types. You could have a work car, a family car, and a fun car that all have the same property and method names that are defined in the car constructor function while sending them different values.

For example, to create a car constructor, you would create a function named Car() and then add your properties and/or methods within the function. The following example shows an outline of a Car() constructor function:

```
function Car() {◄——— The constructor function is defined
   Properties/Methods go here. ◄——— The properties and methods will be listed
}                                     here for the object you are creating
```

Note that the function name begins with a capital letter (C). While this is not required, it is customary to begin the name of a constructor function with an uppercase letter to help distinguish it from other types of functions.

To complete the preceding function, you need to add your properties to the function. Suppose you want to create an object named car with the properties seats, engine, and radio. The following code shows how this is done:

```
function Car(seats, engine, radio) {          The function takes three arguments
    this.seats = seats;
    this.engine = engine;                     The parameter values are assigned
    this.radio = radio;                       to the properties of the object
}
```

In this code, on the first line, you see that the function takes three arguments. The next thing you see is that the values of the arguments are assigned as the property values; however, there is a new keyword named *this*. The keyword this in JavaScript is used to represent the current object being used, or "this object," so to speak. You will see how this works to create the structure for other objects. Note that a return statement is not needed as part of the constructor function.

Once you have the object's properties set with the constructor function, you need to create what is called an *instance* of the object in order to use it, because a constructor function creates only the structure of an object, not a usable instance of an object. To create an instance of an object, you use another JavaScript keyword: *new*. You have used this previously with the array constructor. Arrays are also objects in JavaScript, so using new Array() creates an instance of the JavaScript Array object.

The use of the new keyword to create an instance of your Car object is shown in the following code:

```
var work_car = new Car("cloth", "V-6", "Tape Deck");
```

The first thing you see is that you are creating a new variable named work_car. This variable will be assigned as a new instance of the Car object that uses the arguments provided as its property values. These are the values you want to use for this instance of the Car object. Given the order, you are saying that you want the seats to be cloth, the engine to be V-6, and the radio to be Tape Deck.

You can now access the work_car instance of the Car object. If you want to know what type of engine the work_car has, you can access it with dot notation like this:

```
var engine_type = work_car.engine;
```

This assigns the value of the engine property of the work_car instance of the Car object to the variable engine_type. Since you sent V-6 as the engine parameter to the constructor function, the engine_type variable is assigned a value of V-6.

Putting the Pieces Together

To help you visualize this process, it's time to put all these parts together so that you can see how it works. The following code combines all the code of the previous examples to make things easier to see:

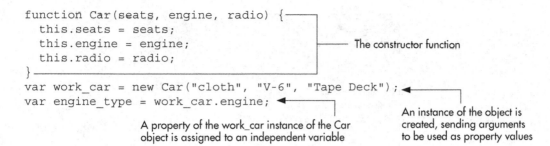

```
function Car(seats, engine, radio) {
    this.seats = seats;
    this.engine = engine;                      The constructor function
    this.radio = radio;
}
var work_car = new Car("cloth", "V-6", "Tape Deck");
var engine_type = work_car.engine;
```

An instance of the object is created, sending arguments to be used as property values

A property of the work_car instance of the Car object is assigned to an independent variable

Now you can see the constructor function, the creation of an instance of the Car object, and the assignment of one of the properties of the object to a variable. When the work_car instance of the Car object is set, it gets the values of cloth for the property work_car.seats, V-6 for the property work_car.engine, and Tape Deck for the property work_car.theradio.

In order to see how an instance of an object works, you will add another instance of the Car object to your code. The following code uses two instances of the Car object, one named work_car and a new one named fun_car:

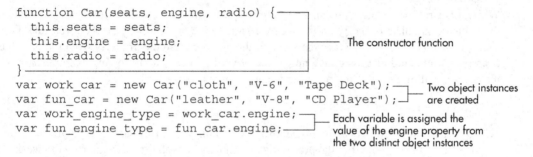

```
function Car(seats, engine, radio) {
    this.seats = seats;
    this.engine = engine;                      The constructor function
    this.radio = radio;
}
var work_car = new Car("cloth", "V-6", "Tape Deck");       Two object instances
var fun_car = new Car("leather", "V-8", "CD Player");      are created
var work_engine_type = work_car.engine;      Each variable is assigned the
var fun_engine_type = fun_car.engine;        value of the engine property from
                                             the two distinct object instances
```

Notice how the new instance of the object uses the same constructor function, but with different values. You could now access any of the features from either type of car. For example, take a look at the following code:

```
function Car(seats, engine, radio) {
    this.seats = seats;
    this.engine = engine;                      The constructor function
    this.radio = radio;
}                                                          New instances of the
                                                           Car object are created
var work_car = new Car("cloth", "V-6", "Tape Deck");
var fun_car = new Car("leather", "V-8", "CD Player");
document.write("I want a car with " + fun_car.seats + " seats.<br>");
document.write("It also needs a " + work_car.engine + " engine.<br>");
document.write("Oh, and I would like a " + fun_car.radio + " also.");
```

Some of the property values from the two instances of Car are displayed in document.write() statements

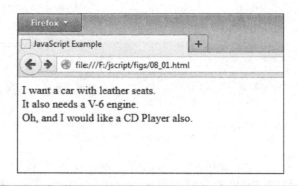

Figure 8-1 The features you like from each type of car are displayed in the browser.

The results of this script are shown in Figure 8-1.

Property Values

While this isn't real estate, you can alter your property values. In your scripts, you can change the value of an object property on-the-fly by assigning it a new value, just like a variable. For example, if you wanted to change the value of the work_car.engine property from the previous examples, you could just assign it a new value of your choice. The following example shows the assignment of a new value to the work_car.engine property:

```
work_car.engine= "V-4";
```

While perhaps not a good change, it could save you money on insurance (and gas)!

It is important to note that the preceding assignment will change the value of the work_car.engine property for any calls made to it after the change. Anything you do with its value before the change would not be affected.

For example, the following code gives a new assignment to the work_car.engine property:

```
function Car(seats, engine, radio) {
  this.seats = seats;
  this.engine = engine;
  this.radio = radio;
}
var work_car = new Car("cloth", "V-6", "Tape Deck");
var fun_car = new Car("leather", "V-8", "CD Player");
var original_work_car_engine = work_car.engine;
work_car.engine = "V-4";
var new_work_car_engine = work_car.engine;
document.write("I wanted a " + original_work_car_engine + " initially.<br>");
document.write("I got a " + new_work_car_engine + " instead to lower gas
costs.");
```

The original value of work_car .engine is assigned to a variable

The value of work_car .engine is changed

The new value of work_car .engine is assigned to a variable

The original value and the new value are displayed in document.write() statements

The work_car.engine property was originally set to "V-6", but it is changed to "V-4". When it is assigned to the original_work_car_engine variable, it was still "V-6" and that variable retains that value. After it is changed, the new value is assigned to the new_work_car_engine, which uses the new value of "V-4". Figure 8-2 shows the result of running this script in a browser.

Adding Methods

To add a method to a constructor function, you can assign a function expression to a property name, as in the following code:

```
function Car(seats, engine, radio) {
  this.seats = seats;
  this.engine = engine;
  this.radio = radio;
  this.describe = function() {
    document.write("This amazing car has these features: ");
    document.write(this.seats + " seats, " + this.engine + " engine, ");
    document.write(this.radio);
  };
}
var work_car = new Car("cloth", "V-6", "Tape Deck");
work_car.describe();
```

A method named describe() is added to the Car constructor

The method is called for the work_car instance of the Car object using work_car.describe()

As you can see, you can call the method once you have an instance of the object using the instance name, dot, and method name. When the method is called for the work_car instance, the string "This amazing car has these features: cloth seats, V-6 engine, Tape Deck" is displayed on the page.

While adding a method to the constructor is straightforward, there is a drawback to including methods within the constructor function. For each new instance of the object, a new method function that does the same thing is created. Effectively, the method is reproduced numerous times, even though it is not seen in the code directly.

As you have seen, a method within the constructor is simply another property. Since each property is unique to each instance, method functions are also unique to each instance. If you have 50 instances of the Car object, then 50 functions will be created, using up resources.

Firefox ▾

JavaScript Example   +

←   file:///F:/jscript/figs/08_02.html

I wanted a V-6 initially.
I got a V-4 instead to lower gas costs.

Figure 8-2   The change in the property value affects the statements that use it after the change, but not those that use it before the change.

To make it a single function that is simply reused, you could move the method function outside of the constructor function, as in the following code:

```
function Car(seats, engine, radio) {
    this.seats = seats;
    this.engine = engine;          The function describe_car is assigned
    this.radio = radio;            to the describe property
    this.describe = describe_car;◄─────────┐   The describe_car function is
}                                               defined outside the constructor
function describe_car() {─────────────────────────────────────────────────┐
    document.write("This amazing car has these features: ");
    document.write(this.seats + " seats, " + this.engine + " engine, ");
    document.write(this.radio);
}─────────────────────────────────────────────────────────────────────────┘
var work_car = new Car("cloth", "V-6", "Tape Deck");─┐   The remaining code
work_car.describe();─────────────────────────────────┘   works as it did before
```

Here, a function named describe_car is defined outside of the constructor, allowing it to be assigned to the describe property inside the constructor to make it a method function. Notice that when it is assigned, no parentheses () are used. This is so that the function itself, rather than the result of the function, is assigned to the describe property. When the instance is created and the method is run, you get the same result you did before, so the move was successful.

However, there is a downside to this technique as well: method functions are now global, which can clutter the global scope with a lot of functions that should really be within the local scope of the Car structure. To fix this issue, you will need to learn about prototypes.

Using Prototypes

Every function in JavaScript has what is known as a *prototype* property, which is an object that contains the properties and methods that are always available for each instance of an object created using that function. This allows code to easily be reused across instances for shared properties and methods.

Working with Prototypes

To see how prototypes work, you will make use of the prototype property with your Car object. Consider the following code:

```
function Car(seats, engine, radio) {─┐
    this.seats = seats;
    this.engine = engine;            ├─ The Car constructor function
    this.radio = radio;
}────────────────────────────────────┘
Car.prototype.locks = "automatic";◄──────── Adds a property to the
                                            prototype of the Car function
```

Notice how the function Car has a prototype property (Car.prototype). Since the prototype is an object itself, you can add a property to the prototype as you could with any other object. Here, a property named locks is added to the Car prototype using Car.prototype.lock and assigning it a value.

So, what exactly does this do? If you add instances of the Car object, you will find that each instance can access the windows property:

```
function Car(seats, engine, radio) {
  this.seats = seats;
  this.engine = engine;
  this.radio = radio;
}
Car.prototype.locks = "automatic";
var work_car = new Car("cloth", "V-6", "Tape Deck");
var family_car = new Car("cloth", "V-4", "CD Changer");
window.alert(work_car.locks);
window.alert(family_car.locks);
```

Both alerts will display the value "automatic", which is not in the Car constructor, but is found in Car's prototype.

How does this happen? In JavaScript, calling a property or method of an object will first check the object that tried to use it. If it does not find the property or method, it does not simply give up at this point. Instead, JavaScript will search the object's prototype to see if there is a match. If so, then the property or method is available to the object that is trying to use it. For example, Figure 8-3 shows how the search for the locks property for the work_car instance is performed.

As you can see, it simply checks the work_car instance for the locks property. When it is not there, the prototype is searched, where the locks property is found and then is available to the work_car instance. Notice that the prototype has a property named constructor that points back to the constructor function.

The constructor function and any instances created by that constructor will point to the prototype. In this case, Car, work_car, and family_car all point to the Car prototype, and can make use of any properties or methods within the Car prototype.

When creating an instance, you can actually add a property to the instance that is the same as the name of a property in the prototype. This will effectively hide the value of the property

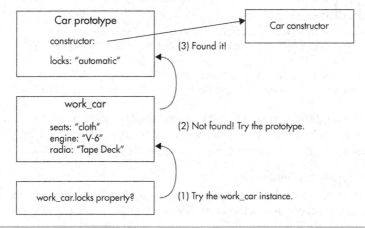

Figure 8-3   Looking for the locks property

by the same name in the prototype for that instance of the object, since the property will always be found in the object and the prototype will not be searched. For example, take a look at the following code:

```
function Car(seats, engine, radio) {
  this.seats = seats;
  this.engine = engine;
  this.radio = radio;
}
Car.prototype.locks = "automatic";
var work_car = new Car("cloth", "V-6", "Tape Deck");
var family_car = new Car("cloth", "V-4", "CD Changer");
work_car.locks = "manual";
window.alert(work_car.locks);
window.alert(family_car.locks);
```

Adds a locks property to the work_car instance

Alerts "manual"

Alerts "automatic"

Here, assigning a value to work_car.locks ensures that the locks property is found in the work_car instance and the prototype will not be searched. Thus, work_car.locks will have a value of manual. Since this does not affect other instances, family_car.locks still must search the prototype to find a value, and thus it still has a value of "automatic".

The hasOwnProperty() Method

There are times when you will want to know whether the property being used was found in the object instance rather than the prototype. The hasOwnProperty() method of an object will return true if the property is found in the instance, and return false otherwise. In the previous example, the work_car instance had a locks property, while the family_car instance did not (it only had a locks property in the prototype). Consider the following code:

```
function Car(seats, engine, radio) {
  this.seats = seats;
  this.engine = engine;
  this.radio = radio;
}
Car.prototype.locks = "automatic";
var work_car = new Car("cloth", "V-6", "Tape Deck");
var family_car = new Car("cloth", "V-4", "CD Changer");
work_car.locks = "manual";
window.alert(work_car.hasOwnProperty("locks")); // true
window.alert(family_car.hasOwnProperty("locks")); // false
```

Here, the first alert displays true, while the second displays false. You will see later in this chapter that this can be useful when you are using a for-in loop when you only want to use properties that are in the instance of the object, rather than its prototype.

Using Prototypes for Methods

Since the prototype is outside of an object's constructor function and not in the global scope, it provides a good location for method functions that will be shared among each instance of an object. You can now give each instance of an object its properties (if they will have unique values) in the constructor function and place its methods in the prototype for reuse in all instances. For the reasons mentioned, this is a common pattern for custom object creation, typically called the combination constructor/prototype pattern.

As an example, the following code will continue to add the properties to the Car constructor, but will add a method to the Car prototype:

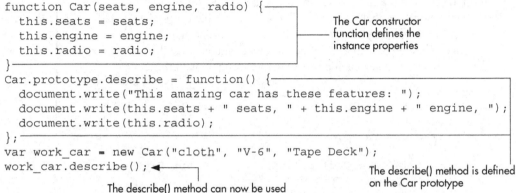

```
function Car(seats, engine, radio) {
   this.seats = seats;
   this.engine = engine;
   this.radio = radio;
}
Car.prototype.describe = function() {
   document.write("This amazing car has these features: ");
   document.write(this.seats + " seats, " + this.engine + " engine, ");
   document.write(this.radio);
};
var work_car = new Car("cloth", "V-6", "Tape Deck");
work_car.describe();
```

The Car constructor function defines the instance properties

The describe() method is defined on the Car prototype

The describe() method can now be used with any instance of the Car object

With the combination constructor/prototype pattern in place, the code now will allow for instance properties and methods as well as shared properties and methods. As you continue through this book, you will see more on prototypes and how they can be used for inheritance for object-oriented programming.

Helpful Statements for Objects

JavaScript allows you to use the for-in loop to help you iterate through object properties and the with statement to access particular objects more easily.

The for-in Loop

The for-in loop allows you to cycle through the properties of an object. The following code shows the structure of a for-in loop:

```
for (var variable_name in object_name) {
JavaScript statements
}
```

The loop begins by naming a variable to represent the property names in the object, along with the name of the object

JavaScript statements go here

Suppose you wanted to cycle through the properties of a work_car instance of a Car object in order to display the values of each property on the page. The for-in loop allows you to do this without the need to type each property name, as in this code:

```
function Car(seats, engine, radio) {
   this.seats = seats;
   this.engine = engine;
   this.radio = radio;
}
```

The Car constructor

```
var work_car = new Car("cloth", "V-6", "Tape Deck");
for (var prop_name in work_car) {
  document.write(prop_name + ": " + work_car[prop_name] + "<br>");
}
```

An instance of the object is created

The for-in loop begins

The value of each property of the work_car instance of the car object is written on the page

This will display each property name and its value (note the use of bracket notation so that the prop_name variable can be used to access the property value).

Note, however, that this loop will grab *all* available properties, including those found in the object's prototype. If you want to be sure that the properties that you are using belong to the instance of the object rather than the prototype, you can use the hasOwnProperty() method you learned earlier to check each property before using it, as in this code:

```
function Car(seats, engine, radio) {
  this.seats = seats;
  this.engine = engine;
  this.radio = radio;
}
var work_car = new Car("cloth", "V-6", "Tape Deck");
for (var prop_name in work_car) {
  if (work_car.hasOwnProperty(prop_name)) {
    document.write(prop_name + ": " + work_car[prop_name] + "<br>");
  }
}
```

Here, the code will ensure that you are getting the property from the object instance rather than the prototype before displaying it on the page.

The with Statement

The with statement allows you to access the properties and methods of an object more easily if you plan to use a large number of statements that use the object. For instance, if you want to write a number of statements using an object named work_car on a Web page, you might grow weary of typing the object name (work_car), the dot operator, and then the property name.

CAUTION

The use of with is often discouraged because of performance drawbacks and because a global variable could accidentally be assigned or overwritten when using this statement. It is also not supported when the "use strict" option is enabled.

The with statement allows you to leave off the object name and the dot operator for statements inside the with block, so that you only need to type the property names to access the properties you need. The following code shows the structure of a with statement:

```
with (object) {
  JavaScript statements
}
```

The name of the object is placed inside the parentheses

JavaScript statements that use the object go here

Chapter 8: Objects **199**

Suppose you have a constructor named Car with the properties seats, engine, and radio, and an instance of the object named work_car. You could use the with statement to avoid typing work_car and the dot operator repeatedly, as in the following example:

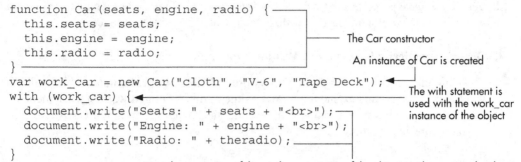

```
function Car(seats, engine, radio) {
    this.seats = seats;
    this.engine = engine;
    this.radio = radio;
}
var work_car = new Car("cloth", "V-6", "Tape Deck");
with (work_car) {
    document.write("Seats: " + seats + "<br>");
    document.write("Engine: " + engine + "<br>");
    document.write("Radio: " + theradio);
}
```

The Car constructor

An instance of Car is created

The with statement is used with the work_car instance of the object

Now the properties of the work_car instance of the object can be accessed without the need to type work_car and the dot operator each time a property is used

This example displays the values of the properties of the work_car instance of the car object on the page. Notice that while inside the with block, the property names could be used without the need to type work_car and the dot operator in front of them.

Now that you have seen how to create objects, properties, and methods of your own, you can better understand how some of the predefined JavaScript objects work. A number of predefined JavaScript objects are discussed as you move through the rest of this chapter and through several other chapters in this book.

Ask the Expert

Q: Do I really have to create an instance of an object every time I want one when I use a constructor function?

A: Yes. The constructor function only gives the browser the structure of an object. To use that structure, you need to create an instance of the object. You need to create instances with some of the predefined JavaScript objects as well.

Q: So what about single objects? I don't have to create instances with them?

A: Single objects don't need to have instances created. Each one is unique and does not reuse code among instances.

(continued)

Q: **Can I use the combination constructor/prototype pattern to share properties as well as methods?**

A: Yes, if you have properties that you do not want unique values for in each instance, you can add them to the prototype instead to share them with other object instances.

Q: **Doesn't JavaScript have classes? Wouldn't that make things easier?**

A: There are plans to implement the class keyword in ECMAScript Harmony, which will allow you to build classes and extend them. At the time of this writing, it was not implemented yet, but it is on the way. You can read more about the changes coming in ECMAScript Harmony in Chapter 16.

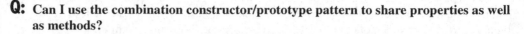

Try This 8-2   Practice with the Combination Constructor/ Prototype Pattern

`pr8_2.html`
`prjs8_2.js`

Suppose you decided to sell certain types of computers: work computers, home computers, and gaming computers. For each computer, there will be different properties and a method to display the properties of each computer.

Step by Step

1. Create an HTML page and save it as pr8_2.html.

2. Create an external JavaScript file and save it as prjs8_2.js. Use it for steps 3–8.

3. Create a Computer constructor and give it the properties type, processor, ram, and hd.

4. Create an instance of Computer named work_computer. The value of type will be "Work", the value of processor will be "2GHZ", the value of ram will be "8GB", and the value of hd will be "1TB".

5. Create an instance of Computer named home_computer. The value of type will be "Home", the value of processor will be "2GHZ", the value of ram will be "4GB", and the value of hd will be "500GB".

6. Create an instance of Computer named gaming_computer. The value of type will be "Gaming", the value of processor will be "4GHZ", the value of ram will be "16GB", and the value of hd will be "2TB".

7. Create a method named describe on the Computer prototype. Use it to display each of the property values on the page.

8. When you are done, your JavaScript file should look like this:

```
function Computer(type, processor, ram, hd) {
  this.type = type;
  this.processor = processor;
  this.ram = ram;
  this.hd = hd;
}
Computer.prototype.describe = function() {
  document.write("<p>" + this.type + ":<br>");
  document.write("Processor: " + this.processor + "<br>");
  document.write("RAM: " + this.ram + "<br>");
  document.write("Hard Disk: " + this.hd + "</p>");
};
var work_computer = new Computer("Work", "2GHZ", "8GB", "1TB");
var home_computer = new Computer("Home", "2GHZ", "4GB", "500GB");
var gaming_computer = new Computer("Gaming", "4GHZ", "16GB", "2TB");
work_computer.describe();
home_computer.describe();
gaming_computer.describe();
```

9. Save the files and open the HTML file in a browser. The properties of each instance should be displayed.

Try This Summary

In this project, you used your knowledge of constructors and prototypes to create a reusable object that has a method on its prototype to display the property values in any instance of the object.

Understanding Predefined JavaScript Objects

In JavaScript, there are many predefined objects you can use to gain access to certain properties or methods you may need. You can make your scripts even more interactive once you learn the various objects and what you can do with them.

This book will be covering a number of the major predefined objects. In this chapter, you are going to look at the navigator and history objects, and what you can do with them.

The Navigator Object

The navigator object gives you access to various properties of the viewer's browser, such as its name, version number, and more. It got its name from the Netscape Navigator browser, which preceded Mozilla Firefox.

The navigator object is part of the window object, which means you can access its properties using window.navigator.*property*, but it can also be shortened to simply navigator.*property*. This is true even for direct properties or methods of the window object as well (for example, window.alert("Hi"); could be shortened to simply alert("Hi"); and it would still be valid). You'll commonly see such properties and methods of the window object shortened in this way to save extra typing or to help shorten the source code. You will see more about the reasons for this in Chapter 11.

First, take a look at the properties of the navigator object.

Properties

The properties of the navigator object cannot be changed, because they are set as read-only. Table 8-1 shows the properties of the navigator object and the values returned by each property. When browser names are shown in parentheses afterward, it means that the property was only known to work with the specified browsers at the time of this writing.

The following sections take a look at some of the more useful properties in more detail.

Property	Value
appCodeName	The code name of the browser
appName	The full name of the browser
appMinorVersion	A string representing the minor version of the browser (Internet Explorer and Opera)
appVersion	The version of the browser and some other information
browserLanguage	The language of the operating system being used (Internet Explorer and Opera)
buildID	The build identifier of the browser being used (Firefox)
cookieEnabled	Specifies whether or not the browser has cookies enabled
cpuClass	The CPU on the user's computer (Internet Explorer)
language	The language of the browser being used (Firefox, Chrome, and Opera)
mimeTypes	An array of MIME types supported by the browser
onLine	Specifies whether or not the browser is in "global offline mode" (Internet Explorer, Firefox, and Opera)
oscpu	The operating system and/or CPU on the user's computer (Firefox)
platform	The machine type for which the browser was created
plugins	An array of the plugins the browser has installed on it
product	The browser's product name (Firefox and Chrome)
productSub	The build number of the product (Firefox and Chrome)
securityPolicy	An empty string—previously returned a value in Netscape 4.7 (Firefox)
systemLanguage	The default language used by the operating system (Internet Explorer)
userLanguage	The natural language of the operating system (Internet Explorer and Opera)
userAgent	The user agent header for the browser
userProfile	Accesses information in the user profile (Internet Explorer)
vendor	The vendor of the browser (Firefox and Chrome)
vendorSub	The vendor version number of the browser (Firefox and Chrome)

Table 8-1 Properties of the Navigator Object

The appName Property This property allows you to determine the name of the browser the viewer is using. If you want to know the value for a particular browser, you can use the following code and open the page in your selected browser:

```
window.alert("You have " + navigator.appName);
```

This property was often used in the past to create a simple browser-detection script, such as the one shown in this code:

```
<script>
if (navigator.appName == "Microsoft Internet Explorer") {
  // Code for IE browsers
}
else {
  document.write("Please get Internet Explorer to run this script");
}
</script>
<noscript>You do not have JavaScript. Get Internet Explorer!</noscript>
```

While this was usable for a time, there are better methods for working with the various browsers you may encounter, such as feature detection and progressive enhancement, which you will learn more about as you proceed through this book.

The cookieEnabled Property This property returns a Boolean value of true if cookies are enabled in the browser, and returns a Boolean value of false if cookies are not enabled in the browser. You can use it to avoid running code to set a cookie if the user does not have cookies enabled:

```
if (navigator.cookieEnabled) {
  // Set cookie
}
```

This allows you to set a cookie for viewers that can make use of it, or to continue with further code if not. You will read about cookies in more detail later in this book.

The plugins Property This array holds the values of all the plugins installed in the viewer's browser. This can be used to detect whether the viewer has a particular plugin available before running code that will use it.

Methods

The navigator object also has a number of methods you can use to perform various tasks. Table 8-2 shows the methods available in the navigator object.

The following section looks at the javaEnabled() method and how it can be used.

The javaEnabled() Method This method returns a Boolean value of true if the viewer has Java enabled in the browser; otherwise, it returns false. The javaEnabled() method could

Method	Purpose
javaEnabled()	Used to test whether or not Java is enabled in the browser
preference()	Allows certain browser preferences to be set. Only allowed in privileged mode (Firefox)
registerContentHandler()	Allows a Web site to set itself as a potential handler of a certain MIME type
registerProtocolHandler()	Allows a Web site to set itself as a potential handler of a certain protocol
taintEnabled()	Returns false—because the method is no longer in use. It was used to specify whether or not data tainting was enabled in the browser

Table 8-2   Methods of the Navigator Object

be useful if you want to display a Java applet to the viewer, but only if the viewer has Java enabled in the browser. The following code would allow you to do this:

```
if (navigator.javaEnabled()) {
  // Insert Java Applet
}
else {
  document.write("No Java? You cannot see my Java Applet!");
}
```

This tests the value returned by the navigator.javaEnabled() method and either displays the Java applet or a message informing the user that Java is not enabled.

The History Object

The history object, which is also part of the window object, provides information on the browser history of the current window.

Property

The history object has only one property, named length (in Firefox, a few more are available, but they do not work with Web content). This property returns the number of pages in the session history of the browser for the current window, which includes the currently loaded page. It could be used in a manner similar to this:

```
alert("Your current window has viewed " + history.length + " pages!")
```

This simply sends an alert to the viewer to say how many pages have been visited in the current browser window.

Method	Purpose
back()	Sends the browser window back one page in the history list
forward()	Sends the browser one page forward in the history list
go()	Sends the browser to a specified page in the history list using an integer value

Table 8-3   Methods of the History Object

Methods

There are three methods of the history object, listed in Table 8-3.

The following sections discuss each of these methods in more detail.

The back() Method   The back() method sends the browser to the last page visited in the history list before the current page, which is like using the browser's "back" button. To use it, you simply call the method in your script where desired:

```
history.back();
```

The forward() Method   The forward() method sends the browser to the page visited in the history list after the current page, which is like using the browser's "forward" button. To use it, you simply call the method in your script where desired:

```
history.forward();
```

The go() Method   The go() method takes an integer as a parameter. The integer can be a negative number to go back in the history list or a positive number to move forward in the history list. For instance, the following code would go back two pages in the window's history:

```
history.go(-2);
```

The following code would go three pages forward in the history list:

```
history.go(3);
```

As with the other two methods, if the page the viewer is attempting to access does not exist (for example, something like history.go(15) may not exist in the window's history), then the method will simply do nothing.

The predefined JavaScript objects can be quite helpful. As you'll see in the next chapter, the document object gives you access to a number of additional properties and methods for working with an HTML document.

✓ *Chapter 8 Self Test*

1. An object is a collection of _____ and _____.

2. When creating single objects, you can use the object _____ or object literal notation.

3. When using object literal notation, the properties and values are enclosed within curly brackets ({ }).

   A. True

   B. False

4. In JavaScript, you typically access object properties through the use of the

   A. addition operator (+)

   B. dot operator (.)

   C. multiplication operator (*)

   D. You can't access the properties of an object

5. When you need to use a variable to access a property name, you can use _____ notation.

6. A _____ function can be used to create an object structure.

7. A(n) _____ of an object can be created using the new keyword.

8. You can only have one instance of an object.

   A. True

   B. False

9. What could you say about the following code:

   ```
   var x = myhouse.kitchen;
   ```

   A. It assigns the string myhouse.kitchen to the variable *x*.

   B. It adds the values of myhouse and kitchen and assigns them to an object named *x*.

   C. Assuming the myhouse object exists, it assigns the value of the kitchen property of the myhouse object to the variable *x*.

   D. Assuming the kitchen object exists, it assigns the value of the myhouse property of the kitchen object to the variable *x*.

10. If a property cannot be found in the object instance, JavaScript will look in the object's _____.

11. Which of the following would send an alert to the viewer that tells the name of the browser being used?

    A. window.alert("You are using " + navigator.appVersion);

    B. window.alert("You are using " + navigator.appName);

    C. window.alert("You are using " + navigator.javaEnabled());

    D. window.alert("You are using navigator.appName");

12. What could you say about the following code?

    ```
    myhouse.kitchen = "big";
    ```

    A. Assuming the kitchen object exists, the myhouse property is assigned a new string value.

    B. Assuming the myhouse object exists, the value of the variable kitchen is added to the string big.

    C. Assuming the myhouse object exists, the kitchen property is assigned a new string value of "big" or is initialized with the value "big".

    D. This wouldn't do anything.

13. In JavaScript, there are many _____ objects you can use to gain access to certain properties and methods you may need.

14. The _____ object gives you access to the various properties of the viewer's browser.

15. Which of the following is not a property of the navigator object?

    A. appName

    B. appCodeName

    C. appType

    D. appVersion

Chapter 9

The Document Object

Key Skills & Concepts

- Defining the Document Object
- Using the Document Object Model
- Using the Properties of the Document Object
- Using the Methods of the Document Object
- Using DOM Nodes
- Creating Dynamic Scripts

Now that you know how objects work and how to use predefined JavaScript objects, it is time to look at some of the major predefined objects in JavaScript.

This chapter covers the document object, which helps you to gather information about the page that is being viewed in the browser. As you will find out in this chapter, some of the document object's properties and methods can be used to get information about the document or to change information about the document. You will also be introduced to the Document Object Model, and see how this can be used with style sheets to create dynamic scripts.

Defining the Document Object

The document object is an object that is created by the browser for each new HTML page (document) that is viewed. By doing this, JavaScript gives you access to a number of properties and methods that can affect the document in various ways.

You have been using the write() method of the document object for quite some time in this book. This method allows you to write a string of text into an HTML document.

To begin your journey through the document object, you will take a look at the Document Object Model (DOM) and the various properties you can access with this object. Many of these properties will turn out to be quite useful when writing scripts.

Using the Document Object Model

The Document Object Model (DOM) allows JavaScript (and other scripting languages) to access the structure of the document in the browser. Each document is made up of structured nodes (for example, the body tag would be a node, and any elements within the body element would be child nodes of the body element). With this structure in place, a scripting language can access the elements within the document in a number of ways, allowing for the modification of the elements within the document.

If you had the following HTML code, you could use JavaScript to access its structure:

```
<body>
<h1>My Page</h1>
<img src="myimage.jpg" alt="My Picture">
</body>
```

Figure 9-1 shows how the body element is a node, and how it can have child nodes and attribute nodes.

The h1 and img elements are both child nodes of the body element. Each element also has its own nodes. The h1 element contains a text node as its child node (the text "My Page"), while the img element contains two attribute nodes (src="myimage.jpg" and alt="My Picture"). This type of structure is available throughout the document, so while this is a simple example, much more complex document structure trees could be drawn for most HTML pages.

You can write scripts to add, remove, or change nodes in the DOM. You can use the document.getElementById() method to access elements by their id attribute values, and even get groups of elements using methods like document.getElementsByTagName() or document .getElementsByClassName().

First, you will look at the properties and methods of the document object.

Using the Properties of the Document Object

Table 9-1 lists the properties of the document object with a short description of each. Following the table, some specific properties are discussed in more detail.

NOTE

Not all of these properties work cross-browser. You can see more information on each of these properties by visiting http://developer.mozilla.org/en/ DOM/document#Properties and http://msdn.microsoft.com/en-us/library/ ms531073(VS.85).aspx.

Collections

A number of the properties (anchors, embeds, forms, images, links, plugins, scripts, styleSheets, and styleSheetSets) return an array that holds a collection of elements or values found in the document. These can be accessed like any array using indexes. The element or value at index zero will be the first, index one the second, and so on.

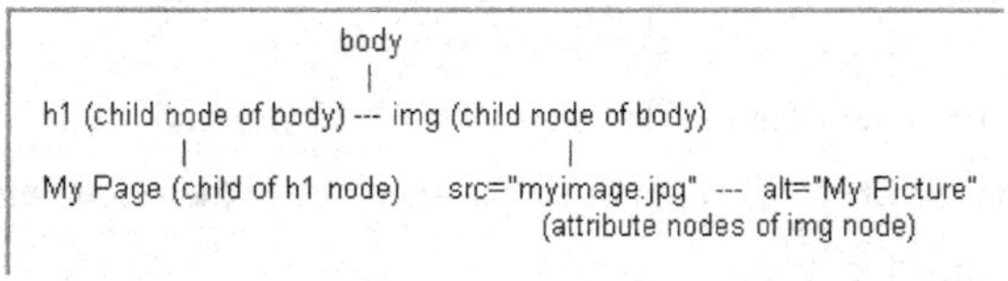

```
                                    body
                                     |
    h1 (child node of body) --- img (child node of body)
             |                          |
    My Page (child of h1 node)    src="myimage.jpg" --- alt="My Picture"
                                       (attribute nodes of img node)
```

Figure 9-1 An example of part of a document's structure

Property	Description
activeElement	Returns the active (focused) element
anchors	Returns an array of all the named anchors in the document
async	Tells the browser whether to load a document with an asynchronous request or a synchronous request
baseURIObject	Returns an object representing the document's URI. Only available in privileged mode.
body	Returns the body or frameset element of the document
characterSet	Returns the character set used in the document
charset	Returns or sets the character set used in the document
compatMode	Returns the string "BackCompat" if the document is rendered in Quirks mode or the string "CSS1Compat" if the document is rendered in Strict mode
contentType	Returns the Content-Type value from the document's MIME header
cookie	Returns or sets a JavaScript cookie in a document
currentScript	Returns the script element that is currently being read
defaultCharset	Returns default character set found in the regional language settings
defaultView	Returns the window object for the document
designMode	Allows a document to be edited
dir	Returns or sets the reading direction of the document
doctype	Returns the doctype declaration associated with the document
documentElement	Returns a string representing the root node of the document
documentMode	Returns the compatibility mode of the document
documentURI	Returns the location of the document
documentURIObject	Returns an object representing the URI of the document (only available to privileged JavaScript code)
domain	Returns the domain name of the server for the document
embeds	An array of all the embed elements in the document
expando	Returns a Boolean value based on whether or not arbitrary variables can be created within the document
fileSize	Returns the size of the document in bytes
fileCreatedDate	Returns the date the document was created
fileModifiedDate	Returns the date the document was last modified
forms	Returns an array of all the form elements in the document
head	Returns the head element of the document

Table 9-1 The Properties of the Document Object

Property	Description
images	An array of all the image (img) elements in the document
implementation	Returns the implementation object of the document
inputEncoding	Returns a string representing the document's encoding
lastModified	Returns the date of the last modification of the document
lastStyleSheetSet	Returns the name of the most recent style sheet set using the selectedStyleSheetSet property.
links	Returns an array of all the hyperlink (<a>) elements in the document
location	Returns the URI of the document
namespaceURI	Returns the XML namespace of the document
parentWindow	Returns a reference to the parent window (the parent window's document object)
plugins	Returns an array of all the plugins used in the document
popupNode	Returns the element where a popup was called in an XUL document
preferredStyleSheet	Returns the preferred style sheet based on the order of style sheet declarations in the document
protocol	Returns the protocol portion of the Web address (URL) of the document
readyState	Returns the loading state of the document
referrer	Returns the URL of the document that referred the viewer to the current document
rootElement	Returns the root SVG element of the document
scripts	Returns an array of all the script elements used in the document
selectedStyleSheetSet	Returns or sets the current style sheet set
styleSheets	Returns an array of all the style sheets used in the document
styleSheetSets	Returns an array of all the style sheet sets in the document
textContent	Returns or sets the text content
title	Returns the text used inside the title tags of the document
tooltipNode	Returns the element that is the target of the tooltip currently in use
uniqueID	Returns a unique ID that is generated for the document
URL	Returns the URL of the current document
URLUnencoded	Returns the URL of the document without any encoding
xmlEncoding	Returns the character encoding found in the declaration of an XML document
xmlStandalone	Returns or sets the standalone value found in the declaration of an XML document
xmlVersion	Returns or sets the version attribute found in the declaration of an XML document
XSLDocument	Returns the root element of an XSL document

Table 9-1   The Properties of the Document Object (*continued*)

For example, the links property can be used to access all of the links in the document. If you need to find the first link in the document, you could use document.links[0] to access that element as an object. You can then use DOM node properties or methods (discussed later in this chapter) to get or set information, or to perform certain tasks on the element.

The cookie Property

The cookie property is used to set a JavaScript cookie to store information for the viewer. A cookie is a small text file saved to the viewer's computer for a particular amount of time (a set date or a browser session). Cookies can be helpful in allowing a site to remember and retrieve information for a viewer (such as the contents of a shopping cart, special settings, or session information).

To set a cookie, you set the value of the document.cookie property to a string that contains the information you want to store for the viewer. The following is the syntax:

```
document.cookie=string;
```

You would replace *string* with a text string that contains the information you want to use. Usually, this is in a format like the one shown in the following example of setting a cookie:

```
document.cookie = "site=homepage";
```

You can see that there is one thing set by the cookie: the site is homepage. In between the two the equal sign is used to help separate the site and homepage when the cookie is read. Note that setting the cookie does not replace the whole cookie; it just adds the new string to it.

You will see how to use advanced string-handling techniques and how to set and read cookies in more detail in later chapters.

The dir Property

The dir property returns a string value that represents the reading direction of the document. This value can be either ltr (left to right) or rtl (right to left). This property is useful for displaying Web pages in languages that are read from right to left rather than left to right, by setting the value to rtl. For fun, you can change the way your page looks on-the-fly with this property, as in the following example code:

```
document.dir = "rtl";
```

Figure 9-2 shows an example of how a page would look with the dir property set to "rtl".

The lastModified Property

The lastModified property holds the value of the date and time the current document was last modified. This is used mostly for informational purposes, such as displaying the date the document was last modified so the viewer knows when you last updated your page. The value of this property depends on your browser, as different browsers have different results if you write the last modified date on the page.

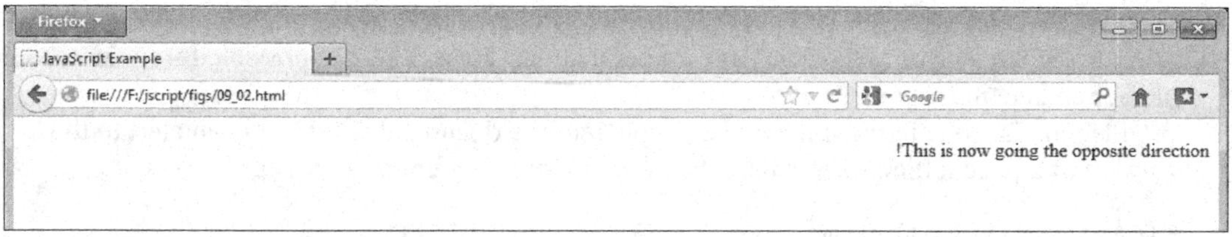

Figure 9-2   A Web page with the direction switched to rtl

Consider the following code, which writes the value of the document.lastModified property into a Web page to display the last modified date and time:

```
<body>
<h1>My Always Updated Web Page!</h1>
<script type="text/javascript">
document.write("Last Updated: " + document.lastModified);
</script>
</body>
```

Figure 9-3 shows the result of this when viewed in Mozilla Firefox.

When writing the date of the last modification on the page, the differences only matter in terms of space on the page. Some layouts may need to have extra space arranged for the longer version of the property.

The referrer Property

The referrer property is used for informational purposes and holds the value of the URL of the page that the viewer was on before arriving at your page (the referring page). While this can be useful, the viewer doesn't always come in with a referring URL (such as when using a bookmark or typing in the address), so the value could be nothing. Also, the value of this

Figure 9-3   The last modified date when viewed in Mozilla Firefox

property isn't always correct, because different browsers may consider different types of things as referring the viewer to the new page, rather than just links, and it is possible for the user to hide or change the referrer.

Placing the code in the following example into the document would send an alert to the viewers of a page telling them where they were before they got to your page:

```
window.alert("You came from " + document.referrer + "!");
```

So, if the referring page were http://www.scripttheweb.com/js/, an alert saying "You came from http://www.scripttheweb.com/js/!" would be sent to the viewer.

The title Property

The title property holds the string value of the title of the HTML document. The title is set inside the <title> and </title> tags of a page.

One way you can use the title property is to display the title of the page to the viewer someplace other than in the top bar of the window. The following code would allow you to do this:

```
<head>
<title>Lions, Tigers and Bears!</title>  ←————— The title of the document is set here
</head>
<body>                                              The title is shown as a
<script type="text/javascript">                    heading to the viewer
document.write("<h1>" + document.title + "</h1>");  ◄——┘
</script>
Lions and tigers and bears were what I saw when I went to ...
</body>
```

This displays your title as a heading on the page. Figure 9-4 shows the result of this when viewed in a browser.

Figure 9-4 The title of the document is shown as a heading on the page.

The URL Property

The URL property holds the value of the full URL of the current document. This information can be useful if you print it at the bottom of your HTML page, because it will show the page URL for anyone who prints out your page.

While you could just type the URL at the bottom on your own, this could become tedious when it needs to be done on numerous pages. This is where this property can be handy, because you can cut and paste a little script to each page rather than type the various URL addresses each time. An example of writing the URL address on the page is shown in the following code:

```
<body>
<h1>Buy Something!</h1>
If you don't buy something I will be really upset so you had better...
<br><br>
<script type="text/javascript">
document.write("You are at: " + document.URL);
</script>
</body>
```

Figure 9-5 shows the result of the preceding code in a browser. The last line of the page tells the viewer the current location. The figure shows a local file address, but it would show a regular URL if the page were online.

The URLUnencoded Property

The URLUnencoded property returns the URL of the document without any encoding. For instance, if there is a filename with a space in it, the property will return the space rather than a %20 in its place. For the URL http://www.scripttheweb.com/my script.html, the document .URL property would return http://www.scripttheweb.com/my%20script.html. The document .URLUnencoded property returns http://www.scripttheweb.com/my script.html, the URL without the encoding for the space. Note that at the time of this writing this property was only available in Microsoft Internet Explorer.

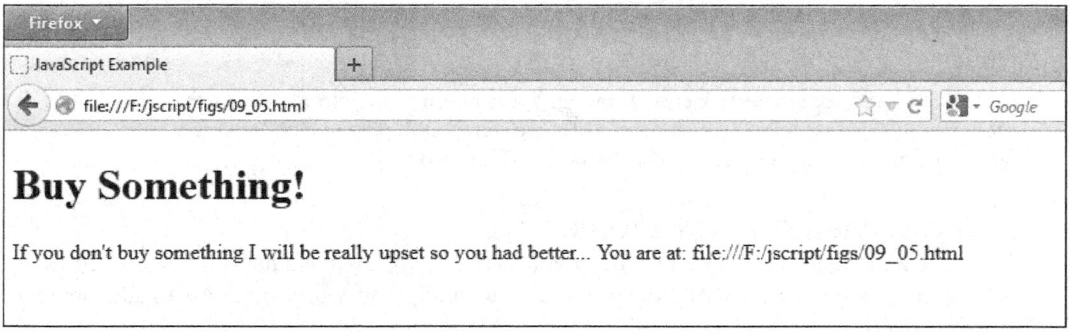

Figure 9-5   The URL of the document is shown at the end of the page contents.

Ask the Expert

Q: **Will learning about the document object and the DOM be helpful to me?**

A: Yes, because they provide a foundation for working not only with Web pages, but other types of documents as well. For example, other types of documents use a similar structure of nodes, so learning how it works for an HTML document is helpful when you need to make use of JavaScript on another platform, such as Adobe Acrobat for PDF files.

Q: **The referrer property is cool! Is there any way I can write that information to a file each time a visitor drops in so that I know where my visitors are coming from?**

A: Client-side JavaScript cannot save information in a file on its own, but can send information to a server-side program where it can then be stored in a file or database. You will learn more about this (using JSON and/or AJAX) in later chapters.

Q: **Other than the arrays that contain element collections, are there any other ways to access elements in the document?**

A: Methods of the document object, such as getElementById(), allow you to be even more specific about the elements you select. You will learn how to use these methods in the next section.

Using the Methods of the Document Object

The methods of the document object allow you to do some new things that you haven't been able to do yet. Table 9-2 lists the methods with a short description of each. Because a number of these methods are browser-specific (as with the properties), only some specific methods are described in more detail following the table.

NOTE

Not all of these properties work cross-browser. You can see more information on these properties by visiting http://developer.mozilla.org/en/DOM/document#Methods and http://msdn.microsoft.com/en-us/library/ms531073(VS.85).aspx.

The get Methods for Elements

There are a number of methods that allow you to get one or more elements in the document for use in your scripts. Each of these provides you a unique way to gain access to any elements you may need.

Method	Description
adoptNode()	Adopts a node from another document
createAttribute()	Creates an attribute with a name that is sent to it as an argument
createAttributeNS()	Creates a new attribute in a particular namespace
createCDATASection()	Creates a new CDATA section
createComment()	Creates a comment with the value that is sent to it as an argument
createDocumentFragment()	Creates a new document fragment
createElement()	Creates an element of the type sent to it as an argument
createElementNS()	Creates an element in a particular URI and a particular type sent to it as arguments
createEvent()	Creates an event
createEventObject()	Creates an event object for the purpose of passing event information
createNodeIterator()	Creates a node iterator object
createNSResolver()	Creates a namespace resolver
createProcessingInstruction()	Creates a processing instruction
createRange()	Creates a range object
createStyleSheet()	Creates a style sheet for the document to use (Internet Explorer only)
createTextNode()	Creates a text string from the value sent to it as an argument
createTreeWalker()	Creates a treewalker object
elementFromPoint()	Returns the element object that appears at the location that is sent to it in two argument values (pixels from left and pixels from top)
evaluate()	Returns a result based on the arguments sent to it
execCommand()	Executes a command on the document when the document is in design mode
getElementById()	Returns a reference to the object with the ID attribute that is sent to it as an argument
getElementsByClassName()	Returns references to the elements with the class name that is sent to it as an argument
getElementsByName()	Returns references to the objects with the name attribute that is sent to it as an argument
getElementsByTagName()	Returns references to the elements with the tag name that is sent to it as an argument
getElementsByTagNameNS()	Returns references to the elements with the tag name and namespace sent to it as arguments
getSelection()	Returns the value of a string of selected text in the document

(continues)

Table 9-2   The Methods of the Document Object

Method	Description
hasFocus()	Returns a Boolean value based on whether or not the document has focus
importNode()	Returns a copy of a node from another document
isDefaultNameSpace()	Returns whether or not the namespace is the default namespace for the current document
isEqualNode()	Returns whether two nodes are equal or not
isSameNode()	Returns whether or not two node references refer to the same node
load()	Loads an XML document
loadOverlay()	Loads an overlay in an XUL document
lookupNameSpaceURI()	Returns a namespace URI
lookupPrefix()	Returns the namespace of a specified prefix
normalize()	Normalizes the nodes in a document so that there are no empty text nodes and so that there are not multiple text nodes next to one another (makes them all a single text node)
open()	Opens a new document that allows you to write its contents using write() or writeln() statements
close()	Closes a new document that has been opened with the open() method
queryCommandEnabled()	Returns a Boolean value based on whether or not a command sent to it as an argument can be executed
queryCommandIndeterm()	Returns a Boolean value based on whether or not a command sent to it as an argument is in the indeterminate state
queryCommandState()	Returns a Boolean value based on whether or not a command sent to it as an argument has executed
queryCommandSupported()	Returns a Boolean value based on whether or not a command sent to it as an argument is supported
queryCommandValue()	Returns the current value of the document for the command that is sent to it as an argument
querySelector()	Returns the first element node that matches the selectors
querySelectorAll()	Returns all of the element nodes that match the selectors
recalc()	Recalculates the dynamic properties in the document
releaseCapture()	Releases the mouse capture from the document
write()	Allows you to write a string of text into an HTML document
writeln()	Allows you to write a string of text into an HTML document, but ends the line with a JavaScript newline character

Table 9-2 The Methods of the Document Object (*continued*)

The getElementById() Method

The getElementById() method allows you access to an element by the value of its id attribute. For example, if you have the following HTML code, you can access the div element with the getElementById() method:

```
<div id="some_text">This is some text.</div>
```

Since the id attribute of the div element has the value of some_text, the document .getElementById() method can access the div element using that value as an argument:

```
var text_element = document.getElementById("some_text");
```

As you go through this chapter, you will see that you can use this and the other selection methods to retrieve information from elements, alter elements, add elements, or delete elements.

The getElementsByClassName() Method

This method allows you to get an array filled with all the elements in the document that have the specified class name (from a CSS class). For example, to obtain all of the elements with a class name of number_one, you could use the following code:

```
var my_class = document.getElementsByClassName("number_one");
```

The getElementsByName() Method

This method allows you to get an array filled with all the elements in the document that have the specified value for the name attribute. In many cases, this value is unique to one element. However, radio buttons that are part of the same group all need to have the same name value (so that only one selection can be made). This is a case where being able to retrieve all of those elements could be handy:

```
<fieldset>
<legend>Choose a dinosaur:</legend>
<input type="radio" name="dino" id="dino_enigmo" value="Enigmosaurus">
<label for="dino_enigmo">The mysterious type</label>
<input type="radio" name="dino" id="dino_spino" value="Spinosaurus">
<label for="dino_spino">One with lots of backbone</label>
<input type="radio" name="dino" id="dino_xeno" value="Xenotarsosaurus">
<label for="dino_xeno">The unique name type</label>
</fieldset>
```

This HTML code has a set of radio buttons, all named dino. If you want to get all of these elements, you could use the following code:

```
var dino_radios = document.getElementsByName("dino");
```

This will retrieve all of the radio button elements with the name dino in an array, which you could then loop through to perform any necessary tasks:

```
for (var i = 0; i < dino_radios.length; i++) {
   // Do some work...
}
```

As you can see, you could now work with all of the elements in a loop, rather than gathering each one by its id to perform the same task.

The getElementsByTagName() Method

This method allows you to get an array filled with all the elements in the document that have the specified tag name. For example, to obtain all of the image elements in the document, you could use the following code:

```
var all_images = document.getElementsByTagName("img");
```

Getting More Specific

The get methods can be used with more specific objects once you have them. For instance, suppose you had the following HTML code:

```
<nav id="sitelinks">
<a href="page1.html">Page 1</a>
<a href="page2.html">Page 2</a>
<a href="page3.html">Page 3</a>
</nav>
<div>
Here is some content and check out <a href="someplace.com">my other site</a>!
</div>
```

If you wanted to get only the links within the nav element, using document .getElementsByTagName("links") wouldn't work, because you would also get the link that is within the div tag (still part of the document). To do this, you can first get the nav element and then use the getElementsByTagName() method on the object created for the nav element, as in the following code:

The nav element is obtained by its id

Each link within the nav element is obtained by its tag name

```
var nav_element = document.getElementById("sitelinks");
var nav_links = nav_element.getElementsByTagName("a");
alert("There are " + nav_links.length + " links in the nav element.");
```

The number of links in the nav element is displayed using the length of the nav_links array that was created by getting each of the a elements within the nav element

Here, you get the nav element by its id, creating the nav_element object. This object is used to get all of the link elements within it and place them into an array named nav_links. This array can now be used to cycle through each link within the nav element or to find out how many links are contained within the nav element. In this case, the number of links is alerted using the length of the nav_links array (3).

The open() and close() Methods

The open() method allows you to open a new document and create its contents entirely with document.write() or document.writeln() statements. When the open() method is called, the browser looks for these statements so that it can write the new page. Once the write() and/or writeln() statements are completed, you need to use document.close() to finish the new page.

NOTE

The open() and close() methods are not necessary (or desirable) when you are writing to the current loading page.

To get an example of the use of the open() method, suppose you want to write a new page based on the name of the viewer. To do this, you not only need to use the open() and close() methods, but also need to create a formName property to use so that you can grab the name entered by the viewer in a text box.

Start with the code for the body section of the initial page. You need a form with a text box and a way to invoke a function that will create the new document. The following code shows a way that you can do this (save the file as document_open.html):

```
<body>
<strong>Enter your name in the box below, then click
  the button to see a personalized page!</strong>
<br>
<form id="newp" onsubmit="newpage();">            The form is given an id and a function
                                                   (newpage) to run when submitted
Name: <input type="text" id="yourname" size="25">
<br><br>
<input type="submit" value="Submit">              The text box is given an id
</form>
<script type="text/javascript" src="document_open.js"></script>
</body>
```

This sets up your script, giving you a form with an id of newp and a text box with an id of yourname. It also has a submit button to submit the form. When the user clicks the submit button, the onsubmit event handler will be triggered, which executes the newpage() function (you will learn more about event handlers later in this chapter and in Chapter 10). You now need to create the newpage() function in your external JavaScript file so that this form will work.

The newpage() function needs to grab the contents of the text box and assign it to a variable. It then needs to open your new customized page in the browser window. The following code shows how this can be done (save the file as document_open.js):

```
function newpage() {                         The value of the text box contents is assigned to a variable
  var thename = document.getElementById("yourname").value;
  document.open();          A setup for a new document is opened
  document.write("<h1>Welcome!</h1>");
  document.write("Hello, " + thename + ", and welcome to my page!");
  document.close();
}
```

The setup for the new document is
closed, allowing it to be displayed

The new document uses these statements
to know what to display

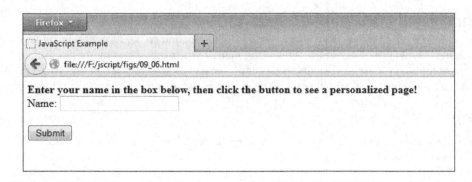

Figure 9-6 This is the page that allows the viewer to enter information.

The first thing the function does is to grab the contents of the text box. To get the contents of the text box, you need to use the value property that is available for form elements, which in this case is accessed using document.getElementById("yourname").value. This value is then assigned to the thename variable for easy use within your document.write() commands.

Once you have that value, you are ready to open the new page. To do this, you use the document.open() command, which allows you to use a series of document.write() statements until the document.close() command is used. You use the document.write() statements to write a greeting to the viewer on the page.

You can now try this out by opening the HTML page in your browser. Figure 9-6 shows the initial page with the form (the page before the form button is clicked). This is where the viewer can enter a name and click the button.

Figure 9-7 shows the result of entering the name "John" in the text box and clicking the button. The new page appears with a greeting!

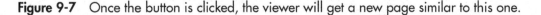

Figure 9-7 Once the button is clicked, the viewer will get a new page similar to this one.

The write() and writeln() Methods

You started using the write() method early in the book, so you know how it works already. The document.write() method is used to display a string value on the page where it is called. The writeln() method works the same way, but adds a newline character (\n) at the end of the statement. Recall that Chapter 3 discussed how the JavaScript newline character works—it only places a new line in the page source code and not in the final appearance of the HTML page.

TIP
While the newline character only affects the appearance of the source code when using document.write(), it can be used to create new lines in display elements created by JavaScript such as alert, prompt, and confirm boxes.

The appearance of the page itself is not affected by the JavaScript newline character. Recall the example from Chapter 3 that split the code into two different lines with the newline character:

```
<body>
<script type="text/javascript">
document.write("<strong>JavaScript Rules!</strong>\n This is fun.");
</script>
</body>
```

Since the document.writeln() method adds a newline character at the end of the statement, you could rewrite the preceding code using the following document.writeln() statements:

```
<body>
<script type="text/javascript">
document.writeln("<strong>JavaScript Rules!</strong>");
document.writeln(" This is fun.");
</script>
</body>
```

This would put the lines of code on two different lines in the page source, but would not affect the appearance of the page in the browser.

Using DOM Nodes

There are methods of the document object (such as createElement(), createAttribute(), and createTextNode()) that allow you to create various elements or nodes on the page using JavaScript. To make use of them, though, the new content must be appended as a child of an existing node in the DOM. This is where DOM node properties and methods are needed.

DOM Node Properties

Each DOM node is an object with properties and methods that can be accessed. The DOM node properties are listed in Table 9-3.

Property	Description
attributes	Returns an array of all of the attributes in the specified node
baseURI	Returns the base URI of the node
baseURIObject	Returns an object representing the base URI of the node
childElementCount	Returns the number of child nodes that are element nodes
childNodes	Returns an array of all the child nodes of the specified node
children	Returns an array of all the child elements of the specified node
classList	Returns a list of the classes within the class attribute of the element
className	Returns the value of the class attribute of the element
clientHeight	Returns the height, in pixels, of the element
clientWidth	Returns the width, in pixels, of the element
clientLeft	Returns the width, in pixels, of the left border of the element
clientTop	Returns the width, in pixels, of the top border of the element
contentEditable	Returns whether or not the element is editable
dataset	Gives access to custom data attributes of the element
dir	Returns the value of the direction of the text in the specified node
firstChild	Returns the first child node of the specified node
firstElementChild	Returns the first direct child element of the specified element
id	Returns the id of the specified node
innerHTML	Returns or sets the HTML code within the specified node
innerText	Returns or sets the inner text of the specified node
isContentEditable	Returns whether or not the content of the element can be edited
lang	Returns the language value of the specified node
lastChild	Returns the last child node of the specified node
lastChildElement	Returns the last direct child element of the specified element
localName	Returns the local portion of the node name

Table 9-3 The DOM Node Properties

Property	Description
name	Returns the name attribute of the specified element
namespaceURI	Returns the namespace URI of the specified node
nextSibling	Returns the node following the specified node
nextElementSibling	Returns the next element on the same level as the specified element
nodeName	Returns the name of the specified node (such as div for a div element)
nodePrincipal	Returns the security context of the specified node (privileged code)
nodeType	Returns the type of the specified node
nodeValue	Returns the value of the specified node (such as the text within a div element or the value of an attribute)
offsetHeight	Returns the offset height of the specified node
offsetWidth	Returns the offset width of the specified node
outerHTML	Returns or sets the HTML code of the specified node (includes the specified element itself)
ownerDocument	Returns the document object that contains the specified node
parentNode	Returns the parent node of the specified node
prefix	Returns the namespace prefix of the specified node
previousSibling	Returns the node before the specified node
scrollLeft	Returns the difference between the left edge and the left edge in view of the specified node
scrollTop	Returns the difference between the top edge and the top edge in view of the specified node
scrollHeight	Returns the entire height (including anything hidden and viewable via a scroll bar) of the specified node
scrollWidth	Returns the entire width (including anything hidden and viewable via a scroll bar) of the specified node
style	Returns the style object of the specified node
tabIndex	Returns the tab index of the specified node
tagName	Returns the tag name (in uppercase) of the specified node
textContent	Returns or sets the text content of a node
title	Returns the value of the title attribute of the specified node

Table 9-3   The DOM Node Properties (*continued*)

When Table 9-3 mentions the specified node, a node works in much the same way as you worked with elements in previous chapters. For instance, you might have the following HTML code:

```
<body>
<div id="div1" title="All about me!">
This page is about me, me, and... me!
</div>
</body>
```

If you wanted to obtain the value of the title attribute of the div element, you could use document.getElementById() to grab the div element by its id of div1. This would be the specified node for the DOM node title property. Then, you could access the title property of the element node, as in the following code:

Gets the element by its id and assigns it to a variable

```
var me_div = document.getElementById("div1");
window.alert("The title of the div element is " + me_div.title);
```

Alerts the value of the element's title attribute to the viewer

This works just like object properties, as you learned in the previous chapter. The me_div.title property returns the string value "All about me!", which is the value of the div element node's title attribute.

Knowing this, you can use the DOM node methods in the same way.

DOM Node Methods

Table 9-4 lists the DOM node methods.

As mentioned earlier, to make the creation methods of the document object useful by adding the created node to the document, a DOM node method, such as appendChild() or insertBefore(), is needed to add the new node to the document.

For instance, you might have the HTML code used earlier, as follows:

```
<body>
<div id="div1" title="All about me!">
This page is about me, me, and... me!
</div>
</body>
```

This code has a div element node with a child text node (and attribute nodes). If you want to create another div element as the last child node of the div1 element node, you could use a combination of document.createElement(), document.createTextNode(), and the DOM node method appendChild().

Each node is an object that can use all of the node properties and methods. Since you have a div node available, you can use getElementById() to access it as an object, which will allow you to add an element within it using the appendChild() method.

Method	Description
addEventListener()	Adds an event listener to the specified node to run a function on the event sent to it as an argument
appendChild()	Appends a node as the last child of the specified node
attachEvent()	Attaches an event to the specified node to run a function on the event sent to it as an argument
blur()	Removes focus from the specified node
click()	Executes the click event on the specified node
cloneNode()	Creates a clone of the specified node
compareDocumentPosition()	Returns a number representing the position of the node in comparison to the node sent as an argument
detachEvent()	Detaches an event from the specified node
dispatchEvent()	Executes an event on the specified node
focus()	Gives focus to the specified node
getAttribute()	Returns the value of the attribute name sent to it as an argument on the specified node
getAttributeNS()	Returns the value of the attribute name and namespace sent to it as an argument on the specified node
getAttributeNode()	Returns the attribute node of the attribute name sent to it as an argument for the specified node
getAttributeNodeNS()	Returns the attribute node of the attribute name and namespace sent to it as arguments for the specified node
getElementsByTagName()	Returns an array of all the child element nodes with the tag name sent to it as an argument in the specified node
getElementsByTagNameNS()	Returns an array of all the child element nodes with the tag name and namespace sent to it as arguments in the specified node
hasAttribute()	Returns true if the attribute name sent to it as an argument exists on the specified node, or false if not
hasAttributeNS()	Returns true if the attribute name and namespace sent to it as arguments exist on the specified node, or false if not
hasAttributes()	Returns true if the specified node has any attribute nodes defined, or false if not
hasChildNodes()	Returns true if the specified node has any child nodes. or false if not
insertBefore()	Inserts a node sent to it as an argument before the node sent to it as a second argument inside the specified node
normalize()	Normalizes the specified node

(continues)

Table 9-4 The DOM Node Methods

Method	Description
removeAttribute()	Removes the attribute node for the attribute name sent to it as an argument from the specified node
removeAttributeNode()	Removes the attribute node for the attribute node object reference sent to it as an argument from the specified node
removeAttributeNS()	Removes the attribute node for the attribute name sent to it as an argument with the namespace sent to it as an argument from the specified node
removeChild()	Removes the child node sent to it as an argument from the specified node
removeEventListener()	Removes an event listener from the specified node
replaceChild()	Replaces the child node sent to it as the second argument with the child node sent to it as the first argument in the specified node
scrollIntoView()	Scrolls the specified node into view in the browser window
setAttribute()	Sets an attribute node's name (first argument) and value (second argument) for the specified node
setAttributeNode()	Sets an attribute node as the attribute node object sent to it as an argument for the specified node
setAttributeNodeNS()	Sets an attribute node as the attribute node object sent to it as an argument with the namespace sent to it as an argument for the specified node
setAttributeNS()	Sets an attribute node's namespace (first argument), name (second argument), and value (third argument) for the specified node

Table 9-4 The DOM Node Methods (*continued*)

First, go into the JavaScript code and grab the div1 element by its id and assign it to a variable:

```
var me_div = document.getElementById("div1");
```

Next, create the new element node using document.createElement():

```
var inner_div = document.createElement("div");
```

After that, create the text node for the inner_div node by using the document.createTextNode() method:

```
var inner_div_text = document.createTextNode("More about me...")
```

Next, use the DOM node method appendChild() to add the text node as a child of the new inner_div node:

```
inner_div.appendChild(inner_div_text);
```

To give the inner_div node a title attribute, you can assign a value to its title property:

```
inner_div.title = "More";
```

Finally, use the DOM node method appendChild() to add the inner_div node to the document structure as the last (and in this case, only) child element of the me_div node:

```
me_div.appendChild(inner_div);
```

The complete JavaScript code looks like this:

```
var me_div = document.getElementById("div1");
var inner_div = document.createElement("div");
var inner_div_text = document.createTextNode("More about me...");
inner_div.appendChild(inner_div_text);
inner_div.title = "More";
me_div.appendChild(inner_div);
```

The div1 element is assigned to the me_div variable

A new div element is created and assigned to the inner_div variable

A text node is created and assigned to the inner_div_text variable

The text node (inner_div_text) is added to the inner_div element (the new div element)

The inner_div element is assigned a value for its title attribute

The inner_div element is officially appended to the DOM structure inside the me_div element using appendChild()

This adds your new div node at the end of the original div element (but before the original element is closed, since it will be a child node). Thus, the document structure for the HTML code would now be like this (though it won't show up when you use the browser's "View Source" command):

```
<body>
<div id="div1" title="All about me!">
This page is about me, me, and... me!
<div title="Me">
More about me...
</div>
</div>
</body>
```

As you can see, the div is added with the text "More about me..." and a title attribute with a value of "Me".

NOTE

Another way to add or alter content is to use the innerHTML property, which is discussed in the next section, "Creating Dynamic Scripts."

If you decide you want to delete a node from the DOM structure, you can use the removeChild() DOM node method. For example, if you want to remove the inner_div node added in the previous example, you can use the following code:

```
me_div.removeChild(inner_div);
```

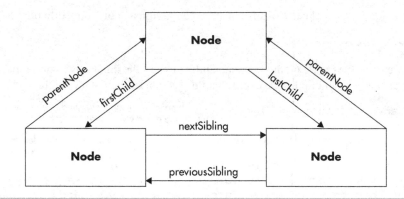

Figure 9-8 DOM node relationships

This will remove the inner_div child node from the me_div parent node.

Each node has one or more relationships with other nodes in the DOM structure. Figure 9-8 shows how the relationships are tied together.

As you can see, there are properties and methods that can be used with each of these relationships (for example, previousSibling, parentNode, firstChild, and so on). You can use these to access or alter any element within the DOM structure as needed. For example, you might have an HTML document like this:

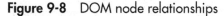

```
                          Parent node of the two "employee" divs within it
<body>
<div id="company">◄─────────┘
<div id="employee1">Marty</div>◄──────── First child node of the outer "company" div
<div id="employee2">John</div> ◄──────── Last child node of the outer "company" div
</div>
</body>
```

Each div element could be accessed in different ways, depending on where you begin. For example, you could access the outer "company" div using any of the following paths:

```
document.getElementById("company"); // direct route
document.getElementById("employee1").parentNode; // from first child
document.getElementById("employee2").parentNode; // from last child
```

Likewise, the "employee1" div can be accessed a number of ways:

```
document.getElementById("employee1"); // direct route
document.getElementById("company").firstChild; // from parent
document.getElementById("employee2").previousSibling; // from its sibling
```

The same, again, goes for the "employee2" div:

```
document.getElementById("employee2"); // direct route
document.getElementById("company").lastChild; // from parent
document.getElementById("employee1").nextSibling; // from its sibling
```

While it may seem easiest to simply use the direct route all the time, there may be situations where you do not know the id of the node you are seeking beforehand. Suppose one of the nodes had been added by another script? If you always wanted to find the last "employee" div, for example, it might be better to use lastChild from its parent node, so that if other employees are added (for example, "employee3", "employee4"), you will always be accessing the last employee:

```
var last_hired = document.getElementById("company").lastChild;
```

This will ensure that last_hired will always point to the last "employee" div that is a child of the "company" div.

Try This 9-1   Add a DOM Node to the Document

pr9_1.html
prjs9_1.js

This project allows you to practice using the new document and DOM node properties and methods you have learned in this chapter.

Step by Step

1. Create an HTML page with the following code for the body section and save it as pr9_1.html:

```
<body>
<div id="div1" title="Gosh!">
Whatever I feel like I want to write...
</div>
<script type="text/javascript" src="prjs9_1.js"></script>
</body>
```

2. Create an external JavaScript file and save it as prjs9_1.js. Use it for steps 3–5.

3. Get the value of the title attribute of the element with the id of "div1" and send that value as an alert to the viewer.

4. Create a new div element with the text "See you!" and a title attribute with the value "Lucky!". Add it to the document structure as a child of the div element with the id of "div1".

5. Save the JavaScript file and open the HTML file in your browser to view the results.

(continued)

Try This Summary

In this project, you used your knowledge of the properties and methods of the document object and the DOM nodes to alert a DOM node property and to create a new div element in the document's structure.

Creating Dynamic Scripts

As you have seen, JavaScript gives you access to all of the elements in the document with the various methods such as document.getElementById() and document .getElementsByTagName().

This allows you to get information, add nodes, alter nodes, and remove nodes, as you have seen. In addition, you can access the style attributes of elements (typically initially set by a style sheet) to make changes to such things as their positions, colors, borders, sizes, or just about any other part of the styles, using the style DOM node property.

Styles in JavaScript

When setting styles using Cascading Style Sheets (CSS), you may set up something like the following in your CSS code (save it as dyn_01.css):

```
#div1 { color:#000000; background-color:#FFFFFF; }
#div2 { border-style:solid; border-width:1px; border-color:#000000; }
```

This gives you style attributes for two ids, div1 and div2. Thus, if you had the following HTML code (save as dyn_01.html), the div elements would use the preceding styles in their presentation on the Web page:

The CSS file is linked to the document here

```
<head>
<link rel="stylesheet" type="text/css" href="dyn_01.css">
</head>
<body>
<div id="div1">
I am in div1. It seems like a nice place.
</div>
<div id="div2">
I am in div2. It's a little fancier here.
</div>
<script type="text/javascript" src="dyn_01.js"></script>
</body>
```

The div element with an id of "div1"

The div element with an id of "div2"

The JavaScript file is called here

The HTML code is linked to the CSS code via the link tag. Thus, the div1 element is going to display as simple black text on a white background and the div2 element is going to have a plain, solid-black border around it.

As you can see, this page is using ids for each div element—so not only can you access those elements' ids with the CSS code, but you can also access the elements via their ids in the JavaScript code. So, you can start out your JavaScript file (called in the preceding HTML code—saved as dyn_01.js) with some code to grab both div elements by their ids by using the document.getElementById() method:

```
var d1 = document.getElementById("div1");
var d2 = document.getElementById("div2");
```

Now you have variables for both elements.

If you want to alter the styles that were set up in the CSS code via JavaScript, you'll need to make use of the style property that is a part of each element node. Then, JavaScript uses the same name as the CSS selector to access that particular property. For instance, if you wanted to change the color of the text in the div1 element to a light gray color, you would use the following code:

```
var d1 = document.getElementById("div1");
var d2 = document.getElementById("div2");
d1.style.color = "#DDDDDD";
```

In the CSS code, the selector color is used to alter the element's foreground color. In JavaScript, it is also the name of the property used to alter it after accessing the element's style property.

What if the CSS selector is not all one single word? For example, the background-color selector would not work in JavaScript if you used it the same way as in the CSS code. The following code attempts to change the background color to green:

```
var d1 = document.getElementById("div1");
var d2 = document.getElementById("div2");
d1.style.background-color = "#DDDDDD";
```

This won't work, because JavaScript doesn't allow the hyphen (-) character as part of a property name. Instead, JavaScript puts both words together and capitalizes the first letter of any additional words after the first word. Thus, the CSS selector background-color becomes backgroundColor in JavaScript. Other selectors would follow the same pattern (for example, border-right-color would become borderRightColor).

The JavaScript code could be rewritten as follows to make the change effective:

```
var d1 = document.getElementById("div1");
var d2 = document.getElementById("div2");
d1.style.backgroundColor = "#DDDDDD";
```

This will change the background color of the div1 element to green. The only issue now is that this will happen as soon as the script runs, which in this case is probably before the viewer ever notices there was another background color on the div1 element in the first place. To make this more useful, you need a way to run portions of your script at a time other than the loading or reloading of the document.

CAUTION
Reading a style isn't as easy as setting it, as there are browser differences and other
issues that occur. For further information and techniques on how to get styles, see
www.quirksmode.org/dom/getstyles.html.

Simple Event Handling

So far, your scripts have simply run during the loading (or reloading) of the Web page. This
is good for a number of tasks, but many, such as node and style changes, would be more
useful if they were executed in response to an action taken by the user. For instance, changing
the background color of an element while the page is loading may not even be noticed by the
viewer, but changing the color in response to a mouse click would allow the viewer to see the
change and provide the choice of leaving the original color or changing to the new color
via a click.

The click Event

The click event is available for most elements within the DOM. This event is triggered when
the user clicks the primary mouse button while the mouse pointer is over a specific element.
One way to gain control of the click event is through onclick, as shown in the following code
(other methods will be covered in the next chapter):

```
var d1 = document.getElementById("div1");
var d2 = document.getElementById("div2");
d1.onclick = function() {
  // Code to execute when the element is clicked
};
```

Here, the d1 element's onclick property is assigned a function expression (refer to Chapter 4
if you need to review function expressions), which can then execute code. Thus, when the d1
element is clicked by the user, any code within the function will be executed.

So, you can now take the code you were using to change styles and perform the task when
the user clicks the element rather than while the page is loading. The following code shows an
example of this:

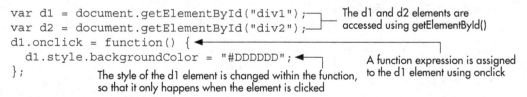

```
var d1 = document.getElementById("div1");     The d1 and d2 elements are
var d2 = document.getElementById("div2");     accessed using getElementById()
d1.onclick = function() {
  d1.style.backgroundColor = "#DDDDDD";       A function expression is assigned
};                                            to the d1 element using onclick
     The style of the d1 element is changed within the function,
     so that it only happens when the element is clicked
```

Figure 9-9 shows what the page looks like after the user clicks on the first div element. The
background color has changed from white to a light gray.

NOTE
Event handling will be covered more thoroughly in Chapter 10. For the time being, only
the click event will be covered using simple DOM0 event handling.

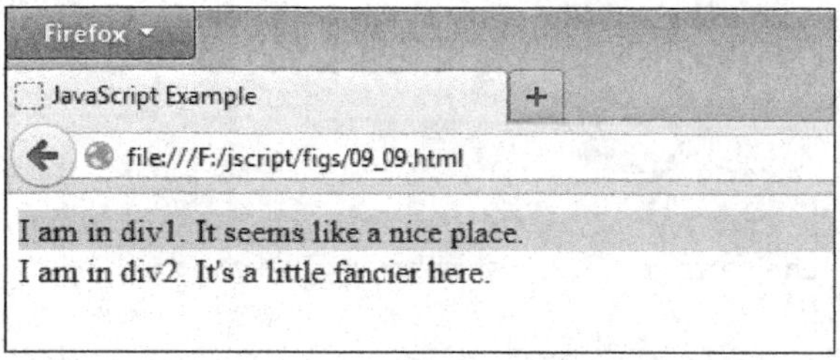

Figure 9-9   The background color of the first div element is changed and is now light gray.

Coding a Dynamic Script

Now that you know how to alter an element's style properties, you can alter them in reaction to user events to create dynamic scripts. In addition, you can alter the entirety of the HTML code within a given element using the innerHTML property.

The innerHTML Property

The innerHTML DOM node property allows you to change the HTML code that is inside a specified element. For instance, you could start out with the following HTML code:

```
<body>
<div id="div1">
What is 2+2?
</div>
<div id="div2">
<a href="answer.html" id="answer_link">Get the answer</a>
</div>
</body>
```

This code sets up a div element node with an id of div1, another div element node with an id of div2, and the link with an id of answer_link. Now, if you want to change the HTML code in the div1 element so that it displays the answer for the viewer when the link is clicked, you can use the click event on the link to start the script in motion and then change the innerHTML property on the div1 element node to change the contents of that element from the question to the answer:

```
var d1 = document.getElementById("div1");
var answer_link = document.getElementById("answer_link");
answer_link.onclick = function() {
  d1.innerHTML = "That is easy, the answer is <strong>4</strong>!";
  return false;
};
```

Note that in order to keep this link from being followed when clicked, you add the return false statement after performing the desired actions. This will be discussed in more detail in the next chapter.

When run, this script changes the content inside the div1 element on the page, so that the HTML code would now be the following (though it will not be seen using the browser's "View Source" command):

```
<body>
<div id="div1">
That is easy, the answer is <strong>4</strong>!
</div>
<div id="div2">
<a href="answer.html" id="answer_link">Get the answer</a>
</div>
</body>
```

TIP

To make the script accessible to those without JavaScript, a default link destination (answer.html) is used. Including the answer text on the linked page allows users without JavaScript to still click the link and obtain the answer to the question.

As you can see, this can be a handy way to make dynamic changes to the content of a Web page. The innerHTML() and appendChild() methods allow you to change information displayed on the page dynamically and without reloading the page. This provides a definite improvement over document.write(), which you have been using up to this point, since document.write() can only change content when the page is loaded or reloaded.

Now that you know the newer methods, you will make use of these methods rather than document.write() as you continue through this book.

Using what you have learned in this chapter to access the DOM and use the properties and methods of the document object and the DOM nodes, you can build scripts to make any number of alterations to the document's appearance or content.

Try This 9-2   Try Out Property Changes

`pr9_2.html`
`prjs9_2.js`

This project allows you to practice using the new style and innerHTML properties you have learned in this chapter.

Step by Step

1. Create an HTML page with the following code for the body section and save it as pr9_2.html:

```
<body>
<div id="div1">
When will I update this page?
```

```
</div>
<div id="div2">
<a href="answer.html" id="c_link">Find out!</a>
</div>
<script type="text/javascript" src="prjs9_2.js"></script>
</body>
```

2. Create an external JavaScript file and save it as prjs9_1.js. Use it for steps 3–5.

3. Write some code so that when the link is clicked, the background color of the div element with the id of div1 changes to #CCCCCC and the content of the same element changes to the following:

```
<strong>Right now!</strong> Was that quick or what?
```

4. When complete, the JavaScript file should look like this:

```
var d1 = document.getElementById("div1");
var c_link = document.getElementById("c_link");
c_link.onclick = function() {
  d1.innerHTML = "<strong>Right now!</strong> Was that quick or what?";
  return false;
};
```

5. Save the JavaScript file and open the HTML file in your browser to view the results.

Try This Summary

In this project, you used your knowledge of the style and innerHTML properties of DOM nodes to make style and content changes to the Web page.

Chapter 9 Self Test

1. The _____ object is an object that is created by the browser for each new HTML page that is viewed.

2. The _____ property of the document object returns the URL of the document that referred the viewer to the current document.

3. You can use the DOM node property style to alter the style sheet attributes of an element.

   A. True

   B. False

4. The _____ method of the document object allows you to get an element by the value of its id attribute.

  A. getElementsByClassName()

  B. createElement()

  C. getSelection()

  D. getElementById()

5. The appendChild() DOM node method allows you to add a child node as the first child node of a specified node.

  A. True

  B. False

6. You cannot remove nodes from the document once they have been added.

  A. True

  B. False

7. The _____ property of the document object is an array that contains all of the anchor (<a>) tags on the page.

8. The _____ DOM node property allows you to change the HTML content of an element node.

9. The _____ property holds the value of the date and time the current document was last modified.

10. The Document Object Model (DOM) allows JavaScript (and other scripting languages) to access the structure of the document in the browser.

  A. True

  B. False

11. You can use the title property to display the title of a Web page someplace other than in the top bar of the browser window.

  A. True

  B. False

12. Which property returns the complete URL of the current document?

  A. domain

  B. referrer

  C. URL

  D. title

13. How does the writeln() method differ from the write() method?

    A. It adds the equivalent of an HTML <br /> tag at the end of the line.

    B. It adds the equivalent of an HTML <p> tag at the end of the line.

    C. It adds a JavaScript newline character at the end of the line.

    D. It is exactly the same as the write() method.

14. What is the getElementsByName() method commonly used to obtain?

    A. All the elements that you know by name.

    B. All the elements that are named but do not have an id attribute.

    C. All the elements that have the same value for the name attribute (most commonly radio buttons).

    D. All of the elements that have property values that are equal to a specified name.

15. What statements are most common between a document.open() and a document.close() statement?

    A. HTML commands

    B. document.write() and document.writeln() statements

    C. Only document.writeln() statements

    D. Only window.alert() statements

Chapter 10

Event Handlers

Key Skills & Concepts

- Understanding Event Handler Locations and Uses
- Learning the Event Handlers
- Other Ways to Register Events
- The Event Object
- Creating Scripts Using Event Handlers

When creating scripts, you will often find that there are user "events" (such as a user moving a mouse over a certain element or clicking a particular element) to which you want your script to react. The way you do this is through the use of event handlers.

To learn how the event handlers work, you need to learn what they are and why they are useful to you. You will then learn where event handlers are placed in a document and how to use them. Finally, you will see the various events in JavaScript and the event handlers that take care of each event. To get started, this chapter presents a general overview of event handlers.

What Is an Event Handler?

An event handler is a predefined JavaScript property of an object (in most cases an element in the document) that is used to handle an event on a Web page.

You may ask the question "What is an event?" An event is something that happens when the viewer of the page performs some sort of action, such as clicking a mouse button, clicking a button on the page, changing the contents of a form element, or moving the mouse over a link on the page. Events can also occur simply by the page loading or other similar actions.

When events occur, you are able to use JavaScript event handlers to identify them and then perform a specific task or set of tasks. JavaScript enables you to react to an action by the viewer and to make scripts that are interactive and more useful to you and to the viewer.

Why Event Handlers Are Useful

Event handlers are useful because they enable you to gain access to the events that may occur on the page. For instance, if you wanted to send an alert to the viewer when he or she moves the mouse over a link, you could use the event handler to invoke the JavaScript alert you have coded to react to the event. You are now making things happen based on the actions of the viewer, which enables you to make Web pages that are more interactive.

In creating this interactivity, many people find that JavaScript starts to become a little more fun to code and to use. With event handlers, you can create scripts that will add more functionality to the page. JavaScript can make a number of things happen on a Web page that will make the page more interesting than a static HTML document.

Understanding Event Handler Locations and Uses

To see how event handlers work, you need to know where you can place them in a document and how to use them to add JavaScript code for an event.

Event handlers can be used in a number of locations. They can be used directly within HTML elements by adding special attributes to those elements. They can also be used within the <script> and </script> tags or in an external JavaScript file.

To understand better where event handlers are located, you need to learn how to add event handlers to your script.

Using an Event Handler in an HTML Element

To use an event handler directly in an HTML element, you need to know the keyword for the event handler and where to place the event handler within the HTML code. To give you an example, I will introduce the onclick event handler, which is used to make something happen when the viewer clicks a specific area of the document.

One element that can be clicked is a form button. So, suppose you want to alert the viewer to something when the user clicks a form button. You would write something similar to the following code:

```
<input type="button" value="Click Me!" onclick="JavaScript code here">
```

To use an event handler, you add it as an additional attribute to an HTML tag. The only difference between an event handler "attribute" and an HTML attribute is that you can add JavaScript code inside an event handler attribute rather than just an attribute value. In the previous code, you would replace the *JavaScript code here* text with some actual JavaScript code.

So, to make an alert pop up when the user clicks the button, you can add the necessary JavaScript code right inside your onclick attribute, as shown in the following example:

```
<form>
<input type="button" value="Click Me!" onclick="window.alert('Hi!');">
</form>
```

Notice how the onclick event handler
works much like an HTML attribute

When the viewer clicks this plain button, an alert will pop up with a greeting. Notice that the rules on the quote marks apply here. Using the onclick event handler as an attribute requires you to use double quotes around all of your JavaScript code, so when you need quote marks for the alert, you use single quotes in order to avoid possible errors.

Also notice that the alert command ends with a semicolon. This enables you to add additional JavaScript code after the alert, which enables you to perform multiple actions on the click event rather than just a single JavaScript statement.

You could code in two alerts if you wanted to do so. All you have to do is remember to include the semicolons to separate the alert commands. This will be a little different because all of the code will be on one line rather than separate lines, as you normally see:

```
<form>
<input type="button" value="Click Me!"
 onclick="window.alert('Hi!'); window.alert('Bye!');">
</form>
```

Notice how the semicolons separate the JavaScript statements

This example is able to perform two JavaScript statements on the same event by using semicolons to separate them. When using event handlers, you can execute multiple commands this way. It is important, however, to keep everything between the event handler keyword (in this case, onclick) and the ending set of quotes (in this case, after the last semicolon in the code) on one line in your text editor; otherwise, a line break in the code could cause it not to run properly or to give a JavaScript error.

If the code you want to use becomes really long, you may wish to put the code in a function instead. The event handler can be used for any JavaScript code, so you can use it to call a function you have defined elsewhere. For example, you could place your two alerts within a function inside an external JavaScript file, and call the function from an event handler in the HTML code. First, code the external JavaScript file (here it will be saved as js_event_01.js) as follows:

```
function hi_and_bye() {
  window.alert('Hi!');
  window.alert('Bye!');
}
```

Next, add the script tags and the event handler to your HTML code:

Notice how the function is called using the event handler

```
<form>
<input type="button" value="Click Me!" onclick="hi_and_bye();">
</form>
<script type="text/javascript" src="js_event_01.js"></script>
```

Notice how the function is called using the event handler just like a normal function call within a script. This enables you not only to shorten the code within the event handler, but also to reuse the function on another button click or event later in the page instead of writing the two alerts out again. The use of a function can help you quite a bit, especially when the code you want to use becomes extremely long.

Using an Event Handler in the Script Code

You can also use an event handler within the script code (whether using the script tags in the HTML document or using an external JavaScript file). One way to do this is to give the element an id attribute and then use the JavaScript method document.getElementById() to access the element, as you learned in Chapter 9.

Add the id Attribute

To use the previous script in this way, you will first add an id attribute to the HTML tag for the input button, as shown here:

```
<form>
<input type="button" value="Click Me!" id="say_hi">
</form>
<script type="text/javascript" src="js_event_01.js"></script>
```

Notice that the button input element was given an id of say_hi. You will use this to access the button and tie it to an event in your script.

Access the Element

The document.getElementById() method allows you to access any element in the HTML document that has an id attribute using the value of its id attribute. In order to access the button input element you have been using with an id of say_hi, you could use the following code:

```
var hi_button = document.getElementById("say_hi");
```

Now, you can place the function code into a function expression in the JavaScript file (js_event_01.js), as shown here:

```
var hi_button = document.getElementById("say_hi");
hi_button.onclick = function() {
   window.alert("Hi!");
   window.alert("Bye!");
};
```

The button input element is accessed via its id (say_hi) and assigned to a variable (hi_button)

The onclick event handler is used to assign the function expression to the onclick event for the button input element

   The function expression (which displays the two alerts) is assigned to handle the click event on the input button. Thus, when the button is clicked, the viewer will see the two alerts!

   This method of handling events allows you to place all of your JavaScript code outside of your HTML elements, which keeps your HTML code cleaner (especially if an external JavaScript file is used). Later in this chapter, you will see that newer methods are also available to handle events.

CAUTION

Make sure an element has been added to the page before accessing it with getElementById(). This can be done by placing the <script></script> tags at the end of the document (just before the closing </body> tag) or by using the load event to determine that the document has loaded before accessing DOM elements.

Ask the Expert

Q: You mean I can just write some JavaScript by using an event handler like an HTML attribute?

A: Yes, but keep in mind that giving an element an id attribute and responding to the event in the JavaScript code will help keep your HTML code cleaner.

Q: Can you use events on elements other than buttons?

A: Yes, almost any element can react to an event. You will learn more about the events that are used in JavaScript in the next section.

Q: Didn't I already learn this in Chapter 9?

A: So far, what you have seen is basically a review of some of the things you learned in Chapter 9. The remaining sections will build on this by providing you with the available events, discussing the event object, learning new event registration techniques, and building example scripts from what you have learned.

Learning the Events

Now that you know what event handlers are and how to use them, you need to see which event handlers are used for various events on a page. Begin by looking at Table 10-1, which lists the most common events, their event handlers, and samples of what actions might trigger each event.

NOTE
Some of these events, such as the copy event, will only work with certain browsers (which may need to be running in their latest versions). There are also events that work only in Internet Explorer (see http://msdn.microsoft.com/en-us/library/ms533051(VS.85).aspx) or that are not necessarily cross-browser as of yet (see www.w3.org/TR/DOM-Level-3-Events/events.html#Events-EventTypes-complete). Drag events for drag-and-drop functionality are discussed in Chapter 16.

Now that you have a general idea about event handlers, you will take a look at some of the most often used ones in detail to see how they work.

Event	Event Handler	Event Trigger
Abort	onabort	An image is stopped from loading before loading has completed
Blur	onblur	Viewer removes focus from an element
Change	onchange	Viewer changes the contents of a form element
Click	onclick	Viewer clicks an element
ContextMenu	oncontextmenu	Viewer opens the context menu
Copy	oncopy	Viewer uses the copy command on part of a page
Cut	oncut	Viewer uses the cut command on part of a page
Dblclick	ondblclick	Viewer double-clicks the mouse on the element
Error	onerror	Viewer's browser gets a JavaScript error or an image that does not exist
Focus	onfocus	Viewer gives focus to an element
Keydown	onkeydown	Viewer presses down a key on the keyboard
Keypress	onkeypress	Viewer presses down a key on the keyboard and the corresponding character is typed
Keyup	onkeyup	Viewer releases a key on the keyboard
Load	onload	Web page finishes loading
Mousedown	onmousedown	Viewer presses the mouse button
Mouseenter	onmouseenter	Viewer moves the mouse over an element (child elements excluded)
Mouseleave	onmouseleave	Viewer moves the mouse away from an element (child elements excluded)
Mousemove	onmousemove	Viewer moves the mouse (moves the cursor)
Mouseout	onmouseout	Viewer moves the mouse away from an element
Mouseover	onmouseover	Viewer moves the mouse over an element
Mouseup	onmouseup	Viewer releases the mouse button
Mousewheel	onmousewheel	Viewer rolls the mouse wheel in either direction
Paste	onpaste	Viewer uses the paste command on part of the page
Reset	onreset	Viewer resets a form on the page
Resize	onresize	A window is resized
Scroll	onscroll	Viewer scrolls an area that is scrollable
Select	onselect	User makes a selection
Submit	onsubmit	Viewer submits a form on the page
Unload	onunload	Viewer leaves the current page

Table 10-1 The Events and Event Handlers

The Click Event

The click event, which you have already been studying, occurs when a viewer clicks on an element in a Web page. For example, you could use a form button and send an alert when it is clicked:

```
<body>                                          The onclick event handler
<form>                                          is used on a button
<input type="button" value="Do not Click Here"
 onclick="window.alert('I told you not to click me!');">
</form>
</body>
```

This will send the viewer an alert once the button has been clicked. Figure 10-1 shows the result of this code when the viewer clicks the button.

To use this event handler to do the same thing with a link, you might be tempted to do something similar to the following:

Oh no! This will give you problems because
the browser will try to follow the link

```
<body>
<a href="http://none" onclick="window.alert('Hey! You clicked me!');">
Don't Click Me</a>
</body>
```

The problem with this code is that the alert will work, but the browser will try to continue the original action of the link tag and attempt to go to http://none. This would probably cause a "Server not found" error in the browser.

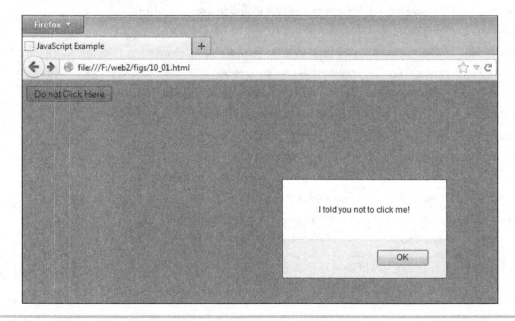

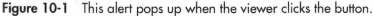

Figure 10-1 This alert pops up when the viewer clicks the button.

One way you can avoid a "Server not found" error is to link to an actual page (which is good for accessibility); however, if the viewer has JavaScript enabled, it may take the viewer away from the current page. To keep the link from being followed when JavaScript is enabled, you need to add an extra statement to the JavaScript in the click event. You need to tell the browser not to continue after you have shown the viewer your alert. To do this, you will add a return false statement, which will keep the browser from following the link after the alert has been shown. The following code shows how to add in the return statement inline:

```
<body>
<a href="http://none"
 onclick="window.alert('Hey! You clicked me!'); return false;">
Don't Click Me</a>
</body>
```

The return false statement keeps the browser from trying to follow the link

With this code in place, the click event will be taken care of by the onclick event handler, and the browser will not need to worry about attempting to follow the link in the href attribute. Later in this chapter, you will learn how to use the modern method of preventing the default action, event.preventDefault().

NOTE
You can also code JavaScript for a link by using the javascript: command—for example, <a href="javascript:window.alert('Hi');">Click</a>—but this method is not recommended for accessibility reasons (if JavaScript is off, the link doesn't go anywhere).

Focus and Blur Events
The focus event occurs when the viewer gives focus to an element or window. A viewer gives focus to something by clicking somewhere within the item, by using the keyboard to move to the item (often via the TAB key), or via a script. For instance, a viewer who clicks a text input box (before entering anything) gives that text box focus. Also, clicking an inactive window and making it the active window gives the window focus. The focus event also has a related method called focus(), which is covered in Chapter 11 and Chapter 14.

To see the focus event in action, you can create a text input box, which is one of the form elements that will enable you to give the element focus. The following example shows how to do this, as well as how to code a reminder alert to pop up when the viewer gives focus to the text box:

```
<form>
Enter Your Name:
<input type="text" onfocus="window.alert('Don\'t forget to capitalize!');">
</form>
```

The focus event in a text box

This code will give the viewer an alert before he or she can begin typing. The alert serves as a reminder to capitalize the name. Figure 10-2 shows the result of the preceding code in the browser when the viewer gives focus to the text box.

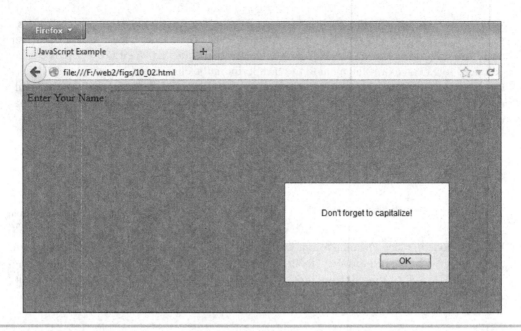

Figure 10-2 This alert pops up when the text box receives focus from the viewer.

The blur event occurs when the viewer takes the focus away from an element or a window. To take the focus off something, the viewer usually gives focus to something else. For instance, the viewer could move from one form element to another, or from one window to another. The blur event also has a related method called blur(), which will be covered in Chapter 11 and Chapter 14.

NOTE
The blur event is triggered only when the viewer gives focus to another area, which is the only way the browser will know the viewer released the focus from the first area. For example, when the viewer presses the ENTER key in an input field, the focus goes from the input field to the document window.

To see the blur event in action, the following example uses two text boxes: clicking the first text box gives it focus, and clicking the second text box invokes the blur event in the first text box.

```
<form>
Give this box focus:<br>
<input type="text" onblur="window.alert('Hey! Come back!');"><br>
Then give this box focus to blur the first one:<br>
<input type="text">
</form>
```

The onblur event in a text box

Clicking this text box after giving the focus to the first one will trigger the blur event on the first text box

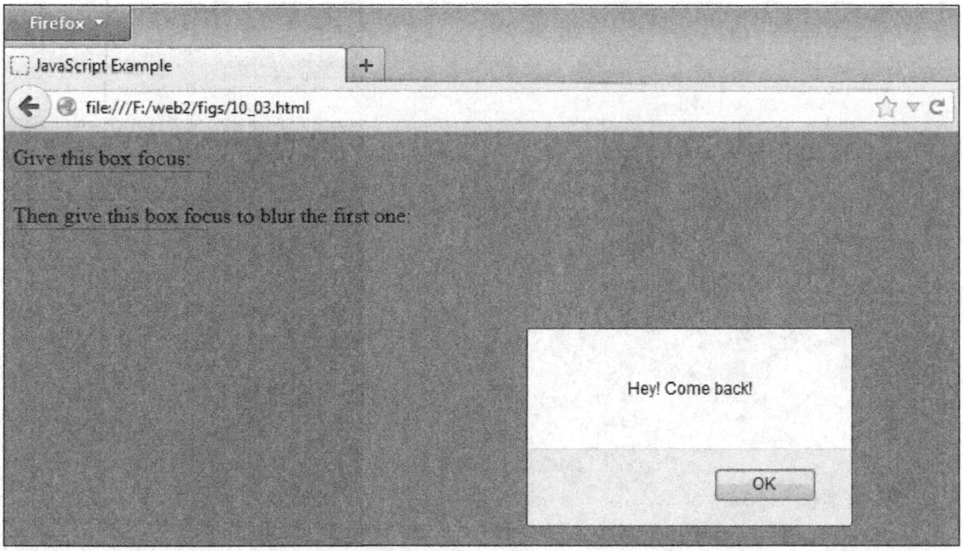

Figure 10-3 This alert pops up when the viewer takes the focus off a text box.

When viewers click the second text box, they get the alert from the first one telling them to come back.

Figure 10-3 shows the result of the preceding code when run in the browser. Notice that the focus is in the second text box when the alert pops up. By clicking the second text box, the viewer invoked the blur event in the first text box.

The Load and Unload Events

The load event occurs when a Web page finishes loading. If you want an alert to be shown when the page has finished loading, you could use the following code:

```
<body onload="window.alert('I\'m done loading now!');">
Text for the body of the page...
</body>
```

Notice that the onload event handler is added in the body tag

When the page has finished loading, viewers will get an alert that tells them it is finished. Figure 10-4 shows how the preceding code example would appear in the browser.

If you want to use the onload event handler in the script code rather than in the body tag, you could write this code into an external JavaScript file (save it as load_alert.js):

```
window.onload = function() {
  window.alert('I\'m done loading now!');
};
```

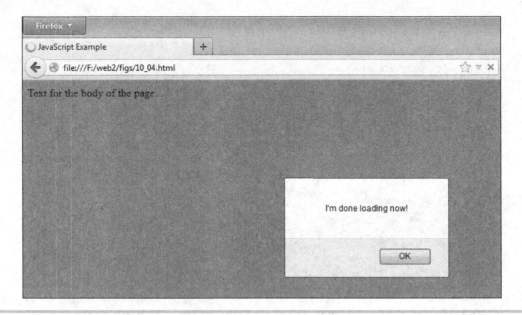

Figure 10-4 This is displayed in the browser window after the page has finished loading.

This will capture the load event for the current window (the window object will be explained in more detail in Chapter 11). You can now access all of the elements in the HTML code, and you can now remove the event handler from the opening <body> tag, as shown here:

```
<body>
<script type="text/javascript" src="load_alert.js"></script>
Text for the body of the page...
</body>
```

NOTE
Once the load event occurs, you can no longer use document.write() to write to the document.

The unload event occurs when a viewer leaves the current Web page. The viewer could leave by clicking a link, typing another address in the browser, or closing the window.

This event is known to annoy viewers, because it enables the site owner to do something while visitors are trying to move on to another page or another Web site (forcing them to wait). To have an alert pop up when the user leaves the page, you could write the following code:

```
<body onunload="window.alert('Be sure to come back, OK?');">
Other HTML code goes here...
</body>
```

The onunload event handler is added to the body tag

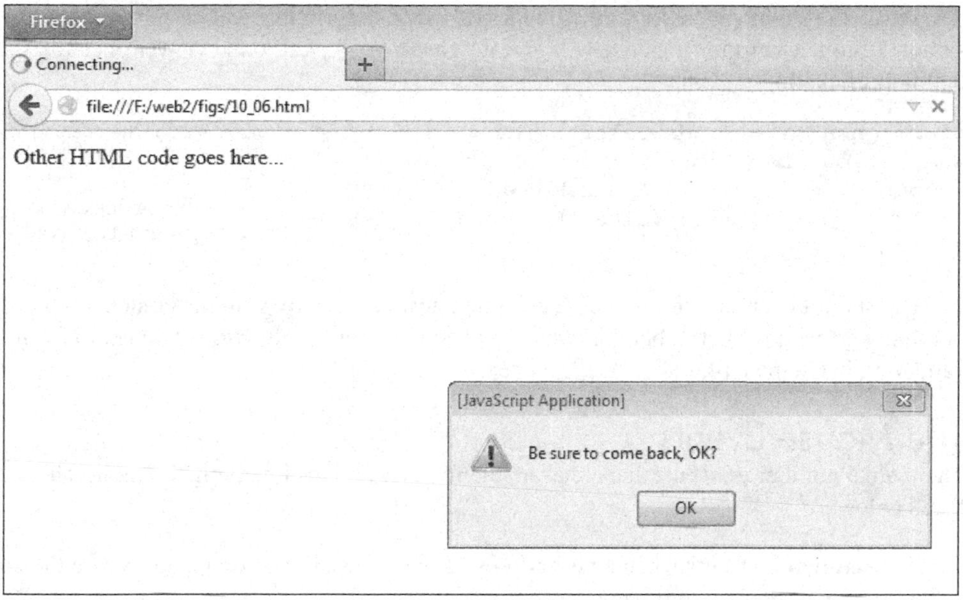

Figure 10-5   This alert pops up when the viewer tries to leave the page.

Figure 10-5 shows the result of the preceding script. As viewers try to leave the page that contains this script, an alert pops up telling them to be sure to come back. Of course, this could cause a viewer to become quite inconvenienced if it is used on an index page or on a number of pages within a Web site.

As with the onload event handler, you can use the onunload event handler in the script code rather than as an attribute of the body tag by using window.onunload.

Overall, be sure to think twice before using the unload event on a live page, because it will almost surely annoy most Web users.

TIP
If onunload does not work properly, you try using onbeforeunload if you need this functionality.

The Reset and Submit Events
Reset and submit events are used when one or more forms are included in a document. A form can have its contents reset or can be submitted for processing. These events allow you to program a response to one of these form actions.

The reset event occurs when a viewer uses a form reset button to reset the form fields in a form. The reset event also has a related method called reset(), which is covered in Chapter 14. The submit event occurs when the viewer submits a form. The submit event also has a related method called submit(), which will be covered in Chapter 14.

To see the submit event at work, you have to create a form that can be submitted with a submit button. The following code will give a "Thank You" alert to the viewer once the submit button is clicked:

```
<form onsubmit="window.alert('Thank You');">◄─onsubmit used in the opening form tag
What's your name?<br>
<input type="text" id="thename"><br>
<input type="submit" value="Submit Form">◄────The submit button triggers the
</form>                                        submit event when it is clicked
```

The submit event doesn't do you much good now (especially with the contents of the form not really going anywhere), but this event will become more useful when you get to form validation in Chapter 14.

The Mouse Events

There are a number of events that are available for user actions involving the mouse. These are listed below.

- **mousedown**   Occurs when a viewer presses the mouse button down but before the click is complete (the button has not yet been released).

- **mouseup**   Occurs when the viewer releases the mouse button after pressing it down.

- **mouseenter**   Occurs when a viewer moves the mouse cursor over an element (excluding child elements

- **mouseleave**   Occurs when a viewer moves the mouse cursor away from an element (excluding child elements)

- **mouseover**   Occurs when a viewer moves the mouse cursor over an element

- **mouseout**   Occurs when a viewer moves the mouse cursor away from an element

- **mousemove**   Occurs when the viewer moves the mouse cursor

- **mousewheel**   Occurs when the viewer scrolls the mouse wheel up or down

An example of using a mouse event can be shown by creating a text link. When you add the onmouseover event handler to the link, you have the option to perform JavaScript commands when the viewer passes the cursor over the link. Thus, if you want an alert to pop up when the viewer moves the mouse over a link, you could code something like the following:

```
<a href="http://www.pageresource.com"
 onmouseover="window.alert('I told you not to try to click me!');">◄─┐
Don't Try Clicking Me!</a>                                            │
                                    The onmouseover event handler in a link tag
```

This time the visitor doesn't even get to click the link before being greeted with an alert. Keep in mind that a script like this could annoy your visitors if it is overused. Figure 10-6 shows the result of this script in a browser. The alert pops up as soon as the mouse cursor moves over the link.

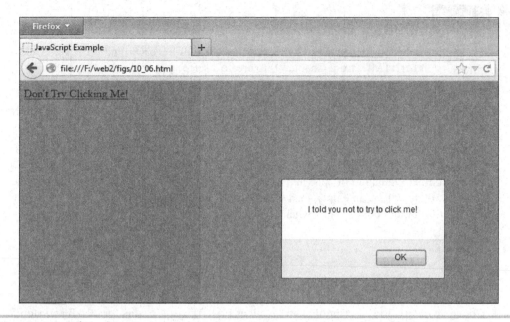

Figure 10-6 This alert pops up when the mouse cursor moves over the link.

Since there is no need to click the link for something to happen, the browser won't try to follow the link afterward. In fact, with this script in place, it is impossible to click the link at all because the alert keeps popping up when you move your mouse over to click it!

The Keyboard Events

Keyboard events occur when the user interacts with a Web page using the keyboard. These allow you to react to each phase of a key being pressed and released by the viewer. The keyboard events are listed here:

- **keydown** Occurs when the viewer presses down a key on the keyboard.

- **keypress** Occurs when a viewer presses down a key on the keyboard and the corresponding character is typed. This occurs between the keydown and the keyup events.

- **keyup** Occurs when the viewer lets go of a key on the keyboard, releasing the key.

For example, if you wanted to send an alert each time a character was typed into a text box, you could use the following code:

```
<input type="text" id="typing" onkeyup="alert('You typed a character!');">
```

This would remind the viewer each time a character is typed into the text box. This can get quite annoying after a couple of characters are typed, but once you learn about the event object later in this chapter, you will learn how to find out what key was pressed, which will give you more flexibility with the keyboard events.

Try This 10-1   Focus and Blur

pr10_1.html
prjs10_1.js

In this project, you will use your knowledge of the focus and blur events and innerHTML (from Chapter 9) to create a script that will remind a user what to type into a text box.

Step by Step

1. Create an HTML page and save it as pr10_1.html. Add the necessary script tags to point to an external JavaScript file named prjs10_1.js. Add code so that there is a text box for a phone number with an id of "pn" and a text area for an address. Beside the phone number text box, there will be an empty span tag with an id of "reminder". The body section of the HTML file should look like this when complete:

```
<form>
Phone Number:
<input type="text" id="pn"> <span id="reminder"></span><br><br>
<textarea></textarea>
</form>
```

2. Create an external JavaScript file and save it as prjs10_1.js. Use this for step 3 and step 5.

3. Get the "pn" and "reminder" elements by their ids and assign them to the variables pn and rm, respectively.

4. When pn receives focus, change the innerHTML of rm to the text "Format: 123-456-7890". When pn is blurred, change the innerHTML of rm to an empty string ("").

5. The JavaScript file should look like this when complete:

```
var pn = document.getElementById("pn"),
    rm = document.getElementById("reminder");
pn.onfocus = function() {
  rm.innerHTML = "Format: 123-456-7890";
};
pn.onblur = function() {
  rm.innerHTML = "";
};
```

6. Save the HTML and JavaScript files, and load the HTML page in your browser. Click inside the text box and a reminder message should appear next to it. Click the text area afterward to blur the text box and make the message disappear.

Try This Summary

In this project, you used your new skills, the focus and blur events, to create a script that could help a user fill out a form.

Ask the Expert

Q: **Why are there so many events?**

A: There are so many things that a viewer (or the browser itself) can do while on a Web page that you end up with a bunch of possible events.

Q: **Do I need to memorize all of these events?**

A: You probably only need to memorize them if you are taking a test, or you are doing this for a job and need to know things quickly, or if you just like knowing the events off the top of your head; otherwise, you can just refer to Table 10-1 in this chapter if you are not sure which event needs to be used.

Q: **Will I be using every single event in this book while doing the projects in this book?**

A: Since this book is a beginner's guide, you will not get to the point where you use every single event.

Other Ways to Register Events

Up to this point, you have been using what are called DOM Level 0 event handlers (onclick, onmouseover, and so on). There are two other methods for registering events in addition to the method you have used: addEventListener() and attachEvent(). These are called DOM Level 2 event handlers, and they offer the ability to attach multiple events to elements, whereas the DOM 0 method only allows one event to be registered on any given element. For example, suppose you had the following JavaScript code:

```
var mydiv = document.getElementById("mydiv");
mydiv.onclick = function() {
  alert("First Click!");
}
mydiv.onclick = function() {
  alert("Second Click!");
}
```

In this case, the second instance of assigning the onclick event handler to the mydiv element will overwrite the first one, so only the "Second Click!" alert will be displayed when a click occurs. DOM Level 2 event handlers allow you to avoid this issue.

The addEventListener() Method

The addEventListener() method is the standard from W3C, and is currently supported in all the most recent browsers (Internet Explorer needs to be version 9+). It allows you to specify an event, a function to execute for the event, and a value of true or false depending on how you want the event handler function to be executed in the capturing (true) or bubbling (false) phase. The general format looks like this:

```
element.addEventListener("event_type", function_name, true_or_false);
```

Thus, if you want to create a linked input button as you did earlier in this chapter, you could adjust the JavaScript code to look like this:

```
var web_page1 = "http://www.yahoo.com";
var b1 = document.getElementById("btn1");
b1.addEventListener("click", function() {
  window.location = web_page1;
}, false);
```

Notice that rather than using the event handler, this method uses the name of the event (instead of onclick, you simply use click). Also, this method will accept a function name or a function expression to handle the event (as shown previously).

Removing an Event

To remove an event, you would use the removeEventListener() method:

```
element.removeEventListener("event_type", function_name, true_or_false);
```

Note that if a function expression is used in the addEventListener() method, the event registration cannot be removed (the function expressions will be seen as two different arguments, even if they use exactly the same code). If there is a chance you will need to remove the event later, it is best to use a separate function and use the function name as the second argument in both method calls. An example of this is shown here:

```
var web_page1 = "http://www.yahoo.com",
    b1 = document.getElementById("btn1");
function go_to_site() {
  window.location = web_page1;          The function is defined
}
b1.addEventListener("click", go_to_site, false);    The event listener is added
b1.removeEventListener("click", go_to_site, false);  The event listener is removed
```

Since this is the standard method for registering events in modern browsers, you will use this method of event registration for the remainder of this book.

Capturing and Bubbling Phases

When you have elements inside other elements that both have the same event type registered to them, which event occurs first will depend on whether the capturing or bubbling phase is used to register the events. If capturing is used, then the outermost element's event occurs first and the innermost element's event will occur last. If bubbling is used, the opposite is the case. It is most common to use the bubble phase, since it has the greatest browser compatibility.

The attachEvent() Method

The attachEvent() method works in a similar way to addEventListener(). However, it only works with event bubbling and does not currently (as of the time of this writing) have a way to use event capturing. It is used like this:

```
element.attachEvent(event_handler, function_name);
```

Thus, if you want to use the same script you have been using, you could write it like this:

```
var web_page1 = "http://www.yahoo.com";
var b1 = document.getElementById("btn1");
b1.attachEvent(onclick, function() { window.location = web_page1; } );
```

Notice that this method does use the name of the event handler (onclick). Also, it does not have the third option; it just uses event bubbling.

To remove an event, you would use the detachEvent() method:

```
element.detachEvent(event_handler, function_name);
```

Browser Support

The attachEvent() method of event registration is the one that is used in Internet Explorer versions prior to version 9 (addEventListener() is unavailable, but DOM Level 0 registration is available). If you need to support prior versions of Internet Explorer, you will want to use a function that allows you to handle events using the method that is available to each browser. If needed, you can find one at http://dean.edwards.name/weblog/2005/10/add-event2/ or you can use a JavaScript library such as jQuery (discussed later in this book) to assist with event registration.

The Event Object

When an event occurs, an object named *event* is created, which stores information about the event. This information can be used by your script to help it perform the required actions. For example, a keyboard event will have information about the key that was pressed stored in the event object. This allows you to program different responses when different keys are pressed.

The event object works a little differently in Internet Explorer (prior to version 9), so you will first take a look at how to use the event object with all browsers that support it.

DOM and Internet Explorer: DOM Level 0 Registration

In most browsers, the event object is accessed by using the name *event*. It can be passed as the lone argument to a function that handles the event, as in the following DOM Level 0 code:

```
var b1 = document.getElementById("btn1");
b1.onclick = function(event) {
  alert("The " + event.type + " event started this!");
};
```

Notice that the argument *event* is passed to the event listener. The *type* property of the event object (which returns the type of event) is then used to display an alert to the viewer, which will let it be known that the click event is what caused the function to run.

Internet Explorer, however, uses *window.event* to access the event object, which means the DOM Level 0 event handler would use the following code:

```
var b1 = document.getElementById("btn1");
b1.onclick = function() {
  alert("The " + window.event.type + " event started this!");
};
```

With DOM Level 0 functions, the event object can be implemented cross-browser by assigning the needed value, based on what the browser supports, to a variable, as in the following code:

```
var b1 = document.getElementById("btn1");
b1.onclick = function(event) {
  var e = event || window.event;
  alert("The " + e.type + " event started this!");
};
```

Notice that the variable is assigned the event object if it is available, or the window.event object if not. The use of the logical OR (||) allows you to provide a preferred value if it is available, or to set another (default) value if not. Now that the variable e will hold the proper value cross-browser, it can be used to alert the event type.

Using event with Modern Event Registration

When using addEventListener() or attachEvent(), the event object is accessible via *event*. This allows you to use the event object as expected. For addEventListener(), you could use the following code:

```
var b1 = document.getElementById("btn1");
b1.addEventListener("click", function(event) {
  alert("The " + event.type + " event started this!");
}, false);
```

For attachEvent(), you could use the following code:

```
var b1 = document.getElementById("btn1");
b1.attachEvent(onclick, function(event) {
  alert("The " + event.type + " event started this!");
});
```

Support for older browsers, if needed, can be achieved using the DOM Level 0 method. Again, you can refer to the resources mentioned in the "The attachEvent() Method" section earlier in the chapter, as they have been coded to handle the various event registration models.

Properties and Methods

You have already seen the type property, but the event object also has other properties and methods that are useful, which are listed in Table 10-2.

Property/Method	Description
bubbles	Whether or not the event bubbles
cancelable	Whether or not the default action of the event can be canceled
cancelBubble	Cancels event bubbling when set to false (Internet Explorer)
currentTarget	The element that is currently handling the event
defaultPrevented	Whether or not preventDefault() has been called
detail	Additional information about the event
eventPhase	The phase in which the event handler was called: 1 = capturing, 2 = at target, 3 = bubbling
preventDefault()	Prevents the default action of the event from occurring
returnValue	Prevents the default action of the event from occurring (Internet Explorer)
srcElement	The element that is the target of the event (Internet Explorer)
stopImmediatePropagation()	Ends all capturing and bubbling on the event, and stops other event handlers from being called
stopPropagation()	Ends all capturing and bubbling on the event
target	The element that is the target of the event
trusted	Whether or not the event was initiated by the browser or the programmer
type	The event type (for example, click, mouseover, and so on)
view	The window object where the event happened

Table 10-2   The Properties and Methods of the event Object

As you will notice, some of the listed properties work with Internet Explorer (prior to version 9), while the others will work with other modern browsers. Since most modern browsers (including Internet Explorer 9 and above) support the standard DOM Level 2 event registration model, you will use this method through the remainder of this book. Notes will be added for cases where you may need to know how to perform a task in Internet Explorer prior to version 9.

Preventing the Default Action

You will recall that when using the DOM Level 0 registration, preventing the default action on a link was achieved using a return statement (return false). However, you can do this without the need to return immediately by using the preventDefault() method of the event object.

For example, the following code can now be used to prevent a link click from loading the specified page:

```
var nlink = document.getElementById("notlink");
nlink.addEventListener("click", function(event) {
  event.preventDefault();
  alert("This link doesn't go anywhere!");
  // Further Code...
}, false);
```

As you can see, you can continue handling the event, rather than using a return statement to leave the function.

NOTE

When using Internet Explorer prior to version 9, you can use the returnValue property. Setting its value to false (for example, window.event.returnValue = false;) will do the same thing as preventDefault().

Event Information

Some events, such as keyboard events, have additional properties that are not shown in the table (which are available to all events).

For example, when a keyboard event occurs, the key code of the key that was pressed is stored in event.keyCode, which allows you to determine which key was pressed. This can be used by your script to react only when a particular key is pressed. For example, you could use this code:

```
var text = document.getElementById("textbox1");
text.addEventListener("keyup", function(event) {
  if (event.keyCode === 80) {
    alert("Please do not press the p key!");
  }
}, false);
```

This will alert the viewer that you do not want the p key to be pressed, since 80 is the key code for the "p" key on the keyboard. You can see more on key codes at: http://protocolsofmatrix .blogspot.com/2007/09/javascript-keycode-reference-table-for.html

Try This 10-2   Using addEventListener()

```
pr10_2.html
pr10js10_2.js
```

In this project, you will use addEventListener to register a mouseover and mouseout event on a piece of text.

Step by Step

1. Create an HTML page and save it as pr10_2.html. Add code so that it links to an external JavaScript file named prjs10_2.js. The body section of the HTML code should look like this:

```
<p>
This is very <span id="int">interesting</span>!
</p>
```

2. Create a JavaScript file and save it as prjs10_2.js. Use it for step 3.

3. When the mouse is moved over the "int" span, change the color to #FF0000. When the mouse moves away, change the color to #000000. When complete, the JavaScript file should look like this:

```
var int = document.getElementById("int");
int.addEventListener("mouseover", function() {
  int.style.color = "#FF0000";
}, false);
int.addEventListener("mouseout", function() {
  int.style.color = "#000000";
}, false);
```

4. Save the JavaScript file and open the HTML file in your browser. Move the mouse over the text and off the text to change colors.

Try This Summary

In this project, you used your skills with event handlers and addEventListener() to change the color of text when the mouse moves over or away from it.

Creating Scripts Using Event Handlers

Now that you have tackled the long list of event handlers and the event object, it's time to have a little fun. In this section, you are going to learn how to do things other than sending alerts.

Show Hidden Content

For this script, create an HTML file with the following code inside the body section and save it as news.html.

```
<div>
<strong>Breaking News Story!!!!!!</strong>
<a href="story.html" id="morelink">More...</a>
</div>
<div id="morediv">
Today, there was a major development in a story that
we have been covering here at my site. We will post
later with further details. Hurry back!
</div>
<script type="text/javascript" src="news.js"></script>
```

Here, you have a "breaking news story" headline. A link (with an id of morelink) is placed so that when clicked, it will display the content of the story. Below this, you have a div (with an id of morediv) that contains the content of the story. At the moment, it is perfectly visible, since no CSS or JavaScript has been applied to change it. Your goal is to hide this content initially, and then display it when the user activates the link.

Next, create a JavaScript file and save it as news.js. The first thing you will want to do is to define some variables that will grab the two needed elements: the morelink and morediv elements.

```
var mlink = document.getElementById("morelink"),
    mdiv = document.getElementById("morediv");
```

These are now assigned as objects to the mlink and mdiv variables. Next, you will need to add an event listener that will allow you to show or hide the mdiv element when the mlink element is clicked, as in the following code:

```
mlink.addEventListener("click", function(event) {
    event.preventDefault();
    mdiv.style.display = (mdiv.style.display === "none") ? "block" :
"none";
}, false);
```

Notice that the event object is passed as an argument, allowing preventDefault to be used. The display property of the mdiv element is changed to "block" if it is "none", or to "none" if it is anything other than "none" (for example, when it has been set to "block" from a previous change).

Now everything is set for the click event, except that you need to hide the mdiv element for the initial page display. This could be done in CSS, but here you will use JavaScript to simply set its display style to "none":

```
mdiv.style.display = "none";
```

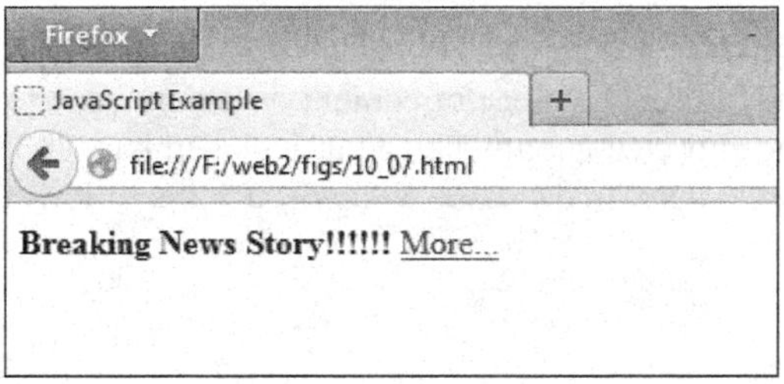

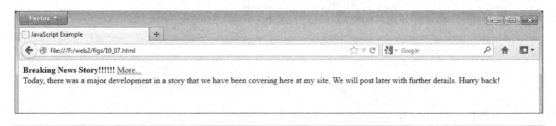

Figure 10-7   The initial view of the page, with only the headline and link displayed

The full code for the JavaScript file now looks like this:

```
var mlink = document.getElementById("morelink"),
    mdiv = document.getElementById("morediv");
mlink.addEventListener("click", function(event) {
  event.preventDefault();
  mdiv.style.display = (mdiv.style.display === "none") ? "block" :
"none";
}, false);
mdiv.style.display = "none";
```

Save the JavaScript file and open the HTML file in a Web browser. You should see the headline and the link, with no additional content. Figure 10-7 shows what the initial page should look like.

Click the link. The story content should now display below the headline and link. Clicking again should hide the story, which you probably will want to do after reading a teaser headline that simply leads to another teaser telling you to check back soon! Figure 10-8 shows the result of clicking the link to display the content.

Figure 10-8   Once the link is clicked, the content is displayed.

Change Content

Instead of showing and hiding one piece of content, you may want to give the viewer several options and display the chosen content when a particular link is clicked. To do this, you will first need an HTML document. In this case, you will use the following HTML and save the file as technews.html.

```
<!doctype HTML>
<html>
<head>
<title>Selected Tech News</title>
<link rel="stylesheet" type="text/css" href="technews.css">
</head>
<div class="wrapper">
  <div class="headline">Nick Delivers Crushing Defeat to John</div>
  <div id="top_story_nav" class="story_nav">
    <a href="#sumdiv" id="sumlink">Summary</a>
    <a href="#statsdiv" id="statslink">Stats</a>
    <a href="#comdiv" id="comlink">Comments</a>
  </div>
  <div id="sumdiv" class="spart">
Earlier today, we attended a JavaScript programming competition, where
we watched a first round showdown between Nick and John. In the beginning,
it looked like this might be a close battle, but Nick got the upper hand
quickly and never looked back.
<p>John started writing some strange code and put everything into the
global scope, while Nick was busy building objects, using inheritance,
and optimizing his code until he had a very slick, clean application.
John's app, on the other hand, just seemed clunky and buggy in comparison.</p>
<p>Perhaps it was an off day for John, but now he can sit back and watch as
the remaining coders go toe to toe. We will write up another report once
we see the next showdown!</p>
  </div>
  <div id="statsdiv" class="spart">
App. Loading Speed: Nick 0.002 ms, John 3043.231 ms
<p>Globals: Nick 1, John 137</p>
<p>JS File Size: Nick 0.5K, John 1.2 MB</p>
<p>Final Score: Nick 15298, John: 12</p>
  </div>
  <div id="comdiv" class="spart">


H3110W0rlD: Is it any wonder John lost with all of those globals?
Really, John? REALLY?
<p>Anne: I saw this coming. Honestly, Nick is just better.</p>
<p>Paul: John, I know the challenge had to do with balloons, but to even
be in this competition you should know better than to overwrite the pop()
method on the Array prototype! Wow!</p>
<p>Sup3rCod3r: This was a schooling! I hope John learns from this...</p>
<p>Con5pir@cy: I think the competition is rigged... can't you all see it?</p>
<p>Doug: @Conspir@cy or whatever- See what? It looked to me like one was
```

```
just a better programmer than the other. John actually used this line:
while (1 == true) { alert('True!'); } ! The judges had to reboot!</p>
<p>Christie: Yikes! How did John fall into that trap?!</p>
<p>Z25S11OO: Has the video been posted yet? I've gotta see this! lol!</p>
</div>
</div>
<script type="text/javascript" src="technews.js"></script>
</body>
</html>
```

Notice that there is a wrapper div, which you will use to contain all of the content. Within it, you have the headline div, the top_story_nav div, and the three content divs (sumdiv, statsdiv, and comdiv). The script will allow each link to display one of the content divs while hiding the other two. This way, the user can view one section at a time rather than scrolling to the desired section.

The next thing you will do is add a little style to the page by creating a CSS file. Include the following code and save the file as technews.css.

```
.wrapper { width:590px; height:390px; padding:5px; overflow:scroll;
           font-size:1em; font-family:Verdana, sans-serif; }
.headline { font-weight:bold; font-size:1.8em; font-family:Arial,
            sans-serif; background-color:#6699CC; text-align:center; }
.story_nav { margin:0 0 10px 0; padding:2px; background-color:#DDD;
            word-spacing:20px; text-align:center; }
.spart { margin-bottom:10px; }
```

This defines the size of the wrapper div, which will be 600×400 pixels when the padding is included. It allows content that is longer to be scrolled by the user within the wrapper. The other styles provide some color, margins, padding, and spacing for the other elements. You can of course adjust these to fit your preferences.

Finally, you will need to create the JavaScript file. Include the following code and save the file as technews.js.

```
var slinks = [document.getElementById("sumlink"),
              document.getElementById("statslink"),
              document.getElementById("comlink")],
    sdivs = [document.getElementById("sumdiv"),
             document.getElementById("statsdiv"),
             document.getElementById("comdiv")];
function change_div(count) {
  slinks[count].addEventListener("click", function(event) {
    event.preventDefault();
    sdivs[count].style.display = "block";
    for (var j = 0; j < sdivs.length; j++) {
      if (j === count) {
        continue;
      }
```

```
    else {
      sdivs[j].style.display = "none";
    }
  }
}
}, false);
}
for (var i = 0; i < slinks.length; i++) {
  change_div(i);
}
sdivs[1].style.display = "none";
sdivs[2].style.display = "none";
```

The three links correspond to the three content divs, and so the elements from both sets are placed into arrays (slinks and sdivs). The change_link() function will be explained shortly, but first notice the for loop after the function. This cycles through the slinks array and calls the change_div() function for each link, passing the value of i along as an argument. This argument will be used to register the click event for each element and to change the appropriate content when each link is clicked.

The change_div() function takes in the passed count variable from the for loop as an argument. The first time through the loop, change_div will be sent a value of 0, the second time a value of 1, and so on. Since the links and content divs are in arrays, this allows you to use the count value to access the desired elements. The function begins by using addEventListener(). The listener is added to the link element found in the slinks array at index *count*. In other words, slinks[0] will be accessed when count is 0. This accesses the first link element, since the value of slinks[0] is document.getElementById("sumlink"). Since this loop is run three times, the event listener will be added with the count values of 0, 1, and 2.

The event listener function first prevents the default action. Then, depending on the link that was clicked, the corresponding div element in the sdivs array is displayed by setting its style display to "block". A loop is used to hide the remaining two div elements. Notice that if the value of j is equal to the count value (the element being shown), then it is skipped so that the element currently being shown remains visible.

Finally, at the end of the script, you will see that the statsdiv and comdiv elements are hidden. This initializes the page with the sumdiv element still visible by default while the other two content divs are hidden. Figure 10-9 shows the initial display of the page when viewed in a browser.

Clicking on the "Stats" link will show the statistics (makes statsdiv visible and the others hidden). Figure 10-10 shows the result of clicking the "Stats" link.

Finally, clicking the "Comments" link will display all of the comments that were directed at me for my embarrassing showing at that programming competition! Figure 10-11 shows the comments being displayed.

This script combines many of the techniques you have learned (events, loops, arrays, and more). The arrays and loops were particularly helpful here as they kept you from typing three versions of addEventListener() with each value hard-coded into the event registration and function. When working with events, it is often helpful to have these handy ways of typing less code.

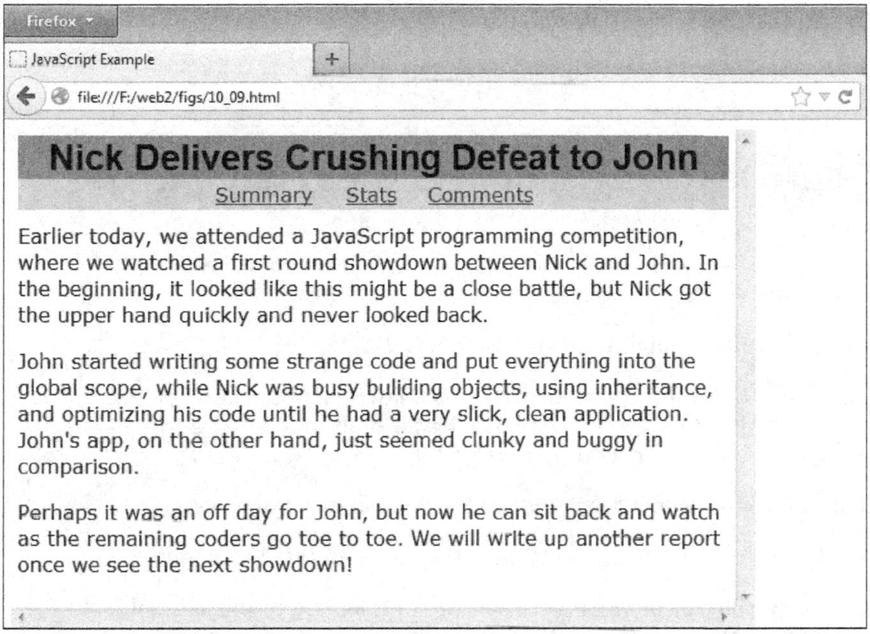

Figure 10-9 The initial display. Notice the links available for the user to click.

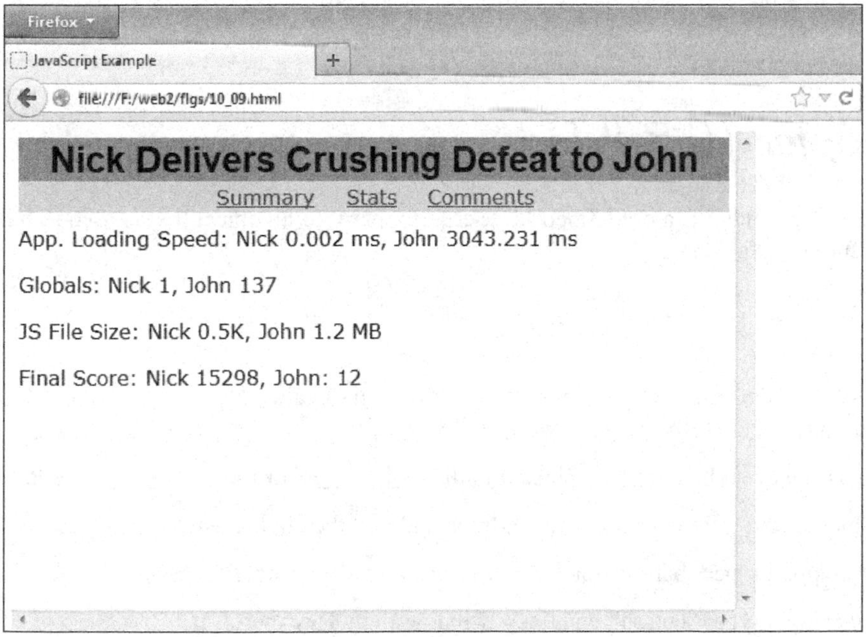

Figure 10-10 The result of clicking on the "Stats" link

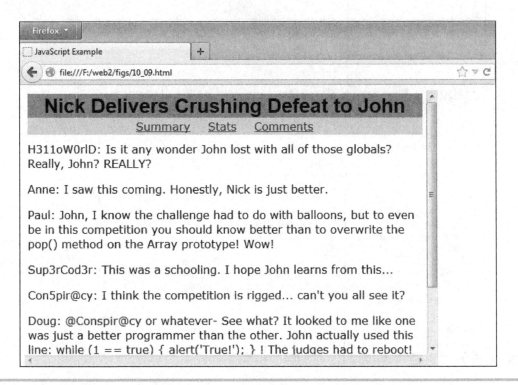

Figure 10-11 The comments display when the "Comments" link is clicked.

✓ Chapter 10 Self Test

1. An event handler is a predefined JavaScript property of an object that is used to handle an event on a Web page.

   A. True

   B. False

2. Event handlers are useful because they enable you to gain _____ to the _____ that may occur on the page.

3. To use an event handler, you place it in the _____ or the _____ code.

4. Which of the following correctly codes an alert on the click event?

   A. <input type="button" onclick="window.alert("Hey there!");">

   B. <input type="button" onClick="window.alert('Hey there!');">

    C. <input type="button" onclick="window.alert('Hey there!');">

    D. <input type="button" onChange="window.alert("Hey there!");">

5. The _____ event occurs when a Web page has finished loading.

6. A mouseover event occurs when:

    A. The viewer clicks the mouse while the cursor is over a button.

    B. The viewer moves the mouse cursor away from a link.

    C. The viewer clicks a link, linked image, or linked area of an image map.

    D. The viewer moves the mouse cursor over an element on the page.

7. A mouseout event occurs when a viewer clicks an element on the page.

    A. True

    B. False

8. The _____ event occurs when the viewer leaves the current Web page.

9. The blur event is the opposite of the _____ event.

10. The _____ object contains properties and methods for an event.

11. The _____ property of an event contains the type of event that occurred.

12. The submit event occurs when the viewer _____ a _____ on a Web page.

13. The keydown event occurs when a viewer presses down a key on the keyboard.

    A. True

    B. False

14. In Internet Explorer prior to version 9, the event object can be accessed by using _____.

15. The _____ method and the _____ method are two new ways to register events.

Chapter 11

Window Object

Key Skills & Concepts

- Window: The Global Object

- Using the Properties of the Window Object

- Using the Methods of the Window Object

- Opening New Windows

The JavaScript window object gives you access to more properties and methods you can use in your scripts, and serves as the global JavaScript object in Web browsers. In this chapter, you will see how it works as the global object, and learn to use a number of its properties and methods.

Window: The Global Object

The window object is created for each window that appears in the browser. A window can be the main window, a frame set or individual frame, a tab, or even a new window created with JavaScript. It differs from the document object in that the window object contains the document object (as well as many other objects, such as history, navigator, and so on). It serves as the global object for JavaScript in Web browsers.

Because it is the global object, any global variables or functions that are defined are also properties and methods of the window object. For example, consider the following code:

```
var fruit = "lemon";
function show_msg(fruit) {
  alert("You have a " + fruit);
}
```

Here, there is a global variable named fruit and a global function named show_msg(). Both of these can now be called as part of the window object, as in the following code:

```
alert(window.fruit); // Alerts "lemon"
window.show_msg(fruit); // Alerts "You have a lemon"
```

Because window is the global object, it is not necessary to use window.fruit or window.show_msg(). The window is assumed, so these can simply be shortened to fruit and show_msg(), which is the way you have already been using them.

For this same reason, objects, properties, and methods within the window object do not need to reference the fact that they are within the window object. As you recall, you have used window.alert(), which can be called by simply using alert(). This also works for objects such as the history object, which are within the window object. Instead of typing window.history.back(), you can type history.back() to access the back() method of the history object.

Using the Properties of the Window Object

To begin your study of the window object, take a look at its properties that you can use, which are listed and described in Table 11-1. Some of the properties are discussed in more detail following Table 11-1.

Property	Description
applicationCache	A reference to the application cache, which stores data on the user's system so that the script can be used offline
closed	Holds the value based on whether or not a window has been closed
console	The console object, which allows access to the debugging console if available
content	The content object representing the primary content window
defaultStatus	Defines the default message displayed in the status bar
document	The document object (discussed in Chapter 9)
frameElement	Returns the element where the window is located (such as iframe) or null if it is the top-level window
frames	An array of the frames in the window
history	Object that provides information on the browser history of the current window (discussed in Chapter 8)
innerHeight	Returns the height, in pixels, of the viewable area within the window
innerWidth	Returns the width, in pixels, of the viewable area within the window
length	Returns the number of frames in the current window
location	Returns or sets the current URL of the window
localStorage	An object that can be used to store data locally
name	Enables a window to be named
navigator	The navigator object (discussed in Chapter 8)
opener	Refers to the window that opened another window
outerHeight	Returns the width, in pixels, of the entire browser window
outerWidth	Returns the width, in pixels, of the entire browser window
parent	Refers to the frame set that contains the current frame
screen	Contains properties to gather information about the screen, including availHeight, availWidth, colorDepth, height, pixelDepth, and width
self	Provides another way to reference the current window
status	Enables a message to be placed in the status bar; overrides defaultStatus
top	A reference to the top window containing a frame, frame set, or nested frame set
window	A reference to the current window

Table 11-1 Properties of the Window Object

NOTE

As in previous chapters, some of the properties and methods listed in this chapter are not cross-browser or only work in modern browsers. For more information and more complete listings, see: https://developer.mozilla.org/en/DOM/window and http://msdn.microsoft.com/en-us/library/ms535873(VS.85).aspx.

The closed Property

The closed property is used to check whether or not a window has been closed by the viewer. The way it is normally used is with the name of a window, followed by the closed property, such as in the following example:

```
if (windowname.closed) {
   JavaScript Statements
}
```

You would replace the *windowname* part with the name of the window that you wish to check. This is often a new window that you opened with JavaScript; you will see how to name a new window later in the chapter in the section "The open() Method."

You can also use the closed property inside a new window to check whether the window that opened it has been closed. To do that, you would use closed after the opener property (discussed in "The opener Property" section), as in the following example:

```
if (window.opener.closed) {
   JavaScript Statements
}
```

This use of the closed property is really handy if you choose to create a new window that enables the viewer to navigate the main window through links in the new window.

The frames Property

The frames property is an array containing each frame within a frame set. It is often used to gain access to the properties of the various frames on a page. You can find the number of frames in a window by using the frames.length property.

The innerWidth and innerHeight Properties

The innerWidth and innerHeight properties hold values for width and height of the area of the window in view (the browser window minus scroll bars, menu bars, toolbars, and so on). These properties work in modern browsers, but not in Internet Explorer prior to version 9 (document.body.clientWidth and document.body.clientHeight can be used for older versions of Internet Explorer).

So, if you wanted to obtain the width of the content area you have available to your script, you could use the following code:

```
var mywin_width = window.innerWidth;
```

Of course, if you want to use different HTML code for the browser depending on the available innerWidth of the window, you could use the following code:

```
var mywin_width = window.innerWidth;
var cont = document.getElementById("container");
cont.style.width = (mywin_width >= 800) ? "750px" : "90%";
```

The value of the innerWidth property is assigned to the mywin_width variable

The conditional operator is used for a quick if-else statement to assign the width of the div element based on the available space

A "container" div is accessed, which will not have a set width and will house the code to be provided via innerHTML

This will determine whether the viewer has 800 pixels of viewable width. If so, the width of the div element will be set to 750 pixels. Otherwise, the div element will have a safer width of 90 percent so that it can display more easily for smaller screens.

The length Property

The length property tells you how many frames are in a window, just like the window.frames .length property. This just shortens it to window.length (which is often more convenient when you are writing code).

The location Property

The location property holds the current URL of the window. You can use the location property to cause instant redirection of the browser to a new page (if your page has moved to a new location, for instance). However, make sure that you don't use this technique on a page that is listed with search engines that do not allow quick redirection, because they may drop the page from their listings.

If a page has been moved and you want to redirect the viewer without any delay, you could just give the location property a new value, as shown in the following code:

```
<body>
<script type="text/javascript">
  window.location = "newpage.html";
</script>
Lacking JavaScript? Click the link below for the new page then!<br>
<a href="newpage.html">New Page</a>
</body>
```

This sends the viewer away instantly, since no action needs to take place to set this in motion

This would just take the viewer to the local URL newpage.html. A standard link was included for browsers without JavaScript. Otherwise, the preceding code would load a blank page for those viewers and nothing would happen.

NOTE

Instant redirection is best suited for testing purposes on pages that are not indexed by a search engine, since the rules on redirection vary from one search engine to the next.

The name Property

The name property holds the name of the current window and also enables you to give a window a name. If you want to give the main window a name, you could assign the name you want to use to this property. The following code shows an example of this:

```
window.name = "cool_window";          The window is given its own name
alert("This window is named " + window.name);          The name of the window
                                                         is alerted to the viewer
```

The script gives the window a name, and then alerts the name to the viewer. Figure 11-1 shows the result of this script in a browser.

The opener Property

The opener property is used to reference the window that opened the current window. This is often used in new windows opened using the open() method, which you will see later in the chapter in the section "The open() Method." By using the opener property in a new window, you could detect whether the main window has been closed using the closed property you learned about earlier. The following example shows how you could perform this test:

```
if (window.opener.closed)
```

This adds the closed property after the opener property to check whether the window that opened the current window has been closed. This is helpful if you want to perform an action in the

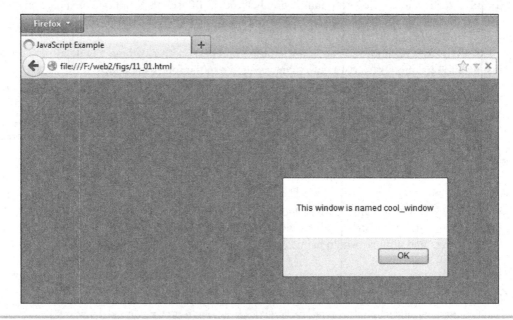

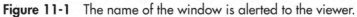

Figure 11-1   The name of the window is alerted to the viewer.

main window through the new one, because you could check to see that it still exists before doing anything.

The parent, self, and top Properties

The parent property is only used when there are frames on a page. It enables you to access the parent frame set of the current frame. This is helpful when you wish to change a property in one frame from another frame.

The self property is another way of saying "the current window" in JavaScript. It is used like the window object and can access the properties of the current window just like the window object. The self property is useful if you have a lot of windows with names and want to be sure you are using a property of the current window and not one in another named window.

The top property is used to access the top window out of all the frame sets (which could be nested). This is a little different from the parent property, which only goes to the top of the current frame set. The top property instead goes all the way to the top window, even if the window contains nested frame sets.

The status and defaultStatus Properties

The status property contains the value of the text set in the status bar of the window. Changing this property overrides the content of the status bar set with the defaultStatus property.

CAUTION

Modern browsers, by default, do not display status bar text altered by JavaScript, in order to keep unscrupulous Web sites from deceiving users with false link destinations in the status bar. Thus, the status and defaultStatus properties will not work unless browser settings are altered by the viewer. Since it is a security risk for the user to change browser settings to allow this, use of these properties is not recommended.

The defaultStatus property sets the text string that is displayed by default in the status bar when nothing has been assigned to the window.status property. A change of the window.status property overrides this setting, because it is only shown as the default. This property is often set in the load event to display a custom message when the viewer is not performing an action that would change the text in the status bar.

Try This 11-1   Use the location and innerWidth Properties

```
pr11_1.html
prjs11_1.js
```

This project enables you to practice using the location and innerWidth properties of the window object.

Step by Step

1. Create an HTML page, leaving the body section blank other than including a set of script tags to reference a JavaScript file named prjs11_1.js just before the closing </body> tag. Save the file as pr11_1.html.

(continued)

2. Create a JavaScript file and save it as prjs11_1.js. Use this file for steps 3–6.

3. Set a default value for a variable named mywin_width.

4. Assign the value of the window.innerWidth to mywin_width.

5. If the value of mywin_width is greater than or equal to 1000, send the viewer to the URL http://www.scripttheweb.com/js/. Otherwise, send the viewer to the URL http://www.scripttheweb.com/css/ (use the window.location property).

6. When complete, the JavaScript file should have the following code:

```
var my_win = window.innerWidth;
if (my_win >= 1000) {
  window.location = "http://www.scripttheweb.com/js/";
}
else {
  window.location = "http://www.scripttheweb.com/css/";
}
```

7. Save the JavaScript file and open the HTML file in your Web browser. Try changing the width and then reopening the page with the new width to see which Web page it gives you.

Try This Summary

In this project, you were able to use your knowledge of the location and innerWidth properties of the window object to create a script that will redirect a viewer based on the available width of the viewing area in the viewer's browser.

Using the Methods of the Window Object

Now that you know how to use the properties of the window object, you can move on to using window methods. Table 11-2 lists a number of the methods of the window object with a description of each, and particular methods are described in more detail next.

The alert(), prompt(), and confirm() Methods

The alert(), prompt(), and confirm() methods all bring up system dialogs that require the user to take an action. For example, the user may click OK to close an alert, or enter information into a text box when prompt() is used.

The alert() Method

You have used the alert() method extensively in earlier chapters in example scripts. This pops up a message to the viewer, and the viewer has to click an OK button to continue.

Method	Description
addEventListener()	Registers an event on the window
alert()	Pops up an alert to the viewer, who must then click OK to proceed
back()	Takes the window back one item in its history list
blur()	Removes the focus from a window
clearInterval()	Cancels the action of a setInterval() method call
clearTimeout()	Cancels the action of a setTimeout() method call
close()	Closes a browser window
confirm()	Displays a confirmation dialog box to the viewer, who must then click OK or Cancel to proceed
escape()	Converts special characters in a string to hexadecimal characters
find()	Enables the viewer to launch the Find utility in the browser to find text on a page
focus()	Gives the focus to a window
forward()	Takes the window one item forward in its history list
home()	Sends the viewer to the home page the viewer has set in the Web browser settings
moveBy()	Moves a window by certain pixel values that are sent as parameters
moveTo()	Moves the top-left corner of the window to the coordinates sent as parameters
open()	Opens a new browser window
print()	Prints the contents of the window
prompt()	Pops up a prompt dialog box asking the viewer to input information
resizeBy()	Resizes a window by moving the bottom-right corner by certain pixel values that are sent as parameters
resizeTo()	Resizes an entire window to the height and width that are sent as parameters
scrollBy()	Scrolls the viewing area of a window by certain pixel values that are sent as parameters
scrollTo()	Scrolls the viewing area of the window to the specified coordinates that are sent as parameters
setInterval()	Calls a function each time a certain amount of time passes
setTimeout()	Calls a function once after a certain amount of time has passed
stop()	Stops the window from loading its content
unescape()	Converts an escaped string back to its normal characters

Table 11-2   Methods of the Window Object

The prompt() Method

The prompt() method is used to prompt the viewer to enter information. You used this method in Chapter 6 to allow the user to enter data into the prompt dialog.

The confirm() Method

The confirm() method can be used to give the viewer a chance to confirm or cancel an action. This method returns a Boolean value of true or false, so its result is often assigned to a variable when it is used. So, if you wanted to assign the result to a variable named is_sure and ask the question "Are you sure?", you could use the following code:

```
var is_sure = confirm("Are you sure?");
```

Figure 11-2 shows a sample confirm dialog box that is displayed by the preceding code. Notice the two buttons the viewer can choose to click: OK and Cancel. If the viewer clicks OK, the method returns true. If the user clicks Cancel, the method returns false. Note that as with alert() and prompt(), you cannot change the value of the text in the buttons, since this is determined by the user's browser and operating system.

As a real example of this method, suppose that you want to create a link to another page, but you want to be sure the viewer wants to leave before being sent away. You could use the confirm dialog box to find out whether or not the viewer wishes to leave the page.

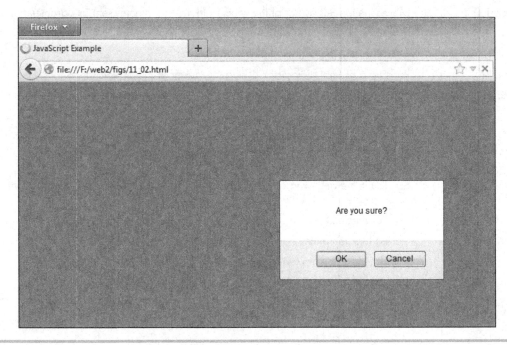

Figure 11-2 An example of a confirm dialog box

The following code shows how you can get a confirmation from the viewer and react appropriately. First, the HTML code:

```
<body>
<a href="http://www.google.com" id="search_link">Go Searching</a>
</body>
```

Next, use JavaScript to confirm whether the user really wants to leave when the link is clicked:

```
var s_link = document.getElementById("search_link");
s_link.addEventListener("click", function(event) {
  var is_sure = confirm("Are you sure you want to leave?");
    if (is_sure === false) {
      event.preventDefault();
      alert("OK. You can stay here.");
    }
}, false);
```

The function confirms whether or not the viewer wants to leave

Notice that if OK is clicked and the confirm() method returns true, the viewer is taken to the linked Web site. If cancel is clicked and the confirm() method returns false, an alert is sent to the viewer and the function returns false so that the link won't be followed by the browser (you can also simply omit the alert and just have nothing happen after Cancel is clicked, by using only the return false statement).

Figure 11-3 shows the browser window after the link is clicked on the page. The confirm dialog box with your "Are you sure you want to leave?" message pops up on the screen.

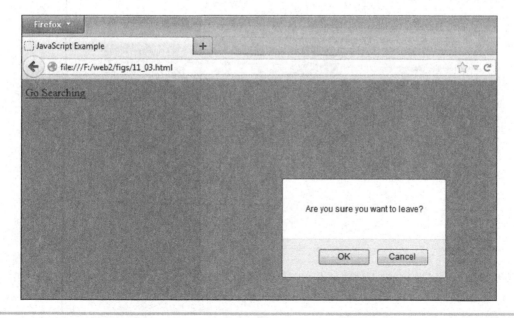

Figure 11-3 A confirm dialog box pops up when the button is clicked.

The find() Method

You can use the find() method to let the viewer find a certain bit of text on your page. It tells the browser to use its built-in Find utility and enables the viewer to type in the text to look for on the page.

For example, if you wanted to create a button for viewers to click when they want to find something on your page, you could use the following code:

```
<form>
<input type="button" value="Click to Find Text" onclick="find();">
</form>
```

This pops up the Find dialog box in the browser and enables the viewer to search for text within the page. Figure 11-4 shows the result of this script when it is added to an HTML document.

This functionality is useful if you have a really long page and want the viewer to be able to find things more quickly by searching the page.

The home() Method

The home() method is used to send the viewer to the home page the viewer has set in the Web browser settings. For instance, you could use it to offer viewers a button that will take them to their selected home page when clicked, as in the following code (at the time of this writing this method worked in Mozilla Firefox and Opera but did not work in Microsoft Internet Explorer):

```
<form>
<input type="button" value="Go Home!" onclick="home();">
</form>
```

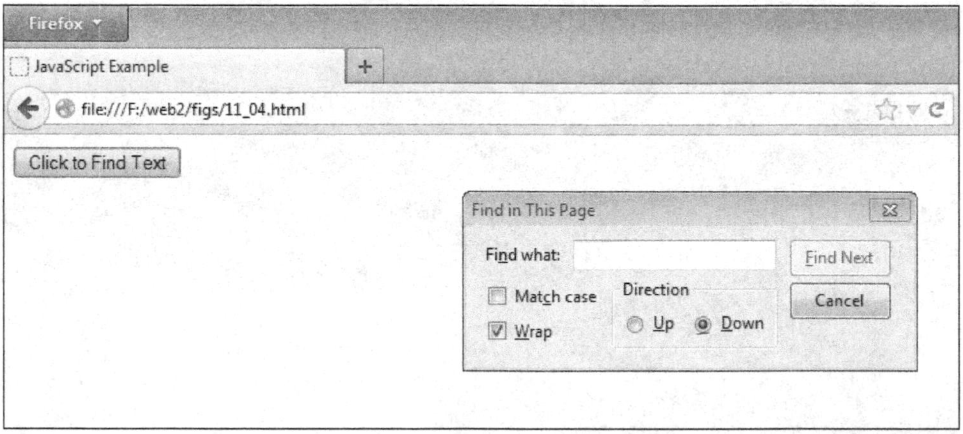

Figure 11-4 A Find dialog box pops up, enabling the viewer to search for text on the page.

The print() Method

The print() method enables the viewer to print the current window. When this method is called, it should open the viewer's Print dialog box so that the viewer can set the printer settings to print the document.

To use it, you could create a button that enables the viewer to print the page they are viewing:

```
<form>
<input type="button" value="Click to Print Page" onclick="print();">
</form>
```

This code should open the user's Print dialog box when the user clicks the Click to Print Page button. Figure 11-5 shows the result of running this script in a browser. This dialog box may appear differently for different viewers, depending on the browser and printer being used.

The setInterval() and clearInterval() Methods

The setInterval() method is used to execute a JavaScript function repeatedly at a set interval. The following is the general syntax for using this method:

```
setInterval(function() { // function content }, time);
```

You replace *function content* with the code you wish to repeat. You then replace *time* with the time (in milliseconds) you want to wait before each repetition of the function.

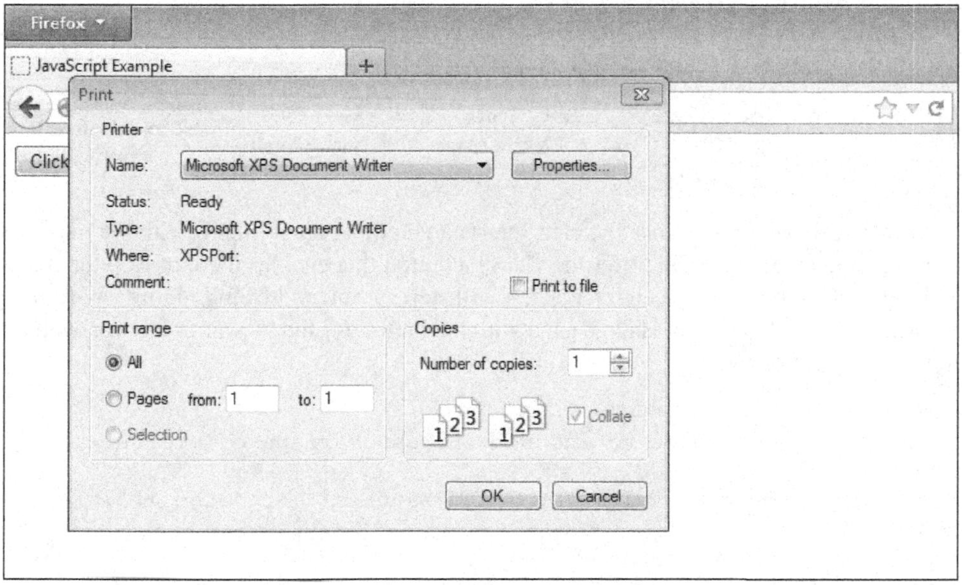

Figure 11-5   The viewer's print options pop up when the print button is clicked.

So, if you really wanted to annoy your viewers, you could use this method to pop up an alert every 10 seconds (10,000 milliseconds) once the page is viewed. You could do this by placing the following script inside the HTML of a document:

```
setInterval(function() {
  alert("Am I bothering you yet?");
}, 10000);
```

An interval is set for 10,000 milliseconds (10 seconds)

This, of course, could become quite annoying. The less time set in the interval, the more annoying it would become. Luckily, the ten-second interval gives you enough time to leave the page before another alert pops up.

CAUTION
You may come across scripts that provide a string value in place of the function as the first argument to setInterval() or setTimeout(). This requires JavaScript to evaluate the string as JavaScript code using the eval() function, the use of which is discouraged in most cases.

To end the barrage of alerts from the previous script, you could use the clearInterval() method. The following is the general syntax for using this method:

```
clearInterval(name);
```

You must replace *name* with a variable name that has been assigned to the setInterval() method call you want to clear. The problem is, you didn't assign your setInterval() call to a variable name in the previous example.

In order to clear it, you need to adjust your code. The following code is updated and assigns the setInterval() call to a variable name:

```
var madness = setInterval(function() {
        alert("Am I bothering you yet?");
      }, 10000);
```

The method call is assigned to a variable for later reference

You now have a way to use the clearInterval() method, by calling it with the madness variable as the parameter. So, offer the visitor a button that enables them to stop the madness. As long as it is clicked between intervals, it will stop the interval from running any further. The following code gives you an HTML page with the button for the viewer to click as well as the updated JavaScript code:

```
<body>
Click the button below to end the endless barrage of alerts.<br>
<form>
<input type="button" value="Stop the Madness!" id="stop_it">
</form>
</body>
```

The updated JavaScript code:

```
var madness = setInterval(function() {                    The method is assigned to a
            alert("Am I bothering you yet?");             variable for later reference
            }, 10000);
var stop_it = document.getElementById("stop_it");
stop_it.addEventListener("click", function(event) {
    event.preventDefault();
    clearInterval(madness);                               This method refers to the first method through
}, false);                                                the variable name to cancel its action
```

Now the viewer can stop the alerts by clicking the Stop the Madness button.

You will see in later chapters that this method can be handy for clocks and other things that need to be updated at regular intervals on the page.

The setTimeout() and clearTimeout() Methods

The setTimeout() method enables you to execute a JavaScript function after a certain amount of time has passed. It differs from the setInterval() method because it is only executed once (unless it is put inside a loop of some sort). The general syntax is the same as that of the setInterval() method.

If you want to have only a single alert pop up after ten seconds and not repeat, you could use the following code:

```
var theguest = setTimeout(function() {                    The timeout is set, and
            alert("Sign my guest book NOW!");             also set to a variable
            }, 10000);
```

This would send the viewer an alert after ten seconds, demanding that the guest book be signed immediately.

The clearTimeout() method enables you to cancel a setTimeout() call if you call the clearTimeout() method before the time expires from the setTimeout() call. The general syntax is the same as that of the clearInterval() method: you use a variable name as a parameter so that it knows which setTimeout() call to cancel.

So, if you want to give viewers a chance to avoid getting an alert, you could add a button for them to click within ten seconds. If the button is clicked in time, the setTimeout() call is canceled and no alert pops up. The following is the example code:

```
<body>
Click the button below within 10 seconds to avoid an alert
message.<br>
<form>
<input type="button" value="No Alert for Me!" id="noalert">
</form>
</body>
```

The JavaScript code:

```
var  theguest = setTimeout(function() {
            alert("Sign my guest book NOW!");
        }, 10000);
noalert.addEventListener("click", function(event) {
    clearTimeout(theguest);
}, false);
```

The timeout is set, and set to a variable for later reference

The timeout is cleared, stopping it from occurring if the button is clicked in time

If the button is clicked in time, the viewer avoids receiving an alert about signing the guest book.

Ask the Expert

Q: There are way too many properties and methods here! How am I ever going to remember all of these?

A: As you begin using them with more frequency, they will be easier to remember. I remember the ones I use more often better than those I don't use much. If you do a lot of coding, it is good to keep a reference handy, such as this book, in case you need to check the details of a property or method now and then. I keep a bunch of books and bookmarks to reference Web sites on hand.

Q: Will I be making window remote controls any time soon?

A: A new window that changes properties (like the location property) in the main window is a "remote control." Though remote controls are not discussed in this book, there are scripts for these at free script sites on the Web. For now, you want to be sure to master the coding that you need to create and manipulate a regular new window. Note that working between two windows could cause security concerns.

Q: Will I be using the timed methods like setTimeout() and setInterval() often?

A: You will have a use for them when you need to build time-dependent scripts such as clocks, slide shows, or Dynamic HTML (DHTML) animations.

Try This 11-2 Use the setTimeout() and confirm() Methods

pr11_2.html
prjs11_2.js

This project enables you to practice using some of the window methods. You will have the browser wait a certain number of seconds and then ask the viewer to confirm whether to stay at the page or move on to an Internet search site.

Step by Step

1. Create an HTML page, with the following code in the body section, and save it as pr11_2.html:

```
<body>
<h1>Breaking News!</h1>
<ul>
<li>An interesting point here...</li>
<li>A very interesting point here...</li>
<li>An incredibly interesting point here...</li>
</ul>
<script type="text/javascript" src="prjs11_2.js"></script>
</body>
```

2. Create a JavaScript file and save it as prjs11_2.js. Use it for steps 3–4.

3. After 20 seconds, have a confirm box display to the viewer asking them if they want to continue using this Web page. If so, do nothing. If not, send them to the URL http://www .google.com to search for more news.

4. When complete, the JavaScript file should have the following code:

```
setTimeout(function() {
        var stay = confirm("Do you want to continue using this Web site?");
        if (stay === false) {
            window.location = "http://www.google.com";
        }
}, 20000);
```

5. Save the JavaScript file and open the HTML file in a Web browser. After 20 seconds, you should see a confirm box.

Try This Summary

In this project, you were able to use your knowledge of the properties and methods of the window object to create a timed, interactive script. This allowed you to give the viewer a choice as to whether to stay at the current Web page or move on to an Internet search site.

The Main Window and New Windows

The main browser window is often protected from being moved, resized, closed, or otherwise manipulated for security reasons (for example, to keep a new window from being opened to a bad site while closing the main window, or to keep microscopic pop-up windows from being opened). Thus, many of the methods mentioned in the previous section, such as resizeTo() or close(), don't do anything when called in the main window or display a warning to the viewer.

In a number of cases, browsers will allow you more control of a pop-up window. The following sections will discuss how to open new windows and how to customize their look and placement on the screen.

CAUTION

Even when using new windows, some browsers will not allow some methods such as resizeTo() or moveTo() to be used. In addition, browsers may simply open the new window content in a new tab or in the main browser window rather than a pop-up window. It is not recommended that pop-up windows be used on Web sites (though they can have uses for local applications or in other JavaScript environments).

The Tale of Pop-up Windows

At one time, pop-up windows were used quite often on Web sites. While there were legitimate advertisements that used pop-up windows, there were also a number of deceptive advertisements that were designed to "trick" the user into clicking them by appearing to be an alert or some other type of system message. Also, the fact that numerous new windows could be opened, could be hidden from the user's view, or could be otherwise manipulated caused many security concerns.

These concerns were addressed in a number of ways:

- Pop-up windows can only be opened in modern browsers when the user performs a click or a key press.

- Pop-up windows may only be opened in the main window or as a tab in the main browser window in some browsers.

- In most cases, the status bar and/or location bar will be displayed regardless of the information provided to design the pop-up window.

- A pop-up window may not be permitted to be resized or moved in some browsers.

- Certain code may be effective working locally, but will not work when the page is online.

For these reasons, it is typically not a good idea to use pop-up windows on Web sites. With that said, the following information is provided should you need to work with new windows in a local environment or a more secure platform.

NOTE

Instead of using new windows, you may wish to use a dialog that overlays the current window, but is not a pop-up window. For more information on this, see jqueryui.com/dialog.

Opening New Windows

The open() method enables you to open a new window with JavaScript. This method is typically used with three arguments, as shown in the following example:

```
window.open("URL","name","attribute1=value,attribute2=value");
```

The first argument, "URL", is replaced with the URL of the HTML document that is to be opened in the new window. The "name" parameter is replaced with the name you wish to give to the window. The third parameter enables you to add attributes for the new window. These attributes are set by using "yes", "no", or a numeric value on the right side of the equal sign. Notice that each time an attribute is set with a value, there is a comma before the next one and no spaces in between.

If you want to open a window with the features of the current window, you could do so by leaving off the third argument with the attributes. The following example would open a new window with a local URL of newpage.html and a name of my_window; it will have the same features as the window that opened it:

```
window.open("newpage.html","my_window");
```

Attributes

If you want to include window features, you need to learn some of the attributes that you can use with the windows. Table 11-3 lists attributes that you can use as part of the third argument in the open() method.

Any "yes or no" attribute not defined will default to "no" if it is not overridden by the browser. For example, the location, menubar, and status attributes will likely default to "yes" in most modern browsers and will be unchangeable. Any numeric values not defined will use the settings of the browser being used. These also may be unchangeable or may only allow certain values. For instance, the new window may be required to have left and top coordinates that place it in a viewable area on the screen, and the width and height may have minimum values that you cannot go under in order to keep a window from being too small to be noticed by the user.

To open a basic new window with a width of 400 pixels and a height of 300 pixels, you can use the following code:

```
window.open("newpage.html","my_window","width=400,height=300");
```

Aside from the width and height, this window will open with the default values for the other attributes, which will depend on the browser being used by the viewer.

Attribute Name	Possible Values	Function
width	number	Defines the width of the new window in pixels
height	number	Defines the height of the new window in pixels
top	number	Defines the top coordinate of the new window
left	number	Defines the left coordinate of the new window
fullscreen	yes, no, 1, 0	Defines whether or not the new window should open maximized. Only works in Internet Explorer
location	yes, no, 1, 0	Defines whether or not the new window has a location box to type in a new URL
menubar	yes, no, 1, 0	Defines whether or not the window has a menu bar (File menu, Edit menu, and so on)
resizable	yes, no, 1, 0	Defines whether or not the viewer is allowed to resize the new window
scrollbars	yes, no, 1, 0	Defines whether or not the new window has scroll bars if the contents of the window are larger than the window's size
status	yes, no, 1, 0	Defines whether or not the new window has a status bar at the bottom
toolbar	yes, no, 1, 0	Defines whether or not the new window has a toolbar (Forward and Back buttons, Stop button, and so on)

Table 11-3   Standard Attributes for a New Window

To set the other attributes, you can assign them a value of "yes" or "no" depending on whether or not you want each feature. You may also use 1 for yes and 0 for no if you prefer, as they will have the same effect. So, if you want to have a 300×200 pixel window with a menu bar added (this adds the Forward, Back, Stop, and other similar buttons), you could use the following code:

```
window.open("newpage.html","cool","width=300,height=200,menubar=yes");
```

This gives you a new window with the contents of newpage.html, a name of "cool," dimensions of 300×200 pixels, and a menu bar.

You can add as many of the attributes as you want inside the quote marks of the third parameter by separating each one with a comma.

NOTE

Due to space limitations, a new window command may occasionally be on more than one line in the code in this book. Be sure that when you use the code, you put everything from window.open to the ending semicolon (;) on one line to avoid JavaScript errors.

The following example opens a window with most of the features mentioned in Table 11-3 (again, this takes up more than one line here, but when you enter it in your text editor, the code should go on a single line):

```
window.open("newpage.html","cool","width=300,height=200,top=0,left=0,
location=yes,menubar=yes,resizable=yes,scrollbars=yes,status=yes,
toolbar=yes");
```

If you want a viewable example, you need to make a page named newpage.html and create the code for the main page to include a window.open() command, as described next.

First, create the code for newpage.html (this is just a short page that has some text in it):

```
<body>
I am a new window! I am newer than that old window
 that opened me, so I am special. Ha, ha!
</body>
```

Now, create the main page (save as mainpage.html):

The link is given an id

```
<body>
Click the link below to open an arrogant new window ...<br>
<a href="newpage.html" id="nwin">New Page</a>
<script type="text/javascript" src="openwin.js"></script>
</body>
```

The external JavaScript is called

Finally, create the JavaScript code (save as openwin.js):

The link element is assigned to a variable

```
var nw_win =  document.getElementById("nwin");
nw_win.addEventListener("click", function(event) {
  event.preventDefault();
  window.open("newpage.html","cool","width=400,height=300,status=yes");
}, false);
```

The function opens the new window and prevents the default action of the link

When the link is clicked, it launches the new window with the contents of your newpage.html document. This window is 400×300 pixels and has a status bar at the bottom. Note that the event.preventDefault() method is added so that the newpage.html file will not also be opened in the main browser window when the link is clicked (if the viewer does not have JavaScript enabled, the link will work normally and open the newpage.html file in the same window).

Figure 11-6 shows the result of opening the main page in the browser and clicking the link to open the new window.

Closing New Windows

The close() method is used to close a window; however, unless your script has certain security rights, this method can only be used to close a window that you have opened using JavaScript. It cannot close the main window (though some browsers will offer the user the option to do so via a confirmation dialog).

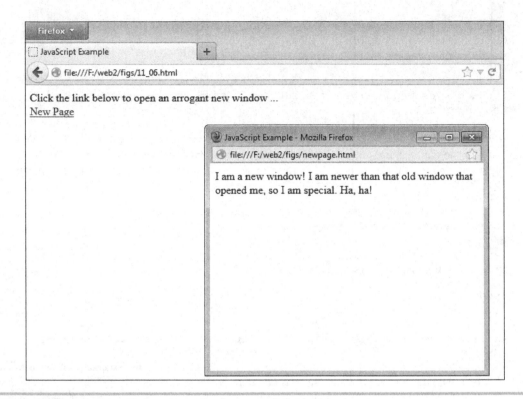

Figure 11-6 A new window is opened when a link is clicked.

To use the close() method, you could modify your newpage.html code to provide a button at the end of the text that enables the viewer to close the window by clicking it. So, you could change the code of newpage.html to look like the following code:

```
<body>
I am a new window! I am newer than that old window
 that opened me, so I am special. Ha, ha!
<form>
<input type="button" value="Close Window" onclick="window.close();">
</form>
</body>
```

The window is closed when the button is clicked

When the button is clicked now, the window.close() method is invoked and closes the window just like the standard Close button at the top right of a window. If you want to try it out, use the main page you used in the previous section and click the button to open the new window. It should offer the new button with the option to close the window, and it should close the window if you click the button.

If you prefer to close the new window from the main window, you can do so by assigning the open() method to a variable, which will provide a reference to the new window. You can then add another link that provides the option to close the window. You can modify mainpage.html to use the following code:

```
<body>
Click the link below to open an arrogant new window ...<br>
<a href="newpage.html" id="nwin">New Page</a>
<a href="mainpage.html" id="cwin">Close New Page</a>
<script type="text/javascript" src="openwin.js"></script>
</body>
```

A new link is added so that the new window can be closed

Next, you will need to alter the openwin.js file to use the following code:

```
var nw_win =  document.getElementById("nwin"),
    cs_win =  document.getElementById("cwin"),
    mywin = "";
nw_win.addEventListener("click", function(event) {
  event.preventDefault();
  mywin = window.open("newpage.html","cool","width=400,height=300,status=yes");
}, false);
cs_win.addEventListener("click", function(event) {
  event.preventDefault();
  mywin.close();
}, false);
```

New variables are added: cs_win to access the "Close New Page" link and mywin, which will be used later as a reference to the new window.

The open() method is assigned to the mywin variable

The window is closed

This allows the window to be both opened and closed via the main window.

Moving, Resizing, and Scrolling New Windows

The moveBy(), moveTo(), resizeBy(), resizeTo(), scrollBy(), and scrollTo() methods allow you to alter the window position, window size, or the beginning viewing position within the window. As with the close() method, browsers typically do not allow these methods to be used on the main window. However, they can often be used on windows created via JavaScript.

The moveBy() and moveTo() Methods

The moveBy() method can be used to move a new window to a new location on the screen. This moves a window by the number of pixels given as arguments in the method call. The following is the syntax for using this method:

```
moveBy(x-pixels, y-pixels);
```

You replace *x-pixels* with the number of pixels you want to move the window from left to right. So, if you want the window to move to the right, you enter a positive number. If you want it to move to the left, you enter a negative number.

You replace *y-pixels* with the number of pixels you want to move the window from top to bottom, with positive numbers pushing the window down and negative numbers pulling the window up.

For example, if you want to give the viewer the option to move the window by the number of pixels of your choice, you could again alter your code to handle this. For mainpage.html, use the following code:

```
<body>
Click the link below to open an arrogant new window ...<br>
<a href="newpage.html" id="nwin">New Page</a>
<a href="mainpage.html" id="awin">Alter New Page</a>  ←———————┐
<script type="text/javascript" src="openwin.js"></script>    │
</body>
```

The link offers an option to alter the new window

Next, use the following code for openwin.js:

```
var nw_win =  document.getElementById("nwin"),
    aw_win =  document.getElementById("awin"),
    mywin = "";
nw_win.addEventListener("click", function(event) {
  event.preventDefault();
  mywin = window.open("newpage.html","cool","width=400,height=300,status=yes");
}, false);
aw_win.addEventListener("click", function(event) {
  event.preventDefault();
  mywin.moveBy(50, 50);  ←——————————————————————————  The window is moved 50 pixels
  mywin.focus();  ←——————————— The window is placed back into    down and to the right
}, false);                      focus so that it can be seen
```

This moves the window 50 pixels to the right and 50 pixels down when the button is clicked. Notice that the focus() method is called after the move. When you click the link in the main window to move the new window, the new window goes out of focus (a blur event). The move still works, but you may not be able to see this if the main window is covering it (since it regains focus when the link is clicked). Placing the focus back on the new window will allow it to be seen in front of any other open windows. Likewise, the blur() method can be used to take a window out of focus, but browsers may disable this as a security feature to ensure that windows are not hidden via scripting. Figure 11-7 shows the initial position of the new window when it is opened from a button on the main page.

Figure 11-8 shows the window after the "Alter New Page" link is clicked. Notice that it has moved to the right and down by 50 pixels in each direction.

The way this works, the viewer could continue clicking the link and moving the window by another 50 pixels in both directions. The window just continues to move by the number of pixels it has been set to move by in the script. Most modern browsers will stop moving the window when the move would take part of the window out of the viewable area of the screen.

The moveTo() method is used to move a window to a specific destination on the screen based on the arguments given in the method call. The following is the general syntax for using this method:

```
window.moveTo(x-value, y-value);
```

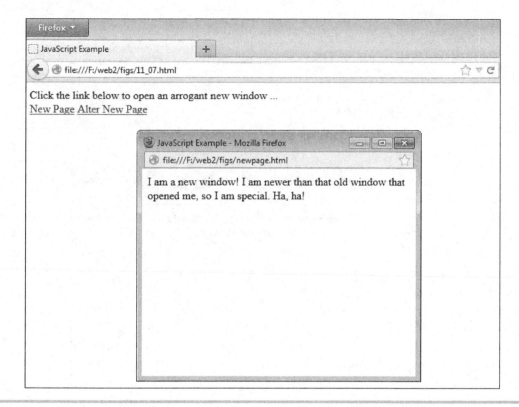

Figure 11-7 The new window in its initial position when it is opened

Here, you replace *x-value* with the number of pixels from the left of the screen where you want the window to be moved. For example, if you input 300, the window is moved 300 pixels from the left of the screen. You then replace *y-value* with the number of pixels from the top of the screen that you want the window to be moved.

As an example, alter your openwin.js code to use moveTo() instead of moveBy(), as in the following code:

```
var nw_win =  document.getElementById("nwin"),
    aw_win =  document.getElementById("awin"),
    mywin = "";
nw_win.addEventListener("click", function(event) {
  event.preventDefault();
  mywin = window.open("newpage.html","cool","width=400,height=300,status=yes");
}, false);
aw_win.addEventListener("click", function(event) {
  event.preventDefault();
  mywin.moveTo(50, 50);  ◄
  mywin.focus();
}, false);
```

The window will move to the coordinates (50,50) on the screen, which is 50 pixels from the left and 50 pixels from the top

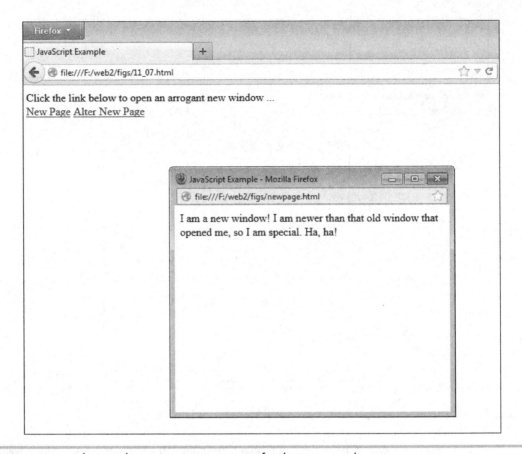

Figure 11-8 The window in its new position after being moved

This time the window will be moved to the coordinates (50,50) on the screen when the link is clicked.

To see that this works differently than the moveBy() method, try clicking the link again. Rather than making another move, it stays in the same place because it has already made it to its destination. If you manually move the new window, however, clicking the link again will move it back to its moveTo() coordinates.

Most modern browsers will not allow any part of the window to be moved off the screen. For example, a window moved to (–10, –10) will likely be moved to (0, 0) by the browser instead.

The resizeBy() and resizeTo() Methods

The resizeBy() method is used to resize a window by the number of pixels given in the arguments sent in the method call. To make the window larger, use positive numbers. To make it smaller, use negative numbers. For example, you could alter your openwin.js code to make the new window smaller when clicked, as in the following code:

```
var nw_win =  document.getElementById("nwin"),
    aw_win =  document.getElementById("awin"),
    mywin = "";
nw_win.addEventListener("click", function(event) {
  event.preventDefault();
  mywin = window.open("newpage.html","cool","width=400,height=300,status=yes");
}, false);
aw_win.addEventListener("click", function(event) {
  event.preventDefault();
  mywin.resizeBy(-100, -100); ◀─────────────  The negative numbers will
  mywin.focus();                               make the window smaller
}, false);
```

This code will make the window smaller by 100 pixels in width and height. Figure 11-9 shows how the new window looks when it is first opened, and Figure 11-10 shows how the new window looks after it has been resized.

As with moveTo(), clicking the link again will continue to resize it. Most modern browsers will stop resizing the window once it gets to a minimum allowable size for security reasons, and will stop once the window size reaches the maximum viewable area on the screen.

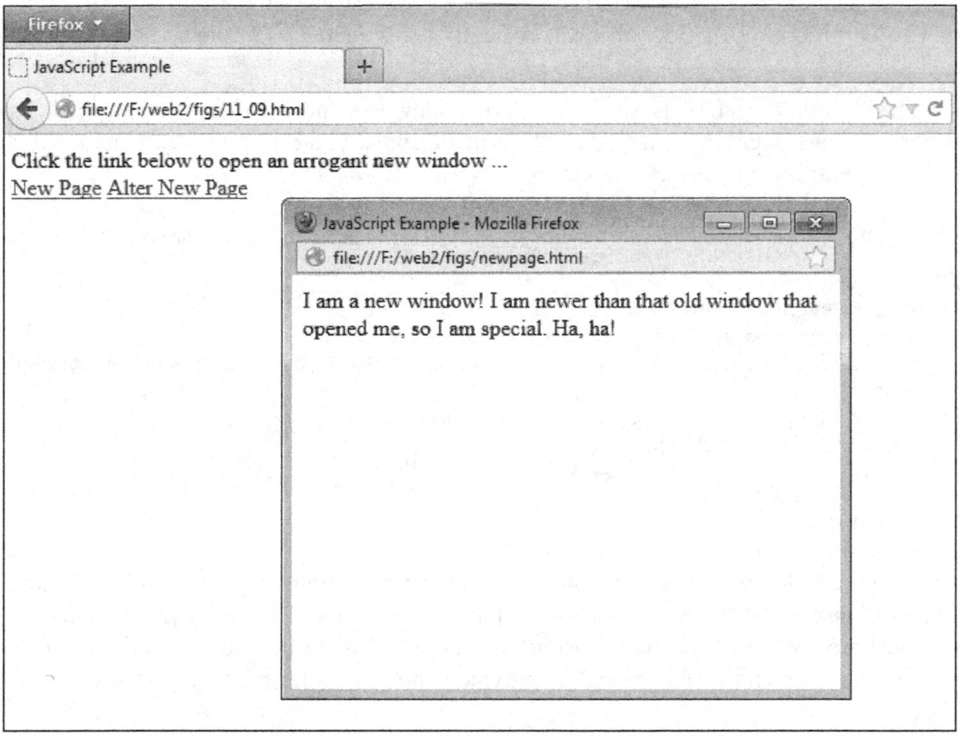

Figure 11-9 The new window when it is originally opened

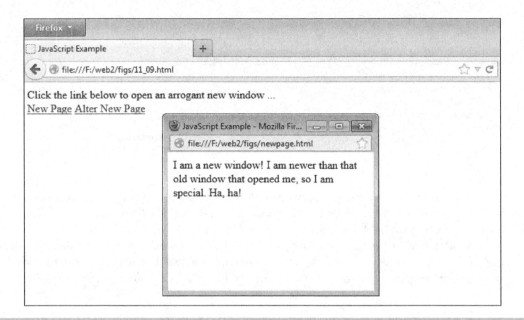

Figure 11-10 The new window after it is resized: it shrinks by 100 pixels in height and width.

The resizeTo() method is used to resize a window to a specific dimension in pixels based on the arguments sent in the method call. As an example, you can again alter your openwin.js file. Use the following code:

```
var nw_win =  document.getElementById("nwin"),
    aw_win =  document.getElementById("awin"),
    mywin = "";
nw_win.addEventListener("click", function(event) {
  event.preventDefault();
  mywin = window.open("newpage.html","cool","width=400,height=300,status=yes");
}, false);
aw_win.addEventListener("click", function(event) {
  event.preventDefault();
  mywin.resizeTo(400, 400); ◄─────────── The window is resized to be
  mywin.focus();                         400 pixels by 400 pixels
}, false);
```

Clicking the "Alter New Page" link in the main window will now resize the new window to 400 × 400 pixels. If the new dimensions will cause the window size to be greater than the viewable area of the screen, then most modern browsers will limit the size of the window to that viewable area rather than using the provided dimensions for security reasons.

The scrollBy() and ScrollTo() Methods

The scrollBy() method is used to scroll a window by the number of pixels given in the arguments sent in the method call. The scrollTo() method is used to scroll a window to a specific destination. The syntax and usage are the same as the other methods mentioned here, and will scroll the new window based on the numbers provided as arguments.

✓ Chapter 11 Self Test

1. A(n) _____ object is created for each browser window.

2. The closed property is used to check whether or not a window has been closed.

   A. True

   B. False

3. The _____ property returns the number of frames within a window.

4. The location property can cause instant redirection of the browser to a new page.

   A. True

   B. False

5. The _____ property holds the name of the current window and also allows you to give the window a name.

6. The calls to properties and methods of the window object can often be shortened because

   A. The window object is the global object for JavaScript in Web browsers.

   B. The window properties and methods are assumed to be part of the navigator object.

   C. There really is no window object.

   D. The browser assumes the window object is part of the document object.

7. The _____ property is another way of saying "the current window" in JavaScript.

8. Why would this code not work:

   ```
   onmouseover="window.status='Page 2'; return true;"
   ```

   A. It should work without a problem.

   B. The quote marks are not set correctly.

   C. Newer browsers do not allow the window status to be changed by default, so the user would need to change security settings in order for it to work.

   D. A change in the status property in a mouseover event must return false afterward.

9. What is the difference between the parent and top properties?

   A. The parent property goes to the top of the current frame set, while the top property goes to the top window of all frame sets on the page.

   B. The top property goes to the top of the current frame set, while the parent property goes to the top window of all frame sets on the page.

   C. The parent property goes to the top of the current frame set, while the top property goes to the top of the current frame.

   D. The parent property goes to the top of the outermost frame set, while the top property goes to the top window of all frame sets on the page.

10. The _____ method pops up a message to the viewer, and the viewer has to click an OK button to continue.

11. What value is returned by the confirm() method if the viewer clicks the OK button?

    A. true

    B. false

    C. "OK"

    D. 25

12. The _____ method enables the viewer to print the current window.

13. The prompt() method is used to _____ the viewer to enter information.

14. When setting the toolbar attribute as part of the third parameter in the open() method, what values may the attribute have?

    A. yes and no only

    B. 1 and 0 only

    C. yes, no, true, and untrue

    D. yes, no, 1, and 0

15. What is the difference between the setInterval() method and the setTimeout() method?

    A. The setTimeout() method is used when the viewer needs to take a break from reading, while setInterval() is used when the viewer needs no breaks.

    B. The setInterval() method is used to repeat a function at a set time interval, while setTimeout() executes a function only once after a set time delay.

    C. The setInterval() method flashes an advertisement across the screen at a set interval by default, while setTimeout() is ad-free.

    D. They both perform the same function.

Chapter 12

Math, Number, and Date Objects

Key Skills & Concepts

- Using the Math Object
- Understanding the Number Object
- Using the Date Object

In this chapter, you will learn about the JavaScript Math, Number, and Date objects, in that order. For each object, a short introduction is provided along with a description of why the object can be useful to you. Following that is a look at the various properties and methods that you can use for that object.

Using the Math Object

The Math object can be useful when you need to perform various calculations in your scripts. To begin, take a look at what the Math object is.

What Is the Math Object?

The Math object is a predefined JavaScript object. Like the other predefined objects you have studied in this book, the Math object gives you properties and methods to use. The Math object is used for mathematical purposes to give you the values of certain mathematical constants or to perform certain calculations or operations.

How the Math Object Is Useful

As mentioned, the Math object is useful when you need to make mathematical calculations in your scripts. For instance, if you need the value of pi for a calculation, the Math object gives you a property to use so you can get that value.

Also, if you need to find the square root of a number, a method of the Math object enables you to do this. Another thing this object provides is a way to generate random numbers in JavaScript, which you will find useful in certain scripts.

Properties

The Math object gives you a number of properties that can help you if you need to perform certain mathematical calculations. Table 12-1 lists the properties of the Math object, with the values of each.

As you can see in Table 12-1, all of the properties simply hold numeric values that can be useful in mathematical calculations. Because these are irrational numbers, the values listed are nonterminating and are thus approximations. Note that these properties are in "all-caps." This is because they are constant values, and the naming convention for such values is that they must be in all capital letters.

Property	Value
E	Value of Euler's constant (E), which is about 2.71828...
LN10	Value of the natural logarithm of 10, which is about 2.302585...
LN2	Value of the natural logarithm of 2, which is about 0.693147...
LOG10E	Value of the base 10 logarithm of E, which is about 0.43429...
LOG2E	Value of the base 2 logarithm of E, which is about 1.442695...
PI	Value of pi, often used with circles, which is about 3.14159...
SQRT2	Value of the square root of 2, which is about 1.4142...
SQRT1_2	Value of the square root of one half, which is about 0.7071...

Table 12-1   Properties of the Math Object

Using the Properties

The properties contain read-only values, which tend to be useful in particular types of calculations. For instance, if you want to find the area of a circle, you use the formula Area = pi*r^2. Knowing that, you could write an application to determine the area of a circle based on the radius input by a viewer. You could use the following code, starting with the HTML code:

```
<form id="getarea">
<label for="radius">Enter a radius:</label><br>
<input type="text" id="radius">
<input type="submit" value="Get the Area!">
</form>
```

Next, the JavaScript code:

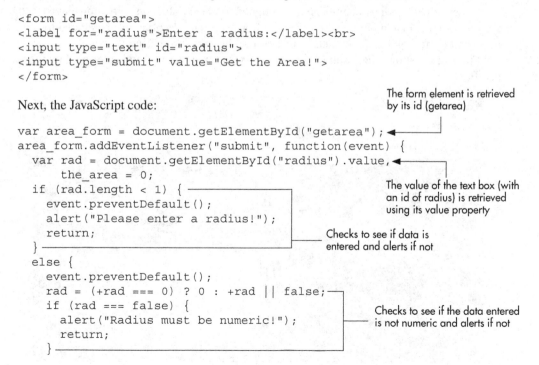

The form element is retrieved by its id (getarea)

The value of the text box (with an id of radius) is retrieved using its value property

Checks to see if data is entered and alerts if not

Checks to see if the data entered is not numeric and alerts if not

```
var area_form = document.getElementById("getarea");
area_form.addEventListener("submit", function(event) {
  var rad = document.getElementById("radius").value,
      the_area = 0;
  if (rad.length < 1) {
    event.preventDefault();
    alert("Please enter a radius!");
    return;
  }
  else {
    event.preventDefault();
    rad = (+rad === 0) ? 0 : +rad || false;
    if (rad === false) {
      alert("Radius must be numeric!");
      return;
    }
```

```
    the_area = Math.PI * (rad * rad);
    alert("The area is " + the_area + " square units. ");
  }
}, false);
```

Performs the calculation and displays the answer

This code first grabs the form element by its id (getarea) and assigns it to a variable named get_area. When the form is submitted, it grabs the value input in the text field for the radius and assigns it to a variable named rad.

Next, the code performs two checks. It checks that the length property of rad is not less than 1, to ensure that the viewer entered data into the field. If it is less than 1, the code gives an alert asking the viewer to enter the information. Next, it checks to see if the value of rad is not numeric. This is done by testing whether or not the value can be coerced into a numeric value using the unary plus operator (except for zero, which is specified so that it remains the numeric zero rather than being coerced to the Boolean value of false). If the number cannot be coerced, it is assigned a Boolean value of false. The if statement will then check the value of rad, and will send the viewer an alert saying that the radius must be numeric if it could not be coerced to a number.

Finally, if the data entered passes those tests, the calculation of the area of the circle is performed and assigned to a variable named the_area. Notice that for now you multiply the radius by itself to get the radius squared. When you get to the math methods in the next section, you will see that the method pow() may be used instead.

Once the calculation is complete and assigned to the variable, an alert is displayed to the viewer with the area in generic "square units." The script could of course be altered to suit your needs or to offer options (centimeters, inches, or other units of measure).

Figure 12-1 shows the result of running this script in a browser and entering 2 into the text field.

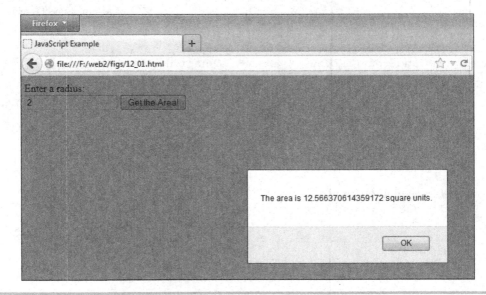

Figure 12-1 The area of the circle is displayed for the viewer.

Methods

The methods of the Math object enable you to perform certain calculations that can be helpful in your scripts. Table 12-2 lists various methods of the Math object and briefly describes the purpose of each. Each method is discussed in more detail in the following sections.

The Basic Methods

For the purpose of this book, "basic methods" are defined as the methods that take in a single number, do a simple calculation with it, and return a value. Grouping the methods in this way avoids the need to list each method with the same sort of example—it is not any sort of official organization of the methods, just a way to expedite this discussion.

Method	Purpose
abs()	Returns the absolute value of the number sent as an argument
acos()	Returns the arccosine of the number sent as an argument, in radians
asin()	Returns the arcsine of the number sent as an argument, in radians
atan()	Returns the arctangent of the number sent as an argument, in radians
atan2()	Returns the arctangent of the quotient of two numbers sent as arguments, in radians
ceil()	Returns the smallest integer greater than or equal to the number sent as an argument
cos()	Returns the cosine of the number sent as an argument, in radians
exp()	Returns the value of E to the power of the number sent to the method as an argument
floor()	Returns the largest integer less than or equal to the number sent as an argument
log()	Returns the natural logarithm of the number sent as an argument
max()	Returns the larger of the two numbers that are sent as arguments
min()	Returns the smaller of the two numbers that are sent as arguments
pow()	Returns the numeric value of the first argument raised to the power of the second argument
random()	Returns a random number between 0 and 1; does not require an argument
round()	Returns the value of the number sent as an argument rounded to the nearest integer
sin()	Returns the sine of the number sent as an argument, in radians
sqrt()	Returns the square root of the number sent as an argument
tan()	Returns the tangent of the number sent as an argument, in radians

Table 12-2 Methods of the Math Object

The following basic methods are the ones that work in generally the same way:

- abs()
- acos()
- asin()
- atan()
- cos()

- exp()
- log()
- sin()
- sqrt()
- tan()

Each of these basic methods takes a numeric value and sends back another value. Since the general usage is the same, this discussion uses sqrt() as an example of how the rest could be used to get their various values. If you need to know what type of value is returned from a different method, refer to Table 12-2 to see what each method does.

The easiest way to use the sqrt() method is to input a positive number as the argument to the method, as shown in the following example:

```
window.alert(Math.sqrt(4));
```

This alerts the value of the positive square root of 4, which is 2.

Instead of calculating a static number, you could get the user to input a number, and then send an alert to the user with the square root of the number input by the user. You could do this using the following code, starting with the HTML code:

```
<form id="getroot">
<label for="sr_num">Enter a (positive) number or zero:</label><br>
<input type="text" id="sr_num">
<input type="submit" value="Get a Square Root">
</form>
```

Next, the JavaScript code:

The value of the text box (with an id of sr_num) is retrieved

```
var root_form = document.getElementById("getroot");
root_form.addEventListener("submit", function(event) {
  var thenum = document.getElementById("sr_num").value;
  thenum = +thenum || false;
  event.preventDefault();
  if (!thenum || (thenum.length < 1)) {
    alert("Input is required and must be numeric!");
    return;
  }
  else if (thenum < 0) {
    alert("Hey! I said to enter a positive number! Try again.");
    return;
  }
```

Checks to see if the input is empty or is not numeric

If the number entered is negative, the viewer has to try again

```
else {
    var theroot = Math.sqrt(thenum);
    alert("The square root of "+thenum+" is "+theroot);
}
}, false);
```

The square root
is calculated and
alerted to the viewer

When the user submits the form, the value input into the text box is assigned to the thenum variable. Next, the function checks to see if the field was left empty or the data entered was not numeric. After that, it checks to see if the viewer entered a negative number. Any of these situations will alert the viewer to the error. Otherwise, the Math.sqrt() method is called using the value of thenum as an argument. This returns the number's square root, which is then assigned to the variable named theroot. Finally, an alert appears telling the user the square root information.

The result of this script when the viewer enters the number 4 is shown in Figure 12-2.

The other methods in this section work in much the same way; they just return different results such as absolute values, tangents, or logarithms.

The Two-Argument Methods

This section discusses the methods that take two arguments instead of just one. These methods include the following:

- atan2()
- max()
- min()
- pow()

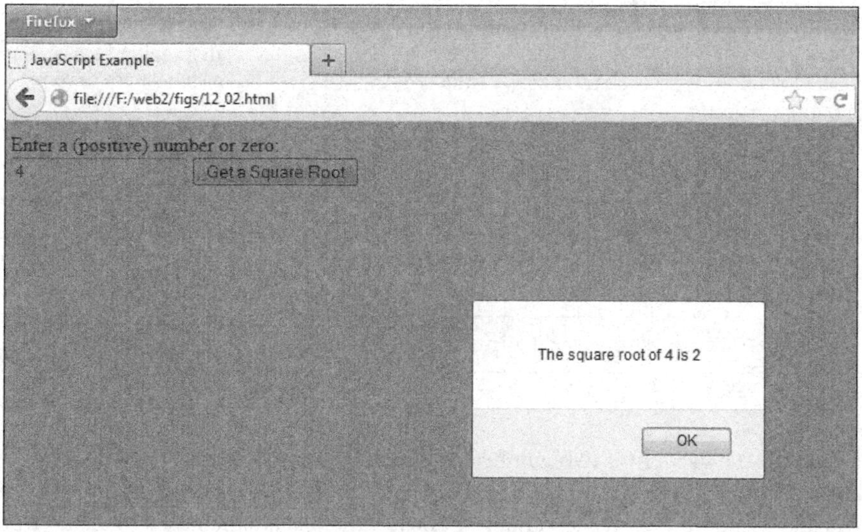

Figure 12-2 The square root is displayed for the viewer.

The max() and min() methods are very similar, while the pow() method does something a bit different.

The max() and min() Methods

The max() method takes two or more numbers and returns the largest number. The min() method also takes two arguments, but returns the smaller number. You could use these methods in a script that enables the viewer to enter two numbers and then alerts the user which number is larger.

The following example code uses both of these methods and gives the viewer the results in an alert. First, the HTML code:

```
<form id="getmax">
Enter two numbers to see which is bigger:<br><br>
<label for="num1">1st Number</label>
 <input type="text" id="num1"><br>
<label for="num2">2nd Number</label>
<input type="text" id="num2"><br><br>
<input type="submit" value="Which Number is Bigger?">
</form>
```

Next, the JavaScript code:

```
var max_form = document.getElementById("getmax");
max_form.addEventListener("submit", function(event) {
  var num1 = document.getElementById("num1").value,
      num2 = document.getElementById("num2").value,
      largenum = 0,
      smallnum = 0;
  num1 = (+num1 === 0) ? 0 : +num1 || false;
  num2 = (+num2 === 0) ? 0 : +num2 || false;
  event.preventDefault();
  if ((num1 !== false) && (num2 !== false)) {
    largenum = Math.max(num1, num2);
    smallnum = Math.min(num1, num2);
    if (largenum === smallnum) {
      alert("Those two numbers are equal!");
    }
    else {
      alert(largenum + " is larger than " + smallnum);
    }
  }
  else {
    alert("Please enter only numeric values.");
  }
}, false);
```

The results of the maximum and minimum are assigned to variables

A check in case the numbers are equal

The alert will display if the numbers are not equal

The alert will display if either value is not numeric

This form asks the viewer for two numbers and assigns them to variables. A check is performed to ensure that numeric values are entered. If so, it takes the maximum and minimum from both numbers and assigns the values to variables. Those variables are then used to check whether they are equal. If so, an alert comes up saying they are; otherwise, an alert pops up with the results.

The following illustration shows the results of this script in a browser if the viewer enters 2 as the first number and 54 as the second number.

The pow() Method   The pow() method takes two arguments and calculates the value of the first argument to the power of the second argument. For instance, the following code would return the value of 2 to the third power:

```
Math.pow(2,3);
```

Other than its difference in calculations, you can use it in the same general way that you used the other two-argument methods by assigning the result to a variable and then using the variable in a script. As an example, you could use the following script, starting with the HTML code:

```
<form id="getpow">
<label for="base">Base Number:</label>
 <input type="text" id="base"><br>
<label for="exp">Exponent:</label>
 <input type="text" id="exp"><br><br>
<input type="submit" value="Find a Power">
</form>
```

Next, the JavaScript code:

```
var pow_form = document.getElementById("getpow");
pow_form.addEventListener("submit", function(event) {
  var base = document.getElementById("base").value,
      exp = document.getElementById("exp").value,
      result = 0;
```

```
    base = +base || false;
    exp = +exp || false;
    event.preventDefault();
    if ((base !== false) && (exp !== false)) {
      result = Math.pow(base, exp);
      alert(base + " to the power of " + exp + " is " + result);
    }
    else {
      alert("Please enter only numeric values");
    }
}, false);
```

Using this code, if the viewer enters 2 as the first number and 3 when asked for a power, the script will compute the result of 2 to the third power. The viewer then is given an alert showing the answer. Clicking the button in the HTML code is how the viewer starts the function. The result of this script when the numbers 2 and 3 are input is shown here:

Now that you know about the two-argument methods, take a look at some other methods that haven't been covered yet.

The Other Methods

These methods take a single argument, but what each does with that argument warrants a closer look. The individual methods include the following:

- ceil()

- floor()

- round()

The ceil() Method   The ceil() method stands for *ceiling* and returns the smallest integer that is greater than or equal to the number sent as the argument. This method is used mainly when there are likely to be numbers after the decimal point in a number. It rounds the number up to the next highest integer, unless the number is an integer already. In that case, the same number is returned (because it can be equal). For instance, Math.ceil(12.23); would return 13, but Math.ceil(12); would return 12.

The following script shows an example of how the ceil() method can be used to return different values, starting with the HTML code:

```
<form id="getceiling">
<label for="num">Number:</label>
<input type="text" id="num">
<input type="submit" value="Find a Ceiling">
</form>
```

Next, the JavaScript code:

```
var ceil_form = document.getElementById("getceiling");
ceil_form.addEventListener("submit", function(event) {
  var num = document.getElementById("num").value,
      ceiling = 0;
  num = +num || false;
  event.preventDefault();
  if (num) {
    ceiling = Math.ceil(num);
    alert("The ceiling of "+ num + " is " + ceiling);
  }
  else {
    alert("Please enter a numeric value.");
  }
}, false);
```

This script displays an alert that states the ceiling of the number entered by the viewer. The following illustration shows the result of this in the browser when the viewer enters 4.55 at the prompt.

The floor() Method The floor() method is like the ceil() method, but it goes the opposite way. The floor() method returns the largest integer less than or equal to the argument sent to the method. This rounds down to the next lowest integer, unless the argument is an integer already. In that case, it returns the same integer since it is already equal to an integer. Basically, this method just removes the decimal part of a number and leaves the integer as the result.

For instance, Math.floor(12.23); will return 12 and Math.floor(12); will also return 12. You can use the floor() method in the same way the ceil() method was used in the preceding section—by assigning the result to a variable.

The round() Method The round() method works like the previous two methods, but instead rounds the number entered as the argument to the nearest integer whether it is greater or less than the number. Any number having the decimal portion's value at .5 or greater will be rounded up, while any decimal portion with a value less than .5 is rounded down.

The .5 cutoff is strict, so Math.round(12.49999999); would return 12 even though your tendency may be to round it up.

The random() Method

The random() method is very useful for creating scripts that require random integers. It returns a random number between 0 and 1. This means that you get a number with a decimal that can be quite long and not useful on its own. For instance, it might return something like 0.36511165498095293.

To get a random integer that you can use, you need to do some things to get the type of value that you want to use.

Random Integers   To get a random integer, the first thing you will want to do is to make the result have a greater range of values so that you are not stuck between 0 and 1. To get a greater range of values, you can multiply the result of the random() method by an integer to create a larger range. Like an array, the range would begin counting from 0; so, to get a range of five possible integers, you would multiply the result by 5. The following code shows how you can do this:

```
var rand_num = Math.random() * 5;
```

This gets the result between 0 and 4, but does not give you an integer yet. The number could still come out as a long decimal number.

To get an integer between 0 and 4, you need to find a way to make all of these decimal numbers convert to integers. Recall that earlier you ran through three methods, floor(), ceil(), and round(), that converted numbers to integers in various ways. The floor() method is the one you will choose here because it simply removes the decimal places after the integer and gives you the integer portion of the number.

To use the floor() method, you could write the following code:

```
var rand_num = Math.random()*5;
var rand_int = Math.floor(rand_num);
```

The floor() method takes in the value of the rand_num variable as an argument and then gives you an integer from it.

If you want to save a line of code, you could get a little fancy. You could just insert the random() method and calculation as the argument to the floor() method. You can do this because the result of the calculation, Math.random*5, is a number, and the floor() method can take a number as an argument. The following code shows how you can code this on a single line:

```
var rand_int = Math.floor(Math.random()*5);
```

Now the variable rand_int will have the value of a random integer between 0 and 4. As you might have noticed, this sort of number range could be quite useful with arrays. This is how you can begin to code some fun scripts with random numbers.

Random Numbers for Scripts   Now you can have a little fun with the Math object by using the random() method. By setting up some arrays, you can create a script that provides random quotes or shows a random image each time the page is loaded.

Random Quotes for Fun   If you have thought about adding a quote to your page but don't want to deal with changing the quote all the time to have something different, a random-quotes script could be just the thing for you.

To make such a script, you first need some quotes to use. Suppose you want to set up ten different quotes that will be displayed in random order each time the page is loaded. Since you have a number of values that are similar (and so that you can use them with the random integer later), you should use an array so that you can store all of these values and retrieve them easily.

So, you need to set up an array with ten elements similar to the following example, in which each element is a random (and perhaps peculiar) quote that I have thrown into the mix for you:

```
var quotes = ["Look in the mirror. Are you looking at me?",
              "It is time for a rhyme, I guess.",
              "Where is my JavaScript book?",
              "If I had a buck for every dollar I spent--Oops, never mind.",
              "I suppose you were expecting a real quote here.",
              "Quotes are great, but don't quote me on that.",
              "What should I write here?",
              "Wut hapns iff eye miss spel ohn purpas?",
              "Mark my words, I will mark my words.",
              "This spot reserved for a better quote."
              ];
```

Now that you have this odd list of quotes in an array, you can use them by generating a random integer.

You need a random integer between 0 and 9 (ten numbers), so you can use the following code to assign a random integer between 0 and 9 to a variable:

```
var rand_int = Math.floor(Math.random() * 10);
```

Now the value of the variable rand_int will be a random integer between 0 and 9. You can use it to access the element of the array whose index number matches the random integer in the rand_int variable. You just need to access the array element using the variable as the index number, as in the following example:

```
quotes[rand_int]
```

You can write this value in the body of the page using the innerHTML property of the div element, as in the following example code. The HTML document is saved as random_quotes.html and the JavaScript file is saved as random_quotes.js. The HTML code:

```
<h1>My Random Quote for You:</h1>
<div id="my_quote">
Look in the mirror. Are you looking at me?
</div>
<script type="text/javascript" src="random_quotes.js"></script>
```

The JavaScript code:

```
var quotes = ["Look in the mirror. Are you looking at me?",
              "It is time for a rhyme, I guess.",
              "Where is my JavaScript book?",
              "If I had a buck for every dollar I spent--Oops, never mind.",
              "I suppose you were expecting a real quote here.",
              "Quotes are great, but don't quote me on that.",
              "What should I write here?",
```

```
            "Wut hapns iff eye miss spel ohn purpas?",
            "Mark my words, I will mark my words.",
            "This spot reserved for a better quote."
            ];
var q_div = document.getElementById("my_quote");
var rand_int = Math.floor(Math.random() * 10);
q_div.innerHTML = quotes[rand_int];
```

The code writes one of the random quotes on the page based on the random integer value in the rand_int variable. A default quote (the first one in the array data) is provided for those without JavaScript, which is then overwritten with the random quote if JavaScript is available. Reloading the page enables the random number to be reset and will probably (though not necessarily, because it is random) show a different quote.

Figure 12-3 shows one of the possible results of this script when run in a browser.

Figure 12-4 shows another one of the possible results of this script when run in a browser. You can keep getting different (or sometimes the same) results by refreshing the page.

Now that you can write random quotes into a page, how about displaying a random image? It is very similar to the last script; you just need to make some small adjustments.

Random Images for the Updated Look   A random-image script can give your page the feel of being updated without requiring you to change an image all the time. Of course, the images all need to fit the content where you decide to place the randomly chosen image. A random-image script could be useful, for example, for an art gallery to display its collection.

The first thing you need is an array of image URL addresses (which can be local or absolute—local addresses are used here). The array used for this script is shown in the following example code:

```
var r_image= ["image0.gif", "image1.gif", "image2.gif", "image3.gif",
              "image4.gif", "image5.gif", "image6.gif", "image7.gif",
              "image8.gif", "image9.gif"];
```

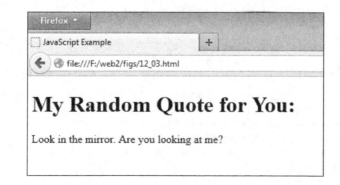

Figure 12-3   A possible result of using the random-quote script

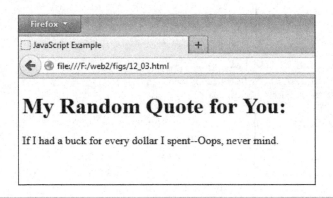

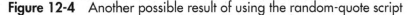

Figure 12-4 Another possible result of using the random-quote script

This array sets up the addresses of images that can be displayed at random each time the page is loaded.

Next, you need a way to get a random integer between 0 and 9. This is the same as in the previous random-quote script:

```
Math.floor(Math.random() * 10);
```

The next step is to access the array in the body section of the document to show a random image from the array when the page is loaded in the browser.

The following code enables you to display the random image using the src property of an img element. The HTML file is saved as random_images.html and the JavaScript file is saved as random_images.js. First, the HTML code:

```
<h1>My Random Image for You:</h1>
<div>
  <img src="cover.jpg" alt="Random Image" id="my_image">
</div>
<script type="text/javascript" src="random_images.js"></script>
```

Next, the JavaScript code:

```
var r_image= ["image0.gif", "image1.gif", "image2.gif", "image3.gif",
              "image4.gif", "image5.gif", "image6.gif", "image7.gif",
              "image8.gif", "image9.gif"],
    im = document.getElementById("my_image"),
    rand_int = Math.floor(Math.random() * 10);
im.src = r_image[rand_int];
```

As you can see, this is quite similar to the random-quote script. Since you are changing an image, you can assign the result to the src property available on image elements to dynamically change the image. If you need to change text as well, you could change this to use innerHTML as you did with the random quotes.

NOTE

For this example, the images are saved as image0.gif, image1.gif, and so on; however, you could save your image files under any name you like.

This discussion of the random() method could go on for some time because there are numerous things that you could randomize. However, you now know the basics of how this feature works, so it's time to move on.

Ask the Expert

Q: **Will I ever have any use for any of the properties of the Math object? They are all numbers that I don't even use!**

A: This depends on how often you perform different types of calculations. It would be unlikely for you to use any of them as a beginner, but there are some scripts out there that use them for various advanced purposes, such as JavaScript calculators, graphical objects (such as the canvas element), and more.

Q: **I have no interest in writing a calculator. Do I really have to bother memorizing all the properties of the Math object?**

A: Well, probably not, since a situation where you need to use them probably won't come up all that often. It is good to have a reference on hand just in case, though, and to know generally what they are, since they appear in scripts on the Web from time to time.

Q: **Some of these properties and methods could be handy if I don't have a calculator around. I could write a little script to calculate some things for myself, couldn't I?**

A: Of course! Just be sure to double-check the numbers with something you know the answer to first to be sure that there are no mistakes in your code.

Q: **The random() method is fun so far, but I can't think of anything else I could use it for. Could you give me some ideas for using it to do other things?**

A: There are a number of other things you could use it for. You can randomize pretty much anything that can be displayed with an HTML tag or plain text, so try out some ideas and see if they work for you. Here are some thoughts off the top of my head for you, though: random links, random linked images, random tasks for a JavaScript game of some sort (like rolling dice or drawing a card), random page greetings, random alerts… and I'm sure there are plenty more.

Try This 12-1 Display a Random Link on a Page

pr12_1.html
prjs12_1.js

This script enables you to work with the random() method a little more by enabling you to create a script to display a random link on a page.

Step by Step

1. Create an HTML page with script tags that point to an external JavaScript file named prjs12_1.js. Add a heading that says "Random Link" and add a div element with an id of random_link. Inside the div element, insert a default link for those without JavaScript. Save the HTML file as pr12_1.html.

2. When complete, the body of the HTML file should look like this:

```
<body>
<h1>Random Link</h1>
<div id="random_link">
<a href="http://www.scripttheweb.com">Random Site!</a>
</div>
<script type="text/javascript" src="prjs12_1.js"></script>
</body>
```

3. Create an external JavaScript file and save it as prjs12_1.js. Use it for steps 4–7.

4. Create a set of five Web addresses in an array. Use the following addresses or some of your own choosing:

   http://www.scripttheweb.com
   http://www.webxpertz.net
   http://www.duckduckgo.com
   http://www.yahoo.com
   http://www.google.com

5. Use the random() method to create a random integer you can use to access the array with the integer as an index number.

6. Display a random link on the page in the format shown next by changing the innerHTML property of the div element with the id of random_link:

```
<a href="random address here">Random Site!</a>
```

7. When complete, the JavaScript file should look like this:

```
var urls = ["http://www.scripttheweb.com",
            "http://www.webxpertz.net",
```

```
                "http://www.duckduckgo.com",
                "http://www.yahoo.com",
                http://www.google.com
                ],
         rdiv = document.getElementById("random_link"),
         rand = Math.floor(Math.random() * 5);
     rdiv.innerHTML = '<a href="' + urls[rand] + '">Random Site!</a>';
```

8. Save the JavaScript file and open the HTML file in your Web browser. Try reloading a few times to see how the random addresses show up for the link.

Try This Summary

In this project, you were able to use your knowledge of the Math object. Using the random() method, you created a Web page that displays a link that goes to a random Web address.

Understanding the Number Object

The Number object is another predefined JavaScript object that offers several useful properties and methods for use with numbers. Its most common use is to access some of its helpful properties that represent certain values that can aid you when creating scripts.

Properties

Table 12-3 lists the properties of the Number object and briefly describes the purpose of each. Each property is described in more detail in this section.

Property	Purpose
MAX_VALUE	Holds a constant number value, representing the largest value before JavaScript interprets a number as infinity
MIN_VALUE	Holds a constant number value, representing the smallest value before JavaScript interprets a number as negative infinity
NaN	Represents the value of "Not a Number"
NEGATIVE_INFINITY	Represents the value of negative infinity
POSITIVE_INFINITY	Represents the value of infinity

Table 12-3   Properties of the Number Object

The MAX_VALUE Property

The MAX_VALUE property is a constant number value, approximately 1.79E+308. The reason this property is helpful is that any number greater than its value is represented as infinity in JavaScript. Thus, using it in a comparison could provide a way to avoid calculations that are too large to display a numerical value. The following code is an example of how this works:

```
var big_num = num1 * num2 * num3;
if (big_num > Number.MAX_VALUE) {
  alert("The number is too large, try smaller numbers.");
}
else {
  alert(big_num);
}
```

Assuming num1, num2, and num3 were entered by the viewer, the alert, instead of displaying the word "infinity" as the answer, informs the viewer to try entering smaller numbers for the calculation if the value of big_num is greater than the value of the MAX_VALUE property.

The MIN_VALUE Property

The MIN_VALUE property is a constant number value, approximately 5e −324. The reason this property is helpful is that any number less than its value is represented as negative infinity in JavaScript. Thus, using it in a comparison could provide a way to avoid calculations that are too small to display a numerical value. The following code is an example of how this works:

```
var small_num = num1 - num2 - num3;
if (small_num < Number.MIN_VALUE) {
  alert("The number is too small, try larger numbers.");
}
else {
  alert(small_num);
}
```

Assuming num1, num2, and num3 were entered by the viewer, the alert tells the viewer to try entering larger numbers for the calculation if the result of the calculation is less than the value of the MIN_VALUE property.

The NaN Property

The NaN property is a value that represents "Not a Number." It is displayed by the browser as a string value of NaN and is not equal to any number or another instance of NaN.

The NEGATIVE_INFINITY Property

The NEGATIVE_INFINITY property is a constant value that represents negative infinity. It can be used in a similar fashion to the way MIN_NUMBER and MAX_NUMBER are used.

The POSITIVE_INFINITY Property

The POSITIVE_INFINITY property is a constant value that represents positive infinity. It can be used in a similar fashion to the way MIN_NUMBER and MAX_NUMBER are used.

NOTE

Infinity behaves differently in mathematical equations than other numbers. For more information on this, see tutorial.math.lamar.edu/Classes/Calcl/TypesOfInfinity.aspx

Methods

Table 12-4 lists the methods of the Number object and briefly describes the purpose of each. The following sections discuss each method in more detail.

The toExponential(), toFixed(), toPrecision(), and toString() Methods

These methods return a string value representing what the Number object would look like formatted in a particular way. Note that these methods cannot be used with a number itself (a numeric value), as in the following code:

```
alert(10.toExponential());
```

This will cause a JavaScript error because it expects a Number object. To avoid this, use the methods by assigning numeric values to variables (which will make them Number objects), as in the following code:

```
var the_num = 10;
alert(the_num.toExponential());
```

NOTE

You could also use the constructor syntax of var the_num = new Number(10); and it will also be valid.

Method	Purpose
toExponential()	Returns a string value that represents the number in exponential notation
toFixed()	Returns a string value that represents the number rounded to the specified number of digits after the decimal
toPrecision()	Returns a string value that represents the number rounded to the specified number of significant digits
toSource()	Returns a string value that represents the source code of the object
toString()	Returns a string value for a Number object
valueOf()	Used by JavaScript internally most often

Table 12-4 Methods of the Number Object

The toExponential() Method

The toExponential() method returns a string representing a Number object in the form of exponential notation. Thus, the following code would write the result of 1.0e+1 (or a similar notation, depending on your browser) on the screen:

```
var the_num = 10;
alert(the_num.toExponential());
```

The toFixed() Method

The toFixed() method returns a string representing a Number object rounded to the specified number of places after the decimal. For instance, if you need to format the results of calculations to appear as monetary values, you could use this method to get the result of your calculation rounded at the second digit after the decimal and displayed in your currency format. For example, this code uses dollars and cents:

```
var kidsmoney = 2000;
var mykids = 7;
var one_share = kidsmoney/mykids;
alert("One share of the money is $" + one_share.toFixed(2));
```

The result of the calculation for one share is 285.7142857142857, but since it is displayed using the toFixed() method on it with 2 as the argument, the sentence displays as follows:

```
One share of the money is $285.71
```

The toPrecision() Method

The toPrecision() method returns a string representing a Number object rounded to the specified number of significant digits. This is for all digits before and after the decimal. Thus, if you wanted a number like 45.57689349 rounded to five significant digits, you could use the following code:

```
var the_num = 45.57689349;
alert(the_num.toPrecision(5));
```

The browser will alert the string 45.577, which is the number rounded to five significant digits (two before and three after the decimal place in this case).

The toString() Method

The toString() method returns the string value of a Number object (or a numerical variable value). This can be useful if you want to convert a numerical value to its corresponding string value (for example, change 10 to "10").

The toSource() Method

The toSource() method returns a string value that represents the source code of the object. With the predefined Number object, this method returns the value of the constructor property. This method is most often called by JavaScript internally and is less likely to be used in code.

The valueOf() Method

This is another method that is mainly used by JavaScript internally. For now, you just need to know that it is a valid method of the Number object.

The parseInt() and parseFloat() Methods

While not methods of the Number object, these two methods are useful when you need to get a numeric value from a mixed string. They work in a similar fashion, with parseInt() only grabbing the integer portion of a number and parseFloat() grabbing the integer and any numbers after a decimal. Here is how they work:

- If the first character in the string is anything other than a number, a plus (+), or a minus (−), then both methods return NaN.

- For parseInt(), if the first character is a number (other than zero), plus, or minus, then each character is evaluated until a non-numeric character is reached (with the exception of hexadecimal values, where certain other characters such as x and A are allowed). The number obtained from this process will be returned. If the first character is zero and the number is not hexadecimal, then zero is returned.

- For parseFloat(), if the first character is a number, plus, or minus, it will evaluate each character and continue if it finds a dot (.) followed by additional numbers, until a second non-numeric character is reached. If the number begins with zero and the number is not hexadecimal, then any leading zeros are ignored until another number is reached. The number obtained from this process will be returned. Hexadecimal numbers return zero.

Some examples of the values returned for each method will show how the rules work:

```
parseInt("14");  // Returns 14
parseInt("cool567"); // Returns NaN
parseInt("+34blah"); // Returns 34
parseInt("-23awesome"); // Returns -23
parseInt("020"); // Returns 0
parseInt("0xA"); // Returns 10 - the hexadecimal value

parseFloat("14"); // Returns 14
parseFloat("blah22"); // Returns NaN
parseFloat("123.456"); // Returns 123.456
parseFloat("123.45.6"); // Returns 123.45 - second dot ends the process
parseFloat("023.44"); // Returns 23.44
parseFloat("0xAF"); // Returns 0
```

When using parseInt(), you are allowed to define a second argument, called the radix. This gives you the opportunity to specify the type of number to be returned. Here are some examples:

```
parseInt("11", 10); // Returns 11
parseInt("11", 2); // Returns 3 - uses the binary value
parseInt("11", 16); // Returns 17 - uses the hexadecimal value
parseInt("11", 8); // Returns 9 - uses the octal value
```

As you can see, the same value can have different results depending on the specified radix. The parseFloat() method does not have this option, since by design it will only parse decimal values.

TIP

When the radix argument is left off, JavaScript decides what type of value to return. In some cases, this can lead to unexpected results. To avoid this, it is best to specify the radix value, even when working with and expecting decimal values (specify the radix as 10).

Using the Date Object

The Date object is another predefined JavaScript object. It enables you to set certain time values and to get certain time values that you can use in your scripts. To use this object, you need to create an instance of the object to which you can refer.

To create an instance of the Date object, you use the new keyword (as you have with a number of other objects), as shown in the following example:

```
var instance_name = new Date();
```

You would replace *instance_name* with a name that you want to use for the instance of the Date object. So, if you wanted an instance named rightnow, you could use the following code:

```
var rightnow = new Date();
```

Now you have an instance of the object named rightnow.

When using the constructor, the default date is the current date; however, you can specify a different date if needed, as in the following code:

```
var go_back = new Date("November 5, 1955");
```

Once you have an instance of the object, you can use the properties and methods of the Date object to perform various tasks (such as create JavaScript clocks). These properties and methods are described in the following sections.

Properties and Methods

The Date object doesn't give you properties (outside of constructor and prototype), but it does have quite a large number of methods you can use. Table 12-5 lists various methods of the Date object and the purpose of each method. Each method is discussed in more detail in the sections that follow.

Now that you have the long list of methods, take a look at them in a little more detail, beginning with the methods used to get date values in an instance of the Date object.

Method	Purpose
getDate()	Returns the day of the month based on the viewer's local time
getDay()	Returns the number of days into the week based on the viewer's local time (0–6)
getHours()	Returns the number of hours into the day based on the viewer's local time (0–23)
getMilliseconds()	Returns the number of milliseconds into the second based on the viewer's local time (0–999)
getMinutes()	Returns the number of minutes into the hour based on the viewer's local time (0–59)
getMonth()	Returns the number of months into the year based on the viewer's local time (0–11)
getSeconds()	Returns the seconds into the minute based on the viewer's local time (0–59)
getTime()	Returns the number of milliseconds since 1/1/1970 for the Date object
getTimezoneOffset()	Returns the time-zone offset (from Greenwich Mean Time) in minutes based on the viewer's local time zone
getYear()	Returns the year based on the viewer's local time (two digits)
getFullYear()	Returns the full year based on the viewer's local time (four digits)
getUTCDate()	Returns the day of the month in Coordinated Universal Time
getUTCDay()	Returns the number of days into the week in Coordinated Universal Time (0–6)
getUTCFullYear()	Returns the full year in Coordinated Universal Time (four digits)
getUTCHours()	Returns the number of hours into the day in Coordinated Universal Time (0–23)
getUTCMilliseconds()	Returns the number of milliseconds into the current second in Coordinated Universal Time (0–999)
getUTCMinutes()	Returns the number of minutes into the hours in Coordinated Universal Time (0–59)
getUTCMonth()	Returns the number of months into the current year in Coordinated Universal Time (0–11)
getUTCSeconds()	Returns the number of seconds into the current minute in Coordinated Universal Time (0–59)
parse()	Returns the number of milliseconds since 1/1/1970 of a date sent as an argument based on the viewer's local time
setDate()	Sets the day of the month for an instance of the Date object
setHours()	Sets the hours for an instance of the Date object
	(continues)

Table 12-5 Methods of the Date Object

Method	Purpose
setMilliseconds()	Sets the milliseconds for an instance of the Date object
setMinutes()	Sets the minutes for an instance of the Date object
setMonth()	Sets the month for an instance of the Date object
setSeconds()	Sets the seconds for an instance of the Date object
setTime()	Sets the time (in milliseconds since January 1, 1970, at midnight) for an instance of the Date object
setYear()	Sets the year for an instance of the Date object (two digits)
setFullYear()	Sets the full year for an instance of the Date object (four digits)
setUTCDate()	Sets the day of the month in Coordinated Universal Time
setUTCFullYear()	Sets the full year in Coordinated Universal Time (four digits)
setUTCHours()	Sets the number of hours into the day in Coordinated Universal Time (0–23)
setUTCMilliseconds()	Sets the number of milliseconds into the current second in Coordinated Universal Time (0–999)
setUTCMinutes()	Sets the number of minutes into the hours in Coordinated Universal Time (0–59)
setUTCMonth()	Sets the number of months into the current year in Coordinated Universal Time (0–11)
setUTCSeconds()	Sets the number of seconds into the current minute in Coordinated Universal Time (0–59)
toDateString()	Returns the date portion of the Date object as a string in American English
toGMTString()	Returns a string that is the date in Greenwich Mean Time (GMT) format (toUTCString() is now used instead)
toLocaleString()	Returns a string that is the date in a format based on the locale
toLocaleDateString()	Returns the date portion of the Date object as a string based on the locale
toLocaleTimeString()	Returns the time portion of the Date object as a string based on the locale
toString()	Returns a string that is the date in American English
toTimeString()	Returns the time portion of the Date object as a string in American English

Table 12-5 Methods of the Date Object (*continued*)

Methods That Get Values

Methods that get values enable you to get various time and date values that you can use in your scripts. The methods that enable you to get values for an instance of the Date object include the following:

- getDate()
- getDay()
- getHours()
- getMilliseconds()
- getMinutes()
- getMonth()
- getSeconds()
- getTime()
- getTimezoneOffset()
- getYear()

- getFullYear()
- getUTCDate()
- getUTCDay()
- getUTCFullYear()
- getUTCHours()
- getUTCMilliseconds()
- getUTCMinutes()
- getUTCMonth()
- getUTCSeconds()

To use these methods, you need an instance of the Date object. Once you have that, you can call any of the methods by using the instance name. The following is the syntax for doing this:

```
instance_name.method();
```

You would replace *instance_name* with the name of your instance of the Date object, and you would replace *method* with the method function you wish to use.

So, if you wanted to use the getDate() method with an instance of the Date object named rightnow, you would use the following code:

```
var rightnow = new Date();
var theday = rightnow.getDate();
```

This assigns the value returned from the getDate() method to a variable named theday.

Because the values returned from the Date methods are often numeric, the methods need to be explained a bit further; thus, the following sections take a look at these methods more closely.

The getDate() Method
The getDate() method enables you to get the day of the month for use in a script. The value returned is a number that represents the day of the month. So, if it is the 5th of the month, the getDate() method would return 5. If it is the 22nd, the getDate() method would return 22. This method is nice because it is fairly straightforward.

The getDay() Method
The getDay() method enables you to get the day of the week; however, rather than returning a name such as Monday or Friday, it returns a number. The number represents the number of days *into* the week (0–6) rather than the day *of* the week you would commonly have in mind (1–7). So, if it is Sunday, the method returns 0; and if it is Wednesday, the method returns 3. You have to remember that it counts from 0 when you begin using it in your scripts. Many of the methods that follow will count beginning at 0.

The getHours() Method

The getHours() method enables you to get the number of hours into the day (0–23). The count begins at 0. So, when it is midnight, the method returns 0; and when it is 2:00 P.M., it returns 14.

The getMilliseconds() Method

The getMilliseconds() method enables you to get the number of milliseconds stored in the instance of the Date object (0–999).

The getMinutes() Method

The getMinutes() method enables you to get the number of minutes stored in the instance of the Date object (0–59). Again, the counting begins at 0. So, if it is 2:00 (either A.M. or P.M.), or any hour on the dot, the method returns 0; and if it is 2:23, the method returns 23.

The getMonth() Method

The getMonth() method enables you to get the number of months stored in the instance of the Date object (0–11). This method also begins counting at 0, which makes the result a little tricky. For instance, if it is January (the month people tend to think of as 1), the method returns 0; and if it is October (the month people tend to think of as 10), the method returns 9. This is one you have to watch a little more closely when you use it in scripts, because you will need to remember to make an adjustment if you want to use numeric dates (like 10/24/2000).

The getSeconds() Method

The getSeconds() method enables you to get the number of seconds stored in the instance of the Date object (0–59). So, if the time is 2:42:23, the method returns 23; and if the time is 2:23:00, the method returns 0.

The getTime() Method

The getTime() method gets the time (in milliseconds since January 1, 1970, at midnight) for an instance of the Date object. So, if you wanted to know the number of milliseconds since that date at your current time, you could use the following code:

```
var rightnow = new Date();
var theday = rightnow.getTime();
```

This assigns the result of the method to a variable so that you can use it later if you need it in your script.

The getTimezoneOffset() Method

The getTimezoneOffset() method gives you the number of minutes that separate the local time from GMT. So, if you are six hours apart from GMT, the method would return 360 (6 × 60); and if you are only one hour apart, the method returns 60.

The getYear() Method

This method returns the last two digits of the year (at least if the year is between 1900 and 1999). For instance, if the year is 1988, the method returns 88. After the year 2000, some browsers will return a three-digit year and others will return a four-digit year. To avoid this, you can use the getFullYear() method, which is supported by the newer browsers and returns a four-digit year.

The getFullYear() Method

The getFullYear() method is very similar to the getYear() method, except it returns a four-digit year consistently to avoid the year 2000 problem.

The getFullYear() method works like the getYear() method, but you do not need to run any extra checks to be sure the year is correct:

```
var rightnow = new Date();
var theyear = rightnow.getFullYear();
```

This assigns the value returned by the method to the theyear variable. This time, the value is already four digits and won't need any adjusting.

The UTC Methods

These methods work the same as their counterparts (for example, getDate() and getUTCDate() work the same), but return the information in terms of Universal Time rather than the viewer's local time.

Now that you have seen the methods that get values, take a look at the methods that enable you to set values for an instance of the Date object.

Methods That Set Values

The methods that set values work with the same types of values as the methods that get values. The methods that enable you to set values for an instance of the Date object include the following:

- setDate()
- setHours()
- setMilliseconds
- setMinutes()
- setMonth()
- setSeconds()
- setTime()
- setYear()
- setFullYear()
- setUTCDate()
- setUTCFullYear()
- setUTCHours()
- setUTCMilliseconds()
- setUTCMinutes()
- setUTCMonth()
- setUTCSeconds()

To set these, you send them a numeric argument based on the time or date you want to use. For instance, if you wanted to set the day of the month for an instance of the Date object, you could use the following code:

```
var rightnow = new Date();
rightnow.setDate(22);
```

This would set the day of the month to the 22nd for the rightnow instance of the Date object.

The other methods work in the same way. In order to know what value needs to be sent to one of these methods, take a look at what type of value is returned by its counterpart in the methods that get values. The argument the method will expect will be a value like the one returned by the method.

Other Methods

The remaining methods perform various tasks that the other methods don't cover in some way.

The parse() Method

The parse() method is used to find out the number of milliseconds since January 1, 1970, at midnight for a date string (such as Dec 12, 1999) input as an argument. This is often used with the setTime() method since it needs an argument in milliseconds to set the time. You could use the parse() method to find the number of milliseconds since January 1, 1970, for the date Dec 12, 1999 at midnight (the rightnow instance of the Date object will use this as the date that all of the methods will use to return values), as shown in the following code:

This method can be used directly from the Date object

```
var rightnow = new Date();
var thenum = Date.parse("Dec 12, 1999");
rightnow.setTime(thenum);
```

This code parses the date into a number of milliseconds, and then sends it to the setTime() method used with the rightnow instance of the Date object.

The toString(), toDateString(), toTimeString(), toLocaleDateString, and toLocaleTimeString() Methods

These methods return a string representing the date and time, or a portion thereof. For instance, the toString() method returns a date in string format. You can use it to get a formatted date for an instance of the Date object, as shown in the following code:

```
var rightnow= new Date();
var thedate= rightnow.toString();
```

This will assign a date string value to the variable thedate. The value of the string depends on what browser the viewer is using to view the page. It can then be written to the page or used with other methods of the Date object in a script.

The toGMTString() Method

The toGMTString() method returns a date string in GMT format. You can use it to get the GMT format for an instance of the Date object, as shown in the following code:

```
var rightnow = new Date();
var thedate = rightnow.toGMTString();
```

This will assign a value, such as Wed, 21 Dec 2003 11:12:44 GMT, to the variable thedate. It can then be written to the page or used with other methods of the Date object in a script.

The toLocaleString() Method

The toLocaleString() method returns a date string in the format of the viewer's locale. You can use it to get the locale format for an instance of the Date object, as shown in the following code:

```
var rightnow = new Date();
var thedate = rightnow.toLocaleString();
```

This will assign a date string value to the variable thedate. The value of the string depends on what browser the viewer is using to view the page. It can then be written to the page or used with other methods of the Date object in a script.

Now that you have the methods down, see if you can have a little fun with the Date object.

How About Some Date Scripts?

With the technical overview out of the way, you are ready to create some scripts that use the methods of the Date object. First you will write a script to display the date on the page, and then you will create a script for a simple status bar clock.

Write the Date on the Page

To write the date on the page, you need to use some of the Date object methods to get the values you need. Suppose you want to write a date with the format of Tuesday, M/D/Y (month, day, year). To do this, you need to find out the day of the week, the month, the day of the month, and the year. You can do this using the getDay(), getMonth(), getDate(), and getFullYear() methods.

The following script will write the date to the page. First, the HTML code (save as write_date.html):

```
<h1>Today's Date</h1>
<div id="write_date">
<!-- call to a server-side script for backup could go here -->
</div>
<script type="text/javascript" src="write_date.js"></script>
```

Note the comment within the div element. If you want to make this accessible to browsers that do not support JavaScript, you can place a call to a PHP (or other server-side technology) script here for those lacking JavaScript. For example, if you had the page set up to parse PHP, you could use the following to display the date much like the JavaScript code will:

```
<h1>Today's Date</h1>
<div id="write_date">
<?PHP
$the_date = date(l, n/j/Y);
echo "$date";
?>
</div>
<script type="text/javascript" src="write_date.js"></script>
```

You will see that the PHP script is much shorter than the JavaScript script due to its built-in date-formatting capability. The date displayed may differ from the viewer's date as it displays the date on the Web server. An in-depth discussion of server-side technology is beyond the scope of this book, but this serves as an example of a way to provide the same basic feature for those without JavaScript.

Next, the JavaScript code (save as write_date.js):

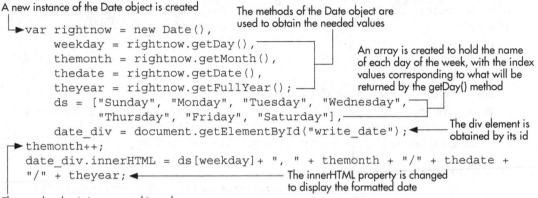

```
var rightnow = new Date(),
    weekday = rightnow.getDay(),
    themonth = rightnow.getMonth(),
    thedate = rightnow.getDate(),
    theyear = rightnow.getFullYear();
    ds = ["Sunday", "Monday", "Tuesday", "Wednesday",
        "Thursday", "Friday", "Saturday"],
    date_div = document.getElementById("write_date");
themonth++;
date_div.innerHTML = ds[weekday]+ ", " + themonth + "/" + thedate +
"/" + theyear;
```

A new instance of the Date object is created

The methods of the Date object are used to obtain the needed values

An array is created to hold the name of each day of the week, with the index values corresponding to what will be returned by the getDay() method

The div element is obtained by its id

The innerHTML property is changed to display the formatted date

The month value is incremented in order to look like its standard numerical month value

This script sets the results of the methods to variables. It then creates an array to hold the days of the week, which are later accessed using the number returned from the getDay() method as the index. The script then makes an adjustment, adding 1 to the number returned by the getMonth() method, so that the month will show up the way you would expect it (recall that it counts months starting at 0 instead of 1, so this ensures that January is represented by the number 1 rather than 0, for example).

The formatted output is written onto the page for the viewer to see. The result of this script when run in a browser is shown in Figure 12-5.

Figure 12-5 The date is shown on the page.

Create a Simple Clock

To create a simple clock, you need the hours, minutes, and seconds of the current time. To get these, you can use the getHours(), getMinutes(), and getSeconds() methods.

The following code will create a clock that is displayed on the page. First, the HTML code (save as clock.html):

```
<h1>Current Time:</h1>
<div id="my_clock">
<!-- call to a server-side script for backup could go here -->
</div>
<script type="text/javascript" src="clock.js"></script>
```

CAUTION

If you use a server-side script as a backup to the JavaScript clock, you almost surely do not want it to update every second because this could put undue strain on the Web server. In such a case, it is often best to simply display the time without updating it.

Next, the JavaScript code (save as clock.js):

```
function startclock() {
  var thetime = new Date(),
      hours = thetime.getHours(),          ┐  The methods of the Date object are used
      mins = thetime.getMinutes(),         ├  to obtain the hours, minutes, and seconds
      secn = thetime.getSeconds(),         ┘
      ap = (hours >= 12) ? "p.m." : "a.m.",◄── A variable is set so that a.m. or p.m.
      clock_div = document.getElementById("my_clock");  may be displayed after the time
  hours = (hours >= 13) ? hours -= 12 : hours;  ┐  The hours, minutes, and
  hours = (hours < 1) ? 12 : hours;             │  seconds are adjusted so
  mins = (mins < 10) ? "0" + mins : mins;       ├  that they will display like a
  secn = (secn < 10) ? "0" + secn : secn;       ┘  typical 12-hour digital clock
  clock_div.innerHTML = hours + ":" + mins + ":" + secn + " " + ap;◄┐
  setTimeout(function() { startclock(); }, 1000);                    │
}                                                  The hours, minutes, seconds, and
startclock();◄── Calling the function here starts the process  ap variables are combined and
                                                   displayed as the new innerHTML
The script is called every second                  for the div element
using the setTimeout() method
```

The script creates a function that sets the results of the methods to variables. It takes the hours variable and sets the ap variable to p.m. if hours is greater than or equal to 12 and sets it to a.m. if hours is less than 12 (at this point the hours variable still holds 13 for 1 p.m., 14 for 2 p.m., and so on). Once this is done, the hours variable is adjusted so that it will display the expected value for a 12-hour clock.

The script then adjusts the values of the variables that show the minutes and seconds by adding a leading 0 when the number is less than 10. This way the clock will show 12:02:34 for 12:02:34, instead of leaving out the 0 and displaying 12:2:34 (this can also be done for the hours variable if you would like it to have a leading zero).

Figure 12-6 The current time is displayed on the page.

At the end, the function displays the output on the page. The function is initially called right after it is defined. The function is repeated at intervals of 1000 milliseconds, or 1 second. This enables the clock to stay current. The results of this script when run in a browser are shown in Figure 12-6.

Try This 12-2 Create a JavaScript Clock

pr12_2.html
prjs12_2.js

This project enables you to work more with the methods of the Date object, as well as learn how to adjust the values that are returned so they can be used in various ways. This creates a JavaScript clock with a few more options than your simple clock in the previous section.

Step by Step

1. Create an HTML page with script tags that point to an external JavaScript file named prjs12_2.js. Add a heading that says "Current Time" and add a div element with an id of my_clock. Save the HTML file as pr12_2.html.

2. When complete, the body of the HTML file should look like this:

```
<body>
<h1>Current Time</h1>
<div id="my_clock"></div>
<script type="text/javascript" src="prjs12_2.js"></script>
</body>
```

3. Create an external JavaScript file and save it as prjs12_2.js. Use it for steps 4–7.

4. Write some code that will display a clock. In this clock, include the following information:

5. The time with hours, minutes, and seconds

6. Whether it is A.M. or P.M.

7. The date in the form mm/dd/yyyy

8. This will be a 12-hour clock, so be sure to adjust the value of the hours so that they stay between 1 and 12. Also, note the format of the date and adjust the month and day values accordingly.

9. Begin the clock, and have it update every second.

10. When complete, the JavaScript file should look like this:

```
function startclock() {
  var thetime = new Date(),
      hours = thetime.getHours(),
      mins = thetime.getMinutes(),
      secn = thetime.getSeconds(),
      ap = (hours >= 12) ? "p.m." : "a.m.",
      themonth = thetime.getMonth(),
      thedate = thetime.getDate(),
      theyear = thetime.getFullYear(),
      clock_div = document.getElementById("my_clock");
  hours = (hours >= 13) ? hours -= 12 : hours;
  hours = (hours < 1) ? 12 : hours;
  mins = (mins < 10) ? "0" + mins : mins;
  secn = (secn < 10) ? "0" + secn : secn;
  themonth++;
  clock_div.innerHTML = hours + ":" + mins + ":" + secn + " " + ap + " " +
                        themonth + "/" + thedate + "/" + theyear;
  setTimeout(function() { startclock(); }, 1000);
}
startclock();
```

11. Save the JavaScript file and open the HTML file in your browser. The time and date should appear on the page.

Try This Summary

In this project, you used your knowledge of the Date object. Using the methods of the Date object, you created a clock with a date that appears on the Web page.

✓

Chapter 12 Self Test

1. What do the properties and methods of the Math object enable you to do?

   A. Take the square roots and other such values of strings and return a number

   B. Perform mathematical calculations

   C. Go to math class to learn new theorems

   D. Nothing, they are useless

2. The _____ property holds the value of Euler's constant.

3. The LN10 property holds the value of the natural _____ of 10.

4. The LOG10E property holds the value of the logarithm of 10*E.

   A. True

   B. False

5. Which of the following would correctly write the value of pi on a Web page?

   A. document.write(Math.Pi);

   B. document.write(Math.pi);

   C. document.write(Math.PI);

   D. document.write(Date.PI);

6. The _____ property holds the value of the square root of 2.

7. The abs() method returns the _____ value of a number sent to it as an argument.

   A. absent

   B. absurd

   C. absolute

   D. absolute square root

8. The _____ method returns the arcsine of a number sent to it as an argument.

9. The pow() method returns the numeric value of the _____ argument raised to the power of the _____ argument.

10. Which of the following would correctly generate a random number between 0 and 7?

   A. var rand_int= Math.floor(Math.random()*7);

   B. var rand_int= Math.floor(Math.random()*6);

   C. var rand_int= Math.floor(Math.random()*8);

   D. var rand_int= Math.sqrt(Math.random());

11. The _____ method returns the square root of a number sent to it as an argument.

12. What must be created in most cases before the Date object's properties and methods can be used?

   A. Nights string

   B. A number for reference to the date

   C. A time for the date to be set

   D. An instance of the Date object

13. The _____ method returns the number of days into the week.

14. The getMonth() method returns the same number as the number that represents the current month (for example, returns 1 if the current month is January).

   A. True

   B. False

15. Which of the following correctly assigns the day of the week for an instance of the Date object named rightnow to a variable named weekday?

   A. var weekday= rightnow.getDate();

   B. var weekday= rightnow.getDay();

   C. var weekday= right now.getDay();

   D. var weekly= rightlater.getMinutes();

Chapter 13

Handling Strings

Key Skills & Concepts

- Using the Properties of the String Object
- Using the Methods of the String Object
- Using Cookies
- Using Regular Expressions

To work with strings in JavaScript, you need to learn about the various methods that handle them. The methods come from the JavaScript String object.

This chapter first explains what the String object is and how to create strings that use its properties and methods. Then, the String object's properties and methods are discussed in more detail so you can see how they work. Finally, you'll code a script that uses some of the properties and methods you've learned.

Introduction to the String Object

The String object provides properties and methods to get information about strings or to modify strings. A String object is created in either of two ways: a programmer creates one by using the new keyword with the constructor function, or JavaScript creates one temporarily when one of the methods is called from a string literal. What makes a String object and what makes a string literal? To find out, take a look at how to create a String object in JavaScript.

The String Object

As just explained, one way to create a String object is to use the new keyword, as you've done with other objects previously. The syntax is shown here:

```
var instance_name = new String("string value here");
```

You replace *instance_name* with the name you want to use for the instance of the String object. You then replace *string value here* with the string of characters to use as the new String object.

So, if you want to create an instance of the String object named guitar_string, you could use the following code:

```
var guitar_string = new String("G");
```

This script creates an instance of the String object for the string "G".

The String Literal

You can create a string literal just by assigning a string value to a variable. This technique is a bit shorter than creating a String object using the new keyword and still allows you to use all the methods of the String object (as well as one of the properties).

A string literal is created in the code that follows. Notice that the code assigns a string value to a variable.

```
var guitar_string = "G";
```

This makes the string "G" a string literal, which you know as a regular text string. With text strings, you're also allowed to use the properties and methods of the String object.

What's the Difference?

The difference between a String object and a string literal is that a regular text string has the value of the string itself, and it can be compared against another string easily, as in the following code:

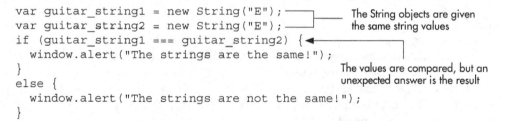

```
var guitar_string1 = "E";
var guitar_string2 = "E";                Both variables have the same string value
if (guitar_string1 === guitar_string2) {      The strings are compared
  alert("The strings are the same!");
}
else {
  alert("The strings are not the same!");
}
```

Because this code uses regular string literals, the result is what you'd expect. An alert says that the strings are the same.

However, if you used String objects to run through the same if block, you would see something unexpected. The code that follows uses String objects instead:

```
var guitar_string1 = new String("E");        The String objects are given
var guitar_string2 = new String("E");        the same string values
if (guitar_string1 === guitar_string2) {
  window.alert("The strings are the same!");
}                                            The values are compared, but an
else {                                       unexpected answer is the result
  window.alert("The strings are not the same!");
}
```

This time the alert would tell you that the strings are not the same, even though the string values are both "E"—because a String object is an object value and not a literal value. Objects aren't going to be equal to one another in the same way regular text strings would be (objects contain name-value pairs, while literal values only contain the value). For most purposes, you would probably use string literals and let them use the String object's methods.

A regular text string is able to use the String object's methods because JavaScript takes the string literal and turns it into a temporary String object. Once the method's execution is complete, it returns a string literal. This allows you to use the String object's methods without having to create String objects.

Using the Properties and Methods of the String Object

The String object has only has one property (aside from the constructor and prototype properties, which can only be used with a String object created via the constructor function). Table 13-1 shows this property.

The length Property

This property returns the length of the string, which is the number of characters contained in the string. You can use it with both String objects and string literals. You've seen this property with other objects as well, such as the Array object. (In that case, the value was the number of elements in an array.)

The following code uses a regular text string. It writes the length of the string variable onto the page.

```
var myname = "John";    ◄──── A string literal is created
alert("The name has " + myname.length + " characters.");  ◄──┘
```

The length of the name is alerted to the viewer

Notice how the name of the variable is used like an object name, and is able to access the String properties and methods. The script writes the result to the page. Because the name has four characters, the length property has a value of 4 here.

Methods of the String Object

The methods of the String object are listed in Table 13-2 (grouped by function).

HTML Methods

Though these are not used often today due to innerHTML(), node creation, and the fact that some of the methods create tags that are no longer valid HTML, the HTML methods of the String object are available for use if needed.

The basic HTML methods (big(), blink(), bold(), fixed(), italics(), small(), strike(), sub(), and sup()) simply add basic HTML tags around a string. For example, to create some small text, you could use the small() method:

```
var little_bit = "I only want a little bit of cake.";
var tagged_phrase = little_bit.small();
document.write(tagged_phrase);
```

Property	Purpose
length	Holds the numeric value of the length of the string (its number of characters)

Table 13-1 Properties of the String Object

Method	Purpose
anchor()	Creates an HTML anchor tag with a target on a page
big()	Adds <big> and </big> tags around a string value
blink()	Adds <blink> and </blink> tags around a string value
bold()	Adds <b> and </b> tags around a string value
fixed()	Adds <tt> and </tt> tags around a string value
fontcolor()	Adds <font color="*color*"> and </font> tags around a string value, which change the color of the string to a specified color
fontsize()	Adds <font size="*number*"> and </font> tags around a string value, which change the size of the string to a specified size given as a number
italics()	Adds <i> and </i> tags around a string value
link()	Creates HTML links using the string as the link text and linking to the URL sent as a parameter
small()	Adds <small> and </small> tags around a string value
strike()	Adds <strike> and </strike> tags around a string value
sub()	Adds _{and} tags around a string value
sup()	Adds ^{and} tags around a string value
charAt()	Finds out which character is at a given position in a string
charCodeAt()	Finds the character code of a character at a given position in a string
concat()	Adds two or more strings together and returns the new combined string value
slice()	Pulls out a specified section of a string value and returns a new string
substr()	Allows a portion of the string specified with a starting position and ending after a certain number of characters to be returned
substring()	Allows a portion of the string specified with a starting position and an ending position to be returned
indexOf()	Searches for a character sent as a parameter in a string: if it's found, the position of the first instance of the character is returned; otherwise, it returns −1
lastIndexOf()	Searches for a character sent as a parameter in a string: if it's found, the position of the last instance of the character is returned; otherwise, it returns −1
toLowerCase()	Converts a string to all lowercase letters and returns the result
toUpperCase()	Converts a string to all uppercase letters and returns the result
toString()	Returns the string literal value of a string
fromCharCode()	Uses character codes sent as parameters to create a new string
localeCompare()	Compares strings based on alphabetical order and returns the result
match()	Compares a regular expression and a string to see if they match

(continues)

Table 13-2 Methods of the String Object

Method	Purpose
replace()	Finds out if a regular expression matches a string and then replaces a matched string with a new string
search()	Executes the search for a match between a regular expression and a specified string
split()	Separates a string into an array of strings based on a character sent as a parameter to the method
trim()	Removes white space from the beginning and end of a string

Table 13-2 Methods of the String Object (*continued*)

This code would then write the following into the HTML code:

```
<small>I only want a little bit of cake.</small>
```

When viewed in the browser, this text would appear smaller than it would normally have appeared without the <small> and </small> tags.

The remaining HTML tag methods (anchor(), fontcolor(), fontsize(), and link()) take parameters and build the tags based on the string value and the argument(s) sent to them.

The anchor() Method The anchor method uses the string as the text for a named anchor. For example, take a look at this code:

```
var anchor_text = "Part 1";        A string literal is created
var full_anchor = anchor_text.anchor("part1");
document.write(full_anchor);        The value of the variable is written on the page
```

The result of the anchor() method is assigned to a variable

The code writes the following link into the code for the page:

```
<a name="part1">Part 1</a>
```

Figure 13-1 shows what this code looks like when viewed in the browser. Notice that the viewer sees only the anchor text for the section.

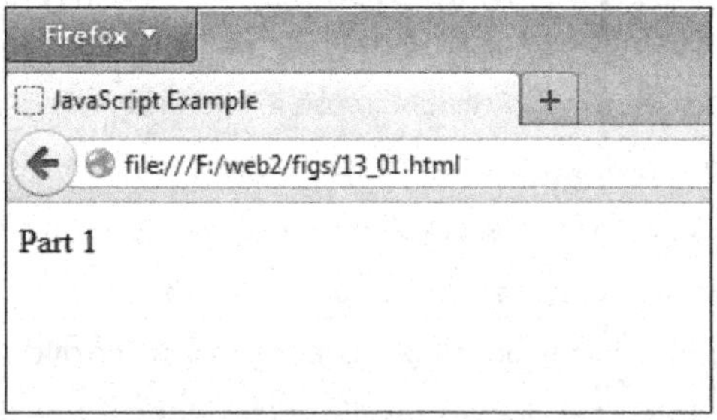

Firefox ▾

JavaScript Example   +

file:///F:/web2/figs/13_01.html

Part 1

Figure 13-1 A named anchor is placed on the page.

The fontcolor() Method   The fontcolor() method adds font color to the text string that is used to call it. It takes an argument indicating what color the text should be, using either the color name or its red-green-blue (RGB) value. For an example, this code creates some red text on the page:

```
var the_text = "I am so mad I am red!";
document.write(the_text.fontcolor("red"));
```

This script places the following code into the page source:

```
<font color="red">I am so mad I am red!</font>
```

You can also use the RGB value in place of the color name. In this code, the RGB value is used instead:

```
var the_text = "I am so mad I am red!";
document.write(the_text.fontcolor("#FF0000"));
```

This time, the code produced would be changed to include the RGB value in place of the color name in the previous example, as shown here:

```
<font color= "#FF0000">I am so mad I am red!</font>
```

The fontsize() Method   The fontsize() method adjusts the font size of the text string that calls the method. It takes a numeric value to represent the size of the text (between 1 and 7). The example that follows shows this method in action:

```
var the_text = "I am pretty small!";
document.write(the_text.fontsize(2));
```

This script provides the code that follows in the page source:

```
<font size="2">I am pretty small!</font>
```

The link() Method   The link() method works like the anchor() method, but instead it creates a typical hyperlink on the page. It takes the URL of the link as an argument, as in the following code:

```
var link_text = "A Web Site";
var full_link = link_text.link("http://www.scripttheweb.com");
document.write(full_link);
```

This code creates the link shown here in the page source code:

```
<a href="http://www.scripttheweb.com">A Web Site</a>
```

The charAt() and charCodeAt() Methods

The charAt() method determines which character resides at a particular position in a string. It takes a number argument representing the position of the character in the string.

When you want to find a character, remember that the position count begins at 0 (as with arrays) rather than 1, so the first character is at position 0. The following code shows how to get the first character in a string by using the charAt() method:

The charAt() method finds the character at position 0 (the first character) in the string

```
var the_text = "Character";
var first_char = the_text.charAt(0);
alert("The first character is " + first_char);
```

This code assigns the result of the charAt() method call to a variable named first_char, which is then used in an alert. The alert will tell the viewer the first character in the text string that called the method. In this case, the alert would say "The first character is C".

If you want to find the last character, either you need to know how many characters are in the string before you use the method, or you can use the length property to determine the number of characters in the string. When using the length property, remember that it returns the number of characters, not the position of the last character.

The length property begins counting at 1, while you must begin counting at 0 when you use the charAt() method. Thus, the last character in a string will be at a position one less than the number of characters it contains. In other words, if the string has 10 characters (1–10), the last position (0–9) is at 9. For example, this code finds the last character in a string:

Subtract 1 from the length property to find the last position available in the string

```
var the_text = "Character",
    position = the_text.length - 1,
    last_char = the_text.charAt(position);
alert("The last character is " + last_char);
```

The charAt() method uses that value to find out which character is in the last position in the string

This code assigns the value of the length of the string minus 1 to a variable named position. The position variable now holds the position of the last character in the string. The result of calling the charAt() method with the value of position sent as the parameter is assigned to a variable named last_char. Finally, an alert provides the last character in the string, which is *r*. Thus, the viewer gets an alert saying "The last character is r".

The charCodeAt() returns the character code for the character at the positions sent as the argument (for further discussion on character codes, you can refer to Chapter 5 or visit www .scripttheweb.com/js/ref/javascript-character-codes.html). For example, you could use the following code:

The charCodeAt() method finds the character code for the character at position 0 (the first character) in the string

```
var the_text = "Hello";
var char_code = the_text.charCodeAt(0);
alert("The character code is " + char_code);
```

An alert would then tell you the character code at position 0 in the string (the letter *H*), which is 72.

The concat(), slice(), substr(), and substring() Methods

These methods are provided to allow you to alter the value of a string in various ways.

The concat() Method   This method works much like the Array object's concat() method. It combines the text string that calls the method with any number of other text strings sent as arguments and returns the combined value. The text string calling the method comes first in the order, while the strings sent as arguments are added in order afterward. The following code shows an example that combines three strings using the concat() method:

```
var string1 = "I went to the store ",
    string2 = "then ",                       The three strings are combined
    string3 = "I played a video game";       in order from left to right
alert(string1.concat(string2, string3));
```

This code combines the strings in the order string1, string2, and then string3. The result is an alert that says "I went to the store then I played a video game".

The slice() Method   This method slices out a portion of a string and returns the value that was sliced. It works much like the slice() method of an array. The first argument tells it the position at which to start slicing, while the second argument is one greater than the position where it will stop. For instance, take a look at the code that follows:

```
var the_text = "Do not cut this short!";
var shorter_string = the_text.slice(0,7);
alert(shorter_string);
```

This code slices the string from position 0 through position 6. Position 7 is where the *c* is in "cut"; but it isn't sliced because the argument that tells JavaScript where to end the slicing is one greater than the position of the last character to slice. Thus, the alert will say "Do not ".

The substr() Method   This method pulls out a portion of a string and returns the portion that is removed as a new string. The first argument specifies the beginning of the removal, and the second specifies how many characters to remove. For instance, the following code removes a portion of a string beginning at position 0 and continues until seven characters are removed:

```
var the_text = "Do not cut this short!";
var shorter_string = the_text.substr(0,7);
alert(shorter_string);
```

This code removes everything from the string from the first "D" up to the beginning of the word cut in the string. The string returned is the portion of the string that has been removed. Thus, the alert will say "Do not ".

The substring() Method   This method works much like the substr() method, but it allows you to send arguments for the beginning position and the ending position of the portion of the string you want to remove. It then returns the removed portion as a new string.

For example, take a look at the code that follows. Rather than specifying the number of characters to remove, you give an ending position. The characters are removed beginning at the starting position and ending at one less than the ending position. (Remember the slice() method.)

```
var the_text = "Do not cut this short!";
var shorter_string = the_text.substring(3,7);
alert(shorter_string);
```

You remove everything between the beginning of the string and the beginning of the word "cut". The alert will say "not ".

NOTE
The slice() and substring() methods are very similar, but they do have their differences in specific cases. To see more about this, go to http://stackoverflow.com/questions/2243824/what-is-the-difference-between-string-slice-and-string-substring-in-javascript

The fromCharCode() Method
The fromCharCode() method creates a string from a series of character codes sent as parameters to the method. The charCodeAt() method returns a numeric code for the character at a given position. This is the type of value you must send to the fromCharCode() method. Also, fromCharCode() is called directly from the String object rather than from an existing string, because it is piecing together a string on-the-fly and doesn't require one to run. Instead, it uses the parameters sent to it to return a string.

So, if you want to alert the text string "HI" to the viewer, you could use the example code shown here:

```
window.alert(String.fromCharCode(72,73));
```

This code takes the first parameter (the character code 72) and converts it to an *H*. It then takes the second parameter (the character code 73) and converts it to an *I*. The two are combined in the order they were sent to form the string "HI", which is sent as an alert to the viewer.

The localeCompare() Method
The localeCompare() method compares two strings and returns a number indicating whether or not the string comes before or after the string argument in alphabetical order. The method will use different ways of calculating this, depending on the locale (country and language) of the browser. It returns one of the following values:

● If the string should come before the argument alphabetically, it returns a negative number.

● If the strings are equal, it returns 0.

● If the string should come after the argument alphabetically, it returns a positive number.

For example, you could use the following code to determine whether the string "orange" comes before or after another string alphabetically:

```
var comp_string = "orange";
    new_string = "apple";
    pos = comp_string.localeCompare(new_string);
if (pos < 0) {
  alert(comp_string + " comes before " + new_string);
}
else if (pos > 0) {
  alert(comp_string + " comes after " + new_string);
}
else {
  alert("The strings are equal");
}
```

In this case, the viewer will get an alert saying, "orange comes after apple".

The indexOf() and lastIndexOf() Methods

The indexOf() method finds out where a certain character or string begins in a string. It returns the position of only the first occurrence of the character or string that is sent as the argument. If the character or string isn't found in the string value, a value of –1 is returned.

The following code looks for the letter *C* in the string "Cool":

```
var the_text = "Cool";
var position = the_text.indexOf("C");
alert("Your character is at position " + position);
```

Remember that the position count begins at 0, so when it finds *C* as the first character in the string, it returns 0. Thus, the alert will say "Your character is at position 0".

Note that the method is case sensitive, so *C* and *c* are two different characters to JavaScript in this case. Thus, the code that follows returns –1 (telling you the character isn't in the string), even though an uppercase *C* is in the string.

```
var the_text = "Cool";
var position = the_text.indexOf("c");
alert("Your character is at position "+position);
```

The alert would now say "Your character is at position –1".

If you want to check for that –1 to keep from getting it as a position, you could use this code to send a different alert in case the character you want to find isn't in the string:

```
var the_text = "Cool";
var position = the_text.indexOf("c");
if (position === -1) {
  alert("Your character is not in the string!");
}
else {
  alert("Your character is at position "+position);
}
```

This time, the if statement checks to see whether the method returns –1 to the position variable. If so, the alert says "Your character is not in the string!" Otherwise, the regular alert will tell you the position. In the previous code, the lowercase *c* isn't in the string, so the "Your character is not in the string!" alert appears.

The indexOf() method returns the position number only for the first occurrence of the character you send as the parameter. So, if you use the code that follows, you will be alerted that your character is at position 1, even though it's also at position 2:

```javascript
var the_text = "Cool";
var position = the_text.indexOf("o");
if (position === -1) {
   alert("Your character is not in the string!");
}
else {
   alert("Your character is at position "+position);
}
```

If you use the second argument to the indexOf() method, the search for your character or string will begin at that position rather than from the 0 position. Thus, one way to find that second "o" would be to skip past the first one at position 1 and start looking at position 2.

```javascript
var the_text = "Cool";
var position = the_text.indexOf("o",2);
if (position === -1) {
   alert("Your character is not in the string!");
}
else {
   alert("Your character is at position "+position);
}
```

This time, the method returns 2 as the result, since it finds it right at the specified starting position.

NOTE

If you want to find all occurrences of a string, you may wish to use a regular expression, discussed later in this chapter.

The lastIndexOf() method finds out where the last instance of a certain character or string is located in the string. It returns the position of only the last occurrence of the character or string that is sent as the argument. If the character or string isn't found in the string value, a value of –1 is returned.

The following code looks for the letter *C* in the string "Cool Cruising Car":

```javascript
var the_text = "Cool Cruising Car";
var position = the_text.lastIndexOf("C");
alert("Your character is at position "+position);
```

This code will display an alert that tells the viewer "Your character is at position 14."

The match(), replace(), search(), and split() Methods

These methods all perform some type of pattern matching.

- The match() method compares a regular expression and a string to see whether they match.

- The replace() method finds out if a regular expression matches a string and then replaces a matched string with a new string.

- The search() method executes the search for a match between a regular expression and a specified string.

- The split() method creates an array of string elements from a string based on the character sent as an argument.

The first three methods deal with regular expressions, so you will learn more about them later in this chapter in the "Regular Expressions" section.

The split() Method   The split() method uses the character sent as an argument as a separator on which to split the single string into a number of parts. It returns an array with each piece of the string minus the separator character.

For instance, the code that follows has a string with a bunch of colons in it:

```
var the_text = "orange:apple:pear:grape",
    split_text = the_text.split(":"),
    end_count = split_text.length;
for (var count = 0; count < end_count; count++) {
  document.write(split_text[count]+"<br>");
}
```

The string assigned to the the_text variable consists of the names of several fruits separated by colons. The next line creates an array named split_text by using the split() method on the text string the_text. The argument sent is a colon, which is what is used to separate the string into array items. In this case, the array ends up with four items.

NOTE

The separator character that is sent as a parameter won't end up in the array: it serves only as a divider between the text so that the method knows where to begin and end each item.

The next line gets the length of the split_text array and places that value in the variable end_count. This information is then used to loop through the new array and print the items on the page.

Figure 13-2 shows the result of this script in a browser, which is a listing of fruit names.

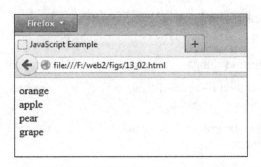

Figure 13-2 The array elements created using the split() method are printed on the page.

The toString() Method

The toString() method returns a string literal value for a string. Here's an example of how you can use this method:

```
var string_obj = new String("Cool");
var string_lit = string_obj.toString();
```

This code takes the String object and uses the toString() method to get its string literal value. It then assigns that value to the string_lit variable.

The toLowerCase() and toUpperCase() Methods

This method returns the string in all lowercase letters. Take a look at this code:

```
var the_text = "I FEEL CALM, REALLY.";
alert(the_text.toLowerCase());
```

This code alerts the string in all lowercase letters, like this sample text:

```
i feel calm, really.
```

The toUpperCase() method returns the string in all uppercase. Here's an example:

```
var the_text = "I am yelling!";
alert(the_text.toUpperCase());
```

This code alerts the string in all uppercase letters, like this sample text:

```
I AM YELLING!
```

The trim() Method

The trim() method removes any excess white space from the beginning and end of a string and returns the result. The original string is left intact. For example, look at the following code:

```
var text = "  Once upon a time...  ",
    trimmed_text = text.trim();
alert(trimmed_text);
```

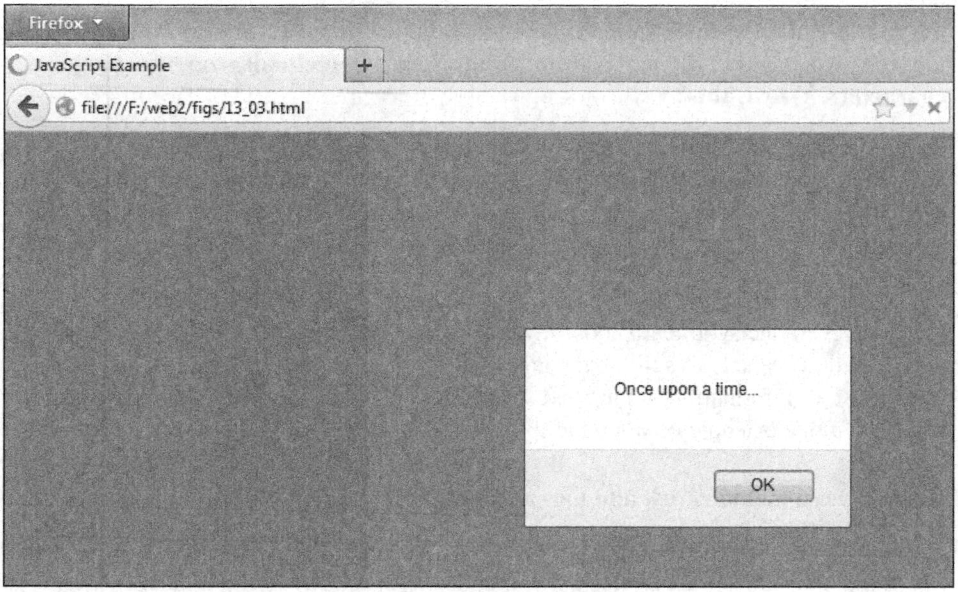

Figure 13-3 The text without the extra spaces is alerted to the viewer.

The spaces from the beginning and end will be removed, and the string "Once upon a time…" is alerted to the viewer. Figure 13-3 shows the result of this script when run in a browser.

NOTE
This method does not work in Internet Explorer prior to version 9.

That's the last of the methods! Now you are ready to test what you've learned.

Ask the Expert

Q: So the length property returns the number of characters in the string, but the string methods start counting at 0. This is a little confusing, just as it is with arrays. Is there an easy way to remember this?

A: The easiest way is probably to remember that the length property begins counting at 1, while the methods count positions beginning at 0. Thus, the length property ends up one greater than the last position in a string. So, if the string has a length of 5, for a method that means the last position in the string is position 4.

(continued)

Q: Yes, but it's also confusing because the second parameter in the slice() and substring() methods is a position higher than the point where the methods stop removing characters. Why is this?

A: It is confusing in the beginning. You just have to get used to how each method works. If you use them often enough, you'll remember which numbers to use in which situations.

Q: Why do I need the split() method? Couldn't I just make my own array and be done with it?

A: Yes. However, once you learn about JavaScript cookies, the split() method will be useful because you'll be able to split up the information stored in the cookie to make use of it. Cookies store information in long text strings, usually with some character as a separator. This is just one example of when the split() method can be useful to you.

Q: A lot of those methods just add tags around a text string. Couldn't I just write out the HTML for that? It seems easier.

A: These methods are not used often any more, due to the ability to use innerHTML or to add DOM nodes to the document. Also, they could cause the HTML code to be invalid, as some of them create tags that are now deprecated in HTML5.

Try This 13-1   Use indexOf() to Test an Address

pr13_1.html
prjs13_1.js

In this project, you practice using the indexOf() method by creating a script that performs a very basic test on an e-mail address that the viewer enters.

Step by Step

1. Create an HTML page that points to a JavaScript file named prjs13_1.js. Create a form with an id of "getemail". Add a text box with an id of "email" and a submit button labeled "Submit E-mail". Save the HTML file as pr13_1.js.

2. When complete, the body of the HTML file should look like this:

```
<body>
<form id="getemail">
<label for="email">Enter E-mail</label>
 <input type="text" id="email"><br><br>
<input type="submit" value="Submit E-mail">
</form>
</body>
```

3. Create an external JavaScript file and save it as prjs13_1.js. Use it for steps 4–7.

4. Assign the value of the "email" text box to a variable named email_add.

5. Use indexOf() to see if the address has an at (@) character in it and to see if the address has a dot (.) character in it.

6. If the address has both an at (@) character and a dot (.) character, send an alert thanking the viewer. If not, send an alert to the viewer saying that he or she needs these characters and to try again.

7. When complete, the JavaScript file should look like this:

```
var getemail = document.getElementById("getemail");
getemail.addEventListener("submit", function(event) {
  var email_add = document.getElementById("email").value;
  event.preventDefault();
  if ( (email_add.indexOf("@") >= 0) && (email_add.indexOf(".") >= 0) ) {
    alert("Thank you!");
  }
  else {
    alert("The @ and . characters are required in the e-mail address.");
  }
}, false);
```

8. Save the JavaScript file and open the HTML file in your browser to try out the script.

Try This Summary

In this project, you used your knowledge of the indexOf() method to test an e-mail address entered by the viewer for certain characters. If one of the characters is missing, an error alert is sent to the viewer. Otherwise, an alert is sent thanking the viewer.

Using Cookies

A *cookie* is a small text file that is stored on the end user's computer. It can be referenced any time the viewer returns to your site, provided the cookie hasn't been deleted or expired. Of course, if the viewer doesn't accept cookies, then a cookie won't be able to be set or referenced later. Keep the following points in mind when using cookies:

- Cookies must be 4KB (4000 characters) each or less.

- A browser can accept up to only 20 cookies from a single domain.

- If a number of viewers don't accept cookies, this eliminates any advantages of your cookie(s) to those viewers.

Cookies can help users browse your site more effectively. For instance, if you use a script on your main page that sends one or more alerts while the page is loading, you won't want that to happen every time the viewer goes to another page on your site and then returns to the home page. It would likely be so aggravating that you wouldn't have a visitor after it happened a few times. The alerts pop up each time the page loads because HTTP lacks state persistence. Cookies fill that gap because they allow the browser to "remember" that the viewer has seen the pop-up alert before and thus not display it on subsequent page visits.

Setting a Cookie

Setting a basic cookie is as easy as giving a value to the cookie property of the document object. The only restriction is that you can't have spaces, commas, or semicolons inside the string. For example, you can set a cookie that will store a name so that you can identify it if you set more than one cookie later. The following code sets a basic cookie:

```
function set_it() {
  document.cookie = "name=tasty1";
}
```

CAUTION

When setting a cookie, remember not to use spaces, commas, or semicolons inside the string that sets the cookie data.

The preceding code sets a cookie with a value of name=tasty1 when the function is called. You can set any delimiter you want, though (or none at all, but setting delimiters allows you to store multiple values like a query string), so the following code would work as well:

```
function set_it() {
  document.cookie = "name:tasty1";
}
```

Adding the additional information isn't very difficult as long as the value does not need a space, as shown in the following code:

```
function set_it() {
  document.cookie = "name=tasty1&fav=Sugar";
}
```

As you can see, the value of the cookie is being formatted in name-value pairs, and each pair is separated with an ampersand (&). Again, you can choose any type of separators you want. The following code is fine as well:

```
function set_it() {
  document.cookie = "name:tasty1|fav:Sugar";
}
```

In this case, the names and values are separated with colons, while the pipe (|) symbol separates them into pairs. You can use anything that you are comfortable using.

The encodeURIComponent() Method

If you want to use spaces, commas, or semicolons in your cookie, you need a way to "escape" them so that they are translated into something a cookie accepts.

A cookie will accept character codes, as a CGI program often does. They may look like %20, %41, or something similar. To turn spaces, commas, and semicolons into these codes, you must use the JavaScript encodeURIComponent() method. It is a method under the window object, so, as you have seen in previous chapters, you can just use encodeURIComponent() rather than window.encodeURIComponent().

The following code shows how you could use the encodeURIComponent() method to set a cookie with a space in it:

```
function set_it() {
  var thetext = "name=tasty1&fav=Chocolate Chip",
      newtext = encodeURIComponent(thetext);
  document.cookie = newtext;
}
```

A string literal is created with information to be used in the cookie

The string is escaped so it can be used in the cookie

The value of the escaped string is placed into a cookie

The thetext variable is set to include the string you want to use in the cookie. The newtext variable is set to hold the result of using the escape() method on thetext. The escaped text is then used as the string for the cookie, which will now have the code for the space character in it (when you want to use this data, you will need to unescape it).

Allowing User Input

By using the escape() method, you can prompt the viewer for the information, escape it, and then use it in the cookie. The following code shows one way to do this to get the viewer's favorite type of cookie:

```
function set_it() {
  var thefav = prompt("Enter your favorite type of cookie", ""),
      thetext = "name=tasty1&fav=" + thefav,
      newtext = encodeURIComponent(thetext);
  document.cookie = newtext;
}
```

The viewer is able to enter information into this prompt

The value entered in the prompt is then added to a string to be used for a cookie

The escaped string is placed into a cookie   The string is escaped so it can be used in a cookie

Now the viewer can help decide the information that will be set in the cookie, and you can use the information your viewers enter on your site on their next visit.

Setting an Expiration Date

Adding an expiration date to a cookie will keep it from being deleted once the browser is closed, or it can be used to expire a cookie you no longer want to use. To set an expiration date, add a little more to your string for the cookie, as shown in the following code:

```
function set_it() {
  var thetext = "quote=I have a quote",
```

```
expdate = ";expires=Mon, 30 Mar 2015 13:00:00 UTC",  ◄──────┐
newtext = encodeURIComponent(thetext);  ◄────┐        An expiration date is given
newtext += expdate;  ◄──────────────┐         The value is escaped before being
document.cookie = newtext;          │         combined with the date to avoid issues
}                                   │    The expiration date is added to the text
```

The cookie is given the value of the
combined text and expiration date

Basically, you are adding on another name-value pair that adds an expiration date (notice that the name-value pairs are separated with a semicolon). It needs to be in this form:

```
expires=date (in UTC format)
```

In the code, an expiration date for the cookie was added by adding the date in UTC format. Then the result is added to the variable that will be used to set the string for the cookie.

If you want a cookie to last a long time, you can set the date far into the future. If you want to expire a cookie you have decided not to use any more, set a date in the past and the cookie will expire.

Reading a Cookie

Reading cookies is straightforward if you have only a single cookie set and want to read it. To read the cookie, you just need to get the value of the document.cookie property from the browser:

```
function read_it() {
  var mycookie = document.cookie;
}
```

However, the preceding code will give you a long and possibly messy string for the value of the mycookie variable. It might look like this:

```
name=tasty1&fav=Chocolate%20Chip
```

The %20 got in the code when the input for the cookie was escaped using the escape() method. To fix that, use the decodeURIComponent() method to get the data in a more readable format.

Thus, the following code would provide the string you need:

```
function read_it() {
  var mycookie = document.cookie,
      fixed_cookie = decodeURIComponent(mycookie);
}
```

Next, you must find a way to extract the information you need from the cookie. Assuming the cookie contained the string just used as an example (name=tasty1&fav=Chocolate%20Chip), the string would now look like this:

```
name=tasty1&fav=Chocolate Chip
```

Notice that the text is divided in two different ways. The ampersand divides the string into name-value pairs, while the equal signs divide the name-value pairs into their names and values.

Assuming the string name=tasty1&fav=Chocolate Chip is what is now in the fixed_cookie variable from the code, you could use that variable to create a new array by splitting the string on the ampersand character:

The value of the cookie property is read

The value is unescaped so the string will have readable characters

```
function read_it() {
  var mycookie = document.cookie,
      fixed_cookie = decodeURIComponent(mycookie),
      thepairs = fixed_cookie.split("&");
}
```

The cookie string is split into an array on the ampersand (&)

The preceding code splits the string into two array values:

```
thepairs[0] with a value of name=tasty1
thepairs[1] with a value of fav=Chocolate Chip
```

You split each of these into a new array that will have a name and a value. Therefore, you need some code like this:

```
function read_it() {
  var mycookie = document.cookie;
      fixed_cookie = decodeURIComponent(mycookie);
      thepairs = fixed_cookie.split("&");
      name = thepairs[0];
      fave = thepairs[1];
      name_propval = name.split("=");
      fav_propval = fav.split("=");
}
```

The values of the array elements are assigned to variables

The new variables are split on the equal sign

Now you have all the information you need using the name_propval[] and fav_propval[] arrays:

```
name_propval[0] with a value of name
name_propval[1] with a value of tasty1
fav_propval[0] with a value of fav
fav_propval[1] with a value of Chocolate Chip
```

You can use them in any way you like, such as placing them in alerts:

```
function read_it() {
  var mycookie = document.cookie;
      fixed_cookie = decodeURIComponent(mycookie);
      thepairs = fixed_cookie.split("&");
      name = thepairs[0];
      fave = thepairs[1];
      name_propval = name.split("=");
      fav_propval = fav.split("=");
```

```
        alert("The cookie's " + name_propval[0] + " is " + name_propval[1]);
        alert("My favorite type of cookie is " + fav_propval[1]);
    }
```

The values obtained from the cookies are used

You might want to be sure document.cookie exists before you try to run all the code in the
function. Any cookie you set to expire later can be read, but those without the cookie may get
an error. By making the check, you can ensure the existence of the cookie or send the viewer
to the function that sets the cookie. To do that, add an if/else block around the code in the
function, as shown here:

```
function read_it() {
  var mycookie = document.cookie;
      fixed_cookie = decodeURIComponent(mycookie);
      thepairs = fixed_cookie.split("&");
      name = thepairs[0];
      fave = thepairs[1];
      name_propval = name.split("=");
      fav_propval = fav.split("=");
    alert("The cookie's " + name_propval[0] + " is " + name_propval[1]);
    alert("My favorite type of cookie is " + fav_propval[1]);
}
if (document.cookie) {
  read_it();
}
else {
  set_it();
  read_it();
}
```

The preceding code assumes that the set_it() function exists and will set the cookie if needed.
It also assumes that this cookie is the only cookie set from this domain and that it is formatted
a particular way. If you plan to use multiple cookies, you will need to do additional testing to
ensure you grab the cookie you need. You can see webmonkey.com/2010/02/advanced_javascript_
tutorial_-_lesson_2/#Reading_and_Writing_Multiple_Cookies for more information on this.

Try This 13-2 Remember a Name

pr13_2.html
prjs13_2.js

In this project, you use a cookie to remember a name when a visitor returns
to the page.

Step by Step

1. Create a new HTML document that uses an external JavaScript file named prjs13_2.js.
   Create a div with an id of "greeting". Save the HTML file as pr13_2.html.

2. Create an external JavaScript file and save it as prjs13_2.js. Use it for the remaining steps.

3. Create a function named set_it() that will set a cookie. Set the expiration to a future date. Allow the viewer to enter a name in a prompt and then use the viewer's entry in the cookie.

4. Create a function named read_it() that will check whether the cookie exists and, if so, read the cookie and write the name on the page in the following format (replace *<name>* with the name read from the cookie):

```
Welcome, <name>!
```

5. If the cookie exists, call the read_it() function. If the cookie doesn't exist, call the set_it() followed by the read_it() function.

6. Save the JavaScript file and open the HTML file in your browser. Enter your name and get your greeting. If you close your browser and open the page again, you should see your name without the need to enter it again.

Try This Summary

In this project, you used your knowledge of setting and reading cookies with JavaScript. You created a Web page that remembers the viewer's name when the viewer returns to the Web page.

Using Regular Expressions

Regular expressions give you much more power to handle strings in a script. They allow you to form patterns that can be matched against strings, rather than trying to use the String object's methods, which may make it more difficult to be precise.

For example, you may want to know whether the value entered in a text box for an e-mail address included at least one character at the beginning, followed by an at (@) symbol, followed by at least one character, followed by a dot (.), followed by at least two more characters (matching a traditional e-mail address like jon@jon.com or the shortest type of e-mail address, j@j.jj).

The String object's methods don't provide a neat and clean way to perform this task (although with enough tinkering, it may be possible). However, a regular expression can shorten the task or even turn a match that seemed impossible with the String object's methods into one that can be completed.

Creating Regular Expressions

To create regular expressions, you must create an instance of the JavaScript RegExp object or a RegExp literal. To create a RegExp literal, you just assign the regular expression to a variable. Instead of using quotation marks to surround the expression, you use forward (/) slashes, as shown here:

```
var varname = /your_pattern/flags;
```

You replace *varname* with the name you want to use for a variable and replace *your_pattern* with the regular expression pattern of your choice. You can follow the last slash with one or more flags (which are discussed in the upcoming section "Adding Flags").

NOTE
JavaScript uses forward slashes to let the browser know that a regular expression is between them, the same way quote marks are used to set off strings. Thus, if a forward slash is used within the regular expression, it must be escaped with a backslash in order to work properly. For instance, instead of writing /02/03/2009/, you would need to write /02\/03\/2009/.

The easiest regular expression pattern to create is one that looks for an exact match of characters. For instance, if you wanted to see if the sequence *our* is present in a string, you could create the following regular expression pattern:

```
var tomatch = /our/;
```

The preceding code creates a RegExp literal named tomatch. Now you need a string against which to test the pattern. If you test the word *our* against the expression, it's a match.

If you test *your*, *sour*, *pour*, or *pouring* against it, then it's a match. If you test *cool*, *Our*, *oUR*, *OUR*, or *souR*, then it won't be a match. So how do you perform this test?

Testing Strings Against Regular Expressions
To test a regular expression against a string, you can use the test() method of the RegExp object. The basic syntax is as follows:

```
regex_name.test(string_to_test);
```

This syntax is similar to using a string method. You replace *regex_name* with the name of the regular expression and replace *string_to_test* with a string or a string variable name. For instance, look at the following example:

```
var tomatch = /our/;
tomatch.test("pour");
```

This code will test the "pour" string against the regular expression named "tomatch." It doesn't use the result, though.

The test() method returns a Boolean value of true or false. It returns true when any portion of the string matches the regular expression pattern. Using the test() method, you can already write a short script, as shown here:

The prompt gets a name from the viewer

```
var thename = prompt("Enter your name",""),
    tomatch = /John/,
    is_a_match = tomatch.test(thename);
if (is_a_match) {
```

A regular expression is set up to see if the name entered will match it

A variable is used to hold the result of the test() method

```
    alert("Wow, we have the same name!");    ◄──── If the result is true, this alert appears
}
else {
    alert("Not my name, but it will work!");◄── If the result is not true, this alert appears
}
```

The prompt gathers a name and holds the value in a variable. The pattern to match is John, and it is case sensitive. Thus, only an entry containing John with a capital *J* followed by lowercase *o*, *h*, and *n* will create a match and return true when it is tested (though it could contain more than just John, so entries such as Johnny or John Doe would also return true—if you want only a specific set of characters, you need to use some additional special characters, which will be discussed later in this section).

The result of the test() method is assigned to a variable named is_a_match. The variable is then used as the condition for the if statement. If the variable holds a value of true, then the viewer gets the "Wow, we have the same name!" alert. If it holds a value of false, the viewer gets the "Not my name, but it will work!" alert instead. Figure 13-4 shows the result of this script when "Steve" is used as the name.

If you want to shorten the script, you can just make the result of the test() method the condition for the if statement (rather than create another variable), as in the following code:

```
var thename = prompt("Enter your name",""),
    tomatch = /John/;
if (tomatch.test(thename)) {  ◄──────── The result of the test() method is used as the condition
    alert("Wow, we have the same name!");
}
else {
    alert("Not my name, but it will work!");
}
```

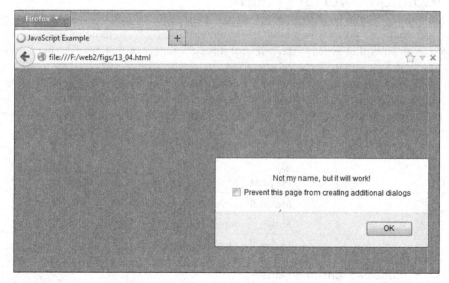

Figure 13-4 The name does not match the regular expression pattern.

Because the method returns true or false, it can be placed as the condition for the if statement on its own. (You could make it (tomatch.test(thename)==true) if you wanted to, though.)

Adding Flags

Flags allow you to make the match case insensitive or to look for every match in the string rather than just the first one (a global test). To add a flag, place it after the last slash in the regular expression. You can use three options, as shown in Table 13-3.

If you wanted to adjust the name script used previously to be case insensitive, you could add an i flag to the regular expression, as shown in the following code:

```
var thename = prompt("Enter your name",""),
    tomatch = /John/i;          The i flag makes this regular expression case insensitive
if (tomatch.test(thename)) {
  alert("Wow, we have the same name!");
}
else {
  alert("Not my name, but it will work!");
}
```

The test() method will now return true as long as the pattern of John is in the string. It can be in any case, so now John, JOHN, john, and even JoHn are all matches and will cause the test() method to return true.

You can also use more than one flag or all three flags at once. For example, if you want to have the match be both case insensitive and multiline, you could use the following:

```
var tomatch = /John/im;
```

Creating Powerful Patterns

Although it's nice to be able to create such an exact pattern, you won't always be looking for a match that is so precise. In many cases, you will be looking to match a more general pattern, such as an entry that needs to have at least three characters or that needs to have two characters of any type followed by a special character.

By using special characters in your expressions, you can create the type of patterns you need to match a given sequence you want. JavaScript regular expressions use the syntax of Perl regular expressions as a model. Thus, if you've used regular expressions in Perl, much of this material will be familiar. Table 13-4 lists a number of the characters to help you create your patterns.

Flag(s)	Purpose
i	Makes the match case insensitive
g	Makes the match global
m	Makes the match work in multiline mode

Table 13-3 Regular Expression Flags

Character	Purpose	Example
^	Matches only from the beginning of a line	/^c/ matches c in *corn* /^c/ does not match c in *acorn*
$	Matches only at the end of the line	/r$/ matches r in *Car* /r$/ does not match t in *Cat*
*	Matches the character preceding it if the character occurs zero or more times	/co*/ matches *co* or *c* /co*/ does not match *pi*
+	Matches the character preceding it if it occurs one or more times	/co+/ matches *co* or *cooooo* /co+/ does not match *ca*
?	Matches the character preceding it if it occurs zero or one time	/o?l/ matches *style* or *column* /co?l/ does not match *cool*
.	Matches any individual character, excluding the newline character	/.l/ matches *al* or *@l* /.l/ does not match \nl or l
(x)	By replacing x with characters, matches that sequence and keeps it in memory to be used later; used for grouping of expressions	/(a)/ matches *a* /(cool)/ matches *cool* /(cool)/ does not match *coal*
|	Used as a logical OR symbol to allow a match of what is on the left of the symbol OR what is on its right	/cool|bad/ matches *cool* /cool|bad/ matches *bad* /cool|bad/ does not match *car*
{x}	Using a number to replace x, matches when there are exactly x occurrences of the character preceding it	/n{1}/ matches *n* /nn{2}/ matches *nnn* /nn{1}/ does not match *nnn*
{x,}	Using a number to replace x, matches when there are x or more occurrences of the character preceding it	/n{1,}/ matches *n* /n{1,}/ matches *nnnnn* /n{3,}/ does not match *nn*
{x,y}	Using numbers to replace x and y, matches when there are at least x occurrences of the character preceding it but no more than y occurrences of it	/n{1,2}/ matches *n* /n{1,2}/ matches *nn* /n{2,3}/ does not match *n* /n{4,7}/ does not match *nnn*
[]	Matches a character set of your choice; will match when any one of the characters in the brackets (such as [abc]) or any one of a range of characters (such as [a–k]) is present	/[abc]/ matches *a* /[abc]/ matches *b* /[abc]/ matches *c* /[a–k]/ matches *j* /[a–k]/ does not match *n*
[^]	Matches when the characters in your character set are *not* present; may be a set (such as [abc]) or a range (such as [a–k]); if it is not within brackets [], then it matches the beginning of the string, as in the first entry in this table.	/[^abc]/ matches *d* /[^abc]/ does not match *b* /[^a–k]/ matches *n* /[^a–k]/ does not match *j* (continues)

Table 13-4 Regular Expression Codes

Character	Purpose	Example
\	Used to escape special characters or to make a normal character special	\@ escapes the @ character \n represents a newline character
[\b]	Matches a BACKSPACE keystroke	/[\b]/ matches a backspace
\b	Matches when the character before or after it is located at a word boundary, such as before or after a space character; to match the beginning of a word, place the character to the right of the symbol (\bc); to match the end of a word, place the character to the left (c\b)	/\bc/ matches c in *my car* /\bm/ matches m in *my car* /\bc/ does not match c in *ace* /\bm/ does not match m in *Sam* /m\b/ matches m in *Sam* /c\b/ matches c in *Mac W* /m\b/ does not match m in *emu* /c\b/ does not match c in *my car*
\B	Matches a character that is not located at a word boundary	/\Ba/ matches a in *car* /\Bc/ does not match c in *car*
\cX	Using a letter character to replace X, matches when the user presses the CTRL key followed by typing the letter X	/\cX/ matches CTRL-X /\cV/ matches CTRL-V /\cS/ does not match CTRL-Z
\d	Matches if the character is a single numeric character	/\d/ matches 4 /\d/ does not match s
\D	Matches a single character if it is *not* a numeric character	/\D/ matches s /\D/ does not match 4
\f	Matches if there is a form feed	/\f/ matches a form feed
\n	Matches if there is a new line	/\n/ matches a new line
\r	Matches if there is a carriage return	/\r/ matches a carriage return
\s	Matches a single character if it represents white space (such as a space or a new line)	/\s/ matches the space in *b c* /\s/ matches the tab in *b c* /\s/ does not match *bc*
\S	Matches a single character if it does *not* represent white space	/\S/ matches d /\S/ does not match a blank space
\t	Matches if there is a tab	/\t/ matches the tab in *b c*
\v	Matches if there is a vertical tab	/\v/ matches a vertical tab
\w	Matches any single character that is a letter, number, or underscore	/\w/ matches 4 /\w/ does not match @
\W	Matches any single character that is *not* a letter, number, or underscore	/\W/ matches @ /\W/ does not match g

Table 13-4 Regular Expression Codes (*continued*)

As you can see, extensive options exist for creating the pattern you need. Now you could easily verify strings according to the standards you decide to set.

Now, if you want to make sure a text field contains one or more digits, you could use the /d and + characters from Table 13-4 with the following HTML and JavaScript code, starting with the HTML code:

```
<body>
<form id="has_digits">
<label for="user_text">Enter some text:</label>
 <input type="text" id="user_text">
<input type="submit" value="Test">
</form>
</body>
```

Next, the JavaScript code:

```
var has_digits = document.getElementById("has_digits");
has_digits.addEventListener("submit", function(event) {
  var has_num = document.getElementById("user_text").value,
      tomatch = /\d+/;
  event.preventDefault();
  if (tomatch.test(has_num)) {
    alert("Your entry contained one or more numbers!");
  }
  else {
    alert("Your entry did not contain any numbers!");
  }
}, false);
```

This code simply checks to see whether any digits are in the string. If you want to ensure that the viewer typed in *only* digits without any other types of characters, you need to be sure the regular expression is written to test from the beginning to the end of the string. Using the ^ and $ symbols from Table 13-4, you can ensure that the string is tested for the match starting at the beginning of the string and ending at the end of the string. The + following the \d ensures that there is at least one number entered. Thus, the following patterns would allow only digits:

```
var tomatch = /^\d+$/;
```

Since the only valid characters from the beginning to the end of the string are digits, this will return true only for entries containing digits without other characters present in the string. This is especially helpful for validating forms and other types of user input to ensure that it is the type of input you expect.

NOTE

Regular expressions can be quite powerful for validation because they allow less erroneous information to be accepted.

Client-side validation of form submissions with data such as e-mail addresses or phone numbers can save unnecessary trips to the server. However, users may disable JavaScript support and make form submissions directly. Therefore, client-side validation should support server-side validation (by a PHP script or CGI script, for example), but should never replace it (it could cause a great security risk to store or display data from a viewer that has not been validated).

Grouping Expressions

You will notice in Table 13-4 that an expression surrounded by parentheses indicates a group that can be stored for later use in the expression (or using a method such as the match() method where it will store each match of a group along with the overall match in an array).

For example, you might decide to use a particular sequence of numbers and to have that sequence repeat a particular number of times. To match the number of times something is repeated, you can use curly brackets ({ }) along with a number or number range. For instance, if you want to match five instances of the number 3, you could use the following expression:

```
/3{5}/
```

If you wanted this to be a match if the number 3 occurs at least five times but no more than ten times, you could use the following expression:

```
/3{5,10}/
```

Now, suppose you wanted the match to start with a 3 and have any digit as the next character, and wanted to match that entire sequence five times (thus, something like 3234353637 would be a match). You might write the following:

```
/3\d{5}/
```

The trouble with this is that it gets the 3 correct, but matches five digits afterward without the need to repeat the 3. Thus, a number like 387643 would match even though you wanted to have five sets of two numbers with each set beginning with a 3. To fix this, you can group the 3 and the \d together with parentheses, and follow that with the number of times it should repeat:

```
/(3\d){5}/
```

This time, the 3 and the second digit are grouped together, and that sequence must be repeated five times.

Grouping is a helpful way to get more out of your use of regular expressions, and you will see more of this when you get to form validation in the next chapter.

The replace(), match(), and search() Methods

These methods of the String object were mentioned earlier in the chapter, and will make more sense now that regular expressions have been introduced.

The replace() Method

To replace information in a string, you can use regular expressions and the replace() method of the String object. The syntax for using the replace() method is as follows:

```
varname = stringname.replace(regex, newstring);
```

You replace *varname* with the name of the variable that will hold the new string value once the information has been replaced. You replace *stringname* with the name of the string variable that will undergo the replacement. You replace *regex* with the name of the regular expression to be used to match against the string. Finally, you replace *newstring* with the string or string variable to replace any matched values in the string.

As an example, the following code replaces the first instance of "car" in mystring with "skunk":

A string literal is created

```
var mystring = "I like the way a new car smells, and cars are fun.",
    toreplace =/car/,          The pattern to replace is set as a regular expression
    newstring = mystring.replace(toreplace, "skunk");
alert(newstring);
```

The alert shows the updated string

The first instance of a match is replaced in the string, and the result is assigned to a variable

The preceding code replaces only the first instance of car, giving the alert "I like the way a new skunk smells, and cars are fun." If you want to change every instance of "car" instead, the g flag is helpful at the end of the regular expression, as shown in the following code:

```
var mystring = "I like the way a new car smells, and cars are fun.",
    toreplace =/car/g,
    newstring = mystring.replace(toreplace, "skunk");
alert(newstring);
```

Adding the g flag causes all matches of the pattern to be replaced when the replace() method is run

The g flag will match every instance of the regular expression it finds in the string. Thus, when the replace() method is run, all instances of "car" will be replaced with "skunk." The viewer will see this alert: "I like the way a new skunk smells, and skunks are fun."

You could also use the replace() method to make a name-changing script that is shorter and somewhat less complex than the one earlier in this chapter. By using the replace() method with a regular expression, the first letter of the first and last name can be changed more easily. The following code shows how:

```
function getname() {
  var tomatch = /^[A-Za-z]+\s[A-Za-z]+$/,
      toreplace = /\b[A-Za-z]/gi,
      thename = prompt("Enter your first and last name", "");
  if (tomatch.test(thename)) {
  newname = thename.replace(toreplace, "Z");
  alert("Now your name is " + newname);
```

```
  }
  else {
   alert("Name invalid. Please Try Again");
   getname();
  }
}
getname();
```

This script changes the first letter of the first and last name to *Z* regardless of what it was before. The regular expression for the replacement simply looks for a letter at the beginning of a word using the word boundary (\b) code. Each time a letter is at the beginning of a word, it is replaced.

The validation of the input keeps the script from getting more than two names and one space, and it also ensures that at least one letter is in each name, with no numbers or special characters. The illustration shows the result of the script if the viewer enters Debra Loo at the prompt: the viewer's name is changed.

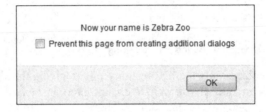

The match() Method

The match() method compares a regular expression and a string to see whether they match. It returns an array containing one or more matches, depending on how it is used. If no match is found, it returns –1.

The basic use of the match() method is as follows:

```
string.match(regex);
```

The *string* will be your string literal, and *regex* will be your regular expression literal. Note the difference in the order between this method and the test() method. You could use it in this way:

```
var mystring = "I am Ironman!",
    tomatch = /Iron/;
if (mystring.match(tomatch)) {
  alert("Your string contains Iron!");
}
else {
  alert("Sorry, no Iron in your string.");
}
```

If this is used with the g flag or with grouping using (), it will remember each match made (including matches on groups or nested groups) and return each match as an array element.

The search() Method

The search() method executes the search for a match between a regular expression and a specified string. If a match is found, it returns the position in the string where the beginning of the match was found. Otherwise, it returns –1. Here is an example of this method in action:

```
var mystring = "I am Ironman!",
    tomatch = /Iron/;
if (mystring.search(tomatch)) {
  alert("Iron found at position " + mystring.search(tomatch) + "!");
}
else {
  alert("Sorry, no Iron in your string.");
}
```

As you can see, the syntax is much like that of the match() method.

More Information

For more information on regular expressions and how to create more complex patterns, you can look at the following online resources:

- www.regular-expressions.info/

- www.regular-expressions.info/javascript.html (includes specifics on the JavaScript engine)

- https://developer.mozilla.org/en/Core_JavaScript_1.5_Guide/Regular_Expressions

    With these techniques down, you are ready to move on to working with forms in JavaScript and working on the validation of form contents.

Chapter 13 Self Test

1. The _____ object provides properties and methods to get information about strings or to modify strings.

2. What are the two ways in which you can create String objects?

    A. Creating an instance of the String object and creating a string literal

    B. Creating an instance of the Array object and creating a string literal

    C. Creating a numeric variable and creating a numeric object

    D. Creating a string and adding numbers

3. You can create a string _____ by assigning a string value to a variable.

4. A regular text string is able to use the String object's methods because:

   A. It is already a String object

   B. It can use other methods as well, so it can use the methods of the String object

   C. JavaScript takes the string literal and turns it into a temporary String object

   D. The String object uses the string literal as-is

5. Which property of the String object can you use with both String objects and string literals?

   A. prototype

   B. constructor

   C. length

   D. color

6. The _____ property returns the length of a string.

7. Which of the following correctly creates a string literal?

   A. var the_text = "Look at me!;

   B. var the_text = "Look at me!";

   C. var the_text = Look at me!;

   D. var the_text = new String("Look at me!");

8. Which method of the String object can you use to find which character is at a given position in a string?

   A. indexOf()

   B. charAt()

   C. charIsAt()

   D. indexOfThePosition()

9. The _____ method adds <big> and </big> tags around a string value.

10. The concat() method _____ two or more strings together and returns the new combined string value.

11. Which one of the following statements is true?

    A. The charAt() method returns a numeric value that is the position of a character sent as a parameter.

    B. The split() method creates a new string by removing a portion of the string and returning the string minus the portion removed.

    C. The length property allows you to add longer properties and methods to the String object.

    D. The indexOf() method returns a numeric value that is the position of a character sent as a parameter, but only the position of the first occurrence of that character.

12. Cookie information is stored in the _____ property.

13. The _____ method returns the string literal value of a string.

14. To replace information in a string, you can use regular expressions and the _____ method of the String object.

15. The _____ method compares a regular expression and a string to see whether they match.

Chapter 14

JavaScript and Forms

Key Skills & Concepts

- Accessing Forms

- Using the Properties and Methods of the Form Object

- Ensuring the Accessibility of Forms

- Validating Forms

- HTML5 and Forms

When you use JavaScript to access forms, you can create new scripts for your Web pages. This chapter begins by explaining how to access a form with JavaScript. Then you'll learn about the various properties and methods to use with forms and form elements. You'll also learn about forms and accessibility, how to validate form elements, and how to use <select></select> elements as navigational tools.

Accessing Forms

Each time you add a set of <form> and </form> tags to an HTML document, a form object is created. To access one of the forms using JavaScript, you can use any one of the following options:

- Use the forms array of the document object

- Name the form in the opening form tag and use that name to access the form

- Give the form an id in the opening form tag and access it using the document .getElementById() method

Using the forms Array

The forms array allows you to access a form using an index in the array. Each set of <form> and </form> tags on the page will create an additional item in the forms array, in the order in which they appear in the document. Thus, you can reference the first form in a document like this:

```
document.forms[0]
```

As you will recall, arrays begin counting at 0, so the previous example will access the first form in the document. If you want to access the second form, you could use the following:

```
document.forms[1]
```

This will work for the rest of the forms on the page in the same way. Just remember to begin counting at 0 rather than 1 to access the correct form.

Accessing the form doesn't do anything on its own. The form that you access is an object. To use it, you need a property or method of the object. The properties and methods of the form object are listed in a later section, "Using the Properties and Methods of the Form Object," but for now, take a look at the length property to see what it does.

A Property Value

The examples in this section use the form object's length property. This property allows you to find out how many elements exist (such as input boxes, select boxes, radio buttons, and others) in an HTML form. For example, take a look at this code:

```
<body>
<form>
<label>Name:</label><input type="text">       The first element is this text box
<label>E-mail:</label><input type="text">      The second element is this text box
<input type="submit" value="Submit">           The third element is this submit button
</form>
</body>
```

The code creates a short form that contains three elements: two text boxes and the submit button. Because it's the only form on the page, it will be the first form, allowing you to access it using document.forms[0]. To use the length property, add it to the end like this:

```
document.forms[0].length
```

Using the preceding code, you can create a short script to tell the viewer how many elements are in the form. The code that follows will write the information on the page after the form:

```
document.write("The form has " + document.forms[0].length + " elements.");
```
The number of elements in the form is displayed on the page

This code informs the viewer that the form has three elements. Figure 14-1 shows this script's results when using the example HTML code shown previously.

Covering Two Length Properties

If you want to try to show the number of elements in the forms on a page when there is more than one form, you can use a more complex script that prints a message for each form on the page. Recall that because there is a forms array, you can find its length.

The length of the forms array is the number of forms on the page (similarly, the length property of a particular form is the number of elements in the form). To find the number of forms on the page rather than the length of a form, you can use the following code:

```
document.forms.length
```

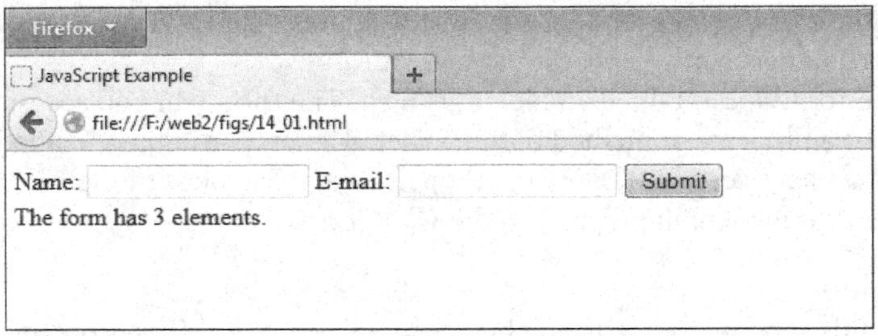

Figure 14-1 The number of elements in the form is displayed to the viewer.

This syntax finds the number of forms on the page. Thus, you need to remember these points:

- document.forms.length finds the number of forms on the page.
- document.forms[*x*].length finds the number of elements in a specific form on the page, where *x* is the index of the form to be accessed.

This syntax might look a bit confusing, but just remember that one length property is for the forms in general, while the other length property is used on a specific form.

CAUTION
Remember the difference between document.forms.length and document.forms[*x*] .length. The former finds the number of forms on the page, while the latter finds the number of elements in a specific form (by replacing *x* with a number).

The following script uses both of the length properties and a loop to cycle through each form. The code displays the number of elements in each form on the page. First, the HTML code (save as lengths.html):

```
<body>

<h1>Form Lengths</h1>

<h2>Form 1</h2>
<form>
<label>Name:</label><input type="text"><br>
<label>E-mail:</label><input type="text"><br>
<input type="submit" value="Submit">
</form>

<h2>Form 2</h2>
<form>
<label>Favorite Color:</label><input type="text"><br>
<label>Favorite Food:</label><input type="text"><br>
<input type="reset" value="Reset">
<input type="submit" value="Submit">
</form>
```

The elements of the first form

The elements of the second form

```
<h2>Results</h2>
<script type="text/javascript" src="lengths.js"></script>

</body>
```

Next, the JavaScript code (save as lengths.js):

The loop to cycle through all the forms on the page begins

```
for (var count=0; count < document.forms.length; count++) {
    var formnum = count + 1;
    document.write("Form " + formnum + " has " + document.forms[count].length);
    document.write(" elements.<br>");
}
```

A variable is created to hold the form number (one more than its index number to look user-friendly)

The results are written on the page

The code creates two forms in the HTML document. The script then opens a loop beginning at 0 (where arrays begin counting) and ending before it gets to the value of document.forms. length, which is the number of forms on the page. Because there are two forms (which will make 2 the value of document.forms.length), the count runs from 0 to 1 and then stops. The count allows you to access the forms array at indexes 0 and 1, which will turn out to be Form 1 and Form 2 in the HTML code.

The formnum variable has the value of the position number in the array plus one, which is the number of the form as seen in the HTML code. The script then writes the number of elements in each form on the page using the document.write() statements.

The forms array is used with the value of the count variable as the index number, which finds the number of elements in the specified form each time through the loop. Figure 14-2 shows the results of this code when run in a browser.

Using Form Names

Using form names allows you to name the forms on the page that you want to access later. This option can help eliminate any confusion between document.forms.length and document .forms[x].length because you won't need to use the latter unless you're trying to loop through each element in each form on the page.

To use a form name, you must add a name="*yourname*" attribute to the opening form tag on the form you want to access. Replace *yourname* with a name you want to use for the form, as in the following code:

```
<form name="info_form">
<label>Name:</label><input type="text"><br>
<input type="submit">
</form>
```

The name of the form is now info_form, and you can use this name to access the form in your script.

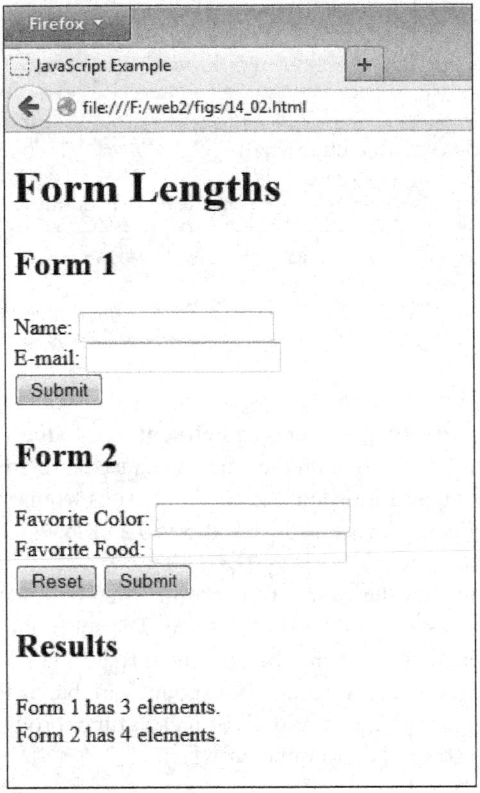
Firefox
JavaScript Example
file:///F:/web2/figs/14_02.html
Form Lengths
Form 1
Name:
E-mail:
Submit
Form 2
Favorite Color:
Favorite Food:
Reset
Submit
Results
Form 1 has 3 elements.
Form 2 has 4 elements.

Figure 14-2 The number of elements in each form is displayed.

The name of the form allows it to become an instance of the form object that you can access through its name. To use JavaScript to access a form that uses a form name, you can use the syntax shown here:

```
document.yourname
```

Replace *yourname* with the name given to the form in the name="*yourname*" attribute in its opening form tag. Thus, if you wanted to write a script to find the number of elements in the named form in this example, you could use the following code:

```
document.write("The form has " + document.info_form.length + " elements.");
```

The number of elements in the named form is written on the page

Notice how the form is accessed in the document.write() statement. Instead of the forms array, the name of the form is in its place. It can now access the properties of the form object and does so by accessing the length property.

Using an ID

The third way to access a form is to use an id attribute and to then use document.getElementById(). This is often the clearest way to access a form and its elements, because you can access each element by using its individual id, whereas the previous two access methods require you to know which array index the form is at or the form name and the element's name.

NOTE

If you need a refresher on accessing elements using getElementById(), you can refer to Chapter 9.

If you wanted to write the script from the previous section using the id method, you could use the following HTML code:

```
<form id="info_form"> ◄─────────── The form is given an id
Name: <input type="text"><br>
<input type="submit">
</form>
```

Next, the JavaScript code:

getElementById() is used to access the form and get its length

```
var f_length = document.getElementById("info_form").length; ◄─┘
document.write("The form has " + f_length + " elements."); ◄─┐
```

The number of elements in the named form is written on the page

Since you are familiar with using document.getElementById() from previous chapters, this should be a straightforward method for you.

The method you use to access a form and its elements will depend on the types of scripts you are writing. If you are using multiple forms on a page, then the forms array can be a handy way to cycle through each form. If you are trying to get as much backward compatibility with older HTML code or browsers as possible, using the name method may be the way to go. On the other hand, trying to validate in XHTML 1.0 Strict will require you to use an id to name each form element, so using the id method would be more appropriate in that case.

Using the Properties and Methods of the Form Object

The JavaScript form object will help you when you need to access certain elements or attributes of the form in a script. The form object has only a few properties and methods. The properties are described first.

Properties

The form object's properties provide information you might need when working with forms in your scripts. Table 14-1 lists the properties of the form object and their values.

Most of these properties just hold values corresponding to the various attributes in an HTML form tag. A few of them have different types of values, though, as explained next.

The action Property

This property allows you to access the value of the action="*url*" attribute in the opening form tag. This attribute is used to send the form to a server-side script for processing (such as a Perl or PHP script). The following example shows how to access the property with a named form. First, the HTML code:

```
<form name="info_form" action="http://someplace.com/php/form.php">
<label>Name:</label><input type="text"><br>
<input type="submit">
</form>
```

An action attribute is defined

Next, the JavaScript code:

```
document.write("The form goes to " + document.info_form.action);
```

This script writes the URL on the page given in the action attribute. Figure 14-3 shows the result of this script when run in a browser.

The elements Property (Array)

The elements property is an array that allows you to access each element within a specific form in the same order it appears in the code, starting from 0. It works much like the forms array but has an entry for each element in a given form.

Property	Value
action	The value of the action attribute in the HTML form tag
autocomplete	Defines whether the browser can use the autocomplete feature, which can assist users when filling in forms by completing certain input for them
elements	An array that includes an array element for each form element in an HTML form
encoding or enctype	The value of the enctype attribute, which varies with different browsers
length	The value of the total number of elements in an HTML form
method	The value of the method attribute in an HTML form tag
name	The value of the name attribute in an HTML form tag
noValidate	The value of the novalidate attribute in HTML, which when present specifies that the form should not be validated (HTML5)
target	The value of the target attribute in an HTML form tag

Table 14-1   Properties of the Form Object

Figure 14-3 The value of the action attribute in the form is printed on the page.

To use the elements array to access an element in a form, use the index number for the element you want to access. For instance, the following form has two elements:

```
<form name="info_form">
<label>Name:</label><input type="text"><br>
<input type="submit">
</form>
```

To access the first element (the text box), you can use the syntax shown here:

```
document.info_form.elements[0]
```

Alternatively, if you want to use the forms array (assume this is the first form on the page), you could use this syntax:

```
document.forms[0].elements[0]
```

Yet another option to access the text box is to name it (as with the form) and access it using its name. You can do this with each element, as well as the form itself; you can choose which method is best for accessing a form and its elements in each situation.

The following code gives the form and the text box a name, and allows you to access them using those names:

```
<form name="info_form">
<label>Name:</label><input type="text" name="yourname"><br>
<input type="submit">
</form>
```

In this case, you could access the text box using the form name and the text box name, as in the syntax shown here:

```
document.info_form.yourname
```

Also, you can of course use the id method:

```
<form>
<label>Name:</label><input type="text" id="yourname"><br>
<input type="submit">
</form>
```

Then, you can access the input element using document.getElementById():

```
document.getElementByID("yourname");
```

The encoding and enctype Properties

These properties both contain the value of the enctype attribute of a form tag, which is the type of encoding used for the data that is sent to the server from the form. The default is "application/x-www-form-urlencoded".

The length Property

The length property holds the number of elements in a given form on a page. This chapter has already covered this property pretty extensively, so there's no need to discuss it again here.

The method Property

This property holds the value contained in the method attribute of a form tag. Thus, if you're sending the form to the server to be processed, you might use something similar to the following code:

```
<form name="f1" method="post" action= "http://site.com/cgi-bin/form.cgi">
<!-- form contents here -->
</form>
```

The value of the method property for this form would be post because it's within the method attribute of the form.

The name Property

This property holds the value of the form's name, which is given to it in the name attribute of the form tag. You might have some code like this:

```
<form name="cool_form">
<!-- form contents here -->
</form>
```

Here, the value of the name property is cool_form, because it's the value inside the name attribute of the form.

The noValidate Property

This property contains the Boolean value of the novalidate attribute in a form tag (added in HTML5). If true, the form is not supposed to be validated when submitted. For more on HTML5 validation, see "HTML5 and Forms" later in this chapter.

The target Property

This property holds the value given in the target attribute in a form tag. For instance, you might have the following code:

```
<form name="cool_form" target="_top" action="program.cgi">
<!-- form contents here -->
</form>
```

Here, the value of the target property is _top, because it's the value inside the target attribute of the form.

Methods

Now take a look at the form object's methods. Selected methods will be discussed following Table 14-2.

The checkValidity() Method

In HTML5, you can have the browser check whether a field contains data or validates against a pattern, which does not require JavaScript. You may wish to perform further actions; however, depending on whether or not all of the fields that require validation pass their respective tests. The checkValidity() function returns true if *all* elements that have validation requirements pass, or returns false if *any* of these elements fail validation. More information on how HTML5 affects forms can be found later in this chapter in the "HTML5 and Forms" section.

Method	Description
checkValidity()	Returns whether or not all form elements that are required to be validated by the browser passed validation (HTML5)
dispatchFormChange()	Creates a formchange event for each form element that is triggered when a change is made (HTML5)
dispatchFormInput()	Creates a forminput event for each form element that is triggered when there is new input (HTML5)
item()	Returns the item in the elements array that is at the specified index (HTML5)
namedItem()	Returns the item(s) in the elements array that have the specified name or id value (HTML5)
submit()	Submits the form
reset()	Resets the form data

Table 14-2   The Methods of the Form Object

The reset() Method

This method enables you to reset a form from your script, which will clear any data entered by the user. For example, you could use the following code to reset a form once you have completed processing previously entered data:

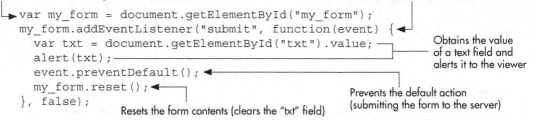

The form element is assigned to a variable

Creates the event listener with the function to execute when the form is submitted

```
var my_form = document.getElementById("my_form");
my_form.addEventListener("submit", function(event) {
    var txt = document.getElementById("txt").value;
    alert(txt);
    event.preventDefault();
    my_form.reset();
}, false);
```

Obtains the value of a text field and alerts it to the viewer

Prevents the default action (submitting the form to the server)

Resets the form contents (clears the "txt" field)

Here, the form is reset after performing a simple operation (an alert) with the data input into a text field.

The submit() Method

This method allows you to submit a form without the viewer clicking the submit button. This can be useful if you need to provide an alternate way (aside from the submit input element) to submit the form. The following code shows an example of this. First, the HTML code:

```
<form id="my_form" action="send_email.php">
<label>E-mail:</label><input type="text" id="email"><br><br>
<a href="submit.html" id="subm">Submit</a>    A submit link is created
</form>
```

Next, the JavaScript code:

```
var my_form = document.getElementById("my_form");
subm = document.getElementById("subm");
subm.addEventListener("click", function(event) {
    var email = document.getElementById("email").value;
    event.preventDefault();
    my_form.submit();    The form is submitted using
}, false);              the submit() method
```

Ensuring the Accessibility of Forms

Ensuring that your forms are accessible to viewers can be somewhat challenging because your preferred layout might not be interpreted properly by an assistive technology (such as Jaws or Homepage Reader). There are several things you can do to help ensure that most of your viewers can access and use your forms. You can place elements and their labels in the expected order, use <label></label> tags, or use <fieldset></fieldset> tags, and be sure not to assume the user has client-side scripting (such as JavaScript) enabled.

Using Proper Element and Label Order

In your HTML code, the order of your label text and form elements can help assistive technology in reading the form. For instance, consider the following input fields:

```
<input type="text" name="yourname" id="yourname"> Name<br>
<input type="text" name="zip_code" id="zip_code"> Zip Code<br>
```

Here, an assistive technology looks for label text to appear before the form element. Since the first input element does not have any label text before it, the viewer is simply prompted for input, with no indication of what information to enter. Afterward, the label text "Name" is associated with the zip_code text box, which can cause the viewer to enter unexpected input.

To correct this, you can simply move the label text and place it before the form element, as in the following code:

```
Name <input type="text" name="yourname" id="yourname"><br>
Zip Code <input type="text" name="zip_code" id="zip_code"><br>
```

Now, the assistive technology likely will pick up the form label and allow the user to enter the expected information. Using both the name and id attributes also helps, because various assistive technologies will pick these up as well.

This works for text boxes, text areas, and select boxes as well. However, when dealing with check boxes and radio buttons, many assistive technologies expect the element first, followed by the descriptive label. Thus, these should be switched around when being used.

When dealing with buttons (such as submit, reset, or created buttons), be sure to use the value attribute to describe what the button does, as that is what assistive technologies will likely expect.

Using <label></label> Tags

Using label tags helps you to further specify which label text belongs with which form element. Here is an example:

```
<label>Name</label>
<input type="text" name="yourname" id="yourname">
```

Here, since the label is in its expected position, you can simply apply the label tag. If you need to be more specific and point directly to the id of a form element, you can add the *for* attribute, as in the following code:

```
<label for="yourname">Name</label>
<input type="text" name="yourname" id="yourname">
```

Here, you assign the for attribute of the opening label tag the value of the id attribute for the form element that will use the label text contained within the <label> and </label> tags. In the preceding example, the for attribute contains yourname, which links the text to the element with the id of yourname in the HTML code.

Using <fieldset></fieldset> Tags

Using a fieldset can be helpful when dealing with radio buttons and check boxes in order to group them together into a logical set. Using a legend tag to label the options to choose from allows the user to know what is expected to be selected. The following code uses a fieldset to group together a group of radio buttons used to select a type of fruit:

```
<fieldset>
<legend>Select a Fruit:</legend>
<input type="radio" name="fruits" id="fruits1" value="Orange">
<label for="fruits1">Orange</label>
<input type="radio" name="fruits" id="fruits2" value="Banana">
<label for="fruits2">Banana</label>
<input type="radio" name="fruits" id="fruits3" value="Apple">
<label for="fruits3">Apple</label>
</fieldset>
```

Here, you group all of the radio buttons within the <fieldset> and </fieldset> tags and use a legend tag after the opening fieldset tag to give the group a label. Then, each element is labeled normally within the fieldset (also using the label tags).

Not Assuming Client-Side Scripting

When coding a form initially, it's best not to assume JavaScript or another client-side technology will be available. If JavaScript is required to make the form usable, then a number of users will not be able to use it because they will have JavaScript disabled for any number of reasons, such as security.

The best practice is to allow the form to be sent to the server side (which will handle the form and provide the most important validation routines) even if JavaScript is unavailable. Code like the following wouldn't be usable for those without JavaScript:

```
<input type="button" onclick="this.form.submit();" value="Submit Form">
```

In this case, a JavaScript event handler and method are required to submit the form. It would be better to use the traditional submit input element to create a submit button.

If you are using some JavaScript validation, you could use code such as the following:

```
<form method="post" action="form.php" id="my_form">
<!-- form contents here -->
<input type="submit" name="submit" id="submit" value="Submit Form">
</form>
```

This allows you to run JavaScript if it is available (by creating an event listener for the submit event). Otherwise, the JavaScript submit event will be ignored and the form will be submitted to the server-side script for validation and handling. If JavaScript is available, the client-side validation routine can save a trip to the server side. If not, the server-side script will need to do the work, but the user will still be able to use the form as expected.

Validation

Validating JavaScript forms is extremely useful. For example, you can validate input before it is submitted, to help reduce the number of forms with incomplete or inaccurate information. Validation of form data prior to submission to, say, a Common Gateway Interface (CGI) script, PHP script, or a Java servlet can save time and reduce load on the server.

Simple Validation

In the last chapter (Try This 13-1), you performed some simple validation on form input by using the submit event to execute a function when the form is submitted and testing the input for particular characters (the @ and . in an e-mail address). You also learned about regular expressions, which can also be helpful when validating form input.

For an example, suppose you had this HTML code for a form:

```
<form method="post" action="form.php" id="my_form">
<label for="yourname">Name:</label>
<input type="text" name="name" id="name"><br><br>
<input type="submit" name="submit" id="submit" value="Submit">
</form>
```

If you use addEventListener() to handle the submit event, you can validate the entered name and allow the default action to occur (submitting the form content to the server), or you can prevent the default action and send an error message if the name does not validate according to your specified rules. Here is an example of this:

```
var my_form = document.getElementById("my_form");
my_form.addEventListener("submit", function(event) {
  var name = document.getElementById("name").value,
  tomatch = /^[A-Za-z'\- ]{2,50}$/;
  if (!tomatch.test(name)) {
    event.preventDefault();
    alert("The name can only contain letters, spaces, apostrophes and hyphens");
  }
}, false);
```

As you can see, this uses a regular expression (see Chapter 13) to limit the type and number of characters that are allowed in the name field. It uses the letter ranges A–Z and a–z to allow all letters, ' to allow apostrophes (for names such as O'Neil), \- to allow hyphens (the hyphen is escaped to avoid being confused with a new range), and a blank space to allow for spaces. It then uses {2,50} to ensure that there are at least two characters in the name and no more than 50 characters. The ^ and $ are used to match the string from beginning to end, rather than stopping after the first valid character. If the name does not validate, the form is not submitted (event.preventDefault() stops the submission) and the user is sent an alert. Otherwise, the form is submitted normally to the server for server-side processing.

If you need to use the DOM0 method in older browsers where the event object is not available, you will want the function that handles the event to return true if the name validates or false if it does not. The function itself can do everything else, but it needs to have a return statement that sends back a value of true or false to the event handler. For example, you could use the following code to perform the same test using the DOM0 method:

```
var my_form = document.getElementById("my_form");
my_form.onsubmit = function() {
  var name = document.getElementById("name").value,
    tomatch = /^[A-Za-z'\- ]{2,50}$/;
    if (!tomatch.test(name)) {
      alert("The name can only contain letters, spaces, apostrophes
and hyphens");
      return false;
    }
    else {
    return true;
  }
};
```

Here, the test is performed. If the name does not validate, the alert is sent and the function returns false. As you will recall, if a function executes a return statement, no statement following it in the function will be executed. Thus, the return statements must come after any actions you wish to perform.

Techniques

For the most part, validation can be as simple or as complex as you need it to be for your purposes. All you need to do is create your own custom functions to validate the form fields of your choice based on the information needed.

For instance, you could check whether a field contains five digits for a typical Zip code by using a regular expression. If it does not, then you can send an alert telling the viewer the Zip code is invalid and asking for it to be reentered. The following code shows a way to do this. First, the HTML code:

```
<form method="post" action="form.php" id="my_form">
<label for="zip_code">Zip Code:</label>
<input type="text" name="zip_code" id="zip_code"><br><br>
<input type="submit" name="submit" id="submit" value="Submit">
</form>
```

Next, the JavaScript code:

```
var my_form = document.getElementById("my_form");
my_form.addEventListener("submit", function(event) {
  var zip = document.getElementById("zip_code").value,
    tomatch = /^\d{5}$/;
  if (!tomatch.test(zip)) {
    event.preventDefault();
    alert("The Zip code must contain exactly 5 digits");
  }
}, false);
```

The code uses the regular expression to check for five digits. If anything other than five digits is entered, then the function will return false. You can, of course, expand this to allow for the extra four digits that are sometimes used to designate more precisely a specific area within a Zip code. To do so, add another input field and require that it have four digits if a value is entered in that second field.

You can make the validation as strict or as loose as you need it in your JavaScript. Keep in mind, though, that at the application layer (your server-side script or program), you will need to take extra care with your validation routines to ensure that bad and/or malicious data cannot be submitted to your application.

TIP

One way to find validation scripts is to try checking some JavaScript sites on the Web. A number of them have special functions that are made to validate different types of data. This can save you some work if you can find a function to suit your purposes.

Check Boxes and Radio Buttons

When using check boxes and radio buttons, you may simply want to know if they have been "checked" by the user. For example, you could have the following form:

```
<form id="signup_form">
<label for="email">E-mail:</label>
<input type="text" name="email" id="email"><br><br>
<input type="checkbox" name="agree" id="agree" value="agree">Agree to Terms
 (<a href="terms.html" target="_blank">View Terms</a>)<br><br>
<input type="submit" name="submit" id="submit" value="Submit">
</form>
```

In this case, you want to be sure the user checks the "agree" box before the form can be submitted for the user to sign up. To check for this in JavaScript, you can use the *checked* property for the checkbox element, which returns true if the element is checked and false if it is not. The following code shows an example of this:

```
var s_form = document.getElementById("signup_form");
s_form.addEventListener("submit", function(event) {
  var agree = document.getElementById("agree");
  if (!agree.checked) {          The if statement checks to see if the element is not checked
    event.preventDefault();
    alert('Error: The "Agree to Terms" checkbox must be checked');
  }
}, false);
```

If the element is not checked, the form is not submitted and an error is alerted to the user

Here, if the "agree" checkbox is not checked, the form will not be submitted. The user will receive the alert saying that the "Agree to Terms" checkbox must be checked.

If you are working with a set of radio buttons and just want to ensure that one of the options has been checked, you can combine the document.getElementsByName() method (see Chapter 9) and the checked property to determine if this is the case. For example, suppose you had the following form:

```html
<form id="signup_form">
<label for="email">E-mail:</label>
<input type="text" name="email" id="email"><br><br>
Choose your favorite food:<br>
<input type="radio" name="food" id="food_pizza" value="Pizza">
<label for="food_pizza">Pizza</label><br>
<input type="radio" name="food" id="food_sandwich" value="Sandwich">
<label for="food_sandwich">Sandwich</label><br>
<input type="radio" name="food" id="food_candy" value="Candy">
<label for="food_candy">Candy</label><br><br>
<input type="submit" name="submit" id="submit" value="Submit">
</form>
```

The name attribute for each radio button of the same category will be the same (here it is "food") so that only one option can be selected. In order to ensure that one of the options was indeed selected, you could use the following code:

getElementsByName() is used to place each "food" radio element in an array

```javascript
var s_form = document.getElementById("signup_form");
s_form.addEventListener("submit", function(event) {
  var food_array = document.getElementsByName("food"),
  selection_made = false;
  for (var i = 0; i<food_array.length; i++) {
    if (food_array[i].checked) {
      selection_made = true;
      break;
    }
  }
  if (!selection_made) {
    event.preventDefault();
    alert('Error: A favorite food must be selected');
  }
}, false);
```

A Boolean variable is created that can be tested after each "food" radio button element has been processed

A loop cycles through each element in the array

If the radio button is checked, then the value of selection_made is set to true and the loop is ended with the break statement

If selection_made does not have a value of true, then none of the radio buttons were checked—the form is not submitted and the user receives the error alert

Ask the Expert

Q: Is validation necessary? After all, couldn't it be handled by the server-side application?

A: Yes, but using client-side validation can help you save strain on your server, since those who have JavaScript enabled won't need to access the server-side application each time invalid information is entered. It can also be helpful to the users, who will not need to reload the entire page to correct any invalid information.

Q: What types of input can I validate?

A: For the most part, you can validate anything you like in the manner you see fit. You can validate dates, names, times, addresses, e-mail addresses, phone numbers, or anything else you might need.

Q: Can I validate the selections in a select box or the text in a text area, or maybe some of the other input types?

A: In some of these cases, you will already have your own values built into the elements. However, if you can, you should still validate those values against other information to be sure the information you receive matches your needs. You just need to adjust your function to perform the needed tasks based on the different types of input devices (text areas, radio buttons, and so on).

Q: I don't use server-side scripts, but I use JavaScript for fun and want to validate the information. Do I really need to add a server-side script?

A: The need for a server-side script depends on your purposes. If you have a form that needs to have information saved, sent by e-mail, or sent to a database, then you need a server-side application.

Here, each of the radio button elements that has "food" as the value of its name attribute is placed into food_array. This allows you to use a loop to cycle through each of the radio buttons to see if it has been checked. A Boolean variable named selection_made is set to false initially. Within the loop, if the script finds that a radio button has been checked, it will set selection_made to true and exit the loop using the break statement. You can do this since only one radio button can be checked—you won't need to continue checking after a positive result is found. If selection_made remains false after running the loop, then the form submission is canceled and the user receives the error alert instead.

Try This 14-1 Request a Number

```
pr14_1.html
prjs14_1.js
```

In this project, you create a script for basic validation of a phone number entered by the viewer, such as 222-222-2222.

Step by Step

1. Create an HTML page with a form and a text box with the label text "Phone Number (XXX-XXX-XXXX):" and an id of "phone". Make sure the form has a submit button. Insert the necessary script tags after the form to call an external JavaScript file named prjs14_1.js. Save the HTML file as pr14_1.html. When complete, the HTML code should look like this:

```html
<body>
<form id="getphone">
<label for="phone">Phone Number (XXX-XXX-XXXX):</label>
<input type="text" id="phone"><br><br>
<input type="submit" value="Submit">
</form>
<script type="text/javascript" src="prjs14_1.js"></script>
</body>
```

2. Create an external JavaScript file and save it as prjs14_1.js. Use it for step 3.

3. Use a regular expression to ensure that the data entered into the text box is in the format XXX-XXX-XXXX. If it is, send an alert saying "Phone number validated." Otherwise, send an alert saying "Invalid phone number entered. Valid format is XXX-XXX-XXXX." When complete, the JavaScript code should look like this:

```javascript
var getphone = document.getElementById("getphone");
getphone.addEventListener("submit", function(event) {
  var phone = document.getElementById("phone").value,
  tomatch = /^\d{3}-\d{3}-\d{4}$/;
  event.preventDefault();
  if (tomatch.test(phone)) {
    alert("Phone number validated.");
  }
  else {
    alert("Invalid phone number entered. Valid format is XXX-XXX-XXXX.");
  }
}, false);
```

4. Save the JavaScript file and open the HTML file in your browser. See if it works by typing various values into the text box and submitting the form.

Try This Summary

In this project, you used your knowledge of JavaScript and forms to create a script to validate a form. The script validates a time entry by the viewer to see if it is a valid phone number by a particular set of standards.

HTML5 and Forms

HTML5 provides several new elements, as well as a number of new input types and attributes. It also provides a way for the browser to perform validation on fields on the client side, easing the burden on JavaScript in browsers that support the new features.

New Elements

The new form-related elements in HTML5 are listed in Table 14-3.

These elements allow you to provide additional information to the viewer or to perform other helpful tasks. You will look at the meter and progress elements in this section, but for more details on any of these elements, including which browsers support each one, see wufoo .com/html5/.

The meter Element

The meter element is used to display a value based on a scale you define. For example, if you decided to use a scale of 0–100, you would give the *min* attribute a value of 0 and the *max* attribute a value of 100. The actual value to be displayed on that scale is provided in the *value* attribute. For example, to show 55 on a scale of 0–100, you could use the following code:

```
<meter min="0" max="100" value="55"></meter>
```

This will display a meter bar in browsers that support it, showing the bar filled to 55 out of the 100 units available. Figure 14-4 shows how this looks in a supported version of Google Chrome.

Element	Description
datalist	A hidden element that provides a set of option elements to be used with the list attribute
keygen	Generates a public key that is submitted with form data and a private key that is stored locally
meter	Displays a value on a particular scale
output	Displays the output of a calculation
progress	Displays the progress of a particular task

Table 14-3   New Form-Related Elements in HTML5

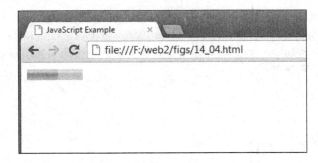

Figure 14-4 A meter bar is displayed.

For browsers that do not support the element, you can provide default text to be displayed by inserting the text within the opening and closing tags, as in the following code:

```
<meter min="0" max="100" value="55">55</meter>
```

This will simply display 55 on the page where the meter would have appeared.

This can be used in combination with JavaScript to display helpful information to the user, such as how many questions have been correctly answered in a quiz. For example, suppose you had the following HTML code:

```
<h1>Math Quiz</h1>
<form id="qform">
<label for="q1">1. 2 + 2 = </label>
<input type="text" name="q1" id="q1"><br><br>
<label for="q2">2. 2 x 255 x 5 = </label>
<input type="text" name="q2" id="q2"><br><br>
<label for="q3">3. 7436 - 2478 = </label>
<input type="text" name="q3" id="q3"><br><br>
<input type="submit" value="Check Answers">
</form><br>
<div id="grade"></div>
```

Here, a form is created for a quick math quiz, allowing the viewer to enter the answers into text boxes and then submit the answers to be checked. An empty div with an id of grade will be used to display the answer via JavaScript. The following code shows how the meter tag could be used as a visual aid in displaying the number of correct answers:

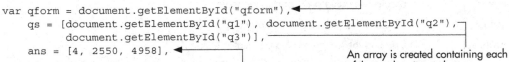

The form element is assigned to a variable

```
var qform = document.getElementById("qform"),
    qs = [document.getElementById("q1"), document.getElementById("q2"),
        document.getElementById("q3")],
    ans = [4, 2550, 4958],
```

An array is created containing each of the text box input elements

The answers to each quiz question are placed into the ans array in the same order as their respective text boxes in the qs array

The grade div is assigned to a variable

An event listener is created for a submit event on the form element

```
grade = document.getElementById("grade");
qform.addEventListener("submit", function(event) {
  var num_correct = 0,
      num_questions = qs.length,
      grade_HTML = "";
  event.preventDefault();
  for (var i = 0; i<num_questions; i++) {
    if (+qs[i].value === ans[i]) {
      num_correct += 1;
    }
  }
  grade_HTML = '<meter min="0" max="' + num_questions + '" ';
  grade_HTML += 'value="' + num_correct + '">';
  grade_HTML += num_correct + '</meter> ';
  grade_HTML += num_correct + '/3 Correct';
  grade.innerHTML = grade_HTML;
}, false);
```

Variables are created to hold the number of correct answers, the number of questions, and a string that will contain the HTML to be placed inside the grade div when the quiz is graded

A loop is created to cycle through the qs array and obtain the value of each of the user's answers

The default action is prevented (which would submit the form to the server)

The grade_HTML variable is assigned the string value of the HTML that will be displayed when the test has been graded

If the numeric value of each user answer is equal to the actual answer in the ans array, then the num_correct variable is increased by one

The innerHTML of the grade div is changed to the content of the grade_HTML variable

Here, the test is graded when the form is submitted. A variable named num_correct is created with an initial value of zero, a variable named num_questions obtains the number of questions in the quiz by grabbing the length of the qs array, which contains each text box input element, and a variable name grade_HTML is assigned an empty string that will be filled in with the meter tag and other text to display the results.

A loop is created to iterate over the qs array, get each value, and determine if it is equal to its corresponding correct answer in the ans array. Notice that the unary + operator is used to attempt to coerce the user's entry into a number before comparing it to the correct answer, since each text box will return a string by default. If the answer is correct, the one is added to the num_correct variable.

The next lines of code create the HTML string that will eventually be placed within the grade div. Notice how the max attribute of the meter tag is assigned the value of the num_questions variable, and how the value attribute is assigned the value of the num_correct variable. An additional message is displayed after the meter element to show the user what type of results the meter is displaying (for example, if two answers were correct, the message "2/3 Correct").

In this case, if the user does not get all the answers correct, the entries can be edited and submitted to be checked again until a 3/3 is obtained. Figure 14-5 shows the result of this script when two of the answers are correct.

The progress Element

The progress element is similar to meter, but displays a percentage rather than a scalar value. For example, to show 25 percent out of 100 percent on a progress bar, you could use the following code:

```
<progress max="100" value="25">25%</progress>
```

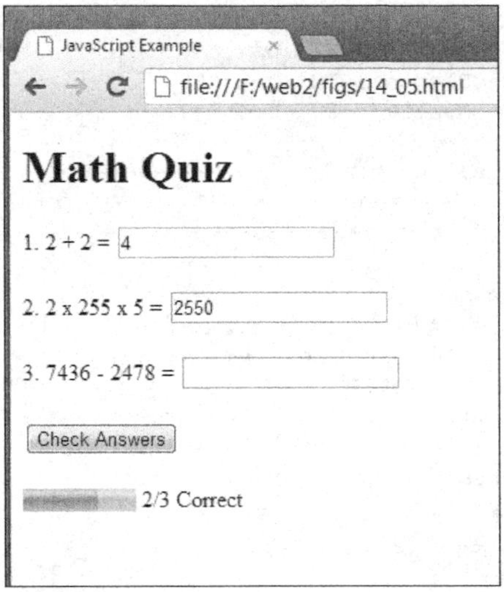

Figure 14-5 The meter is displayed to show how many questions were answered correctly.

As with meter, you can use the max attribute to set the maximum and the value attribute to set the percentage value within a range if zero up to the max value. You could edit the previous meter JavaScript code to use a progress bar to display a percentage grade for the quiz if desired, using the following code:

```
var qform = document.getElementById("qform"),
    qs = [document.getElementById("q1"), document.getElementById("q2"),
        document.getElementById("q3")],
ans = [4, 2550, 4958],
    grade = document.getElementById("grade");
qform.addEventListener("submit", function(event) {
  var num_correct = 0,
      num_questions = qs.length,
      grade_HTML = "",
      score = 0;
  event.preventDefault();
  for (var i = 0; i<num_questions; i++) {
    if (+qs[i].value === ans[i]) {
        num_correct += 1;
    }
  }
  score = Math.round(num_correct / num_questions * 100);
  grade_HTML = '<progress max="100" ';
  grade_HTML += 'value="' + score + '">';
  grade_HTML += score + '%</progress> ';
  grade_HTML += 'Grade: ' + score + '%';
  grade.innerHTML = grade_HTML;
}, false);
```

A new variable named score is added to calculate the score

The score is calculated based on the number correct and the number of questions, then rounded to a nondecimal percentage

A progress element is displayed rather than a meter element, showing the percentage score

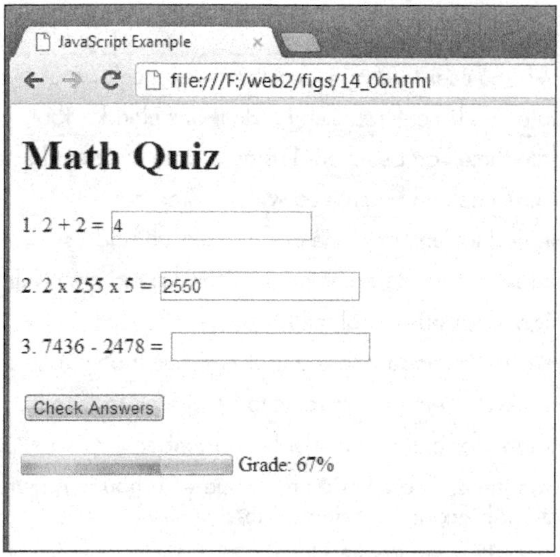

Figure 14-6   The result is displayed as a percentage using the progress element.

Here, some changes are made to calculate the percentage score that will be used in the progress element. The progress element is then generated based on the percentage score. Figure 14-6 shows the result of this script when two out of three answers are correct.

New Input Types

In addition to new elements, HTML5 adds a number of new input types that can be used for the input element. Table 14-4 lists the new additions.

You will notice that some of these input types allow for the use of a tool by the user, such as the color input type. Browsers may implement these in different ways, but those that support one or more of the new input types often make it easier for the user to enter each specific type of value and/or make the value entered easier to validate. An example of using the new color type is shown in this code:

```
<input type="color" name="mycolor" id="mycolor">
```

As you can see, you can plug in the specific *type* inside the type attribute to make use of it. Since these fields ask for specific types of values, the browser is able to perform its own validation on the fields, which is helpful when it is supported. This will be discussed further in the "HTML5 Form Validation" section later.

New Attributes

HTML5 also brings new attributes that can be used with forms and/or form elements. These are listed in Table 14-5.

Type	Description
color	Allows the user to choose a color using a color tool
date	A date can be entered using a date or calendar tool
datetime	A date/time can be entered using a date or calendar tool; time zone set to UTC
datetime-local	A date/time can be entered with no time zone
email	Designed for entering one or more e-mail addresses
month	A date can be entered with a year and a month; no time zone
number	Designed for numerical input
range	Allows for a range where a user can select a value using a range tool
search	Designed for entering a value to be placed in a search
tel	Designed for entering a telephone number
time	Allows the user to enter a time value with hours, minutes, seconds, and fractional seconds; no time zone
url	Designed for entering a URL
week	For entering a week; no time zone.

Table 14-4   New Input Types in HTML5

Attribute	Description
autocomplete	Can be set in the form tag (to affect all form fields) or within any specific input tag (to affect a single field). If the value is set to "off", the field(s) will not use the browser's autocomplete feature to present suggestions for field completion
autofocus	Tells the browser to give focus to the element when the page loads
dirname	Submits an indication of the direction of the input for an element with the form
form	Allows you to specify the form(s) that the element is part of
formaction	Allows a submit element to override the action attribute of its form element
formenctype	Allows a submit element to override the enctype attribute of its form element
formmethod	Allows a submit element to override the method attribute of its form element
formnovalidate	Allows a submit element to override the novalidate attribute of its form element
formtarget	Allows a submit element to override the target attribute of its form element
pattern	Allows you to validate the contents of a form field against a regular expression
placeholder	Allows you to specify a placeholder (light-colored text that gives the user a better idea what type of input is expected) in a form field
novalidate	Disables the validation performed by the browser when the contents of the form are submitted; may be used for the entire form or for individual form elements
required	Indicates that the form field is required be completed

Table 14-5   New Attributes in HTML5 Forms/Form Fields

Many of these allow you to override attributes in the main form element using the submit element. There are also some attributes such as required, novalidate, and pattern that assist with form validation, which is discussed in the next section.

HTML5 Form Validation

HTML5 allows the browser to validate various input types automatically. This can be overridden by using the *novalidate* attribute in the form tag to disable browser input validation for all of a form's fields or by using it in individual form fields so that they are not validated.

If you decide to allow the browser to validate fields, the new input types will have certain validation methods used on them to ensure that the expected type of information is entered. Each field is optional by default, though you can make it required by adding the *required* attribute to each field that needs to be completed. For example, the browser will validate the following form and will require that the URL field be completed:

```
<form id="signup_form" method="post" action="send.php">
<label for="name">Name:</label>
<input type="text" name="name" id="name"><br><br>
<label for="url">URL:</label>
<input type="url" name="url" id="url" required><br><br>
<input type="submit" value="Submit">
</form>
```

Figure 14-7 shows what happens when the required field is not completed in a supported browser. Figure 14-8 shows the result of entering an invalid URL in the URL field in a supported browser.

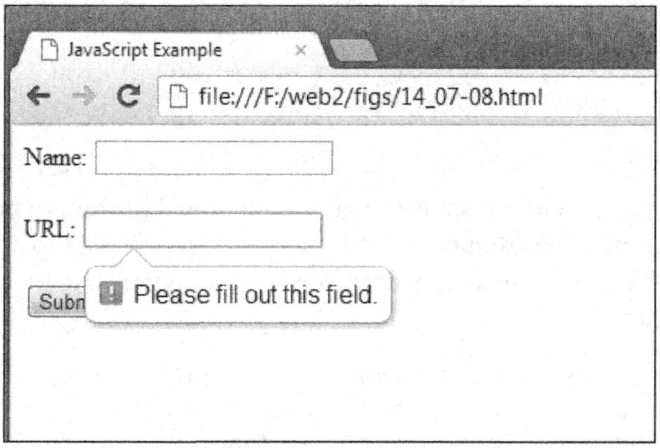

Figure 14-7 The field must be completed to validate.

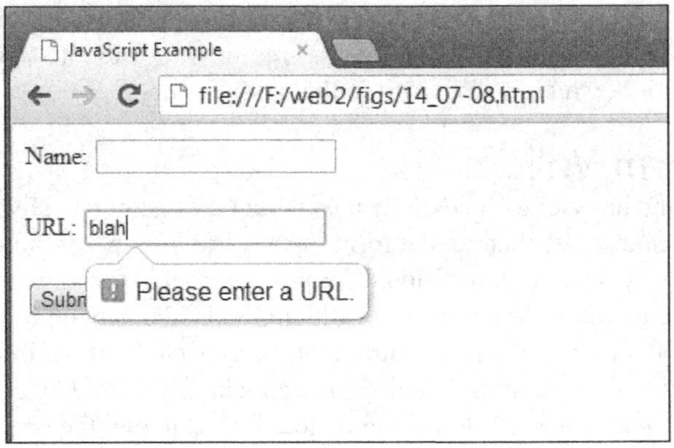

Figure 14-8 The field must contain a valid URL to validate.

You can also use the pattern field so that the browser will validate a field according to a regular expression. For example, if you want the name field from the previous form to contain only letters and spaces, you could use the following code:

```
<label for="name">Name:</label>
<input type="text" name="name" id="name" pattern="[A-Za-z ]+"><br><br>
```

The only drawback is browser support. If you need to validate the input on the client side in browsers that do not support the particular input types or validations used in HTML5, then you will need to write some JavaScript as a backup. For example, suppose you had the following form:

```
<form id="signup_form" method="post" action="send.php">
<label for="name">Name:</label>
<input type="text" name="name" id="name" pattern="[A-Za-z ]+"><br><br>
<input type="submit" value="Submit">
</form>
```

If a browser does not support the pattern attribute and you still want to make sure the field contains only letters and spaces, then you will need to write a script to ensure that the field is still validated. In this case, you could simply use the following code to validate the name field when the submit button is clicked.

```
var sform = document.getElementById("signup_form");
sform.addEventListener("submit", function(event) {
  var name = document.getElementById("name").value,
      pattern = /[A-Za-z ]+/;
  event.preventDefault;
  if (!pattern.test(name)) {
    alert("Name must contain only letters and spaces");
  }
}, false);
```

This simply uses the desired pattern as a regular expression in JavaScript and runs the test method to see if the input matches the pattern. If not, an alert is sent to the viewer so that the name can be corrected.

HTML5 provides numerous new and helpful features to forms. At the time of this writing, JavaScript backups may be necessary for client-side validation. As more users move to newer browsers and browser support for all of the new features is increased, these new tools will become even more helpful to you as a developer.

NOTE

For more details on any of the HTML5 form improvements, including which browsers support each one, see wufoo.com/html5/.

Try This 14-2 | Validate a Phone Number with HTML5 or JavaScript

pr14_2.html
prjs14_2.js

In this project, you will build on the previous project by creating a form that will validate a phone number using the new HTML5 pattern attribute. If the browser does not support HTML5, a backup JavaScript validation is run instead.

Step by Step

1. Create an HTML document and add script tags so that the HTML file will call an external JavaScript file named prjs14_2.js. Create a form with an id of "getphone", and add a text box with an id of "phone" to obtain a phone number. The text box should use the pattern attribute with a regular expression that will validate the phone number if the format is XXX-XXX-XXXX. It will also be a required field. Make sure the form contains a submit button. Save the HTML file as pr14_2.html. When complete, the HTML code should look like this:

```
<body>
<form id="getphone">
<label for="phone">Phone Number (XXX-XXX-XXXX):</label>
<input type="number" id="phone" pattern="/^\d{3}-\d{3}-\d{4}$/"
required><br><br>
<input type="submit" value="Submit">
</form>
<script type="text/javascript" src="prjs14_2.js"></script>
</body>
```

2. Create a JavaScript file and save it as prjs14_2.js. Use it for step 3.

3. Create a script that will back up the HTML5 validation when the form is submitted. If the field does not validate, send an alert saying "Invalid phone number entered. Valid format is XXX-XXX-XXXX." Otherwise, allow the form to be submitted. When complete, the JavaScript code should look like this:

```
var getphone = document.getElementById("getphone");
getphone.addEventListener("submit", function(event) {
  var phone = document.getElementById("phone").value,
      tomatch = /^\d{3}-\d{3}-\d{4}$/;
  event.preventDefault();
  if (!tomatch.test(phone)) {
    alert("Invalid phone number entered. Valid format is XXX-XXX-XXXX.");
  }
}, false);
```

4. Save the JavaScript file and open the HTML file in your browser. Check to see whether the validation system works.

Try This Summary

In this project, you used your knowledge of JavaScript and HTML5 forms to create a validation system that checks for a valid phone number in HTML5 and backs up the validation with JavaScript code.

Chapter 14 Self Test

1. Each time you add a set of <form> and </form> tags to an HTML document, a(n) _____ object is created.

2. The forms _____ allows you to access a form using an index number.

3. Which of the following would access the fourth form on a page?

   A. document.forms[4]

   B. document.forms[3]

   C. document.forms(4)

   D. document.forms(3)

4. Which of the following would find the number of elements in the third form on a page?

   A. document.forms[2].length

   B. document.forms[3].length

   C. document.forms.length

   D. document.forms(3).length

5. Which of the following holds the value of the number of forms in a document?

   A. document.forms[0].length

   B. document.form.length

   C. document.forms.length

   D. document.forms[1].length

6. Using form _____ or _____ allows you to name the forms on the page that you want to access later.

7. Which of the following accesses the value of an element named e1 in a form named f1?

   A. document.f1.e1.value

   B. document.e1.f1.value

   C. document.f1.e2.value

   D. document.forms1.e1.value

8. The _____ property allows you to access the value of the action="*url*" attribute in the opening form tag.

9. The _____ property is an array that allows you to access each element in a specific form.

10. The _____ attribute in HTML5 allows you to give a form field a regular expression it must validate.

11. The _____ method allows you to reset a form using your script.

12. Which of the following would add a valid meter tag to the document to show 8 on a scale of 0 to 10?

   A. <meter min="0" max="10" value="7">8</meter>

   B. <meter min="4" value="8">8</meter>

   C. <meter min="0" max="10" value="8">8</meter>

   D. <meter min="0" max="100" value="8">8</meter>

13. One way to help with form accessibility is to use the _____ tags to identify what field a piece of text is describing.

14. The _____ method allows you to submit a form without the viewer clicking the submit button.

15. Which of the following HTML5 form attributes is used for fields that must be filled in by the user to validate?

   A. obligatory

   B. needed

   C. required

   D. compulsory

Chapter 15

An Introduction to Advanced Techniques

Key Skills & Concepts

- Working with Images

- JavaScript and Frames

- Debugging Scripts

- JavaScript and Accessibility

- JavaScript Security

- AJAX and JSON

Working with Images

JavaScript uses the image object to preload images, create rollover effects, and even create slide shows or animations. The image object's properties will help when you want to create such scripts. Table 15-1 lists and describes the image object's properties.

Rollovers

Image *rollovers* (also known as hover buttons, image flips, and other similar names) can add some zest to your navigational images. With the recent advances in browsers and CSS, rollovers are commonly implemented via CSS rather than JavaScript now. You can see an example of this at www.netmagazine.com/tutorials/create-progressively-enhanced-3d-css-rollovers.

Property	Purpose
name	Holds the value of the image's name from the name attribute
src	Holds the value of the URL from the src attribute
width	Holds the value of the width from the width attribute
height	Holds the value of the height from the height attribute
border	Holds the numeric value of the border property from the border attribute
hspace	Holds the numeric value of the hspace property from the hspace attribute
vspace	Holds the numeric value of the vspace property from the vspace attribute
lowsrc	Holds the value of the URL from the lowsrc attribute
complete	Indicates whether an image has finished loading

Table 15-1   Properties of the Image Object

A Simple JavaScript Rollover

A simple rollover just changes one image to another when the mouse moves over the initial image. First, you create two images and make the second image different in some way. For example, examine the two images shown here:

Shoe Page Shoe Page

NOTE

For each JavaScript rollover effect you create, you need two separate images.

Once you have two images, you can begin working on the code for the image rollover. You can code your initial image into your HTML document, giving it an id:

```
<h1>The image below changes! Move your mouse over it!</h1>
<img src="image1.gif" id="pic1" border="0">
```

In your JavaScript code, you will just need to get the image element by its id and assign it a new value for the src property on a mouseover event. Then you will simply change it back on a mouseout event. The following is the JavaScript code:

```
var im = document.getElementById("pic1");
im.addEventLister("mouseover", function() {
  im.src = image2.gif;
}, false);
im.addEventLister("mouseout", function() {
  im.src = "image1.gif";
}, false);
```

The closest you can get to seeing the results here is to see a before and after set of images. Figure 15-1 shows the initial image, while Figure 15-2 shows the result when the mouse is moved over the image.

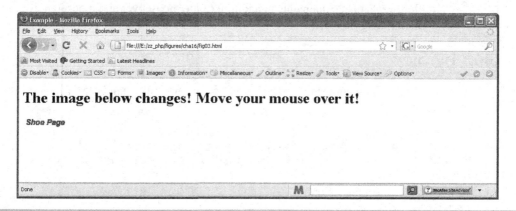

Figure 15-1   The initial image

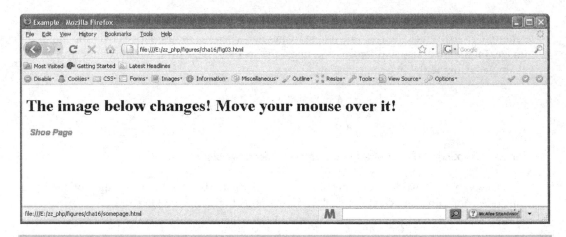

Figure 15-2 The new image appears when the mouseover event occurs.

NOTE

To make this more accessible to users without a mouse, you can use the code to perform the change on the focus and blur events of the <a> element. You will do this in your first project in this chapter.

Try This 15-1   A More Accessible Rollover

`pr15_1.html`
`prjs15_1.js`

To make a JavaScript rollover more accessible, you will use the same set of images and will write code that will change the image on the focus and blur events of <a> elements in addition to the mouseover and mouseout events on the <img> element.

Step by Step

1. Create an HTML document named pr15_1.html and use the following HTML code for the body section:

```
<body>
<h1>The image below changes! Move your mouse over it!</h1>
<a href="page.html" id="imlink"><img src="image1.gif" id="pic1"
border="0"></a>
<script type="text/javascript" src="prjs15_1.js"></script>
</body>
```

2. Create a JavaScript file named prjs15_1.js. In this file, start with the following code:

```
var im = document.getElementById("pic1");
im.addEventLister("mouseover", function() {
  im.src = image2.gif;
}, false);
im.addEventLister("mouseout", function() {
  im.src = "image1.gif";
}, false);
```

3. Make changes to the code so that the image will also change when the focus and blur events occur on the <a> element. You can do this either by moving some of the code to a separate function or by simply pasting the code from the appropriate event listener to its companion event listener (i.e., mouseover and focus will use the same code). If you move the event listener code to a separate function, it will look like this:

```
var im = document.getElementById("pic1"),
    imlink = document.getElementById("imlink");
function on_image() {
  im.src = "image2.gif";
}
function off_image() {
  im.src = "image1.gif";
}
im.addEventListener("mouseover", on_image, false);
imlink.addEventListener("focus", on_image, false);
im.addEventListener("mouseout", off_image, false);
imlink.addEventListener("blur", off_image, false);
```

4. Save the HTML and JavaScript files and open the HTML file in your browser. The image should now change when the focus and blur events occur on the <a> element.

Try This Summary

In this project, you used your knowledge of JavaScript, images, and events to create an image rollover that works with the mouseover, focus, mouseout, and blur events.

JavaScript and Frames

The decision of whether or not to use frames on your Web site is up to you. However, it should be noted that frames do have accessibility/usability issues. In fact, <frameset> and <frame> are no longer valid in HTML5. The <iframe> element (an inline frame) is still available.

Purpose of Frames

Frames divide a window into two or more separate areas (a *frame set*), each containing different content. This differs from tables in that the divisions in a frame set each contain a separate Hypertext Markup Language (HTML) document, and you can change one of the sections without affecting the other sections.

NOTE

Each frame shown on a Web page is actually a separate HTML document.

For example, Figure 15-3 shows a Web page with two frames. Each frame is actually a separate HTML document. The HTML document that creates the frames uses a set of <frameset> and </frameset> tags to create a frame set.

Accessing Frames

How do you access a frame in JavaScript? You can either use the frames array or name the frame and use the frame name instead. To begin, take a look at how to access a frame using the frames array.

The frames Array

You use the frames array to access frames based on their order in the source code. You will access one frame from within another frame, so you must be able to find the frame you want to access.

Recall that the frames array comes from the window object. Frames carry most of the same properties and methods as regular windows, but you access them differently. For instance, take a look at this code, which creates a frame set with two frames. Name it frameset1.html.

```
<html>
<frameset cols="60%,40%">
<frame src="frame1.html"></frame>
<frame src="frame2.html"></frame>
</frameset>
<noframes>
Use the link below to go to the frameless version of the site.<br>
<a href="noframes.html">Frameless Site</a>
</noframes>
</html>
```

If you're coding some script inside the first frame (frame1.html) and want to know the value of the location property in the second frame (frame2.html) to display it for the viewer,

Figure 15-3 A frame set containing two frames

you must figure out how to access the second frame. To access the other frame, you need to find a way to get back to the main window and reference the frame. Recall that the window object's top property allows you to access the topmost window in a frame set (the main window).

You can now use the frames array because you have access to that main window, which contains the code for the frame set. The frames array contains an item for each frame tag in the code. The count starts at 0, so to access the first frame in a frame set, you could use the following syntax:

```
top.frames[0]
```

Using the top property allows you to access the main window and the frameset code. Then, frames[0] is used to access the first frame in the source code. So, if you're coding within the second frame and want to access the first frame, you would use this syntax:

```
top.frames[0]
```

Now, you can make the code in the second frame access the needed information in the first frame for the viewer. The following code is for the first frame (frame1.html):

```
<body>
I am frame 1 and the other frame took information from me! How rude!
</body>
```

To complete this script, you could use the following code for frame2.html:

```
<body>
The first frame is from: <br>
<script type="text/javascript">
  document.write(top.frames[0].location);
</script>
</body>
```

The value of the location of the left frame is printed on the page using the frames array to access the information in the frame

Now you can see the result by opening the main window (frameset1.html). The right frame should tell you the location of the document used for the left frame. Figure 15-4 shows how this may appear in a browser. (Your location value will probably be different from the filename.)

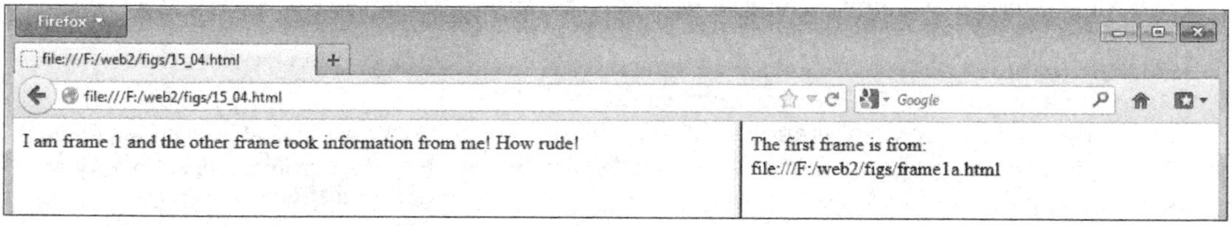

Figure 15-4   The second frame shows information taken from the first frame.

Using a Frame Name

Another way to access one frame from another is to use the name of the frame (much like the way you used form names in the previous chapter). For example, this code gives each frame a name by adding the name attribute to the frame tag (call this frameset3.html):

```html
<html>
<frameset cols="50%,50%">
<frame src="frame1.html" name="left_side"></frame>
<frame src="frame2.html" name="right_side"></frame>
</frameset>
<noframes>
Use the link below to go to the frameless version of the site.<br  />
<a href="noframes.html">Frameless Site</a>
</noframes>
</html>
```

You can now access one of the frames from the other using the frame name rather than the frames array. Thus, if you want to access the second frame (right_side) from the first one, you could use this syntax:

```
top.right_side
```

In the same way, you could access the first frame from within the second frame with this syntax:

```
top.left_side
```

Now you can make each frame tell the viewer the location of the other frame by coding the frames with a short document.write() statement in each. The document for the first frame (frame1.html) could be coded like this:

```html
<body>
The second (right) frame is from: <br>
<script type="text/javascript">
  document.write(top.right_side.location); ◄──── The name of the right frame is
</script>                                         used to print information from
</body>                                           it in the left frame.
```

After that, frame2.html could be coded as follows:

```html
<body>
The first (left) frame is from: <br  />
<script type="text/javascript">
  document.write(top.left_side.location); ◄──── The name of the left frame is used
</script>                                        to print information from it in the
</body>                                          right frame
```

Each frame now gives out information about the other one.

NOTE

Frames and iframes have potential security risks when they are used. For more on these risks, see appliedlife.blogspot.com/2011/02/html-frames-and-security.html.

Breaking Out of Frames

Sometimes another Web site will code links that don't break the user out of the site's frames before arriving at your site. Your site is then left in a smaller portion of the viewer's window with the navigation from the other site still showing in other frames. When this happens, you may want to offer your viewers a way to break out of the other site's frames.

You can place a link on your page for viewers to click to break out of frames. You need to add a special target in the <a> tag, as shown here:

```
<a href="http://yoursite.com" target= "_top">Break Out of Frames</a>
```

The target of _top tells the browser to use the full window when opening the URL in the link, rather than opening the link inside a frame. You just need to replace the URL in the tag with your own.

Debugging Scripts

Even though JavaScript is fun, sometimes it can also be quite frustrating. One error in the code can cause an entire script to run incorrectly or not run at all. Debugging a script can be a time-consuming and arduous process, but there are a few techniques you can use that may help save some time while looking over the code. The first step in debugging a script is to figure out what type of error is likely to be causing the problem.

Types of Errors

The two main types of errors are syntax errors and logical errors. A syntax error occurs when the coder forgets to add a semicolon, forgets a quotation mark, misspells a word, and so on. A logical error occurs when the code is implemented incorrectly.

For example, a while loop could go on infinitely if the condition for executing the loop never becomes false. While it may be coded with the correct syntax, the results won't be what the programmer expected.

Find the Syntax Errors

A syntax error could be as simple as leaving out a necessary semicolon. For example, the following code is missing a semicolon between statements:

```
var greet = function() { say_hi() say_welcome(); };
```

In this case, the semicolon is very important because the two statements are on the same line. To fix this, you just need to add the needed semicolon, as shown here:

```
var greet = function() { say_hi(); say_welcome(); };
```

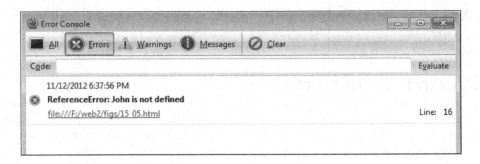

Figure 15-5 A JavaScript error message

Syntax errors often cause the browser to display an error message so that you can debug the script. For example, you might see a message like the one in Figure 15-5.

NOTE
Most modern browsers hide these error messages by default, but you can enable them if you wish to view them.

These messages can help you figure out what's causing the problem. The line number shown in the error message often tells you where the error is. For instance, if the message says the error is on line 15, you would start at the 15th line from the top of your document and see what's there. The rest of the message might tell you what's missing or what has been placed improperly.

However, sometimes the line stated in the message is not the line where the actual problem is located. It could be on the preceding line, a few lines away, or even somewhere else entirely. You may need to do a little searching to figure out where the problem started.

Scanning the Script
If the error message doesn't help you locate the problem, you can try scanning the script for errors on your own. This solution can be more tedious, but it may help you find the problem if the error message isn't helpful. Table 15-2 shows some items you should try to find.

Item	Appearance
Missing semicolon	;
Missing curly or square brackets	{ } [ ]
Missing parenthesis	( )
Missing single or double quote	' "
Misspelling	*ture* instead of *true*, for example

Table 15-2 Items to Look for When Scanning a Script for Errors

The following code is riddled with errors; see how many of them you can find.

```
var mymoney = 0;
var mycar = "Mustang";
function send_alert()
 alery("You like + mynar + "!");
 alert("Cool";
}
var somearray = neq Array(2)
somearray[0] = "Me";
somearray1] = "Me2";
for var count = 0; count < somearray.length; count ++) {
  document.write(somearray[0 + " and " + somearray[1]);
```

The code is missing a number of necessary items. Following is the list of items you should have found:

- Between lines 3 and 4: The function is missing its opening curly bracket

- Line 4: The word *alert* is misspelled as *alery*; the double quote mark is missing after the word *like*; the mycar variable is misspelled as *mynar*

- Line 5: The alert method is missing a closing parenthesis

- Line 7: The word *new* is misspelled as *neq*

- Line 9: The array index number is missing its opening square bracket

- Line 10: The opening parenthesis for the loop is missing

- Line 11: The index number for somearray[0] is missing its closing square bracket

- Between lines 11 and 12: The closing curly bracket to end the loop is missing

You probably won't make that many errors, but the example provides a nice way to see how to catch them while scanning a script. After you become more experienced with locating these small errors, you'll be able to find them quickly when you have a problem in a script.

Find the Logical Errors

Logical errors are often tougher to find because the syntax of the code is correct. You will be trying to find a mistake in how the code was implemented. For example, look at the following code (but do not run it!):

```
x = 1;
y = 2;
while (x <= y) {   ◄──────  Problem: x is never greater than y!
  alert("Hi");
}
```

The code has no syntax errors. All the semicolons and quote marks are where they should be. The problem here is that the variable *x* is never greater than the variable *y*. This situation would cause an infinite loop, possibly crashing the browser.

You can fix the code by adding a line inside the loop to increase the value of *x*, decrease the value of *y*, or both increase *x* and decrease *y*. The important point is that something must be done to make the condition false. The following code shows a possible fix for this problem:

```
x = 1;
y = 2;
while (x <= y) {
  alert("Hi");
  x++;          ◀———————— Increasing x within the loop will allow x to become greater than y over time
}
```

Alerts and Using the Console

If there are values that don't seem to be correct, they can be quickly checked at any point in the script by using an alert or sending the value to the console. For example, suppose you have the following code:

```
var x = 2,
    y = 0;
// other code...
var z = x/y;
alert(z);
```

When run, the alert will display "Infinity", which probably is not the intended result. With additional code between the initial variable definitions and the assignment of the calculation (*x/y*) to the *z* variable, it may be difficult to see that a division by zero is taking place while scanning the code. To find out where the error is, you could place an alert in the code prior to the calculation of the *z* variable to see if it can help you see what is happening, as in the following example:

```
var x = 2,
    y = 0;
// other code...
alert("Calculation will be: " + x + "/" +y);   ◀———— This alert will display the
var z = x/y;                                          calculation that is about to
alert(z);                                             be performed
```

When the alert shows that the calculation will be "2/0", you can see that the *y* variable having a value of zero is causing the issue. Knowing that, you can now look for any lines of code that assign a value to the *y* variable to see if it results in *y* being given a value of zero. In this case, it happens on the second line of the code, and can be corrected by assigning a different value to *y*.

If you decide to add several checks, or simply do not want to have alert messages popping up with the values as the script runs, you may opt to use the console.log() method. This allows you to place a message in the console, which many modern browsers use to track errors, warnings, or other messages that occur when the HTML, CSS, and JavaScript code is read by the browser.

NOTE

It is best to remove your testing code when you are finished debugging, as it could cause errors or other issues with the script when run by the user.

The console can typically be displayed in a browser by looking in the "Tools" menu and looking for a menu option such as "Web Developer" or "Developer Tools". For example, you can display the console in Firefox by opening the "Tools" menu, going to "Web Developer", and selecting "Web Console".

The script used previously can now be changed to display the message in the console, as in the following code:

```
var x = 2,
    y = 0;
// other code...
console.log("Calculation will be: " + x + "/" +y);    ◄─── The message is now
var z = x/y;                                                 displayed in the console
                                                             rather than in an alert
```

The script will now log the message in the console, and will not bring up an alert. When you need to place multiple messages to check for values at various points in the script, this is a good way to obtain the necessary information without being overrun with pop-up alert messages.

Using a Lint Tool

Thanks to some expert Web developers, there are tools available that can assist you in finding JavaScript errors, while also encouraging the use of best practices in your JavaScript code. A lint tool (a tool that looks at the code for anything that might not be correct) can be very useful in tracking down any problems (or potential problems) in your code.

Two popular lint tools for JavaScript are listed here:

- JSLint (www.jslint.com)
- JSHint (www.jshint.com)

Both tools allow you to paste your JavaScript code into a text area and have it checked. The tools will check for various issues such as:

- Variables defined without the var statement (making them global)
- Missing semicolons
- Use of eval()
- == vs. ===
- Other issues

For example, suppose you had the following code:

```
var x = 1
var y = "1";
function isEqual() {
    if (x == y)
        alert("Equal");
    else
        alert("Not Equal");
}
isEqual();
```

There are some problems with this code that will give you unexpected results when the code is run. Running the code through JSLint, for example, will give you a number of errors. Included in the list are some important notes that will assist you in fixing the code:

- **Line 1: Expected ';' and instead saw 'var'.**
  The end of Line 1 is missing a semicolon to complete the first var statement. Since these could be combined, the best practice would be to use a comma between the two variable definitions and remove the second var keyword, as in this code:

  ```
  var x = 1,
      y = 0;
  ```

- **Line 4: Expected '===' and instead saw '=='.**
  The comparison (x == y) could give an unexpected result here due to type coercion being performed. With x = 1 and y = "1", JavaScript will evaluate x ==y to be true. If you intended to ensure both values were in fact the numeric value of 1, you would not want this to be the case. Using === is safer and avoids any potentially odd results:

  ```
  if (x === y)
  ```

- **Line 5: Expected '{' and instead saw 'alert'.**
  To avoid any potential pitfalls and make the purpose of the code easier to read, it is best to place brackets around if and else statements, even if they only contain one line of code (allowing the shortcut of not adding the brackets). This error is picked up for both the if and else statements, and can be fixed by adding the brackets to both:

  ```
  if (x == y) {
      alert("Equal");
  }
  else {
      alert("Not Equal");
  }
  ```

As you can see, a lint tool can pick up on potential problems before you run your code, keeping any remaining debugging tasks to a minimum. By following the suggestions of the tool for this code, you can avoid the number 1 being equal to the string 1, and you also allow the if and else statements to have additional lines of code added within each block without causing problems later (forcing you to figure out what happened and then add the brackets at that time).

Browser Developer Tools

Most of the major modern browsers have a set of developer tools that are available either natively or via an add-on. These tools can prove helpful in debugging JavaScript as well. Some links to tutorials on how to access/acquire and use some of these are provided here:

- **Chrome Debugger** www.nsbasic.com/app/tutorials/TT10.htm

- **Firebug for Firefox** https://getfirebug.com/javascript

- **Internet Explorer Debugger** blogs.msdn.com/b/cbowen/archive/2011/06/24/internet-explorer-9-developer-tools-deep-dive-part-3-debugging-javascript.aspx

Ask the Expert

Q: The error message I get says something I don't understand. What should I do?

A: Error messages don't always make sense and don't always point to the right line in the code. You may need to trace any variables or functions you have called on the line that the message gave you or check the lines near it for errors. Once you've seen an error message a few times, its meaning becomes easier to figure out.

Q: Something in my code crashed the browser when I tried to run it, and I can't try adding alerts to help find the problem because it crashes every time! What should I do?

A: If the script crashes the browser, look closely at your variables, loops, objects, and functions. You might also try a browser add-on, such as Firebug, which will allow you to set break points in the script as needed. As a last resort, write some new code from scratch.

Q: An error in my code crashed not only the browser, but also the computer! What do I do?

A: Restart the computer but *do not* run the code again. Check it very carefully to see if you can find the problem.

Q: Can any other strategies help me debug my scripts?

A: Some text editors use color coding to mark HTML tags, JavaScript code, or other types of code. Color coding helps you see the code more clearly and makes it easier to detect an error. (Try the Vim or NoteTab text editor.)

JavaScript and Accessibility

One topic you have seen many times in this book is how a script or HTML code for the script relates to accessibility. In some cases, such as Web sites of government agencies, a state or federal law (such as the Americans with Disabilities Act) might require that the Web site be accessible to viewers with disabilities. Even if it is not a legal issue for your Web site, it is still a usability issue: you will want as many visitors as possible to be able to use your site and access the information you have for them.

The general theme for accessibility is that content needs to be made accessible to all browsers and other software that may access a Web site. This means that your content should be readable not only by various Web browsers, but also by assistive technologies like screen reading software (for example, JAWS from Freedom Scientific), or Web browsing software on portable devices like cellular phones.

Separate Content from Presentation

Typically, the first step in making your Web site content accessible is to build the accessibility into your HTML/XHTML code, but you'll also need to tweak your JavaScript code. As you may already know, when coding your HTML you can use Cascading Style Sheets (CSS) for presentation of the content (how many columns are displayed, the font style, the width of various divisions, and so forth) while using HTML to simply mark up the content itself (such as dividing it into sections with <div></div> tags or inserting objects like images). This takes care of issues dealing with plain HTML content because the use of a style sheet rather than HTML markup for presentation ensures that you can offer different CSS styles for different types of browsers, or that those not using browsers with CSS capabilities will still get the structural markup of the plain text (for example, there won't be columns or font colors, and so on), which allows them to still view the content of the page.

With JavaScript, making the content accessible often means making sure that the content you use in your script is already displayed on the page or is available through a link or other means. One thing that may help is to move all JavaScript code (or as much as possible) into external JavaScript files while leaving as little JavaScript code in the HTML code as possible.

For example, you might have a Web page that uses the following code:

```
<body>
<script type="text/javascript">
function send_alert() {
  window.alert("Hi, there is a sale today! 20% off everything!");
  return false;
}
</script>
<a href="#" onclick="send_alert();">Hi</a>
</body>
```

This code will function just fine for those with JavaScript. However, having the script in the HTML code makes for a lot of extra scrolling through the file when you need to update the HTML code (especially if you have a long script). Thus, the first move you may want to make is to move the script to an external file, as shown in the following code samples. First the new HTML code:

```
<body>
<a href="#" onclick="send_alert();">Hi</a>
<script type="text/javascript" src="myscript.js"></script>
</body>
```

Next, the myscript.js JavaScript file:

```
function send_alert() {
  window.alert("Hi, there is a sale today! 20% off everything!");
  return false;
}
```

This makes the HTML file shorter and easier to read because the JavaScript functionality is placed in its own file and out of the way of the HTML code.

The next move you may want to make is to change the use of the onclick event handler in the HTML tag. Though valid, it becomes troublesome if you decide to use a function with a different name or decide to make it a normal link without JavaScript, because you will need to update each HTML file to accommodate the change cleanly (you can simply change the script to have the new function use this function name or just do nothing when called, but this could be confusing for those who may need to update the code later). To get this onclick event handler out of the HTML code, you could rewrite the JavaScript slightly and give the anchor tag an id (much like what you have done earlier in this book). First, the updated HTML code:

```
<body>
<a href="#" id="sale">Hi</a>
<script type="text/javascript" src="myscript.js"></script>
</body>
```

Next, the myscript.js JavaScript file:

```
function send_alert() {
  window.alert("Hi, there is a sale today! 20% off everything!");
  return false;
}
var s_alert = document.getElementById("sale");
s_alert.addEventListener("click", send_alert, false);
```

Now the HTML code has no JavaScript commands sprinkled in with it, just a call at the end to the external script. The anchor tag is given an id of sale, which can be used by the JavaScript code to capture the click event on that element. The JavaScript code now uses document.getElementById() to grab the anchor element and then assigns it a function to run when clicked.

The final note here is that the link simply does nothing for those without JavaScript. Since the content of the alert is something you need the visitor to know (so that they will know there is a sale), you will want to be sure that even those visitors without JavaScript can get this message. You can either display it elsewhere on the page, use a set of <noscript></noscript> tags to display the message inline, or code the link so that it leads to an HTML page with the message, as in the following code:

```
<body>
<a href="sale_alert.html" id="sale">Hi</a>
<script type="text/javascript" src="myscript.js"></script>
</body>
```

Then, you can place your message in a file named sale_alert.html:

```
<body>
Hi, there is a sale today! 20% off everything!
</body>
```

This ensures that all users can access the message with or without JavaScript.

Enhancing Content

One technique for ensuring wide accessibility that has become widely used is one that provides the content for the viewer first, then uses JavaScript to make the experience more appealing for those who can run it. This is typically called "progressive enhancement" and allows all viewers to use the site while providing a richer experience for those with modern browsers.

This is what you did (on a small scale) with the script in the previous section. By offering the "sale" message when the link is clicked, you made it accessible to all viewers. However, those with JavaScript were able to view the alert without leaving the page and needing to go back, enhancing their experience somewhat.

This process can be simple, as in the previous example, or it can be as complex as adding a lot of JavaScript code to work with various browsers and/or adding server-side scripting to aid those without JavaScript. You can learn more about progressive enhancement at http:// developer.yahoo.com/yui/articles/gbs/#progressive-enhancement. Yahoo! has a very detailed and organized system of progressive enhancement that allows the JavaScript code to work with as many browsers as possible, but also provides server-side scripts or HTML content for those without JavaScript.

TIP

For information on accessibility with JavaScript and forms, refer to Chapter 14, which discusses this topic and the use of forms with JavaScript.

Try This 15-2 Make This Code Accessible

pr15_2.html
sales.html
prjs15_2.js

To practice making JavaScript more accessible, you will take an HTML page and work with it to separate the JavaScript and HTML code as much as possible. You'll also use code that ensures that those without JavaScript can also obtain any additional content.

Step by Step

1. Create an HTML document named pr15_2.html and use the following HTML code for the body section:

```
<body>
<script type="text/javascript">
function new_win() {
   window.open('sales.html', 'newwin', 'width=300,height=200');
}
</script>
<div>
<h1>Sales:</h1>
</div>
<div>
<a href="#" onclick="new_win(); return false;">Click for Sale
Information</a>
</div>
</body>
```

2. Create an HTML document named sales.html and use the following HTML code for the body section:

```
<body>
<h1>Sales:</h1>
Clothes: 25% off<br>
Electronics: 10% off<br>
Appliances: 15% off (with coupon)
</body>
```

3. Make the code accessible and usable for those without JavaScript by making any necessary adjustments and moving as much JavaScript code as possible to a JavaScript file named prjs15_2.js.

4. One possible solution is shown in the following HTML code (for pr15_2.html) and the JavaScript code (for prjs15_2.js).

HTML Code:

```
<body>
<div>
<h1>Sales:</h1>
</div>
<div>
<a href="sales.html" id="slink">Click for Sale Information</a>
</div>
<script type="text/javascript" src="prjs15_2.js"></script>
</body>
```

JavaScript Code:

```
var slink = document.getElementById("slink");
slink.addEventListener("click", function() {
  event.preventDefault();
  window.open('sales.html', 'newwin', 'width=300,height=200');
}, false);
```

5. Save the HTML and JavaScript files and open the HTML file in your browser. The content should now be accessible in any browser with which you choose to open the page.

Try This Summary

In this project, you used your knowledge of accessibility to make a document and script more accessible for the viewer.

JavaScript Security

You may have noticed that when you try to use the window.close() method on the main browser window, a confirmation box appears asking if you really want to allow the window to be closed. This situation is one of the issues of JavaScript security. The browser does not want a site to close a window that the viewer opened without permission from the viewer. If that were allowed, the programmer would have some control of the viewer's computer, which could be a problem.

Another aspect of security is the mistaken belief that you can "protect" Web pages with passwords or keep the source code of the page from being viewed by a user.

Yet another aspect of security is protecting against cross-site scripting, the use of JavaScript to grab information from a server-side application that didn't properly filter user input.

Security and Signed Scripts

To get viewer permission to close the main browser window or to use certain properties or methods in JavaScript, you must use signed scripts. Signed scripts will open up some more JavaScript features, but you must do some additional work.

Basically, you digitally sign the script using a special tool. The viewer then gets a message when entering the page that asks whether to allow the signed script, with some information about the signed script. If the viewer accepts, then you will be able to use the additional features. If not, you'll need to have alternative code ready to avoid JavaScript errors.

For further information about this subject, go to the Web site www.mozilla.org/projects/security/components/signed-scripts.html.

Page Protection

Many scripts attempt to keep viewers out in some way, such as by using password protection or by using a "no-right-click" script to keep the source code of the page from being viewed.

However, these security strategies are largely ineffective because these "password" and "no-right-click" scripts can often be bypassed by turning off JavaScript or by doing a little extra work.

Passwords

Some password systems are better than others, but none really seems to offer true Web page security. If you don't want someone to view a page, much better methods exist than using a JavaScript system, such as using server-side languages or using certain setups on your Web server.

If you are on a free Web-hosting service, the better methods may or may not be available. However, keep in mind that a JavaScript password system is not foolproof and that you should not protect anything important with such a system.

Hiding Web Page Source Code

Many people would love to hide the source code of a Web page. However, JavaScript isn't going to do the trick. A number of scripts try various means of disabling the right-click. Basically, these strategies don't work because they can be bypassed in a couple of ways:

- If the right-click is disabled, you can always try selecting View | View Source.

- If the preceding method does not work, you can always turn off JavaScript or look in your cache folder on your computer. The browser must have the code to display the page, so a copy of it goes into the browser's cache.

In the long run, these scripts just make viewing the source code more difficult (and they can be annoying). For more information about this topic, go to http://webhome.idirect.com/~bowers/copy/copy1.htm.

Cross-Site Scripting

Cross-site scripting (often shortened to XSS) uses JavaScript code (or other types of code) in a malicious way to obtain information from users of various Web sites with vulnerable applications. With this information, a person can use someone else's cookie or session information and access the Web site as though they were the user from whom they obtained the information. This, of course, can lead to big trouble, especially if that user is an administrator in that application or if the application deals with money (such as a banking or shopping application).

While JavaScript is one of the ways used to perform such an attack, the vulnerable application is usually one that is server-side and displays user input on the page. If the user input is not sanitized (validated) in the server-side application, then any number of possible malicious scripts could be entered instead of the expected input.

For example, you might have a form that uses a server-side script to allow people to send comments. The script displays the comment the user submitted back to the user as a confirmation. If the input is not sanitized, it is possible to enter something like this into the comments field: <script>alert("You've been had!");</script>. If someone submits this and sees an alert on the response page, the person will know there is a potential vulnerability and could simply direct a subsequent user to a malicious URL where the user's cookie or session information can be taken. Figure 15-6 shows how a vulnerable application would display such an alert (this one also included some comment text to help disguise the intent of the person submitting the form).

Cross-site scripting has evolved over the years. In the beginning, it was that a bad Web site could load a good Web site in a frame (or in a pop-up browser window) and then access the text boxes, cookies, and other data (user id and password) using JavaScript—thus the name "cross site." It should be noted that modern browsers, within the past four or five years, don't allow this type of cross-site scripting. One domain cannot access the contents of a different domain. Most of the modern cross-site scripting attacks are injection attacks like the example here (though often much more complex).

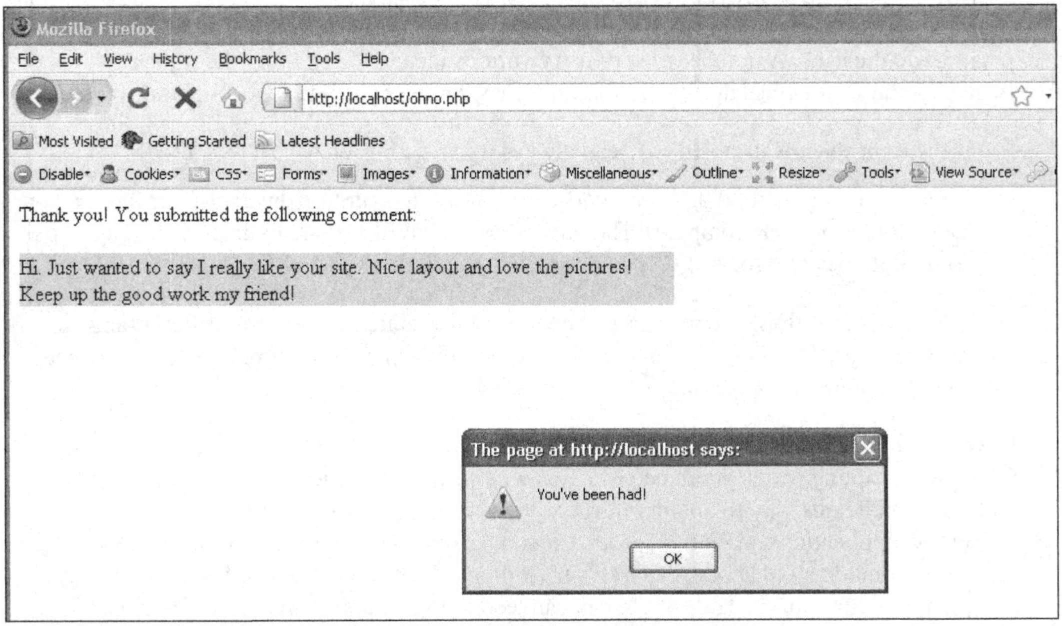

Figure 15-6 Oh no! This would not be good for users of this Web site!

This introduction just scratches the surface of this type of security issue. The main thing to remember is that when you are using server-side applications, you must sanitize any user input to be sure that you receive the type of input you expect. For more information on this topic, go to www.owasp.org/index.php/Cross_site_scripting.

AJAX and JSON

AJAX provides a method of obtaining data from a server-side script using the XMLHttpRequest object. The data obtained can be returned as a usable JavaScript value such as an array or object by using JSON. Both of these are explained in more detail in the following sections.

AJAX

AJAX stands for Asynchronous JavaScript and XML, which is a way JavaScript can obtain data from a server-side file or application without the need to reload a page. For example, a synchronous request to the Web server requires that the current page be reloaded to use the new information. An asynchronous request allows the information to be obtained and used without the need to wait for the entire page to reload.

The data obtained from the server can be any number of things (for example, a text file, an XML file, the result of running a server-side script). The value returned does not actually need to be in XML format, in spite of the AJAX terminology. This gives you a lot of flexibility as to how you can retrieve the data you need.

This type of scripting is useful in progressive enhancement, as it allows applications to enhance the user experience for those with JavaScript enabled in modern browsers. Instead of waiting for a page to load again, the information can be obtained and used on-the-fly.

The XMLHttpRequest Object

In JavaScript, an XMLHttpRequest object is created, which can then be used to make HTTP requests to the server in the background and allow the user to continue using the application without interruption. This object is often referred to as XHR in text as a shorthand for the full object name (XMLHttpRequest).

To create an XHR object, you simply use its constructor, as shown in the following code:

```
var xhr = new XMLHttpRequest();
```

This object is available in most modern browsers. In Internet Explorer versions before version 7, you would need to create an ActiveX object. Workarounds for earlier versions of Internet Explorer can be found on the Web, such as the one at github.com/ilinsky/xmlhttprequest. If you do not need the functionality in older browsers, you can use the standard constructor.

The open() and send() Methods

The open() method allows you to prepare a request to be sent to the server. It takes three arguments: the request method (for example, "get" or "post"), the URL to open, and a Boolean value (true if the request is to be asynchronous and false if the request is to be synchronous). So, to use the "get" method to open a PHP script named get_info.php as an asynchronous request, you could use the following code:

```
var xhr = new XMLHttpRequest();
xhr.open("get","get_info.php", true);
```

Now that the request is prepared, you can send it using the send() method. The send() method takes one argument, which is data to be sent as part of the request. If you are using a "get" request, you can simply use *null* as the argument, as in the following code:

```
var xhr = new XMLHttpRequest();
xhr.open("get","get_info.php", true);
xhr.send(null);
```

This will send the request to the server. Once the request has been sent, you will need to wait for a status to be returned and for the data to be received to complete transmission.

The status Property, the readystatechange Event, and the responseText Property

The first thing you will need to know when trying to retrieve data from the server is whether or not the request received a valid response from the server. This can be determined using the *status* property. Basically, any status code in the 200 range is a successful response. Also, a status code of 304 is successful, since data will be available from the browser cache.

To see what data is returned, you can use the responseText property (or, if using a response MIME type of "text/xml" or "application/xml", the responseXML property can be used). If the get_info.php PHP script is expected to return a string of data, then that data will be available in the responseText property.

Finally, for an asynchronous request, you will want to be able to determine when the data you are trying to retrieve is available for use. This is done using the readystatechange event. This event is fired whenever an update occurs to the readyState property of your XHR object. The readyState property can have the following values:

- 0 – Uninitialized. The open() method has not been called.
- 1 – Open. The open() method has been called.
- 2 – Sent. The send() method has been called.
- 3 – Receiving. Data has been received, but is still not complete.
- 4 – Complete. All of the data has been received and can be used.

For most applications, you only need to worry about whether the response code is 4, since you won't do anything until you have all of the data.

To send a request and receive data, you need to put all of this together. The request needs to be open and sent, a good response status is needed, and you need to know when the value of readyState is equal to 4 by using the onreadystatechange event. This can be accomplished using the following code:

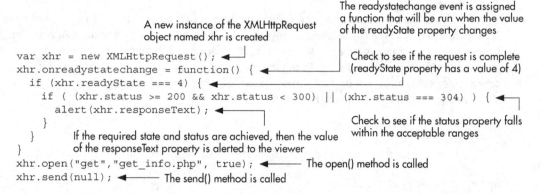

A new instance of the XMLHttpRequest object named xhr is created

The readystatechange event is assigned a function that will be run when the value of the readyState property changes

```
var xhr = new XMLHttpRequest();
xhr.onreadystatechange = function() {
  if (xhr.readyState === 4) {
    if ( (xhr.status >= 200 && xhr.status < 300) || (xhr.status === 304) ) {
      alert(xhr.responseText);
    }
  }
}
xhr.open("get","get_info.php", true);
xhr.send(null);
```

Check to see if the request is complete (readyState property has a value of 4)

Check to see if the status property falls within the acceptable ranges

If the required state and status are achieved, then the value of the responseText property is alerted to the viewer

The open() method is called

The send() method is called

A couple of notes on this code: due to browser compatibility issues, the DOM 0 method of handling the readystatechange event is used, and the open() and send() methods are called after the function that handles the readystatechange event. These two things help to minimize the risk of unexpected errors occurring in various browsers. If the response passes all of the tests, then the user receives an alert with the text received from the PHP script.

The text received in the responseText property can be anything from a simple value to a complex string of data. Whether the script returns "John" or "x=34&y=25&z=50", that value will be placed in the responseText property.

Note that since this is a beginner's guide, you will use "get" requests to retrieve data and won't change the HTTP headers. For additional details on these features of AJAX, see the "Further Reading" section later in this chapter.

An Example AJAX Script

The best way to show how the response data is created is to apply an example. Suppose you had the following HTML to create a simple poll:

```
<body>
<form method="post" id="poll" action="show_results.php">
<h2>Who will win the JavaScript coding contest?</h2>
<input type="radio" name="winner" id="John" value="John">
  <label for="John">John</label><br>
<input type="radio" name="winner" id="Nick" value="Nick">
  <label for="Nick">Nick</label><br>
<input type="radio" name="winner" id="Doug" value="Doug">
  <label for="Doug">Doug</label><br>
<input type="radio" name="winner" id="Paul" value="Paul">
  <label for="Paul">Paul</label><br><br>
<input type="submit" name="submit" id="submit" value="Vote!">
</form>
<div id="results"></div>
</body>
```

In this case, the form action will be a separate PHP script that will run if JavaScript is not available. If JavaScript is available, you will call a script named get_winner.php in your AJAX code.

The get_winner.php will be a server-side application that returns data. This could be results from a database query, a calculation, or any other task a server-side application can perform. In this case, the script is going to add your vote to a database and query the database for the person who has the most votes, declaring that person the current winner of the poll. Since server-side programming is beyond the scope of this book, the get_winner.php script will be shortened to describe its purpose. Here is the script:

```php
<?php
function get_winner() {
// Code to add new vote and obtain current winner from the database
}
$winner = get_winner();
echo "<p>The current winner is $winner!</p>";
?>
```

Here, a function is run to determine the value of the $winner variable from the database. The echo command sends a string of text as a response. If this were run as a standalone script, the string would simply be written in the browser window. When responding to an XHR request, however, this string is returned to the JavaScript application as the value of the responseText property. You can now make use of this data returned from the server-side application in JavaScript!

NOTE

When you're using a server-side application to return data, it does not need to be written in PHP. Any server-side language (for example., Perl, ASP, Python, Java) can be used based on your background and server setup.

With this in mind, the bulk of the remaining work is performed in your JavaScript code. Since you want to display the current winner, the value returned for the responseText property will give you the data you need. Here is the JavaScript code to retrieve and use the information from the get_winner.php script:

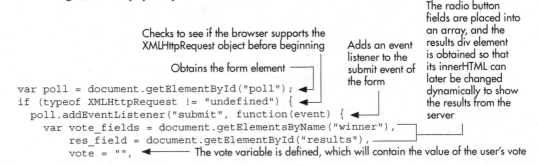

Checks to see if the browser supports the XMLHttpRequest object before beginning

Obtains the form element

Adds an event listener to the submit event of the form

The radio button fields are placed into an array, and the results div element is obtained so that its innerHTML can later be changed dynamically to show the results from the server

```javascript
var poll = document.getElementById("poll");
if (typeof XMLHttpRequest != "undefined") {
  poll.addEventListener("submit", function(event) {
    var vote_fields = document.getElementsByName("winner"),
        res_field = document.getElementById("results"),
        vote = "",
```

The vote variable is defined, which will contain the value of the user's vote

```
      count = 0,                        ──────────  The count variable is defined, which will be used later
      xhr = new XMLHttpRequest(),  ◄───             to help verify that a radio button has been selected
      ustring = "";                ◄───────────────  The xhr object is created
  event.preventDefault();          ◄───
  for (var i = 0; i < vote_fields.length; i++) { ─┐    The ustring variable is
    if (vote_fields[i].checked) {                      defined, which will be used
      vote = vote_fields[i].value;                     to build the URL that will be
      break;                                           sent as part of the request
    }
    else {                                        ──┐  The default action (submitting
      count++;                                          the form) is prevented
    }                                                 The radio button element values
  }                                                   are looped over to determine
  if (count === vote_fields.length) {           ──┐  if one has been checked; if so,
    alert("You must make a selection to vote!");       that value is obtained; if not,
    return;                                            an error message is alerted to
  }                                                    the viewer
  ustring += "get_winner.php?vote=" + encodeURIComponent(vote);  ◄───
  xhr.onreadystatechange = function() { ─────────────
    var results;
    if (xhr.readyState === 4) {
      if ( (xhr.status >= 200 && xhr.status < 300) || (xhr.status === 304) ) {
        res_field.innerHTML = xhr.responseText;
      }
    }
    return false;
  }
  xhr.open("get", ustring, true); ─┐  The open and send      The function that is run when
  xhr.send(null); ─────────────────┘  methods are called to  the readyState changes; this
}, false);                            get a response from the gets the responseText and
}                                     server-side application displays it in the results div
```

The URL string is created to call the get_winner.php script with a query string containing the user's vote value; the value of the vote variable is URL encoded using the encodeURIComponent() method so that it will be sent properly in the get request

This looks like quite a long process, but most of it is preparing the user's vote to be sent (checking that a selection was made before submitting, and so on). This obtains the user's vote, which is stored in the vote variable. This variable is then used as part of a query string that will be added to the URL when get_winner.php is called. For example, if the user voted for "Paul", then the URL sent to the server in this case would be "get_winner.php?vote=Paul". Notice that the encodeURIComponent() method is used on the vote variable, which ensures that the value can be part of a valid URL. This will give the PHP script the data it needs to add that vote to the database. The remainder of the script uses what you learned in this chapter to obtain the data (the current winner of the poll). Since the data is already in the desired format, the results div innerHTML is updated to show the current poll winner. Figure 15-7 shows how the HTML page appears initially, while Figure 15-8 shows how the page appears when the result is displayed.

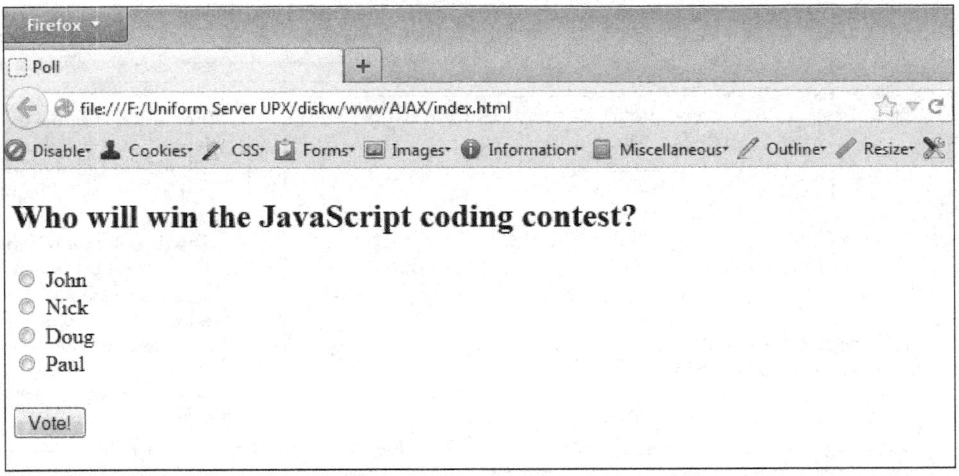

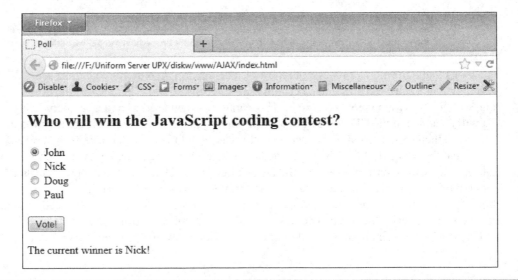

Figure 15-7 The initial HTML page

This script conveniently returned a simple text string, but you may wish to have more data returned that you could use to display more detailed results. Returning this data could result in a string that you have to break apart to get the values (for example, "John=2&Nick=34&Doug =32&Paul=25"). This can be used, but it would be even better if this data could be returned in a format that JavaScript could use more easily. JSON makes this possible, and is discussed in more detail shortly.

Figure 15-8 The page after retrieving the data

Further Reading

More information on AJAX and how to use it in your applications can be found at the following Web sites:

- https://developer.mozilla.org/en/AJAX

- www.w3schools.com/Ajax/Default.Asp

JSON

JSON stands for JavaScript Object Notation. It is a data format that can be used in numerous programming languages, which makes it a perfect companion when making use of AJAX. If you send JSON data to a server-side application, most of these languages have JSON parsers that can take the information and place it in a usable form in that language—be it a value, array, object, and so on. When sending JSON data back to JavaScript, it can easily be used either via the JSON object (newer browsers) or with a JavaScript JSON parser (older browsers).

JSON Object or JSON Parser?

Most modern browsers support the JSON object: Firefox 3.5+, Internet Explorer 8+, Chrome, and others. If you need to use JSON data in JavaScript in older browsers, you can get a parser written by Douglas Crockford at github.com/douglascrockford/JSON-js.

JSON Formatting

Often, you will send or receive an array or object containing data. JSON formatting simply takes the array literal and object literal notation from JavaScript. For example, an array in JSON format could look like this:

```
[2, 5, "Cool"]
```

Notice that this is not assigned to a variable; it is simply the data itself that is passed along in JSON format. The JSON object or JSON parser will convert the data to the desired format for the language that makes use of the information.

For objects, JSON also requires quotes around all strings, including property names. For example, a JavaScript object could look like this:

```
var info = { num: 77, color: "red" }
```

In JSON format, the property names would also need to be quoted, as in the following code:

```
{ "num": 77, "color": "red" }
```

Notice that the property names are also quoted in this case. So, if you need to write or parse JSON data, keep these rules in mind to avoid errors sending or receiving the data.

Using the JSON Object

The JSON object has two methods: stringify() to send JSON data to another application and parse() to turn JSON data into JavaScript values. For example, if you were going to send data from JavaScript to another application, you could convert it into JSON format easily using JSON.stringify(), as in the following code:

```
var info = { num: 77, color: "red" },
    j_data = JSON.stringify(info);
```

The j_data variable could then be sent via the send() method once you have an XHR object.

When receiving JSON data, you would use the JSON.parse() method to convert the data from JSON format into usable JavaScript values. For example, suppose you are receiving the following JSON data in JavaScript:

```
{ "num": 77, "color": "red" }
```

If this JSON data were read into the responseText of an XHR object named xhr, you could convert this data into a usable JavaScript object, as in the following code:

```
var info = JSON.parse(xhr.responseText);
```

The info object would now be created, which would be the same as if you had written this code:

```
var info = { num: 77, color: "red" };
```

With this ability to quickly convert data into a usable JavaScript value, JSON can make data collection and use much easier for your AJAX scripts.

AJAX and JSON Example

Suppose you wanted to change your AJAX script from earlier in the chapter, which displayed the current winner of the poll. Instead of just displaying the current winner, you would like to show all of the current results. Recall that without JSON, you would need to send back and parse a string of names/values or an XML document from the server-side application. With JSON, you could simply send back the data in JSON format, where you could then quickly use the parse() method to make it usable JavaScript.

Here, you will use the same HTML code, a PHP script named get_results.php, and will alter your JavaScript code to make use of JSON data.

First, the PHP script: It will add your vote to the database, then retrieve the current results from the database, then send those results back to JavaScript in JSON format. Here is the example:

```
<?php
function get_winner() {
// Code to add new vote and obtain names and vote totals from the database
}
```

```php
$loopcount = 0;
$results_array = get_winner();
echo "{ ";
foreach ($results_array as $key => $value) {
  $loopcount++;
  if ($count === $loopcount) {
      echo "\"$key\": $value";
  }
  else {
    echo "\"$key\": $value, ";
  }
}
echo " }";
?>
```

In summary, this will send back a string of JSON data to your JavaScript application (here the JSON string is built, but PHP has methods for converting PHP objects to JSON as well), which could look like the following:

```
"John": 2, "Nick": 35, "Doug": 32, "Paul": 25 }
```

You can now alter your JavaScript code to show the names and vote totals for each of the people in the poll. Here is the updated JavaScript code:

```javascript
var poll = document.getElementById("poll");
if (typeof XMLHttpRequest != "undefined") {
  poll.addEventListener("submit", function(event) {
    var vote_fields = document.getElementsByName("winner"),
        res_field = document.getElementById("results"),
        res_HTML = "",
        vote = "",
        count = 0,
        xhr = new XMLHttpRequest(),
        qstring = "";
    event.preventDefault();
    for (var i = 0; i < vote_fields.length; i++) {
      if (vote_fields[i].checked) {
          vote = vote_fields[i].value;
          break;
      }
      else {
          count++;
      }
    }
    if (count === vote_fields.length) {
      alert("You must make a selection to vote!");
        return;
    }
```

```
qstring += "get_results.php?vote=" + encodeURIComponent(vote);
xhr.onreadystatechange = function() {
  var results;
  if (xhr.readyState === 4) {
    if ( (xhr.status >= 200 && xhr.status < 300) || (xhr.status === 304) ) {
      results = JSON.parse(xhr.responseText);
      res_HTML += '<h3>Current Results</h3>';
      for (var prop in results) {
        if (results.hasOwnProperty(prop)) {
          res_HTML += prop + ' : ' + results[prop] + '<br>';
        }
      }
      res_field.innerHTML = res_HTML;
    }
  }
  return false;
}
xhr.open("get", qstring, true);
xhr.send(null);
}, false);
}
```

The responseText contains JSON data that is parsed using the JSON.parse() method

Each property and value is added to the res_HTML variable to be displayed on the page

Checks to ensure that each property is within the results object itself

Once the res_HTML variable has all of the necessary data, it is assigned to the innerHTML of the results div, displaying the results on the page

The parsed data is now an object named results, which now allows you to cycle through its properties using a for-in loop

Here, you are able to simply parse the responseText to obtain a usable JavaScript object named results. A for-in loop cycles through each of the object's properties, which are the names of each person in the poll. The property names and values are then added to a variable named res_HTML, which is then displayed as the innerHTML of the results div on the HTML page.

With the ability to easily use data obtained from a server-side application, you can enhance your scripts to provide your users more options without the need to reload the entire page to get results.

Further Reading
More information on JSON is available from the following Web sites:

- www.json.org/

- developer.mozilla.org/en-US/docs/JSON

✓ Chapter 15 Self Test

1. _____ divide a window into two or more separate areas, each containing different content.

2. Frames differ from tables because the divisions in a frame set contain separate _____ documents.

3. The _____ tags are used to create a frame set.

4. A single frame is created with the _____ tags.

5. The _____ attribute divides a frame set into columns.

6. The _____ property of an <img> element allows you to change an image.

7. What are two methods that can be used to access frames?

   A. The frames array or a frame name

   B. The frame array or a frame name

   C. The frames array or a special code

   D. There is only one way to do it

8. Using JavaScript, you can get information from the server.

   A. True

   B. False

9. Which of the following is a valid Lint tool for JavaScript?

   A. jsChecker

   B. JavaScript Linter

   C. jsLint

   D. <Script> the Web

10. What two methods can be used to test JavaScript values when debugging?

   A. test() and show()

   B. alert() and console.log()

   C. print() and show()

   D. None of the above.

11. What is used to access the main window so that you can access another frame?

   A. top

   B. self

   C. window

   D. this

12. What object allows you to get data from the server in JavaScript?

    A. XMLServerRequest

    B. XMLHttpRequest

    C. JSONRequest

    D. XMLFileGet

13. _____ stands for Asynchronous JavaScript and XML.

14. JavaScript can retrieve data from the server other than an XML document.

    A. True

    B. False

15. The acronym for JavaScript Object notation is _____.

Chapter 16

JavaScript Libraries, HTML5, and Harmony

Key Skills & Concepts

- Using jQuery
- Other JavaScript Libraries
- JavaScript and HTML5
- ECMAScript Harmony
- Further Reading

This chapter introduces a number of advanced techniques that you may wish to pursue further once you have finished this book. First, you will be introduced to jQuery, which is a good JavaScript library for creating DOM-related scripts that work cross-browser. You will also learn a little about other JavaScript libraries that are available, such as php.js and MooTools. After covering these libraries, you will look at how JavaScript is incorporated into HTML5, and then learn about things that are on the horizon for the future of JavaScript in ECMAScript Harmony.

Using jQuery

One of the reasons to learn JavaScript is so that you can more easily work with jQuery. The jQuery library has become a very popular tool for easily creating dynamic effects that work cross-browser, which avoids many of the issues you may face trying to do so, such as the differences in how to handle events in each browser. At the time of this writing, jQuery had support for Internet Explorer 6.0+, Firefox 10+, Safari 5.0+, Opera, and Chrome.

Obtaining jQuery

The first thing you will need to do is to grab a copy of jQuery or to use a remote copy. If you wish to use a local copy, you can download the latest version from jquery.com. Once you have it, you call it using a <script> tag as you would any other external JavaScript file, as in this code:

```
<script type="text/javascript" src="jquery-1.8.2.min.js"></script>
```

If you decide to use a remote copy, such as one from Google (which can be helpful as the user may already have the file cached, which will speed up load time), you can grab the latest code from https://developers.google.com/speed/libraries/devguide#jquery. Here is an example of using a copy from Google:

```
<script src="//ajax.googleapis.com/ajax/libs/jquery/1.8.2/jquery.min
.js"></script>
```

You can choose the method that works best for you. Once you have the code included in your HTML, you are ready to make use of what jQuery has to offer.

NOTE

When including JavaScript from external sites, there can be security concerns. For more on this, see www.securitee.org/files/jsinclusions_ccs2012.pdf.

Getting Started: document.ready()

The first thing jQuery needs is to be sure that all DOM elements are available for scripting. The document.ready() method determines when the DOM structure is loaded, and then will run the code within, usually a function, as in this code:

```
$(document).ready(function() {
  // JavaScript/jQuery code here...
});
```

This is placed in your regular JavaScript code (for example, your .js file). Notice the $ at the beginning of the code. This is the jQuery selector, and is used when you invoke jQuery in your JavaScript code.

Using Selectors

In jQuery, you can select elements via CSS syntax, rather than using the typical JavaScript methods such as document.getElementById() or document.getElementsByClassName(). For example, suppose you had the following code:

```
var story = document.getElementById("story");
story.addEventListener("click", function() {
  story.style.color = "#009";
  story.style.fontSize = "2em";
}, false);
```

This simply changes a couple of CSS style properties, though it does take several lines of code to do so. In jQuery, this can be shortened like this:

```
$("#story").click(function() {
  $("#story").css({'color':'#009', 'font-size':'2em'});
});
```

First, you will notice that the "story" div is selected using CSS syntax ("#story") rather than document.getElementById("story"). This makes the selection of the element a little shorter. Also, you will see that event handling simply attached the event name ("click" in this case) followed by the function to execute when the event occurs. This keeps you from needing to write cross-browser event-handling code. Next, you are able to alter the CSS of the element by using the css() method on the story element. The css() method accepts an object as a parameter, and it contains each property to change along with its new value (all quoted much like JSON syntax). In this way, you do not need to code a separate statement for each CSS property change you want to make.

To see this example in action, you will need to create an HTML page with a "story" div, as in the following code:

```
<body>
<div id="story">
This is my story. It is full of interesting stuff for you to read
when you have time. I can keep going and going and going...
</div>
<script src="http://ajax.googleapis.com/ajax/libs/jquery/1.8.2/jquery.min.js">
</script>
<script src="jqexample.js" type="text/javascript"></script>
</body>
```

If you are using a local copy of jQuery, you can call that in place of the Google copy here. You can save this HTML page as jqexample.html. Next, you will want to create a JavaScript file, which you will save as jqexample.js. Here is the code:

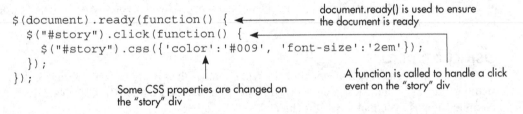

Once you have the code in place, open jqexample.html in your browser and click on the div element. The text should become larger and turn blue. Figure 16-1 shows the page before the changes, while Figure 16-2 shows the page after the changes:

There are a number of selectors available in jQuery to help you select the element(s) you need in your scripts. Some of the most common are

- (*)   Selects all of the elements in the document

- (.*class_name*)   Selects all elements with the provided class name

---

Figure 16-1   The original page

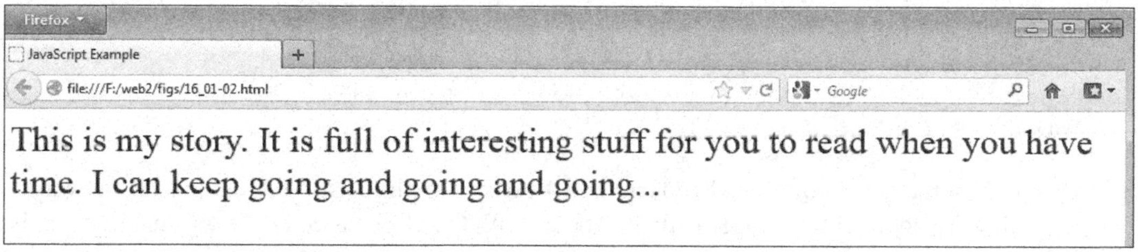

Figure 16-2 The page after the div element is clicked

- (*#id*) Selects the element with the provided id

- (*element_name*) Selects all *element_name* elements

- (*element_name.class_name*) Selects all *element_name* elements with the *class_name* class

- (*element_name[attribute="value"]*) Selects all *element_name* elements that have the provided attribute with the provided value

Further selection options are available if needed at api.jquery.com/category/selectors.

Altering Classes

The addClass() and removeClass() functions make it very easy to change the style of elements in jQuery. If you already have classes coded in your CSS, then you can use these methods to add or remove them at any time. For example, suppose you had the same HTML page (jqexample.html), and altered it to include a CSS file named jqexample.css. You could then write CSS classes that could be added or removed from the "story" div. Here is the updated HTML code:

```
<head>
<link rel="stylesheet" type="text/css" href="jqexample.css">
</head>
<body>
<div id="story">
This is my story. It is full of interesting stuff for you to read
when you have time. I can keep going and going and going...
</div>
<script src="http://ajax.googleapis.com/ajax/libs/jquery/1.8.2/jquery.min.js">
</script>
<script src="jqexample.js" type="text/javascript"></script>
</body>
```

The next step is to create jqexample.css and include some CSS declarations:

```
.style1 { font-weight:bold; }
.style2 { color:#009; font-family:Arial; font-size:2em; }
.style3 { font-style:italic; }
```

This gives three possible styles. Each can now be easily applied to an element or taken away as needed. To add a class, simply call addClass() with the class name as the argument, as in the following code:

```
$("#story ").addClass("style2");
```

If you later decide to remove it, you can do the same thing with removeClass():

```
$("#story").removeClass("style2");
```

You can also add more than one class to an element at a time by separating each class name with a space, as in the following code:

```
$("#story").addClass("style2 style3");
```

This will not only make the text larger and blue, but will also make it italic. You can make use of this along with the existing code in order to add or remove classes on a click.

If you decide you want to toggle one or more classes, you can use the toggleClass() method. This will add a class if the element does not have it and will remove a class if the element already has it. Here, you will update your jqexample.js code to toggle the style2 and style3 classes when the div is clicked. The updated script is shown in the following code:

```
$(document).ready(function() {
  $("#story").click(function() {
    $("#story").toggleClass("style2 style3");
  });
});
```

With this code, each click will add or remove both the style2 and style3 classes, depending on the current style of the element.

If you want to check whether or not an element has a class before adding or removing it, you can use the hasClass() method. The method returns true if the element has the class applied to it, and false if not. For example, the following code would make sure the "story" div does not already have the style3 class before adding it:

```
$(document).ready(function() {
  $("#story").click(function() {
    if (!$("#story").hasClass("style3")) {
        $("#story").addClass("style3");
      }
  });
});
```

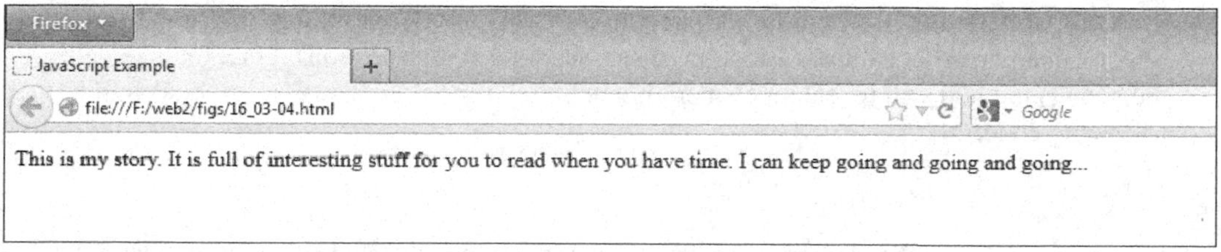

Figure 16-3   The initial page

As you can see here, the JavaScript if statement and the logical NOT operator (!) are used here along with the jQuery code. jQuery is a JavaScript library, so all of the code is still JavaScript code. Since this is the case, you can use any JavaScript code you need as well—operators, statements, arrays, functions, and more. Figure 16-3 shows what the initial page looks like, while Figure 16-4 shows how the page looks after the link is clicked.

Methods for Effects

The jQuery library has a number of methods that make creating specific dynamic effects easier. Table 16-1 lists some of the most commonly used jQuery effects.

Method	Description
show()	Shows an element
hide()	Hides an element
slideDown()	Shows an element using a "slide down" animation
slideUp()	Hides an element using a "slide up" animation
fadeIn()	Shows an element using a "fade in" animation
fadeOut()	Hides an element using a "fade out" animation

Table 16-1   Common Methods Used for Effects in jQuery

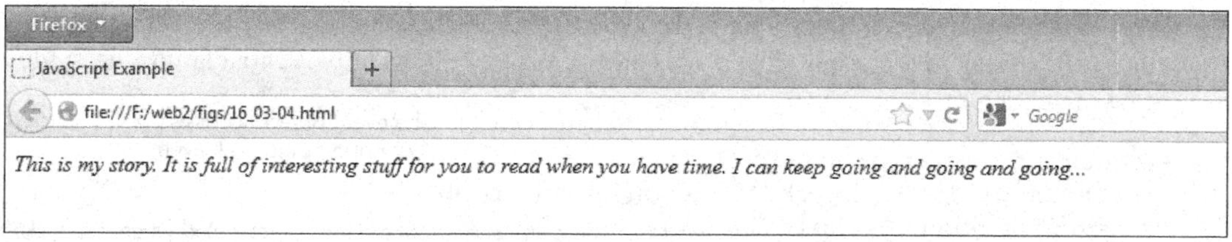

Figure 16-4   After the link is clicked, the class is added.

Each of these methods can take two arguments: the amount of time to take to perform the effect and an optional callback function (discussed later in this section). For example, calling the show() method will reveal an element immediately if no arguments are used, as in the following code:

```
$("#story").show();
```

If you want to show the element over time, you can send the number of milliseconds to the show method as an argument:

```
$("#story").show(1000);
```

When this argument is provided, the element will fade in while increasing in width and height during the specified span of time. Here, the "story" element would fade in and increase in size over a period of 1000 milliseconds (1 second). Alternatively, there are some preset values you can use in place of a specific time: "fast" and "slow", as in the following code:

```
$("#story").show("fast");   ◄─────── Using "fast" shows the element over 200 milliseconds
$("#story").show("slow");   ◄─────── Using "slow" shows the element over 600 milliseconds
```

The other methods work the same way, but perform different animations: slideDown() shows an element by sliding it down into position, slideUp() hides an element by sliding it up and out of sight, fadeIn() shows an element by gradually fading it in, while fadeOut() hides an element by gradually fading it out.

If desired, you can provide a second argument to any of these methods, which is a callback function that will be executed as soon as the effect completes execution. This can be useful to string two or more effects together, executing each one after the previous one has been completed. For instance, the following code will show the "story" element over 500 milliseconds, then fade it out over 2000 milliseconds:

```
$("#story").show(500, function() {
  $("#story").fadeOut(2000);
});
```

You could continue the process by using a callback function as the second argument of the fadeOut() method, and continue adding callback functions as needed until your desired effects have all been completed.

Finally, if you need to prevent the default action when an event occurs on an element (such as when you need a link to not be followed), you can use the jQuery event registration while still passing in the event object. This allows you to call event.preventDefault(), as in the following code:

```
$(document).ready(function() {                    The event object is passed to the function
  $("#changelink").click(function(event) {  ◄──── that handles the click event
    event.preventDefault();   ◄─────── The default action of the link is prevented when it is clicked
    $("#story").show("fast");  ◄─────┐
  });                                The "story" element is shown
});
```

The jQuery library can prove to be a very useful tool if you need to get scripts working across a larger number of browsers (for example, older versions of Internet Explorer). Since it helps with element selection, event handling, and display/animation methods, it allows you to do less work when you need cross-browser code. The next section will give you some resources to look at if you wish to delve further into the jQuery library.

Further Reading

You can read more about jQuery and how to use it at the following Web sites:

- docs.jquery.com/Main_Page

- webdesignerwall.com/tutorials/jquery-tutorials-for-designers

Try This 16-1 — Using jQuery to Create Effects

pr16_1.html
prjs16_1.js

You have a link and a div element with some text that you would like to have initially hidden, but to display when the link is clicked. Once it displays, you want the div element to slowly fade out. You want to use jQuery to accomplish the task.

Step by Step

1. Create an HTML document named pr16_1.html and use the following HTML code for the body section:

```
<body>
<h1>Read a Short Story</h1>
<p>
<a href="page.html" id="changelink">See Story</a>
</p>
<div id="story">
I was walking down the street, and I saw this guy. He was<br>
sitting in the street, and then he said "Hi!"
</div>
<script src="http://ajax.googleapis.com/ajax/libs/jquery/1.8.2/
jquery.min.js">
</script>
<script type="text/javascript" src="prjs16_1.js"></script>
</body>
```

2. Create a JavaScript file named prjs16_1.js. In this file, you need to wait until the document is ready, then immediately hide the "story" element. Next, register the click event for the "changelink" link, prevent its default action, and then show the "story" element using a

"slide down" animation over 3000 milliseconds. The "story" element should then fade out over 10,000 milliseconds. When complete, your JavaScript code should look like this:

```
$(document).ready(function() {
  $("#story").hide();
  $("#changelink").click(function(event) {
    event.preventDefault();
      $("#story").slideDown(3000, function() {
        $("#story").fadeOut(10000);
      });
  });
});
```

3. Save the HTML and JavaScript files and open the HTML file in your browser. Click the link to view the story. It should slide down, then fade out over time.

Try This Summary

In this project, you used your knowledge of JavaScript and jQuery to create animations in response to a user event. The jQuery made it easier to write the code and have it work cross-browser at the same time.

Other JavaScript Libraries

There are a number of JavaScript libraries available that can help you write higher-level scripts with less effort than it would take to write all of the code from scratch. Some of these are listed here in case you would like to look into them further:

jQuery Mobile

The jQuery mobile library is part of the jQuery Mobile framework. It is an HTML5-based framework that uses progressive enhancement so that you can write applications or Web sites that work in the most popular handheld devices or in the browser. More information on jQuery Mobile can be found at jquerymobile.com.

php.js

The php.js library is a useful one if you have been programming in PHP and would like to use functions you are familiar with from PHP, for example, in_array(), array_key_exists(), and others. These functions are set up to work like their PHP counterparts, taking the same arguments and returning the same results. You can find out more about php.js at phpjs.org.

node.js

While node.js isn't actually a library, but a software system that allows you to build server-side applications in JavaScript, it is a popular system worth a mention here. The applications run asynchronously and are event-based. More information on node.js and how it is implemented can be found at nodejs.org.

MooTools

The MooTools library is an object-oriented framework designed to make writing object-oriented code easier and cross-browser. More information on MooTools can be found at mootools.net.

Three.js

The Three.js library allows you to create 3D graphics in the browser using your choice of methods: HTML5 <canvas>, WebGL, or SVG. You can find out more about Three.js at mrdoob.github.com/three.js/.

Ask the Expert

Q: There are a lot of libraries! How do I know which one to use?

A: What you decide to use will depend on your needs and your coding style. For example, if you want to make event registration and handling work across a larger number of browsers using a shorter syntax, jQuery is a good choice. On the other hand, if you want to use object-oriented programming and want to make it easier to write, MooTools would be a good choice. If you have other needs that aren't met by one of these libraries, searching the Web should provide additional options that may be helpful.

Q: Do I need to learn jQuery? Couldn't I just write the JavaScript code?

A: This will also depend on your needs. If your boss wants you to use it or you need to code for maximum cross-browser compatibility, then you probably will want to learn it. If your script is designed to work only with the latest browsers (and does not need to be functional in older ones), then you may not need to learn it. It all depends on your needs at any given time.

Q: Does jQuery do more than what I saw here?

A: Yes, it can do quite a bit. There are more advanced selectors, additional effects, and numerous plugins to fill any additional needs that are not met with the library itself. You can find out more and read more advanced information at docs.jquery.com/Main_Page.

Q: Are there any libraries for developing JavaScript games?

A: Yes! If you would like to delve into game development, you can check out some of the following links to see some of the available libraries and how to use them.

- Crafty   craftyjs.com
- Impact   impactjs.com
- GameQuery   gamequeryjs.com
- Jaws   jawsjs.com

JavaScript and HTML5

HTML5 provides an API (application programming interface) for a number of elements and markup that allow you to create more dynamic Web pages or application. Some of these include dynamic drawing via the <canvas> element, local storage, and the dragging and dropping of elements. These are possible in browsers that support HTML5 and the corresponding JavaScript interfaces. To begin, you will look at the HTML5 <canvas> element.

The <canvas> Element

The <canvas> element allows you to create graphics with JavaScript as the page is rendered. When a <canvas> element is placed on the page, it creates a rectangular area (based on its width and height attributes) where graphics can be drawn. For example, the following code will create a drawing area of 400×400 pixels:

```
<canvas width="400" height="400" id="graphic"></canvas>
```

Anything inside the opening and closing tags will be displayed in browsers that do not support the <canvas> element, as in the following code:

```
<canvas width="400" height="400" id="graphic">My fabulous drawing!</canvas>
```

To begin working with the <canvas> element in JavaScript, you will need to get the element by its id, and then use the getContext() method to create a drawing context. The getContext() method takes one argument, which is the type of context being created. Most modern browsers support a 2D context. A 3D (three-dimensional) context is in the works. Here is an example that opens a 2D context for the <canvas> element you have been using:

```
var graphic = document.getElementById("graphic"),
    ctx = graphic.getContext("2d");
```

Once you have the context, you can begin using it to draw lines, shapes, text, and more.

Rectangles

Rectangles can be drawn in a context by using the fillRect() or strokeRect() methods. The fillRect() method will create a rectangle that is filled in with color, while strokeRect() will create a rectangle that is outlined but has no fill color. Both methods take four arguments: the x-coordinate of the top-left corner, the y-coordinate of the top-left corner, the width, and the height. For example, the following code will draw a filled rectangle beginning at (70, 70) that is 50 pixels wide and 30 pixels tall:

```
var graphic = document.getElementById("graphic"),
    ctx = graphic.getContext("2d");
ctx.fillRect(70, 70, 50, 30);
```

Figure 16-5 shows how this would look in a browser. Notice that the canvas is not outlined. If you want to outline it, you can use CSS to add a visible border.

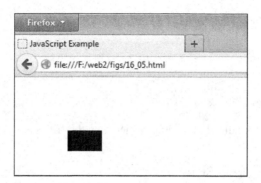

Figure 16-5   A canvas with a filled rectangle

The origin on a canvas is the top-left corner, so a higher *x*-coordinate will move the point further to the right, while a higher *y*-coordinate will move the point further down. Figure 16-6 shows how the canvas grid is laid out when the example rectangle is drawn.

If you decide you would rather have an outlined rectangle that is not filled with color, you can use strokeRect() instead, as in the following code:

```
var graphic = document.getElementById("graphic"),
    ctx = graphic.getContext("2d");
ctx.strokeRect(70, 70, 50, 30);
```

If you need to clear a rectangular area on the canvas, you can use the clearRect() method. It uses the same four arguments as fillRect(), but clears (makes transparent) the area that

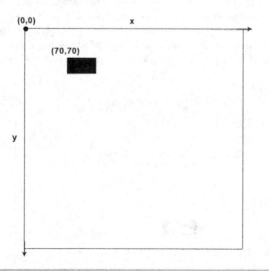

Figure 16-6   The example showing the canvas layout

it affects. For example, you could clear out a rectangle within a filled rectangle using the following code:

```
var graphic = document.getElementById("graphic"),
    ctx = graphic.getContext("2d");
ctx.fillRect(70, 70, 50, 30);
ctx.clearRect(80, 80, 20, 10);
```

Figure 16-7 shows the result of this code. Notice how the filled rectangle now has an area cleared inside of it.

Using fillStyle and strokeStyle

The default color of a shape or outline is black (#000000). To use different colors, you can set these using the fillStyle property for fill color and strokeStyle property for the color of a stroke (outline or line). For example, consider this code:

```
var graphic = document.getElementById("graphic"),
    ctx = graphic.getContext("2d");
ctx.fillStyle = "#FF0000";  ◄———— The fill color of shapes is set to #FF0000 (red)
ctx.fillRect(70, 70, 50, 30);  ◄———— A rectangle is drawn, and will use the new fill color
```

Here, fillStyle is set to #FF0000 (red), and any shapes after this assignment will use red for the fill color. This can always be changed as you go to use shapes with different colors, as in the following code:

```
var graphic = document.getElementById("graphic"),
    ctx = graphic.getContext("2d");
ctx.fillStyle = "#FF0000";  ◄———— fillStyle is set to red
ctx.fillRect(70, 70, 50, 30);  ◄———— This rectangle will be red
ctx.fillStyle = "#00FF00";  ◄———— fillStyle is set to green
ctx.fillRect(10, 10, 50, 30);  ◄———— This rectangle will be green
ctx.fillStyle = "#FF0000";  ◄———— fillStyle set to red again
ctx.fillRect(120, 120, 50, 30);  ◄———— This rectangle will be red
```

Figure 16-7 The rectangle now has an empty rectangular area within it.

If you have particular settings such as fillStyle and strokeStyle that you want to save for later, you can use the save() method. You can then restore those settings using the restore() method, as in the following code:

```
var graphic = document.getElementById("graphic"),
    ctx = graphic.getContext("2d");
ctx.fillStyle = "#FF0000";  ◄———— fillStyle is set to red
ctx.save();  ◄———— The currently set properties are saved (saves the fillStyle value here)
ctx.fillRect(70, 70, 50, 30);  ◄———— This rectangle will be red
ctx.fillStyle = "#00FF00";  ◄———— fillStyle is set to green
ctx.fillRect(10, 10, 50, 30);  ◄———— This rectangle will be green
ctx.restore();  ◄———— Using restore() brings back the saved property values (the saved fillStyle here)
ctx.fillRect(120, 120, 50, 30);  ◄———— This rectangle will be red
```

You can use strokeStyle in the same way as fillStyle to set the color of a shape outline or a drawn line (path). For example, the following code will create a rectangle with a red outline:

```
var graphic = document.getElementById("graphic"),
    ctx = graphic.getContext("2d");
ctx.strokeStyle = "#FF0000";
ctx.strokeRect(70, 70, 50, 30);
```

Using Paths

The canvas context also allows you to draw lines and curves (paths), which gives you the opportunity to create more complex drawings. You begin a path by calling the beginPath() method, and then end a path by calling one of several methods. In between, you can use a number of methods to draw lines, curves, and more. Table 16-2 lists the methods that can be used within a path:

Method	Description
arc(x, y, radius, start_angle, end_angle, counterclockwise)	Draws an arc that is centered at (x,y) with the provided radius and between the start_angle and end_angle (in radians). The counterclockwise argument is set to true if the angles should be calculated counterclockwise and false if clockwise
arcTo(x, y, x2, y2, radius)	Draws an arc from the previous point that runs through (x,y) and ends at(x2,y2) with the provided radius
bezierCurveTo(cpx, cpy, cpx2, cpy2, x, y)	Draws a curve from the previous point to (x,y) using the control points (cpx,cpy) and (cpx2,cpy2)
lineTo(x, y)	Draws a line from the previous point to (x,y)
moveTo(x, y)	Moves the cursor to (x,y) without drawing anything
quadraticCurveTo(cpx, cpy, x, y)	Draws a curve from the previous point to (x,y) using the control point (cpx,xpy)
rect(x, y, width, height)	Draws a rectangle beginning at (x,y) with the provided width and height

Table 16-2 Methods for Drawing Paths

Method	Description
closePath()	Ends the path by drawing a line back to the point where the path began
clip()	Creates a clipping region based on the drawn path
fill()	Fills the path (if complete) with the current fillStyle
stroke()	Strokes the path with the current strokeStyle

Table 16-3   Methods to End a Path

Once you have completed drawing a path, you can end the path in several ways. Table 16-3 lists the available methods.

As an example, suppose you decided to draw a path using lines and arcs, and then stroke the path. You could use the following code:

```
var graphic = document.getElementById("graphic"),
    ctx = graphic.getContext("2d");
ctx.strokeStyle = "#000000";  ←—— Sets the strokeStyle
ctx.beginPath();  ←——————— Begins the path
ctx.moveTo(10, 10);  ←—— Moves the cursor to (10,10) without drawing
ctx.lineTo(10, 50);  ←—— Draws a line from (10,10) to (10,50)
ctx.arcTo(80, 20, 10, 10, 20);  ←—— Draws an arc back to (10,10)
ctx.stroke();  ←—— Strokes the path using the strokeStyle (draws the path with a red line)
```

Figure 16-8 shows the result of this code. It draws a half-oval on the canvas.

Adding Text
The canvas API provides two methods for adding text to the context: fillText() and strokeText(). Both take the same arguments: the text string, *x*, *y*, and an optional argument to

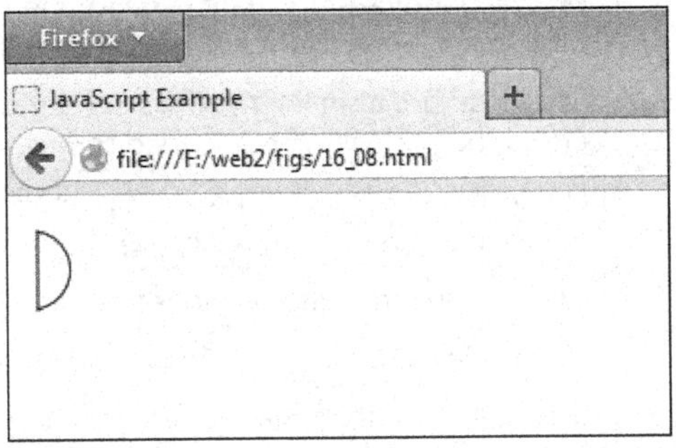

Figure 16-8   A stroked path on the canvas

set a maximum width (which will attempt to condense the text string if it is longer than the set width). For example, the following code will draw the text string "I am some text on a canvas" beginning at (10,10) with a maximum width of 200 pixels:

```
var graphic = document.getElementById("graphic"),
    ctx = graphic.getContext("2d");
ctx.fillStyle = "#000000";
ctx.fillText("I am some text on a canvas", 10, 10, 200);
```

There are also three properties that you can use to style text:

● **font**   Sets the font properties using CSS format, for example, "bold 1em Verdana"

● **textBaseLine**   Sets the text baseline. Possible values are "alphabetic", "bottom", "hanging", "ideographic", "middle", and "top".

● **textAlign**   Sets the alignment of the text. Possible values are "center", "end", "left", "right", and "start".

Thus, if you wanted to change the font and align the text, you could set font and fontAlign, as in the following code:

```
var graphic = document.getElementById("graphic"),
    ctx = graphic.getContext("2d");
ctx.fillStyle = "#000000";
ctx.font = "bold 1em Verdana";
ctx.textAlign = "end";
ctx.fillText("I am some text on a canvas", 10, 10, 200);
```

The text will now be a bold Verdana font with "end" alignment. Figure 16-9 shows the result of this code when run in a browser.

Figure 16-9   The font is now a bold Verdana with "end" alignment.

Further Reading

The basics of using canvas have been covered, but there are even more things you can do. You can learn more about using canvas at the following sites:

- developer.mozilla.org/en-US/docs/Canvas_tutorial/Drawing_shapes

- www.html5canvastutorials.com/

Drag and Drop

HTML5 provides native drag-and-drop capabilities to the browser with the help of JavaScript. Some elements, such as links, images, and selected text, are draggable by default. If you want to make another element draggable, or if you want to ensure an element is not draggable, you can use the *draggable* attribute in its HTML tag, as in the following examples:

The div element is made draggable by setting the draggable attribute to true

```
<div id="story" draggable="true">Some div content...</div>
<img src="me.jpg" id="me" alt="Me" draggable="false">
```

Though the draggable attribute is true by default, setting it to false will make sure the image is not draggable

The next thing you will need is a valid drop target. To set this, you will need to get the element in JavaScript and ensure that its dragover, dragenter, and drop events prevent the default action, which is to not allow dropping. To do this, you can simply add event listeners to each event for the element, as in the following code:

```
var dropdiv = document.getElementById("dropdiv");
dropdiv.addEventListener("dragover", function(event) {
  event.preventDefault();
}, false);
dropdiv.addEventListener("dragenter", function(event) {
  event.preventDefault();
}, false);
dropdiv.addEventListener("drop", function(event) {
  event.preventDefault();
}, false);
```

Doing this will allow items to be dropped into the dropdiv element.

The Drag-and-Drop Events

There are seven events involved in the drag-and-drop process, and each is described in Table 16-4.

Each of these can have event listeners added in order to perform further scripting. Depending on what you need to do, you may use any number of these events when creating a drag-and-drop script.

Event	Event Target	Description
dragstart	Dragged Item	Occurs when the mouse button is held down and dragging begins
drag	Dragged Item	Occurs immediately after dragstart and continues to fire for the duration of the drag
dragend	Dragged Item	Occurs when the drag ends by releasing the mouse button and dropping the item, whether or not the drop is on a valid target
dragenter	Drop Target	Occurs when the item is first dragged onto the drop target
dragover	Drop Target	Occurs immediately after dragenter and continues to fire as long as the item is being dragged inside the drop target
dragleave	Drop Target	Occurs when the item is dragged out of the drop target
drop	Drop Target	Occurs when the item is dropped into the drop target

Table 16-4 The Drag-and-Drop Events

The dataTransfer Object

While you can currently drag an item and drop it with what you have so far, you will probably want to be able to access data stored within the item being dragged, so that it can be used when it is dropped. This is where the dataTransfer object can be used.

The dataTransfer object is part of the event object, and has two methods for setting and retrieving data from the dragged item: setData() and getData().

The setData() method can be used to set custom data, but is also called by default when selected text, and image, or a link is dragged. For selected text, it will store the dragged text; for an image, it will store the image URL; and for a link, it will store the link URL. If you need to store custom data rather than using these defaults (or if you are dragging a different type of element), you can store either text or a URL using the following code:

```
event.dataTransfer.setData("text", "String of text... ");
event.dataTransfer.setData("URL", "http://www.mysite.com");
```

Note that you can store both "text" and "URL" types in a single dataTransfer object, but cannot have more than one of either type. HTML5 extends this to allow for any MIME type to be passed ("text" and "URL" are still valid and are the same as using the "text/plain" and "text/uri-list" MIME types, respectively). Just remember that only one piece of data from each MIME type can be stored in a dataTransfer object.

The getData() method is used to retrieve any data stored in a dataTransfer object. Due to browser compatibility issues, it is best to use the following example code when retrieving text or URL information from the dataTransfer object:

```
var droptext = event.dataTransfer.getData("Text");
var dropURL = event.dataTransfer.getData("URL") ||
          event.dataTransfer.getData("text/uri-list");
```

Notice the capital "T" when retrieving text, which allows older versions of Firefox to get the text value while still working for other browsers. Also, note the method for getting the URL tests first for the "URL" and then for the MIME type "text/uri-list", in order to help with older versions of Internet Explorer.

A Quick Drag-and-Drop Script

As an example to put all of this together, you will create a script to drag a link into a div element in order to display the link URL. First, begin with the following HTML code:

```
<h1>Quick Drag and Drop</h1>
<p>
Drag the link to the box below it to view the link URL
</p>
<p>
<a href="http://www.mysite.com" id="mylink">My Web Site</a>
</p>
<div id="dropdiv" style="border: 1px solid #000;
padding:5px;"> </div>
```

Since links are draggable by default, the draggable="true" attribute is not necessary here. The div element is given a border so that the user can see where to drag the link. Next, you will need the JavaScript code:

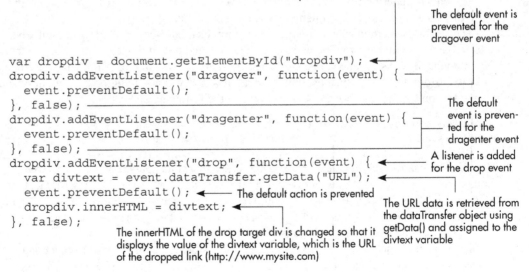

You will notice that since you are dragging a link, you do not need to call setData() to store the URL in the dataTransfer object (if you needed to do this, for example, to store text, you would also need to get the link element by its id, then add an event listener for the dragstart event

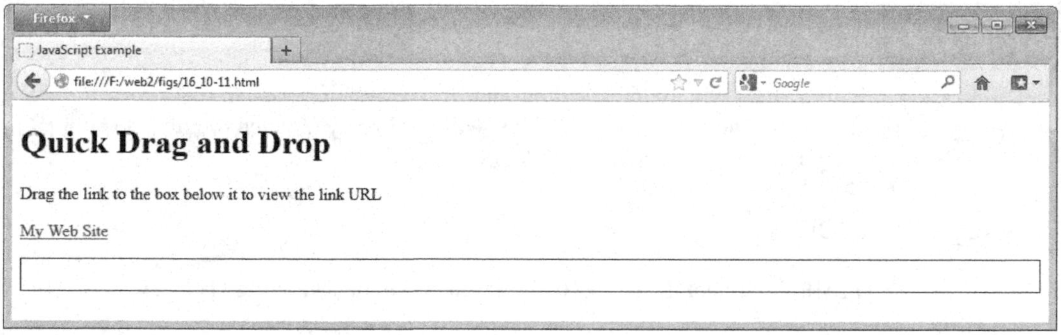

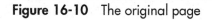

Figure 16-10 The original page

and use setData() within that function). The action here occurs on the drop event for the target div element. When the link is dropped inside the target div, then the URL that was stored in the dataTransfer object is displayed in that div using innerHTML. Figure 16-10 shows the page before the item is dragged and dropped, and Figure 16-11 shows the page afterward.

Further Reading
While this book introduces the drag and drop, you may decide to delve deeper into the topic to create more advanced drag-and-drop scripts. The following resources will provide you with more information on using the drag-and-drop capabilities of HTML5.

- http://html5doctor.com/native-drag-and-drop/
- dev.opera.com/articles/view/accessible-drag-and-drop/

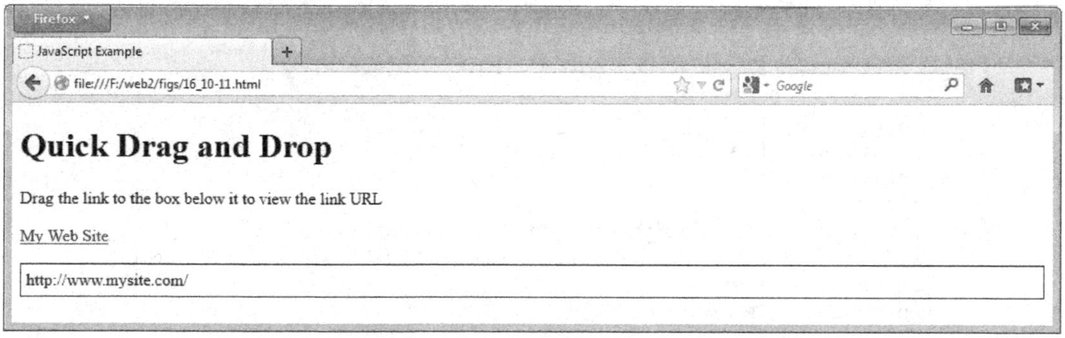

Figure 16-11 The page after the item has been dragged and dropped

Try This 16-2   Drag and Drop

```
pr16_2.html
prjs16_2.js
```

This project will update the drag-and-drop example script so that it stores descriptive text about the link. This will be displayed when the link is dropped in the target div rather than the link URL.

Step by Step

1. Create an HTML document named pr16_2.html and use the following HTML code for the body section:

```
<body>
<h1>Quick Drag and Drop</h1>
<p>
Drag the link to the box below it to view a description of the link.
</p>
<p>
<a href="http://www.mysite.com" id="mylink">My Web Site</a>
</p>
<div id="dropdiv" style="border: 1px solid #000; padding:5px;"> </div>
<script type="text/javascript" src="prjs16_2.js"></script>
</body>
```

2. Create a JavaScript file named prjs16_2.js and begin with the code from the drag-and-drop example from this chapter. Alter the code so that the text "This links goes to my Web Site!" is stored in the dataTransfer object when the link is dragged and then is displayed in the drop target div when the link is dropped inside it. When complete, the code should look like this:

```
var dragdiv = document.getElementById("mylink"),
    dropdiv = document.getElementById("dropdiv");
dragdiv.addEventListener("dragstart", function(event) {
  event.dataTransfer.setData("text", "This links goes to my Web Site!");
}, false);
dropdiv.addEventListener("dragover", function(event) {
  event.preventDefault();
}, false);
dropdiv.addEventListener("dragenter", function(event) {
  event.preventDefault();
}, false);
dropdiv.addEventListener("drop", function(event) {
  var divtext = event.dataTransfer.getData("Text");
  event.preventDefault();
  dropdiv.innerHTML = divtext;
}, false);
```

3. Save the JavaScript file and then open the HTML file in a browser that supports HTML5 drag and drop (the latest Firefox or Chrome browsers should work). Drag the link into the div to display the link's description.

Try This Summary

In this project, you updated your drag-and-drop script so that it stores and retrieves text from the dataTransfer object. This text is then displayed when the link is dragged and dropped into the target div element.

ECMAScript Harmony

ECMAScript Harmony will be the next update to the JavaScript language, and it will add some new features to the language, as well as updating some existing features. Some of the highlights are covered in this section so that you can get a preview of the future of JavaScript.

The const and let Keywords

Currently, JavaScript does not have a formal way to define constants and does not use block-level scope (only function scope). The *const* and *let* keywords will provide a means to use both of these features.

Using const

A constant is a variable that cannot have its value changed once it has been defined. The typical standard for naming a constant is to use all capital letters, for example, TEXT, MAGIC_NUMBER, MONEY. For example, to define a constant named MAGIC_NUMBER with a value of 7, you could use the following code:

```
const MAGIC_NUMBER = 7;
```

With this in place, the value of MAGIC_NUMBER cannot be changed afterward; it will remain constant even if code attempts to change it. The following code shows an example of this:

```
const MAGIC_NUMBER = 7;
alert("The magic number is " + MAGIC_NUMBER);
MAGIC_NUMBER = 42;
alert("Now the magic number is " + MAGIC_NUMBER);
```

Figure 16-12 shows the first alert, and Figure 16-13 shows the second alert. Notice that the value remains 7, even though the code attempted to change it to 42.

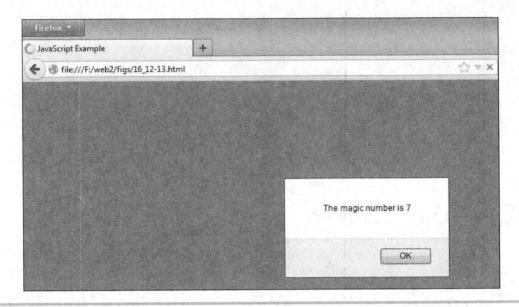

Figure 16-12 The value is 7.

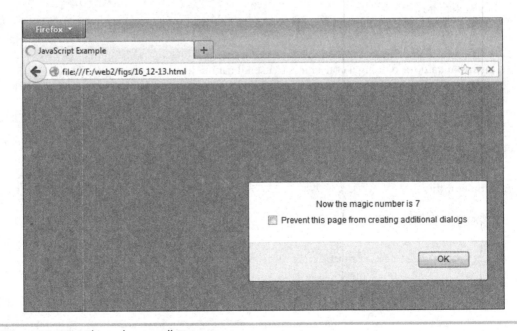

Figure 16-13 The value is still 7.

Using let

The let keyword allows you to define a variable that exists only within the block-level scope in which it is defined. Using this, you can localize a variable to a block rather than only to a function. For example, the following code defines a variable that is only available within the while loop by using let:

```
var i = 0;
while (i < 5) {
  let name = "John";
  if (i === 2) {
    alert(name);
  }
  i++;
}
alert(name);
```

In this code, the name variable is only available for use within the while loop. Trying to alert the value outside the loop results in name being undefined. Figure 16-14 shows the alert that occurs within the loop, and Figure 16-15 shows the alert that occurs outside the loop.

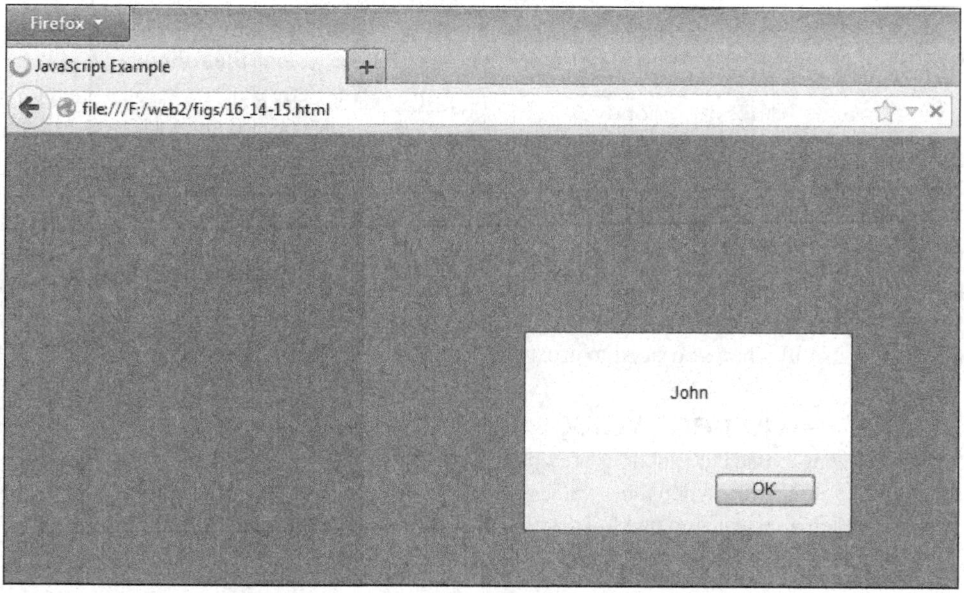

Figure 16-14 The name variable has a value inside the loop block.

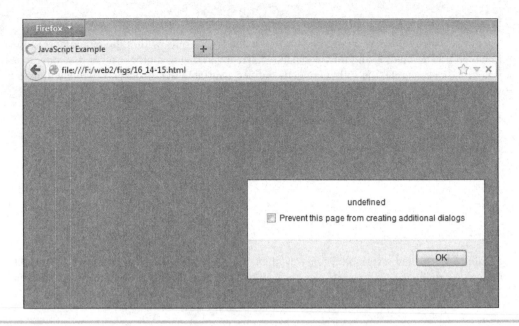

Figure 16-15 The name variable is undefined outside of the block.

You can also use the let keyword to create a block-level statement where one or more variables are defined only within that block. For example, consider the following code:

```
let (name =  "John", money = 30) {          Creates a block where the variable is
  alert(name);                Alerts "John"  only defined inside this block
}
alert(name);           Alerts "undefined"
```

Here, a let statement block is created, and any variables defined within the parentheses will have block-level scope within this block. The name variable will have a value of "John" in the first alert, but will be undefined in the second alert, which is outside the block. As you can see, this can be useful when you need to create a block-level scope without defining a new function.

Default Argument Values

Since arguments passed to functions are optional, it sometimes helps to be able to set a default value for particular arguments when those values are not passed to the function. In Harmony, this can be done by adding an equal sign and the default value to the argument, as in the following code:

```
function multiply_by_five(num=0) {
  return num * 5;
}
var my_num = multiply_by_five(3),
    default_num = multiply_by_five();
```

Here, the variable my_num will have a value of 15 (3*5). Since the value of 3 is passed to the function, the default value of 0 for num is not used. The default_num variable will have a value of 0 (0*5), since no argument was passed to the function, requiring it to use the default value of 0 for num. In this way, you can avoid using additional code to check whether a value was passed to the num variable.

Classes

Harmony will add the ability to use the *class* keyword to define objects using a format similar to Java. Note that this simply provides a format for defining classes—the object is still technically created by JavaScript using the constructor/prototype combination you learned in Chapter 8. For example, suppose you had the following code to define an object named Car:

```
function Car(seats, engine) {
  this.seats = seats;
  this.engine = engine;
}
Car.prototype.show_engine = function() {
  alert("The engine is " + this.engine);
}
```

This creates a constructor for the properties and places the method on the Car prototype. The following code would create a class that is equivalent to the code shown previously:

```
class Car {  ◄─────── The class is created and given a name
  constructor(seats, engine) {  ◄─── The constructor function is defined with two arguments
    public seats = seats;  ─┐    Properties are created using the arguments as values;
    public engine = engine;  ─┘    the properties are public
  }
  show_engine() {  ──────────────────┐
    alert("The engine is " + this.engine);  ─┤   The show_engine() method is defined;
  }  ───────────────────────────────┘    notice that it does not need to use the
}                                          prototype or function keywords
```

As you can see, the class keyword is used, followed by the name of the class, which is defined within the block. A class can contain any number of functions that are used as methods. When inside a class, a method named constructor will always operate as the constructor function for the class. Any other methods will be added to the object's prototype, allowing for maximum reuse of their code. Being able to define a class allows all of the object's code to be in one place (the code block for the class) while still utilizing the advantages of the constructor/prototype pattern.

You will also notice that the constructor defined the properties using the *public* keyword. This allows the properties to be accessed publicly (for example, using Car.seats outside of the class will work). You can also use the *private* keyword if you want a private property—one that cannot be accessed from outside of the class. The syntax for using private members is still in the process of being finalized. The links in the next section may prove helpful in finding out when this has been completed.

More on Harmony

There are other new and/or changed features coming in Harmony, and some of the listed features could have a change in syntax before implementation. To find the latest updates or read more on the ECMAScript Harmony update, you can browse the following Web sites:

- wiki.ecmascript.org/doku.php?id=harmony:proposals

- developer.mozilla.org/en-US/docs/JavaScript/ECMAScript_6_support_in_Mozilla

- www.nczonline.net/

Further Reading

If you wish to delve into JavaScript further, some recommendations for more advanced JavaScript books are listed here:

- *JavaScript: The Complete Reference* by Thomas Powell and Fritz Schneider

- *Professional JavaScript for Web Developers* by Nicholas C. Zakas

- *JavaScript: The Good Parts* by Douglas Crockford

- *JavaScript Patterns* by Stoyan Stefanov

Need Help?

If you find that you are stuck and need help, feel free to get online and visit the JavaScript discussion forums on the Web Xpertz Web site at www.webxpertz.net/forums. Either I or another fellow coder may be able to help you with your questions.

If you would like to contact me, you can send me a message on my Web site (www .scripttheweb.com/about/contact.html) or you can find me on Twitter (@ScripttheWeb).

Ask the Expert

Q: Where can I find free cut-and-paste JavaScript code on the Web?

A:
- http://javascript.internet.com
- http://webdeveloper.earthweb.com/webjs
- www.javafile.com

Q: Where can I learn more about JavaScript?

A:
- developer.mozilla.org/en/JavaScript
- www.javascriptkit.com
- www.quirksmode.org/js/contents.html
- www.scripttheweb.com/js

Q: Where can I learn more about Cascading Style Sheets?

A:
- www.scripttheweb.com/css
- www.csszengarden.com

Q: Where can I learn more about HTML5?

A:
- www.scripttheweb.com/html
- www.html5doctor.com
- www.html5rocks.com

Chapter 16 Self Test

1. Which of the following is used to see if a document is ready in jQuery?

   A. docReadyState()

   B. $documentReady()

   C. $(document).ready()

   D. $(document).done()

2. Which of the following lines would hide an element with an id of "story" using jQuery?

   A. $(getElementById("story")).hide();

   B. $("#story").hide();

   C. $#story.hide();

   D. $("story".hide)();

3. _____ syntax is used to select elements in jQuery.

4. The jQuery library makes it easier to write code that is _____.

5. The _____ element allows you to use JavaScript to draw on a defined area of the page.

6. When drawing on a canvas, you can use the fillCircle() method to draw a circle.

   A. True

   B. False

7. The _____ attribute of an element defines whether or not the element can be dragged.

8. JavaScript _____ may make some advanced coding tasks easier by making the code easier to write.

9. By default, all elements are draggable.

   A. True

   B. False

10. The _____ event occurs when an element begins being dragged.

11. Which object can be used to store or retrieve data during the drag and drop process?

    A. event.dataStorage

    B. event.dataTransfer

    C. event.data

    D. event.dataMove

12. Which method is used to get data stored during a drag and drop?

    A. retrieveData()

    B. getInfo()

    C. getItems()

    D. getData()

13. What keyword can be used in Harmony to declare a constant?

    A. constant

    B. const

    C. let

    D. var

14. What keyword can be used in Harmony to give a variable block-level scope?

    A. block

    B. blockScope

    C. let

    D. secret

15. Is JavaScript fun?

    A. Yes!

    B. Maybe for you!

    C. I was forced to learn this by my boss, so it can never be fun!

    D. I'm curious to know if that coding contest back in Chapter 10 was real, and if so, why John got crushed so badly? That doesn't sound like much fun!

Appendix

Answers to Self Tests

Chapter 1: Introduction to JavaScript

1. C. HTML

2. A. A Web browser

3. C. JavaScript

4. B. False

5. C. ECMAScript

6. A. True

7. C. LiveScript

8. A. prototype-based

9. B. client

10. B. It can validate the information before it is sent to the server.

11. C. scripting

12. A. True

13. D. The client/Web browser

14. D. It is added to an HTML document.

15. A. <script> and </script> HTML tags

Chapter 2: Placing JavaScript in an HTML File

1. D. All of the above

2. B. To ensure the Web page validates when using XHTML

3. A. Yes

4. The noscript tag provides **content** for those without **JavaScript**.

5. A. .js

6. B. <script type= "text/javascript" src="yourfile.js"></script>

7. In HTML, the script tag is not case sensitive. However, with XHTML, the script tag must be in **lowercase**.

8. D. semicolon

9. A. document.write()

10. C. When the script is very long or needs to be placed in more than one HTML document

11. JavaScript comments can be very useful for the purpose of **documenting** or **debugging** your code.

12. C. //

13. A. /*

14. D. */

15. A. close

Chapter 3: Using Variables

1. A variable **represents** or **holds** a value.

2. A. They can save you time in writing and updating your scripts, and they can make the purpose of your code clearer.

3. To declare a variable, you use the **var** keyword.

4. D. =

5. C. var pagenumber = 240;

6. B. False

7. A variable name must begin with a **letter**, a **dollar**, or an **underscore** character.

8. A. True

9. B. var my_house;

10. In JavaScript, the data **types** include number, string, Booleans, null, and undefined.

11. To denote an exponent in JavaScript, you use a letter **e** right after the base number and before the exponent.

12. C. var mytext = "Here is some text!';

13. D. document.write("John said, \"Hi!\"");

14. **Special** characters enable you to add things to your strings that could not be added otherwise.

15. B. document.write("I like to " + myhobby + " every weekend");

Chapter 4: Using Functions

1. In general, a function is a little **script** within a larger **script** that is used to perform a single **task** or a series of **tasks**.

2. B. They provide a way to organize the various parts of the script into the different tasks that must be accomplished, and they can be reused.

3. On the first line of a function, you **declare** it as a function, **name** it, and indicate whether it accepts any **arguments**.

4. C. function

5. A. Curly brackets – { }

6. A. True

7. B. False

8. C. function get_text()

9. **Arguments** are used to allow a function to import one or more values from somewhere outside the function.

10. B. parentheses – ()

11. D. Comma

12. D. window.alert("This is text");

13. B. some_alert("some", "words");

14. A. var shopping = get_something();

15. A **global** variable can be used anywhere in JavaScript.

Chapter 5: JavaScript Operators

1. A(n) **operator** is a symbol or word in JavaScript that performs some sort of calculation, comparison, or assignment on one or more values.

2. **Arithmetic** operators are most often used to perform mathematical calculations on two values.

3. The **addition** operator adds two values.

4. When the increment operator is placed **before** the operand, it increases the value of the operand by 1, and then the rest of the statement is executed.

5. D. $#

6. A. Assigns a new value to a variable

7. The add-and-assign (+=) operator adds the value on the **right** side of the operator to the variable on the **left** side and then assigns that new value to the variable.

8. C. Compares two values or statements, and returns a value of true or false

9. A. 4!=3

10. D. 4<=3

11. The **logical** operators allow you to compare two conditional statements to see if one or both of the statements is true and to proceed accordingly.

12. B. !(17>=20)

13. B. (4>=4) && (5<=2)

14. **Bitwise** operators are logical operators that work at the bit level.

15. In JavaScript, the operators have a certain order of **precedence**.

Chapter 6: Conditional Statements and Loops

1. A conditional statement is a statement that you can use to execute a bit of code based on a **condition**, or do something else if that **condition** is not met.

2. You can think of a conditional statement as being a little like **cause** and **effect**.

3. A. True

4. B. if $(y < 7)$

5. C. Curly brackets

6. The **switch** statement allows you to take a single variable value and execute a different line of code based on the value of the variable.

7. A **loop** is a block of code that allows you to repeat a section of code a certain number of times.

8. B. False

9. A. for (var $x = 1$; $x < 6$; $x += 1$)

10. A **while** loop looks at a comparison and repeats until the comparison is no longer true.

11. B. while $(x = 7)$

12. A. True

13. B. False

14. B. False

15. D. As many times as you like

Chapter 7: JavaScript Arrays

1. An array is a way of storing a **list** of data.

2. In JavaScript, there are **two** ways to define an array.

3. In an array, access to an element is achieved through the use of a(n) **index**.

4. You can use a **loop** to cycle through all of the items in an array.

5. B. False

6. D. var if = new Array[10];

7. B. False (this accesses the sixth item, cool[4] accesses the fifth)

8. C. Creates an array with five items

9. A. The length property

10. Array **literal** notation allows you to create an array using square brackets, without the need to write out "new Array".

11. The **concat**() method is used to combine the elements of two or more arrays and return a new array containing all of the elements.

12. The join() method is used to combine the elements of an array into a single **string**, with each element separated by a specified character.

13. The **pop**() method is used to remove the last element from an array.

14. C. It sorts the contents using string character codes.

15. **Nested** arrays provide the ability to create arrays of more than one dimension.

Chapter 8: Objects

1. An object is a collection of **properties** and **values**.

2. When creating single objects, you can use the object **constructor** or object literal notation.

3. A. True

4. B. dot operator

5. When you need to use a variable to access a property name, you can use **bracket** notation.

6. A **constructor** function can be used to create an object structure.

7. An **instance** of an object can be created using the new keyword.

8. B. False

9. C. Assuming the myhouse object exists, it assigns the value of the kitchen property of the myhouse object to the variable *x*.

10. If a property cannot be found in the object instance, JavaScript will look in the object's **prototype**.

11. B. window.alert("You are using " + navigator.appName);

12. C. Assuming the myhouse object exists, the kitchen property is assigned a new string value of "big" or is initialized with the value "big".

13. In JavaScript, there are many **predefined** objects you can use to gain access to certain properties and methods you may need.

14. The **navigator** object gives you access to the various properties of the viewer's browser.

15. C. appType

Chapter 9: The Document Object

1. The **document** object is an object that is created by the browser for each new HTML page that is viewed.

2. The **referrer** property of the document object returns the URL of the document that referred the viewer to the current document.

3. A. True

4. D. getElementById()

5. B. False (it is added as the last child node rather than the first)

6. B. False

7. The **anchors** property of the document object is an array that contains all of the anchor (<a>) tags on the page.

8. The **innerHTML** DOM node property allows you to change the HTML content of an element node.

9. The **lastModified** property holds the value of the date and time the current document was last modified.

10. A. True

11. A. True

12. C. URL

13. C. It adds a JavaScript newline character at the end of the line.

14. C. All the elements that have the same value for the name attribute (most commonly radio buttons).

15. B. document.write() and document.writeln() statements

Chapter 10: Event Handlers

1. A. True

2. Event handlers are useful because they enable you to gain **access** to the **events** that may occur on the page.

3. To use an event handler, you can place it in the **HTML** or the **JavaScript** code.

4. C. <input type="button" onclick="window.alert('Hey there!');">

5. The **load** event occurs when a Web page has finished loading.

6. D. The viewer moves the mouse cursor over an element on the page.

7. B. False

8. The **unload** event occurs when the viewer leaves the current Web page.

9. The blur event is the opposite of the **focus** event.

10. The **event** object contains properties and methods for an event.

11. The **type** property of an event contains the type of event that occurred.

12. The submit event occurs when the viewer **submits** a **form** on a Web page.

13. A. True

14. In Internet Explorer prior to version 9, the event object can be accessed by using **window.event**.

15. The **addEventListener()** method and the **attachEvent()** method are two new ways to register events.

Chapter 11: Window Object

1. A **window** object is created for each window that appears on the screen.

2. A. True

3. The **length** property holds the value of the number of frames within a window.

4. A. True

5. The **name** property holds the name of the current window and also allows you to give the window a name.

6. A. The window object is the global object for JavaScript in Web browsers.

7. The **self** property is another way of saying "the current window" in JavaScript.

8. C. Newer browsers do not allow the window status to be changed by default, so the user would need to change security settings in order for it to work.

9. A. The parent property goes to the top of the current frame set, while the top property goes to the top window of all frame sets on the page.

10. The **alert()** method pops up a message to the viewer, and the viewer has to click an OK button to continue.

11. A. true

12. The **print()** method enables the viewer to print the current window.

13. The prompt() method is used to **prompt** the viewer to enter information.

14. D. yes, no, 1, and 0

15. B. The setInterval() method is used to repeat a function at a set time interval, while setTimeout() executes a function only once after a set time delay.

Chapter 12: Math, Number, and Date Objects

1. A. Take the square roots and other such values of strings and return a number

2. The **E** property holds the value of Euler's constant.

3. The LN10 property holds the value of the natural **logarithm** of 10.

4. B. False

5. C. document.write(Math.PI);

6. The **SQRT2** property holds the value of the square root of 2.

7. C. absolute

8. The **asin()** method returns the arcsine of a number sent to it as an argument.

9. The pow() method returns the numeric value of the **first** argument raised to the power of the **second** argument.

10. C. var rand_int= Math.floor(Math.random()*8);

11. The **sqrt()** method returns the square root of a number sent to it as an argument.

12. D. An instance of the Date object

13. The **getDay()** method returns the number of days into the week.

14. B. False

15. B. var weekday= rightnow.getDay();

Chapter 13: Handling Strings

1. The **String** object provides properties and methods to get information about strings or to modify strings.

2. A. Creating an instance of the String object and creating a string literal

3. You can create a string **literal** by assigning a string value to a variable.

4. C. JavaScript takes the string literal and turns it into a temporary String object

5. C. length

6. The **length** property returns the length of a string.

7. B. var the_text = "Look at me!";

8. B. charAt()

9. The **big()** method adds <big> and </big> tags around a string value.

10. The concat() method **combines** two or more strings together and returns the new combined string value.

11. D. The indexOf() method returns a numeric value that is the position of a character sent as a parameter, but only the position of the first occurrence of that character.

12. Cookie information is stored in the **document.cookie** property.

13. The **toString**() method returns the string literal value of a string.

14. To replace information in a string, you can use regular expressions and the **replace**() method of the String object.

15. The **match**() method compares a regular expression and a string to see whether they match.

Chapter 14: JavaScript and Forms

1. Each time you add a set of <form> and </form> tags to an HTML document, a **form** object is created.

2. The forms **array** allows you to access a form using an index number.

3. B. document.forms[3]

4. A. document.forms[2].length

5. C. document.forms.length

6. Using form **names or ids** allows you to name the forms on the page that you want to access later.

7. A. document.f1.e1.value

8. The **action** property allows you to access the value of the action="*url*" attribute in the opening form tag.

9. The **elements** property is an array that allows you to access each element in a specific form.

10. The **pattern** attribute in HTML 5 allows you to give a form field a regular expression it must validate.

11. The **reset**() method allows you to reset a form using your script.

12. C. <meter min="0" max="10" value="8">8</meter>

13. One way to help with form accessibility is to use the **<label></label>** tags to identify what field a piece of text is describing.

14. The **submit**() method allows you to submit a form without the viewer clicking the submit button.

15. C. required

Chapter 15: An Introduction to Advanced Techniques

1. **Frames** divide a window into two or more separate areas, each containing different content.

2. Frames differ from tables because the divisions in a frame set contain separate **HTML** documents.

3. The **<frameset></frameset>** tags are used to create a frame set.

4. A single frame is created with the **<frame></frame>** tags.

5. The **cols** attribute divides a frame set into columns.

6. The **src** property of an <img> element allows you to change an image.

7. A. The frames array or a frame name

8. A. True

9. C. jsLint

10. B. alert() and console.log()

11. A. top

12. B. XMLHttpRequest

13. **AJAX** stands for Asynchronous JavaScript and XML.

14. A. True

15. The acronym for JavaScript Object notation is **JSON**.

Chapter 16: JavaScript Libraries, HTML5, and Harmony

1. C. $(document).ready()

2. B. $("#story").hide();

3. **CSS** syntax is used to select elements in jQuery.

4. The jQuery library makes it easier to write code that is **cross-browser**.

5. The **<canvas>** element allows you to use JavaScript to draw on a defined area of the page.

6. B. False

7. The **draggable** attribute of an element defines whether or not the element can be dragged.

8. JavaScript **libraries** may make some advanced coding tasks easier by making the code easier to write.

9. B. False

10. The **dragstart** event occurs when an element begins being dragged.

11. B. event.dataTransfer
12. D. getData()
13. B. const
14. C. let
15. Any answer is correct!

Index

Symbols

" " (double quotes), 42, 45–46, 420
>= (is-greater-than-or-equal-to operator), 107
<= (is-less-than-or-equal-to operator), 107
!= (is-not-equal-to operator), 104–105
*= (multiply-and-assign operator), 100
- (unary negation operator), 97–98
. (dot notation), accessing property values, 185–186, 188
/= (divide-and-assign operator), 100
/ (division operator), 94
/* (forward slash/asterisk), multiple-line comments, 28–30
// (forward slashes), comments, 28
; (semicolon). *See* semicolon (;)
\ (backslash)
    defined, 48
    escaping characters, 45–46
    special characters, 43–45
\ (newline character), writeln() method, 225
_ (underscore), beginning variable names, 39
|| (OR operator), 108–109, 125
+ (addition operator), 90–93
++ (increment operator), 95–96
+ (unary plus operator), 96–97
= (assignment operator), 37, 99, 121
== (equal to) operator, 37

== (is-equal-to operator), 102–104, 121
=== (strict is-equal-to operator)
    avoid mistyping of, 121
    is-equal-to operator vs., 102
    overview of, 105
!== (strict is-not-equal-to operator), 105
! (NOT operator), 109
&& (AND operator), 108, 125
$ (dollar), beginning variable names, 39
%= (modulus-and-assign operator), 100–101
% (modulus operator), 95
() parentheses. *See* parentheses ()
*/ (asterisk/forward slash), multiple-line comments, 28–30
* (multiplication operator), 93–94
[] (bracket notation), object property values, 187–188
{ } (curly brackets). *See* curly brackets { }
< (is-less-than operator), 106–107
> (is-greater-than operator), 106

A

abs() method, Math object, 309–311
accessibility
    creating rollovers for, 414–415
    enhancing content, 428

489

G

Essential Web Development Skills—Made Easy!

The Beginner's Guide series provides everything you need to get started in modern web development. Featuring a practical, hands-on approach, these fast-paced tutorials contain expert insights, sample projects, and downloadable code to help you create dynamic websites quickly and easily.

HTML: A Beginner's Guide, Fifth Edition
Willard | 0-07-180927-9

JavaScript: A Beginner's Guide, Fourth Edition
Pollock | 0-07-180937-6

Also available

HTML5 Multimedia Developer's Guide
Bluttman | 0-07-175282-X

jQuery: A Beginner's Guide
Pollock | 0-07-181791-3
(Available Winter 2014)